Gender and American Social Science

Gender and American Social Science

THE FORMATIVE YEARS

EDITED BY HELENE SILVERBERG

PRINCETON UNIVERSITY PRESS

PRINCETON, NEW JERSEY

Copyright © 1998 by Princeton University Press
Published by Princeton University Press, 41 William Street, Princeton, New Jersey 08540
In the United Kingdom: Princeton University Press, Chichester, West Sussex

Library of Congress Cataloging-in-Publication Data

Gender and American social science : the formative years / edited by Helene Silverberg
p.   cm.
Includes bibliographical references (p.) and index.
ISBN 0-691-01749-2 (CL : alk. paper).—ISBN 0-691-04820-7 (PB : alk. paper)
1. Social sciences—United States—History. 2. Women social scientists—
United States—History. 3. Women—United States—History
4. Sex role—United States—History. I. Silverberg, Helene, 1958–
H53.U5G45   1998   305.4′0973—dc21   97-42951   CIP

This book has been composed in Caledonia

Princeton University Press books are printed on acid-free paper and meet the guidelines for
permanence and durability of the Committee on Production Guidelines for Book
Longevity of the Council on Library Resources

http://pup.princeton.edu

Printed in the United States of America

1   2   3   4   5   6   7   8   9   10

1   2   3   4   5   6   7   8   9   10

(pbk.)

CONTENTS

ACKNOWLEDGMENTS

THREE WOMEN have been crucial to the completion of this volume. Mary Murrell of Princeton University Press believed in this project from the start and was unflagging in her patience and her labors on its behalf. I would also like to thank Dorothy Ross for her exemplary collegiality toward a younger scholar and her scrupulous respect for deadlines. Finally, I am grateful to Victoria Kahn for her dry wit, constant encouragement, and profound sense of the absurd, which helped to guide me through the "Fens, Bogs, [and] Dens" of a collected volume of essays.

Cambridge University Press kindly granted me permission to reprint Kathryn Kish Sklar's essay, *"Hull-House Maps and Papers:* Social Science as Women's Work in the 1890s." The University of California provided financial support for a portion of this work.

GUY ALCHON is Professor of History at the University of Delaware. He is writing a biography of Mary van Kleeck.

NANCY K. BERLAGE is a Ph.D. candidate in the Department of History at the Johns Hopkins University. She is completing her dissertation, which describes the political, economic, and social aspects of local Farm and Home Bureaus and the roles of family, community, and professionals in those organizations.

DESLEY DEACON is Associate Professor of American Studies and Sociology at the University of Texas at Austin. She is author of *Elsie Clews Parsons: Inventing Modern Life* (Chicago: University of Chicago Press, 1997) and "Brave New Sociology? Elsie Clews Parsons and Me," in *Feminist Sociology: Life Histories of a Movement*, ed. Barbara Laslett and Barrie Thorne (New Brunswick, N.J.: Rutgers University Press, 1997), and has written a new introduction to Elsie Clews Parsons, *Fear and Conventionality* (1914; Chicago: University of Chicago Press, 1997). She is now working on a feminist biography of Mary McCarthy.

MARY G. DIETZ is Professor of Political Science and Adjunct Professor of the Center for Advanced Feminist Studies at the University of Minnesota. Author of *Between the Human and the Divine: The Political Thought of Simone Weil* (Totowa, N.J.: Rowman and Littlefield, 1988) and editor of *Thomas Hobbes and Political Theory* (Lawrence: University Press of Kansas, 1990), she is presently completing a volume on feminism, citizenship, and the strategic work of politics.

JAMES FARR teaches political theory at the University of Minnesota where he is Professor of Political Science and project director of the Center for Democracy and Citizenship. Author of several essays in the history and philosophy of political science, he is also coeditor (with Raymond Seidelman) of *Discipline and History* (Ann Arbor: University of Michigan Press, 1993) and (with John Dryzek and Stephen Leonard) of *Political Science in History* (Cambridge: Cambridge University Press, 1995).

NANCY FOLBRE, Professor of Economics at the University of Massachusetts at Amherst, focuses her work on the interface between feminist theory and political economy. She is author of *Who Pays for the Kids* (New York: Routledge, 1994), as well as numerous articles on gender and economics. She is also an associate editor of the journal *Feminist Economics*.

DOROTHY ROSS is Arthur O. Lovejoy Professor of History at the Johns Hopkins University. She is author of *G. Stanley Hall: The Psychologist as Prophet* (Chicago: University of Chicago Press, 1972) and *The Origins of American Social Science* (Cambridge: Cambridge University Press, 1991), and editor of *Modernist Impulses in the Human Sciences* (Baltimore: Johns Hopkins University Press, 1994), and has published many articles on the history of the social and behavioral sciences and American social and political thought.

HELENE SILVERBERG, editor of this volume, is currently a student at Boalt Hall School of Law, University of California, Berkeley. She has taught in the departments of political science at Princeton University and the University of California, Santa Barbara. She is currently writing a book on the American welfare state, sex discrimination law, and women's position in the labor market.

KATHRYN KISH SKLAR is Distinguished Professor of History at the State University of New York at Binghamton. She is author of *Catharine Beecher: A Study in American Domesticity* (New Haven: Yale University Press, 1973) and *Florence Kelley and the Nation's Work* (New Haven: Yale University Press, 1996), coeditor (with Martin Bulmer and Kevin Bales) of *The Social Survey in Historical Perspective* (Cambridge: Cambridge University Press, 1991) and (with Linda Kerber and Alice Kessler-Harris) of *U.S. History as Women's History: New Feminist Essays* (Chapel Hill: University of North Carolina Press, 1995), and has published numerous articles on American women's history.

KAMALA VISWESWARAN teaches anthropology at the University of Texas, Austin. She is author of *Fictions of Feminist Ethnography* (Minneapolis: University of Minnesota Press, 1994) and is currently finishing a manuscript titled "Family Subjects: Women, Feminism, Indian Nationalism."

Gender and American Social Science

Introduction: Toward a Gendered Social Science History

HELENE SILVERBERG

THIS VOLUME examines American social science during its formative years using gender as its analytical lens. It is not a book about women in the social sciences, although women and the subfields in which they came to specialize are central subjects of some of the essays. Rather, this volume seeks to explore the many ways in which the reorganization of gender relations in the late nineteenth and early twentieth centuries shaped the development of the American social sciences as bodies of expert knowledge, forms of social practice, and methods of cultural critique. Building on recent developments in history and feminist theory, these essays seek to provide not just a new history of women but a new history of the social sciences during their formative years.

American social science was fundamentally reorganized in the years between 1870 and 1920. The nineteenth-century American social science tradition joined claims of science and disinterested expertise with the democratic and humanitarian impulses associated with moral reform. Its practitioners included independent scholars, civil servants, and both male and female social reformers. By the end of the century this tradition began visibly to break apart. In the 1870s and 1880s, the male pioneers of the academic social sciences founded the first university departments and set out to establish them on a scientific footing. After 1900, an extraordinary group of women built their own rich network of social research settings outside the universities to serve their own sense of the social and practical purposes of social science. But by the mid-1920s, American social science—and men's and women's respective places within it—had been narrowed and transformed. The prestigious academic social sciences, under the firm control of their male practitioners, had fortified their boundaries through their commitment to a technocratic vision of social science modeled on the natural sciences. Women had achieved an enduring role in other, lower-status forms of social science, housed elsewhere in the university as well as in federal and state agencies and private research institutes. But the range and scope of their participation even within this realm had been reduced and narrowed to such female-dominated fields as home economics, social work, and school-based guidance counseling.

The long Progressive Era also saw the breakup of the Victorian gender synthesis and the birth of a more modern system of relations between the sexes.

Throughout the nineteenth century, social practices had largely (though not completely) consigned women to the sphere of social reproduction. But beginning in the 1880s, (middle-class) women increasingly challenged the system of ideas and cultural practices that had limited their freedom. New opportunities for work and education, the broad political mobilization of women in the suffrage movement, and the sexual revolution (underwritten by the increasingly wide use of birth control) enabled women to contest and recast the Victorian polarities of manhood and womanhood and to place gender relations on a more egalitarian footing. The independent New Woman of the 1920s, who sought to combine career and marriage, embodied one new possibility within the terms of this new gender system.

Separately, these developments are well known to scholars of the early twentieth century. Historians of the social sciences have provided many fine studies of the ascendance of the modern university, the processes of professionalization and specialization, the sources of social science's cultural authority, and the liberal ideological parameters of American social science. Meanwhile, historians of gender history have provided numerous excellent studies of women's reform work and political activity, the reconstruction of sexuality and gender roles, the crisis of masculinity, and the birth of feminism during these years. But these two fields of research have long operated independent of each other, obscuring their shared intellectual interests and overlooking the meaning and significance of some of the period's most crucial transformations.

This volume departs from the standard historiography of American social science in two key ways. First, the essays explore the history of social science through the lens of gender. They focus specifically on the ways in which the shifting gender relations of this period shaped and marked the production, reorganization, and practice of the social sciences during their formative years. They trace the workings of gender as it shaped men's and women's respective places within the matrix of social science institutions. They attend also to the ways in which gender became encoded in the analytical tools, investigative practices, and conceptual categories of this field of social knowledge. Second, the essays work with a broad notion of social knowledge and empirical social research that self-consciously challenges the distinctions between academic social science and other forms of social knowledge that have sustained the privileged position of the academic disciplines. Several essays focus on women reformers and independent scholars who produced and practiced social science from a variety of nonacademic institutions. Other essays explore the fluid boundaries between science and reform that so haunted male academicians yet mark this period as a "golden age" for women social scientists. Working from this perspective, the volume reevaluates the social knowledge, scientific commitments, and epistemological moorings of *both* male and female researchers in university and nonuniversity settings, and examines more fully the connections between these domains. Together, the essays propose that the reorganization of gender relations was central to the transformation of American social science that occurred during these years. They also suggest that the social sciences had a richer, more variegated, and more oppositional life than the historiography suggests.

A gender analysis of the history of American social science, however, involves special difficulties of terminology and focus that must be addressed at the outset. The terms *social science* and *social scientist* are most often reserved for university-based empirical social research and its male producers such as Richard T. Ely in economics, Albion W. Small in sociology, Charles Merriam in political science, and James McKeen Cattell in psychology. A few especially successful academic women such as Margaret Mead in anthropology, Mary Whiton Calkins in psychology, or Jessie Bernard in sociology have been accorded this appellation (along with its prestige), but this narrow formulation cannot easily accommodate women's variegated relationship to, and involvement with, the social sciences. As Mary Furner has noted, this phrase was an invidious and opportunistic distinction crafted by unversity-based academics to enhance their prestige and distinguish themselves from politically vulnerable "reformers."[1] Men and women outside the universities continued to use the term *social science* well into the twentieth century to describe a wide variety of social practices and forms of knowledge about contemporary problems.[2]

The authors in this volume also work with this broader understanding of empirical social knowledge. In addition to its greater historical accuracy, this wider usage has several advantages. First, it permits investigation of the many forms of social knowledge and the diverse venues outside the universities where women studied, produced, and used social science. Second, it sidesteps a major problem encountered in the historiography, in which a rigid notion of "science" is used to distinguish between "real" social scientists (i.e., male academics) and "amateurs" or "reformers" engaged in empirical social research, the category to which women are most often consigned. The more comprehensive formulation allows us to cut across these categories in ways that more closely capture women's experience. Finally, this broader definition acknowledges that science was not the only source of authority for new knowledge during these years. Pragmatist currents established the authority of experience, for example, and middle-class women's clubs elaborated and deployed idioms of female domesticity to bolster their influence over social welfare policy.

This essay sets out the broader historical and historiographical context for those that follow. In the next section, I briefly sketch the historical context required for our reconsideration of social science. This history ranges widely, drawing together material (often treated separately) from social history, gender history, and the history of the social sciences. I draw attention to the large and complex domain of American social science, as well as the diverse but closely linked meanings of social science invoked by men and women in their struggles for professional authority and cultural advantage. I then review the historiographical literature as it has sought to make sense of these developments. My concern in this section is to identify the conceptual roadblocks that have worked to represent social science as an all-male project and to demonstrate the significance of gender analysis for an understanding of the development and reorganization of social science during these years. Finally, I briefly review the themes and concerns of the collection's essays.

THE NINETEENTH-CENTURY TRADITION AND ITS HEIRS

Historians of American social science frequently begin with the American Social Science Association (ASSA), and it is an appropriate beginning here too. Modeled on the British National Association for Promotion of Social Science, the ASSA was founded in 1865 to extend social knowledge and provide a more authoritative basis for addressing contemporary social problems. The ASSA served as the institutional locus for a wide variety of male reformers as well as those who sought to raise the standards of competence in American scientific investigation. Its members included public officials such as Carroll Wright and Francis Amasa Walker, many important liberal economists, and such prominent university reformers as Daniel Coit Gilman, president of Johns Hopkins, and Charles W. Eliot, president of Harvard. But the ASSA was also "the first large organization . . . in the country to admit women on an absolute equality with men,"[3] and it attracted an unusually large female membership. Two of the original twelve members of the Executive Board were women, and women played an active role in the departments of health, education, and social economy where they constituted between 20 and 30 percent of the membership.[4]

The ASSA embodied a tradition of social science that provided an unusually welcoming context for women's concerns. Its commitment to social empiricism combined claims of science and disinterested expertise with the democratic and humanitarian impulses associated with moral reform—a discourse with which women had long allied themselves. The ASSA's ethos was also practical and it understood knowledge to be comprehensive and synthetic; its guiding spirits (both male and female) were openly skeptical of arguments for academic specialization, which rested on a rigid separation of knowledge and reform. The ASSA strongly encouraged research, but its aim was not scholarship per se. Rather, it sought the application of the best available intelligence to the amelioration of social problems. This view enabled women to carve out a prominent place for themselves in the wider social science movement.[5]

The strong affinities between the new empiricist sensibility and emerging feminist currents in America also attracted women to the new social science organization. Many women's rights advocates recognized their need for new epistemological ground outside custom, "nature," and especially the religious tradition of the established churches, that had long been used to justify women's subordinate status. They viewed science as both the most authoritative form of modern knowledge and a source of free inquiry that could be marshaled against these pillars of women's oppression. Elizabeth Cady Stanton's well-known anticlericalism was a part of these larger currents, and feminists' search for alternative sources of authority led them to embrace the goals and aspirations of social scientists. These feminist sensibilities were widely shared by the men of the ASSA (a commitment to social science seemed both to reflect and to inspire a skepticism toward all traditional relations of authority), and the ASSA was highly sympathetic to the women's rights agenda.[6]

This social empiricist tradition began to split apart in the 1870s and 1880s. The rise of the modern research university, the professionalization of the academic social sciences, the expansion of higher education for women, and the emergence of the "woman movement" quickly eroded the unity of the earlier tradition. In the new universities, Richard Ely, G. Stanley Hall, John Burgess, Albion Small, and other (mainly German-trained) men reworked and embellished the scientific impulses of the nineteenth-century social science tradition. They remained strongly committed to empirical investigation as the chief criterion of science but focused their efforts on specialization, theory building, and the development of a more "objective" professional stance. The more comprehensive and practical tendency of the nineteenth-century social science tradition was taken up by middle-class women based in female institutions such as the National Consumers' League, Hull House, and the Chicago School of Civics and Philanthropy in the years after 1890.

The opening of institutions of higher learning to women laid the foundations for women's new role in the world of social science. The expansion of the American university system in the 1870s and 1880s helped inspire a broad-based—and highly successful—campaign to open higher education to women. In the East, where the major universities successfully resisted the demand for coeducation, the elite Seven Sisters colleges, including Vassar (1865), Wellesley (1875), and Bryn Mawr (1884), created unprecedented new opportunities for women. In the West and Midwest, the great land-grant universities also came under pressure to admit women.[7] By 1900, women constituted 36.8 percent of all college students, up from only 21 percent in 1870.[8] Yet opportunities for them to use their new skills in socially useful ways were limited, especially if they sought also to support themselves and build lives outside the family. The research-and-reform organizations they created and staffed in the 1880s and 1890s would do much to address this dilemma.[9]

The academic freedom "trials" that swept American universities between 1886 and 1894 helped to widen the distance between the academic and the reform realms of social science. Henry Carter Adams at Cornell, Richard T. Ely at Wisconsin, and Edward Bemis at the University of Chicago were among the many university social science faculty who for a time spoke out forcefully on union activities and the ethical foundations of the market. But their frank, and socialist-leaning, advocacy provoked a backlash among conservative university presidents, trustees, and colleagues that resulted in the discharge of some and the intimidation of many others. This wave of academic repression ended the openly reform-oriented engagements of male academics, who subsequently recast themselves as "objective" experts, and broke the links between male academic social scientists and popular movements for social justice.[10] Women's colleges and social science institutions, by contrast, were considerably more tolerant of such views; their destinies were more often shaped by their founders and resident communities who strongly supported the social activists in their midst. College-based women social scientists such as Wellesley's Vida Dutton Scudder, Emily Greene Balch, and Katharine Coman participated openly in the vibrant reform politics of the early twentieth century. The settlement houses, the Russell Sage Foundation, and the National Consumers' League also supported the social reform agenda, and they helped to sustain a corps of college-educated women devoted to a broad and action-oriented program of social investigation.[11]

The American Collegiate Alumnae's study of the health consequences of higher education for women, published in 1885, was emblematic of women's vision of the practical and reform-oriented purposes of social science. In 1873, Dr. Edward Clark, a member of Harvard's Board of Overseers and a former member of its medical faculty, had launched a broadside attack on college study for women. Drawing on the authority of medical knowledge, Clark argued that the rigor of college instruction placed undue strain on women's minds and irreparably damaged their bodies. The ACA responded to this challenge with a pioneering analysis of the health of women college alumnae that built directly on the conceptual resources and personnel of the ASSA. Emily Talbot (a cofounder of the ACA) discovered the reform possibilities of statistics in her work as secretary of the ASSA's education department, and she helped pattern the ACA's inquiry on earlier ASSA surveys. The study was guaranteed a wide audience when Carroll Wright, a friend of the Talbots', president of the ASSA, and chief of the Massachusetts Bureau of Labor Statistics, published it as a bureau monograph. The study was brought to the attention of an even wider audience the following year when John Dewey, then a young instructor in philosophy at the University of Michigan, reviewed its findings at length in the *Popular Science Monthly*. Though the report seemed to have had little impact on the debate over higher education for women, it exemplified a vision of social science's purposes that women—both inside and outside the university—embraced and reworked over the next three decades.[12]

THE UNIVERSITY AND THE ACADEMIC SOCIAL SCIENCES

The social sciences took root in the universities as separate disciplines during the 1870s and 1880s. Four of the five disciplines formed their first graduate programs in the 1880s, and sociology followed in the early 1890s. National organizations and professional journals, along with procedures and standards for recruiting and training students, followed in the next decade as the number of men with distinct professional identities as social scientists grew. In economics, this group was composed of men trained in German historical economics like Richard Ely of Johns Hopkins. In psychology, it consisted of laboratory men trained in the new German physiological psychology like G. Stanley Hall, founding president of Clark University and the man who introduced Americans to Freudian psychoanalysis. In the years after 1900, these men pursued the more difficult tasks of identifying the distinct methods, theories, and objects of investigation of their respective disciplines.[13]

In the process, the academic social sciences became marked as masculine cultural terrain in several ways. Most obviously, major university social science departments simply refused to hire women faculty. Although graduate programs were opened to women in the 1890s, and patterns of recruitment remained highly irregular until the 1920s—drawing in lawyers, ministers, and social reformers alongside men who had received formal advanced training in the social sciences—university social science departments declined to appoint women to faculty positions. Even the brilliant Helen Thompson Woolley, who was awarded her Ph.D. summa cum laude by the psychology department at the University of Chicago and regarded by John Dewey as the department's best student, could not break through the custom against hiring women.[14] Women with Ph.D.'s were consigned to ancillary departments at these institutions (such as "Household Administration" at the University of Chicago) or to the women's colleges. The land-grant universities would employ a small group of women faculty in the 1890s, but the majority of private, four-year research universities would not reach even 10 percent until the 1930s.[15] But the "maleness" of the academic social sciences went beyond the sex of their practitioners.

Gender also became encoded in the conceptual apparatus and professional ethos of the new disciplines. Gendered narratives of contemporary social relations, embedded in textbooks and scholarly treatises, established both the primacy of male experience and male social scientists' right to speak authoritatively about those social relations. Economists regularly represented the market as an arena of production and exchange among male workers and male employers—even as the number of working women increased and women's consciousness as consumers became politicized. Political scientists depicted the city and city government as exclusively male terrain—though the women's club and suffrage movements had brought women into prominent new roles in the public sphere. America's first generation of academic social scientists also sought to bolster the prestige of their disciplines with a repertoire of metaphors borrowed from masculine professional and cultural realms of life. Political scientists routinely employed language drawn from the business and financial worlds, while psychologists drew upon metaphors from engineering and medicine.[16] "If I did not believe psychology affected conduct and could be applied in useful ways," James McKeen Cattell wrote, "I should regard my occupation as nearer to that of the professional chess-player or sword-swallower rather than to that of the engineer or scientific physician."[17]

The breakup of the Victorian gender system may also have provoked a crisis of masculinity that fueled the academic disciplines' search for science and social control. "Professionalizing the social sciences in late nineteenth- and early twentieth-century America had a gendered meaning," Barbara Laslett has argued; "It was connected to the gender interests of the male social scientists who were its supporters." These interests included, for example, their need to earn a living to uphold their gender roles as the family breadwinner, as well as their socialized disdain for emotion and feeling. William Ogburn and L. L. Bernard in sociology, and G. Stanley Hall and James McKeen Cattell in psychology, also seem to have supported wavering masculine identities with extreme commitments to scientism. Moreover, women's real and symbolic association with reform also seemed to threaten the scientific standing of the new social sciences (at least in the eyes of their male practitioners). In this way, they hoped, would scientism served to set the boundaries of the masculine social sciences against the feminine domains of social work and reform.[18]

A few iconoclasts with feminist sensibilities wrestled openly with gender in their work. W. I. Thomas's *Sex and Society: Studies in the Social Psychology of Sex* (1907) argued that contemporary gender roles were the products of cultural habits formed in earlier stages of evolution and were now outmoded.[19] Thorstein Veblen criticized woman's place at the turn of the century, labeling the patriarchal household a "predatory institution" and marriage an arrangement based on "coercion and ownership." His radical critique of gender relations grew directly out of his criticism of both capitalism and orthodox economic theory, and he was among the first to expose the gendered vision at the foundation of economic theory. Reviewing John B. Clark's *The Essentials of Economic Theory*, Veblen noted that "there is, of course, no 'solitary hunter,' living either in a cave or otherwise, and there is no man 'who makes by his own labor all the goods that he uses . . . since mankind reached the human plane, the economic unit has not been a 'solitary hunter,' but a community of some kind; in which, by the way, women seem in the early stages to have been the most consequential factor."[20] Although the family quickly became an important area of interest within sociology's "social problems" literature, few social scientists joined these brave pioneers in their open challenge to conventional gender roles and sexual and familial relations.[21]

Women's entrance into social science graduate programs in the 1890s began slowly to challenge the masculinity of the new disciplines. The decision by the University of Pennsylvania, Stanford, Brown, Columbia, and especially Yale and the University of Chicago (which quickly became the two largest producers of women doctorates) to admit women on an equal basis with men and to award them doctor of philosophy degrees, provided a crucial opening wedge for women into the higher reaches of academic life. (Of the women's colleges, only Bryn Mawr, at the insistence of M. Carey Thomas, included a Ph.D. from the beginning in 1885.)[22] Though trends across the disciplines varied, women's interest in graduate education in the social sciences was very high, especially in areas (such as social economics) that were directly relevant to the emerging women's professions. Data on the Johns Hopkins Department of Political Economy suggest a far greater interest in academic social science among

women than the small number of Ph.D.'s awarded to women (the figures usually cited) would suggest. Of the 252 people who completed at least one year of
graduate work between 1876 and 1926 in that department, nearly 35 percent
(seventy-seven) were women.[23]

Many of these pioneering women used their training in academic social science to directly contest the Victorian underpinnings of turn-of-the-century
American society. In psychology, Helen Thompson Woolley, Leta Stetter
Hollingworth, and Jessie Taft challenged rigid notions of biologically rooted
sexual difference with their studies of sex-linked variation in intelligence, the
social roots of personality, and the effect of women's menstrual cycles on their
motor and mental abilities.[24] Anthropologist Elsie Clews Parsons, as explored
in this volume by Desley Deacon, combined evolutionary theories with
fieldwork on the Zuni to critique the strictures imposed by the family on
women. In economics, Edith Abbott's lifelong investigation of women workers
openly disputed the contemporary view of their paid labor as a radical departure from a long history of female domesticity.[25] As Rosalind Rosenberg has argued, this research provided both a new language and a scientific basis for
broader feminist currents replacing the Victorian ideal of "True Womanhood"
with the modern vision of the "New Woman." Helen Thompson Woolley's conviction that there was "no reason why science should not guide reform nor why
reform should not direct the use of science" was shared by many women academics of this generation.[26]

This vision of social science made limited headway in university social science departments in the early twentieth century. The refusal of these departments to hire women meant that their research traditions went largely unchallenged. Nor could women scholars at the women's colleges, with their heavy
teaching loads and limited research resources, undertake the kind of work that
might put into question the paradigms and practices of the higher-prestige university departments.[27] Equally important, many women with advanced education and degrees preferred to put their training to practical use and never
sought academic careers. Many had been active in settlement and reform work
prior to entering graduate school, and saw graduate education as a means to advancing nonacademic pursuits. Katharine Bement Davis, Miriam van Waters,
and Frances Kellor exemplified this alternative as they moved directly from
completing their doctorates to nonuniversity positions, from which they
launched nationally prominent careers concerned with issues of female delin-
quency, female penology, and immigration.[28]

Nevertheless, the social sciences were still sufficiently fluid during these
years to accommodate diverse perspectives and interests. The brief appearance
of such female-dominated fields as social economy and sanitary science testified to women's desire (and ability) to reshape academic social science in ways
more congenial to their outlook and purposes. These fields enabled women social scientists to combine their commitment to university-based research with
the social and practical purposes their male counterparts had rejected as con-

trary to the scientific spirit. They often also directly engaged questions of gender and aimed to be useful to women. Jessica Peixotto of Berkeley and Susan Kingsbury of Bryn Mawr joined economic research with social welfare concerns to build a body of knowledge concerning family budgets and cost-of-living studies (a field we now call consumer economics). Similarly, the University of Chicago's Marion Talbot envisioned a program in sanitary science that offered courses in chemistry, physics, physiology, political economy, and modern languages that would train both men and women to address problems of urban planning and consumer protection and discredit the stark lines of Victorian society between male and female abilities. Although home economics and social work would acquire their own separate schools in the 1890s and thereby gain a permanent place in the university, other "hybrid" fields fell victim to the increasingly rigid patterns of training in, and recruitment to, the academic social sciences, and to their fixed departmental structures.[29]

The proliferation and, often, disappearance of these fields reflected complicated processes about which we need to know a great deal more.[30] In some cases, the creation of these separate female-dominated fields was initiated by women and expressed their interest in securing institutional autonomy for their distinct vision of social science. The University of Chicago's Marion Talbot, for example, sought from the outset a separate department of public health and sanitary science and had to settle for a place in the sociology department. A decade later, again at her request, President William Rainey Harper established a new Department of Household Administration, placed her in charge, and transferred the field of sanitary science there.[31] The founding of the Chicago School of Civics and Philanthropy (later the University of Chicago's School of Social Service Administration) seems more ambiguous. After receiving their Ph.D.'s at the University of Chicago, neither Edith Abbott nor Sophonisba Breckinridge was able to find an academic position suitable to her enormous talents and abilities. It was only at the then-autonomous Chicago School that they were able to create professionally and intellectually satisfying careers at the cusp of social science and social work.[32]

BEYOND THE UNIVERSITY: THE MANY LIVES OF SOCIAL SCIENCE

The rise of the universities in the 1870s did not immediately displace other venues for the production and practice of social science. To the contrary, in the years between 1890 and 1920 women social researchers helped to dramatically expand the domain of social science, diversifying its research questions, investigative practices, and political commitments. In reform organizations, child guidance clinics, museums, and even government agencies, women recast and modernized the comprehensive and practical side of the nineteenth-century social science tradition. Located beyond the reach of conservative university administrators and the constraints of academic specialization, these women created new forms of social knowledge that were frankly reformist and policy-oriented. They also engaged questions of gender more openly than did their male (and, sometimes, female) counterparts in the colleges and universities.

The most prominent of these new venues was the female research-and-reform nexus that took shape in cities around America, but especially in New York, Boston, and Chicago. The work of the settlement houses, the National Consumers' League, the Women's Education and Industrial Union, and the Russell Sage Foundation were part of a broader process of public inquiry into social problems that began in the 1830s but reached its heyday at the turn of the century.[33] This network of institutions and organizations provided a wide range of new opportunities for middle-class women to gain economic independence, pursue worthy work, and acquire a voice in important national debates. Crystal Eastman, Frances A. Kellor, Mary Simkhovitch, Florence Kelley, Mary van Kleeck, and Josephine Goldmark each built careers and national reputations outside conventional professional channels on the basis of the new social knowledge they produced within this context. In addition to the means for making a living, the careers in social investigation supported by these institutions provided a new personal and professional identity that better suited the experience and aspiration of college-educated women than had the maternalist idiom that sustained the political influence of middle-class clubwomen. Social science enabled college-educated women to challenge conventional gender roles, and to create new ones, even as they pursued a gender-specific reform agenda.[34]

This unusual intellectual milieu encouraged methodological innovation and generated distinct forms of social knowledge. The unique combination of research-oriented women, college-educated male academic social scientists, and progressive politicians inspired wholly novel approaches linking research to reform. The National Consumers' League's legal brief for *Muller v. Oregon* (1908) (known as the "Brandeis brief" but written by Josephine Goldmark) drew on the fields of law, sociology, and public health in a completely novel fashion to describe the health consequence of overwork for women and to request that the court uphold the Oregon law setting a ten-hour limit on their workday. This brief successfully challenged the liberty-of-contract jurisprudence that had stymied labor legislation for two decades, and helped pioneer the field of sociological jurisprudence.[35] *Hull-House Maps and Papers*, as explored in this volume by Kathryn Kish Sklar, pioneered the use of maps to convey both the character and scope of urban poverty and the moral relationships that governed neighborhood life.

The origin and subsequent political career of the first study published by the Russell Sage Foundation's Committee on Women's Work, *Women in the Bookbinding Trade* (1913), illustrates the connections among politics, social problem-solving, and the production of new knowledge. Interest in the bookbinders had been sparked by the New York Court of Appeals' decision in *People v. Wil-*

liam (1907), which had declared unconstitutional a law that prohibited night work for women in factories. The test case involved a woman on the night shift in a bindery; though the law was struck down, the language of the decision implicitly invited advocates of state labor laws to present facts about the harm that night work inflicted on women to the court. The Committee on Women's Work took up the challenge in the spring of 1908 for purposes of the appeal. In the meantime, the New York State Factory Investigating Commission used the committee's preliminary findings as evidence of the need for new legislation. After the new law was passed in 1913, the material was again used in the test case, *People v. Charles Schweinler Press* (1915), that upheld the new legislation.[36]

Strong links existed between these women social researchers and male social scientists, especially in New York and Chicago. Despite the view of many historians that only male social scientists were concerned to keep their distance, the desire for autonomy existed on both sides. The close ties and mutual respect between the women of Hull House and the University of Chicago social scientists are well known. However, the men played little role in the settlement's research, and the university's brief interest in acquiring Hull House sparked a major crisis at the settlement house and was firmly rejected by Jane Addams.[37] Similarly, the National Consumers' League's list of honorary vice presidents included S. McCune Lindsay, Henry Carter Adams, Richard T. Ely, John Commons, and Arthur N. Holcombe. But Florence Kelley and Josephine Goldmark developed their brilliantly innovative approach to social and legal research independent of these men.[38] More important, the direction of intellectual and methodological influence seems to have run more often from the women to the male academics. The urban sociology that flourished at the University of Chicago in the 1920s built directly on the tradition of urban exploration and the novel research techniques of Hull House. Similarly, the sociological jurisprudence that flourished in American law schools in the 1920s clearly drew its inspiration from the National Consumers' League's briefs for *Muller v. Oregon* and its other labor law cases.[39]

The leading social work schools also, for a time, pioneered new practice-oriented forms of social science. With the help of grants from the Russell Sage Foundation in 1907, three schools—the Chicago School of Civics and Philanthropy, the New York School of Philanthropy, and the Boston School for Social Workers—established bureaus of research to train students in social investigation and to support the research of their faculty. At the New York School, the bureau was directed by Pauline Goldmark (sister of Josephine) and produced several innovative studies of the industrial working conditions and social life of the middle West Side. The bureau's training program could count among its alumnae such New Deal reformers as Josephine Roche and Frances Perkins. At the Chicago School, the links among social research, social work, and social reform were vigorously nurtured and defended by the social science–trained Abbott and Breckinridge, who served for many years as the directors of the school's Bureau of Research. Abbott rejected the view that "social reseach could only be 'scientific' if it had no regard for the finding of socially useful results and no interest in the human beings whose lives were being studied." She and Breckinridge hoped to tie the professionalization of social work not to the perfection of casework techniques but to the creation of specialized practical knowledge organized around "a body of authoritative data upon which programs for social reform and recommendations for changes in social legislation may be based."[40]

The federal government became a third major venue in which women developed their practical and reform-oriented social science. Here, the close proximity to policy making tied their research agenda more directly to the emergence of the positive state. The U.S. Children's Bureau, created in 1912, became the beachhead for this work in the emerging federal bureaucracy. Under the leadership of longtime Hull House resident Julia Lathrop, the bureau's small staff of university-trained female statisticians and health personnel pioneered the sociological and environmental approach to the study of infant mortality. Moreover, in contrast to Britain where male physician-researchers blamed infant mortality on working mothers, the Children's Bureau cited low wages and family poverty as the primary culprit. These conclusions, in turn, inspired and assisted the bureau's successful campaign for the nation's first national social welfare policy and its only universal health policy for mothers and children. [41] The U.S. Women's Bureau in the Department of Labor and the Bureau of Home Economics in the U.S. Department of Agriculture broadened the realm of government-based female social science in the early 1920s. The Women's Bureau's social scientists, though not as methodologically innovative as those working under Lathrop's dynamic leadership, regularly furnished policymakers with studies of women's wages and working conditions, as well as their family responsibilties, that called attention to women's structural disadvantages in the labor market. The Bureau of Home Economics, under Yale Ph.D. Louise Stanley, innovatively combined the social, physical, and nutritional sciences with its studies on the new consumer products and practices that were expanding the scientific content of the home.[42]

Postwar Transformations and Legacies

Following the failure of Progressivism and the disillusionment of war, many male social scientists intensified their search for a more rigid scientific approach. Responding to postwar reactionary movements and the evidence that public opinion was governed by ideology and not science, these men embraced a science of facts and numbers that would, they hoped, moderate the rising conflicts before them. The decision of the major foundations to fund academic social science research greatly strengthened this turn toward scientism. The Social Science Research Council (SSRC), established by the Rockefeller Foundation in 1923, channeled large sums of money into fellowships, summer conferences for university faculty, and, importantly, studies of social science methods for the first time. The creation of the Brookings Institution and the National Bureau of Economic Research (NBER), funded by the Russell Sage Foundation, also expanded the realm of the academic social sciences. Although Brookings and the NBER would develop a more policy-oriented outlook, they shared the growing interest in "scientific" methods, the pose of neutral expertise, and the rejection of advocacy of their university-based counterparts.[43]

These new institutional and funding patterns also helped consolidate academic social science as male terrain. Developments at the University of Chicago provide a good illustration. Since the 1890s, the University of Chicago had been among the most prominent producers of women social scientists. Like men, women were compelled to piece together the financial resources to sustain themselves while pursuing their graduate education. The advent of SSRC money at Chicago, however, introduced new structural disadvantages for women, since the university reserved the precious SSRC fellowships for its male graduate students. Not surprisingly, the important "Chicago School" of sociology and political science in the 1920s (which would set the research and methodological agenda of the social sciences for the next forty years) was associated exclusively with male faculty and their male graduate students.[44] The rise of the NBER and Brookings Institution had a similar effect. Although they were somewhat more open to women than were the universities, they too maintained a research staff that was overwhelmingly male.[45] The rising prestige of these institutions, in turn, sealed the identification of "scientific" scholarship with male academics. The SSRC's volume *Methods in Social Science*, perhaps the most important project of the period, revealed and reinforced the increasing invisibility of women in social science. The essays by the all-male list of contributors critiqued the methodology of key works in the social sciences written by other men. Mary van Kleeck's name, listed among the members of the SSRC committee sponsoring the project, provided the only evidence of women's former prominence in this domain.[46]

Meanwhile, the political and institutional supports of women's social science were eroding. Within academia, women's marginalization was greatly reinforced by their exclusion from wartime government projects. These activities created new relationships among male social scientists that often laid the basis for the discipline's postwar leadership. All the key jobs in the famous Army Psychological Testing Programs, for example, were held by male professors, including many, like its director Robert Yerkes of Yale University, whose previous specialty and experience did not include mental testing, which had been a female-dominated field. Later, when contacts developed in Washington, D.C., were turned into top positions at the National Research Council and elsewhere, women found themselves far from their discipline's centers of power.[47] Moreover, the postwar suppression of dissent took an especially large toll on women academics and social researchers, who had remained active in progressive causes, including the antiwar campaign. Jane Addams, Florence Kelley, Mary van Kleeck, Sophonisba Breckinridge, and others became the objects of vicious attacks by political extremists that eroded their public authority and weakened their political alliances with mainstream politicians. At Wellesley, Emily Greene Balch was forced to resign from the economics department because of her outspoken pacifism (she, like Jane Addams, would later be awarded a Nobel Peace Prize), and the social science program was virtually closed down for a decade.[48]

The Republicans' unbroken national ascendancy in the 1920s also redirected the efforts of the organizations and institutions that had spearheaded the search for the new practical forms of social knowledge. The Supreme Court's decision in *Adkins v. Children's Hospital* (1923), which struck down the District of Columbia's minimum wage law, put a halt to the campaign for state labor laws for women. The National Consumers' League's long battle to reverse the decision turned its attention to the more conventional strategy of reinterpreting the doctrine of substantive due process, since the *Adkins* court had rejected the sociological approach of *Muller*. Social work schools, and social workers, also narrowed their conceptual horizons in response to the contraction of opportunities for political reform. The rise of psychiatry in social work in the 1920s, with its emphasis on "personality" and individual adjustment rather than "environment," led social work schools (with the notable exception of the Chicago School) to discontinue any remaining commitment to social research. Finally, the settlement houses, too, increasingly abandoned their pioneering role in social investigation. The postwar reaction, the rise of the Community Chest system, and the arrival (appearance) of a generation of residents formally trained in social work would lead them to substitute the direct provision of social services for social research.[49]

During these years, however, the university reached an accommodation with some of the once-excluded female social sciences. The formal merger of the Chicago School of Civics and Philanthropy (renamed the School of Social Service Administration) with the University of Chicago in 1924 conferred academic prestige on social work; it also conferred on the university the benefits of having a closer interest in the concerns of the community outside its gates. An extensive network of university-based child welfare institutes, funded by the Laura Spelman Rockefeller Memorial Foundation, similarly created new places in the university for women to develop new forms of psychological knowledge. These accommodations, however, required the imposition of new hierarchies within the social sciences. The distinction between "basic" and "applied" research became more pronounced, and each realm took on an increasingly gendered character. Sociology, which had attracted an especially large number of women, now sought to distance itself from—and subordinate—social work. The University of Chicago's Robert Park actively discouraged sociology students from taking courses at the new School of Social Service Administration and openly castigated women reformers' role in social welfare matters. Occupational segregation by sex within the increasingly differentiated social sciences also became more common. In psychology, the clinical, educational, and industrial branches of the discipline became female enclaves distinguished by their lower pay and status.[50]

HISTORIOGRAPHY: CONCEPTUAL BLINDERS AND NEW DEPARTURES

What has the historiographical literature made of these developments? Most studies have traced the emergence and development of the social sciences to the epistemological shifts and political conflicts of industrial America in the latter half of the nineteenth and early twentieth centuries. But historians of the social sciences have left unexplored the impact of the upheaval in gender relations that also occurred at this time. Before we can integrate gender into the history of American social science, we need first to identify the conceptual blinders that have prevented previous scholars in this field from doing so.

The modern historiography of American social science can be dated from the publication of two now-classic books: Mary Furner's *Advocacy and Objectivity* and Thomas Haskell's *The Emergence of Professional Social Science*. Published in 1975 and 1977, respectively, at a time when the authority and objectivity of social science were under attack from many quarters, both books were concerned to explain the rise of professional social science in modern America. Haskell focused on the mid–nineteenth century and sought to explain the rise of the social scientific mentality and its eventual consolidation in the universities and the allied professional social science associations. Furner focused on the late nineteenth century and provided a social history of developments within the academic social sciences to 1905. She sought primarily to explain the form of the contemporary social sciences, especially their specialization and their pose of objectivity and value-neutrality. Together, these books provided the historiographical framework that shaped research in this area for nearly twenty years. Recently, Dorothy Ross's *Origins of American Social Science* entered upon this ground, providing a second conceptual framework for work in this field. Ross sought to explain the scientism and liberal ideological boundaries of American social science. Because these texts have provided the periodization, identified the key institutional contexts and actors, and set out the key conceptual issues and terms of explanation for research in this field, they are worth examining at some length.[51]

Furner and Haskell entered their history through the concept of professionalization, though they employed this term in slightly different ways. Haskell understood the term to refer to a particular intellectual outlook, one that embraced a model of causality dependent upon the principle of "interdependence." Furner borrowed her definition from sociology; in her view, professionalization involved the acquisition of such attributes as a unique social mission, a systematized body of specialized knowledge that provides the basis for practice, and a code of ethics to govern behavior within the profession. Haskell's definition led him to identify professional status exclusively with the academic disciplines. Furner, by contrast, saw the ASSA and the academic disciplines as representing different forms of professionalism with different professional strategies and ideals. In both cases, however, professionalization represented the story of the emerging dominance of academic social science.

The central characters and key institutional contexts presented in these texts followed from the teleology implied by the concept of professionalization. Both Furner and Haskell wrote their history through the categories of "professionals" and "amateurs."[52] Both books designated university-based social scientists the "professionals," though they did so for slightly different reasons: Haskell conferred this title because they embraced the "interdependent" model of causality, while Furner viewed them this way because social science was their full-time career and they derived their cultural authority from their esoteric knowledge and technical skill. Academic social scientists were juxtaposed with a second group of men, identified as their principal precursors, who were the "amateurs" of the ASSA. Both books represented the ASSA as a group of "best men" or "men of affairs" who derived their authority from their broad general knowledge, their individual character, their class privilege, and other forms of influence associated with the classical learned professions of religion, law, and medicine.

This material was woven together through a historical narrative that rested for its periodization on the key stages of professionalization. Haskell hews closely to the history of the ASSA, marking historical time with the key turning points in its development. He chronicles the ASSA's rise in the 1860s, its decline in the 1870s, and the proposed merger in 1878 of the ASSA and Johns Hopkins University. He shifts his attention from the ASSA to the professional, academic associations in the 1880s, following what he takes to be the decisive and irreversible transfer of authority from the amateur ASSA to the university that occurred during that decade. Furner's time line focuses on a later period and is punctuated by events wholly internal to the academic social sciences. Although she, too, begins with the ASSA, she focuses primarily on academic social scientists' changing conceptions of their social roles and responsibilities. In her telling, the key turning point occurred between 1884 and 1905, when the academic freedom trials compelled social scientists to recognize new constraints on their social roles and to recast their reform outlook in the language of objectivity and professional expertise. Both books end their narrative around 1909 when, having served as the staging ground for several professional organizations, the ASSA finally disbands. With this acknowledgment of the triumph of the academics, both books seem to suggest that the terrain of social science has been abandoned by all competitors and left wholly to its academic practitioners.

Finally, this historiographical framework recognized, though in a highly muted fashion, the role of class in shaping the social sciences during these years. Both Haskell and Furner set their study of social science against the background of an industrializing America preoccupied with the operation of the market, the distribution of wealth, and the emergence of a permanent working class. Both also saw social scientists as centrally struggling with the "social question." Haskell's gentry were clearly responding to the erosion of their authority by the emerging social relations of capitalism, and both they and the academics who succeeded them are represented as struggling mightily both to explain and to master the new pattern of interdependent human relations. Furner's social scientists, too, are deeply embedded in the social relations of the market economy. They grapple with it in their scholarship; different points of view about it tear apart their professional associations; and their outspoken view of its inequities brings down the wrath of conservative university presidents and trustees.

Ross's *Origins* presents a second historiographical framework that shares several assumptions of the earlier one. First, she, too, focuses on the university and her central characters are male academics. Ross also sets her study against the background of industrializing America, though class conflict and the threat of socialism figure centrally in her analysis. Ross, however, enters this history through the concept of American exceptionalism, the discursive frame within which the social sciences worked and sought to understand historical change. Ross's core chronological framework overlaps with that of Furner and Haskell, but historical time is marked by a different dynamic. Ross traces the social sciences' increasing commitment to science by focusing on their response to two key periods of political crisis: first, the Gilded Age, which she dates from the great strike wave of 1877 to the great depression of the mid-1890s; second, the second decade of the twentieth century, which encompassed Progressive reform, the First World War, and their disillusioning aftermath. Each period of upheaval severely tested the exceptionalist faith, Ross shows, prompting social scientists to revise their conception of America's place in history and their own disciplinary traditions.

Though ostensibly gender-neutral, both historiographical frameworks have operated to turn social science into an all-male project. The assumption that the founders of American social science were primarily concerned with "the social question" obscured the theoretical significance of the ASSA's large female membership and the centrality of feminist currents to the ASSA's vision of social science. These studies also concealed the distinctive trail that women blazed out of the ASSA into their own research and reform institutions, following only men's route to the university and representing it as gender-neutral. Finally, the analytical prominence of the universities marginalized the institutions in which women practiced social science during those years. The use of concepts such as professionalization and specialization further reinforced this focus on academic—hence male—social sciences. As a result, the centrality of men and academic social science to the history of American social science has been overstated, and the importance of women and their institutions to this history has been diminished.

The gendered, partial perspective of these conceptual frameworks is perhaps best demonstrated by the difficulty of fitting women's experience of, and encounter with, social science within it. The opposing categories of "amateur" (or reformer) and "professional," for example, cannot fully comprehend the careers and commitments of women like Mary van Kleeck or Florence Kelley who possessed specialized knowledge (most of which they had helped to create), embraced a distinctive social mission, and supported themselves with their research, yet also worked outside the universities and embraced a practical vision of social science that more closely resembled that of the ASSA than the academic social sciences. Similarly, periodization schemes linked to the rise of professional associations, the controversies of the academic trials, or the crises of class conflict and world war do not accord well with the key turning point of women's involvement with empirical social research. A more inclusive framework would have to give analytical weight to such developments as the opening of Harvard's psychological laboratory to women, the founding of Cornell's School of Home Economics, or the invention of sociological jurisprudence by Goldmark and Kelley in the National Consumers' League's brief for *Muller v. Oregon* in 1908.

Even as Furner and Haskell wrote, however, feminist challenges to social science were achieving a new level of visibility and authority. Feminism joined deconstruction, critical legal studies, and a host of other new theoretical approaches in critiquing the objectivity and value-neutrality of the social sciences. These concerns were given wide visibility with the publication of *Another Voice: Feminist Perspectives on Social Life and Social Science*, edited by Marcia Millman and Rosabeth Moss Kanter, two prominent sociologists, in 1975.[53] The collection turned the spotlight of feminist criticism on contemporary social science and revealed the gendered perspective of its conceptual tools and substantive conclusions. A large literature extending this approach emerged over the next decade and a half.[54] But the historical dimension of these questions remained largely unexplored.

In the early 1980s, feminist scholars began to turn their attention to the historical issues and to challenge the standard representation of American social science during its formative years. The early studies were usually inspired by a desire to recover the names of "lost" women social scientists and find female role models. They scrupulously documented women's extensive presence in turn-of-the-century social science and emphasized their achievements and contributions along with their experience of discrimination and exclusion. Later studies also highlighted their links to intellectual and reform currents and described the unconventional niches they often constructed as they sought to remain professionally active outside the university. These studies, combined with new research on the history of higher education, provided an important corrective to male-centered histories of social science. They placed the few well-known women—academic pioneers such as Margaret Mead and reformers such as Jane Addams—in a broader framework. These women were now viewed in the context of the struggles of two generations of women who strove to reshape early-twentieth-century social science.[55]

This research also raised broader and more fundamental questions about both the history and the historiography of social science. It disputed the narrative of women's slow but steady advance in the social sciences. The new research revealed, instead, that women's position in the social sciences had peaked in the 1920s and then fallen off, suggesting that women in the 1970s were only beginning to recover lost ground. Most important, it challenged the conventional definition of social science by revealing its roots in a male social biography. Because the term *social scientist* was reserved for individuals with advanced degrees and university appointments, it excluded many women in the wider realm of social science almost by definition. These women, feminist scholars noted, often lacked Ph.D.'s, and even those with doctorates frequently worked in nonacademic settings. Yet they were often intellectual innovators and made significant contributions to the social sciences, broadly construed.

These studies provided valuable material for a better understanding of the place and contributions of women in the American social sciences. They complicated distinctions between academic and applied knowledge, and between science and reform. Perhaps more fundamentally, they highlighted the need for a new interpretive framework for illuminating the development of American social science. A different institutional landscape and set of actors, along with different battle lines and conceptions of science, came clearly into view when the history of American social science was viewed through women's experience.

In the end, however, the approach implied in this work proved also to have limitations. The focus on women—their contributions, their reform activities, their experience of discrimination—seemed implicitly to assume that women are the only gender-marked category. This work persuasively demonstrated that turn-of-the-century women social researchers' conception of the meaning and purposes of social knowledge was marked by their experience as women; but it failed to extend that crucial insight to male social scientists and their research. Even where explicit comparisons between male and female social scientists were drawn, men's conception of knowledge and science was represented (even if only implicitly) as gender-neutral. The belief that gender is an attribute only of female persons placed the academic social sciences—their investigative practices, bodies of social knowledge, scientific communities—beyond the reach of this approach. To address *these* issues—to rethink not just the place of women in the social sciences but the social sciences themselves—requires additional analytical tools.

Gender analysis as a distinct method came into extensive use in the mid-1980s, though it describes research strategies, theoretical approaches, and epistemological commitments that reach back to the earliest days of feminist scholarship. Taking inspiration from a wide range of theoretical developments showing the constructed character of knowledge, gender analysis offered scholars the interpretive tools to reach beyond women to explore how understandings of sexual difference become embedded in language, institutions, social practices, and structural relationships. Gender analysis enables us to see that both men and women are gendered subjectivities, and it compels us to ask how people construct and understand their experience of masculinity and femininity, how these meanings are related to the conditions under which they live and work.[56]

The essays in this volume begin the task of extending gender analysis to the history of the American social sciences during their formative years. Gender analysis promises to shed new light on the history of American social science in at least two ways. First, gender analysis invites us to reconsider academic social science as a gender-marked body of knowledge, social practice, and form of cultural commentary. From this perspective, such ostensibly gender-neutral issues as the cultural authority of expertise, the division of labor among the academic social sciences, or the meaning of professionalization and specialization take on new meanings. Second, gender analysis invites us to broaden our scope of inquiry and to reevaluate the social science that women practiced and produced outside the university. This perspective compels us to consider the role of gender in setting the boundaries between applied and academic, reform and science, and establishing the meanings of these polarities.

New Contributions

Part One, "Discourses of Gender in the Social Sciences," explores the ways in which sexual difference was discussed and represented within three academic social sciences. Although the breakdown of the Victorian gender system in the late nineteenth century provoked widespread popular debate over the meaning of sexual difference, these controversies were only partially articulated—if at all—in the individual disciplines themselves. The essays in this section explore how these debates were mediated by each discipline's own distinct intellectual traditions, strategies of cultural authority, and internal gender politics. The essays reveal the diversity of gender discourses operating within the social sciences during their formative years and challenge fundamentally the long-standing view of the academic disciplines as gender-neutral bodies of knowledge. They also call attention to important methodological issues in their differing approaches to explaining the character and salience of these discourses.

Nancy Folbre's "The 'Sphere of Women' in Early-Twentieth-Century Economics" examines an important paradox in turn-of-the-century economics. Despite the raging popular controversies over women's entrance into paid employment, the discipline proved resolutely uninterested in this pressing social problem. Folbre's explanation focuses on the relationship between gender and research topics during these crucial years. Women economists, she notes, were far more likely than their male counterparts to pursue research on women workers. But their intellectual concerns never became a permanent part of the discipline's agenda. Folbre argues that the increasing number of women receiving advanced degrees in economics provoked the defensive response on the part of male economists of refusing to hire women as faculty members into their departments. The effort to maintain economics as a male project was also sanctioned by prevailing theories of political economy, which saw women primarily in domestic terms. With women economists unable to obtain permanent university positions, research on women workers was also eliminated from the academic discipline's ambit. Gender continued to permeate economic theory, primarily in disciplinary debates about the family wage, but this patriarchal de-

piction of sexual difference clearly indicated the defeat of the women economists' challenge.

Mary G. Dietz and James Farr's "'Politics Would Undoubtedly Unwoman
Her': Gender, Suffrage, and American Political Science" explores the debate
over woman suffrage as it was articulated in late-nineteenth-century political
science. Focusing on texts by Francis Lieber, Theodore Dwight Woolsey,
Johann Bluntschli, and W. W. Willoughby, Dietz and Farr argue that the discipline's gendered images of State and Citizen facilitated and motivated its arguments against women's enfranchisement. With the domain of the State figured
as male, and the Citizen celebrated for his manhood, the inclusion of women in
civic life clearly threatened to undermine the masculinity of the political realm.
Yet ultimately, Dietz and Farr conclude, late-nineteenth-century political science proved unable to provide a convincing case for denying women the vote.
The arbitrary and often conflicting assignment of gender to other elements of
political life prevented the elaboration of a coherent argument against woman
suffrage.

Kamala Visweswaran's essay, "'Wild West' Anthropology and the Disciplining of Gender," examines the discourse of gender in a field unusually hospita-
ble to women. Visweswaran seeks to explain the emergence and character of
feminist analysis in anthropology at the turn of the century. She argues that its
advent was not simply a result of the large number of women in anthropology.
Rather, she suggests, it also reflected the ways in which the discipline's dominant paradigm both invited and constrained research on the relations between
the sexes. Victorian evolutionary theory, which implicitly viewed sex roles not
as "natural" but as the achievement of civilization, strongly encouraged research on gender relations by women anthropologists. Ultimately, although
early women anthropologists were among the most likely women of their class
to argue against racial and gender stereotypes, their failure to perceive the racial hierarchies embedded in the evolutionary paradigm prevented them from
fully reversing its assumptions about gender relations.

Part Two, "Gender as Constitutive of Social Science," examines the ways in
which gender shaped the production, organization, and uses of social knowledge in the late nineteenth and early twentieth centuries. These essays explore
three different types of social science during the years when they acquired
their characteristic styles of reasoning, methodological orientations, and professional ethos. The processes through which the social sciences took on their distinct identities have most often been analyzed in terms of such macrohistorical,
and ostensibly gender-neutral, processes as modernization and professionalization. But these essays suggest that gender also played a critical role in the social
construction of the new social knowledge. They show how the intellectual and
professional projects of both women and men were patterned by institutional
and conceptual structures deeply informed by gender.

In "*Hull-House Maps and Papers*: Social Science as Women's Work in the
1890s," Kathryn Kish Sklar examines a distinctly female social science tradition
that emerged in the last decade of the nineteenth century. Sklar focuses on

Hull-House Maps and Papers, the most significant product of this tradition, and explores the several ways in which gender informed its production, its content, and the purposes for which it was assembled. Sklar calls our attention, first and foremost, to the network of female-controlled settlement houses and private institutions that sprang up in the hollows of America's liberal state. It was this unique institutional setting, itself a consequence of nineteenth-century gender relations, that produced and sustained a distinct female social science tradition. Untouched by the repressive policies of university presidents and boards of trustees, the women of Hull House were free to combine their interest in women's sphere with innovative social science methods to emphasize the need for state initiatives for women and children. Thus *Hull-House Maps and Papers*, which set new standards for social investigation, sharply illuminates the gendered features of contemporary social science.

In "'A Government of Men': Gender, the City, and the New Science of Politics," I tackle the question of how gender informed the processes through which the boundaries of political science were set in the early twentieth century. Although these years were, in many ways, a "golden age" of women's activism in the public sphere, political scientists conceived their intellectual terrain—the domain of "politics"—in terms that wholly excluded their remarkably extensive presence. This view, I argue, was not a straightforward result of the male bias of this most masculine of all social science fields. Rather, it emerged as political scientists puzzled over what they perceived to be the central problem of their day: the party machines' control of city politics and government. In assembling their new science of politics out of the diverse elements of this problem, political scientists brought both an inherited intellectual tradition and ideas, drawn from their own experience as middle-class men, of the shape of the well-run city, which they unwittingly assimilated into their new science.

In "The Establishment of an Applied Social Science: Home Economists, Science, and Reform at Cornell University, 1870–1930," Nancy K. Berlage examines the rise of home economics, a unique female-dominated academic discipline devoted to the home and family. Focusing on developments at Cornell University, where the first and most distinguished program would take shape, Berlage explores the ways in which home economists combined elements of both the female reform tradition and the academic practices pioneered by male social scientists to create a new "applied" form of social knowledge. Berlage rejects the view that home economics was simply an expression of late Victorian separate spheres ideology or a repository for academic women excluded from other disciplines; she sees instead an innovative search for power and authority, in which home economists capitalized on domestic discourse and the clout of the women's reform community to make a place in the university both for themselves and for their new knowledge about home and family.

The third part, "Social Science as Cultural Critique," explores social science as a vehicle of social commentary rather than a body of expert knowledge or a new university discipline. The volume's methodology shifts here, turning away from disciplinary history to explore the rich complexity of individual experience. Converging with the recent renaissance of feminist biography, these essays examine the lives and work of three extraordinary women—Jane Addams, Elsie Clews Parsons, and Mary van Kleeck—whose engagement with social science helped pioneer the passage from the late Victorian to the modern world. The essays illuminate the ways in which social science's rich public life was both informed by, and transformed, contemporary discourses about gender. Addams, Parsons, and van Kleeck each drew upon the cultural resources of their gender as they struggled to make sense of the central problems of their day. Their effort to reach a broad popular audience through women's clubs, public speaking, and popular journals was only one of several ways they differed from their academic counterparts. These essays call our attention to forms of social science that did not simply encode existing relations of power, as much social science history suggests, but instead helped to generate new, critical understandings of class, family, and community.

In "Gendered Social Knowledge: Domestic Discourse, Jane Addams, and the Possibilities of Social Science," Dorothy Ross explores the role of domestic ideology in shaping Addams's interpretive sociology. Ross retrieves Addams from the margins of social science history, where the appellation "social reformer" had long consigned her, and relocates her within a broader, more complex history of social science. Ross argues that Victorian domestic discourse did not operate simply as a constraint on Addams's life but also offered her unique resources for a new approach to social knowledge. Drawing on notions of feminine intuition and women's higher morality, an appreciation of emotion in women's lives, as well as pragmatist and romanticist intellectual currents, Addams's interpretive sociology enabled her to conceive of a mutual social connection with her urban neighbors that Ross characterizes as "social democracy on the domestic model." Addams's gendered social knowledge also offered an important alternative to the academic social sciences then emerging in the university. Addams's practice-oriented approach, in which knowledge emerged from democratic social action and interpretation rather than from science, was, Ross suggests, one of many paths not taken by American social science.

In "Bringing Social Science Back Home: Theory and Practice in the Life and Work of Elsie Clews Parsons," Desley Deacon explores Parsons's social science as it critiqued the conventions of middle-class family life. Parsons was a wealthy socialite and modernist New Woman; her own struggle to combine a productive work life and family inspired her radical challenge to the domestic paradigm at the heart of the Victorian gender system. Acting as a native informant in her own milieu, Parsons combined ideas drawn from sociology and anthropology with new feminist currents to lay bare the debilitating effects of family life on women's capacity for social and sexual development. Her public refashioning of the family, which echoed conflicts in her own life, replaced Victorian concepts of self, gender, and home with a vision of the modern family based on equality and the autonomy and personal development of both partners. Deacon's essay illuminates the significance of the personal conflicts generated by

America's Victorian gender legacy for the production of new social knowledge in the early twentieth century.

In "The 'Self-Applauding Sincerity' of Overreaching Theory, Biography as Ethical Practice, and the Example of Mary van Kleeck," Guy Alchon takes on the meaning of gender analysis through an exploration of the life and work of the pioneering industrial sociologist and social worker Mary van Kleeck. Alchon challenges a perceived dichotomy in the historiography between female practitioners of a reform-oriented social science and male academics' commitment to a "scientific" and "objective" social science, and he offers van Kleeck as an example of a woman who defies this categorization. He represents van Kleeck as a Christian radical, motivated by a fusion of "evangelical faith and social science mysticism" rather than female values or feminist agendas. As he traces van Kleeck's life from her days at Smith College through her involvement with the International Industrial Relations Institute, he emphasizes her commitment to a technocratic social science, which fused scientific management and social work, to remedy the terrible instability of early-twentieth-century American economic life. In doing so, Alchon cautions us against constructing new dichotomies even as gender analysis seeks to dismantle them in other areas.

NOTES

I would like to thank Mary Furner and Dorothy Ross for helpful comments on an earlier draft of this essay.

1. Mary Furner, *Advocacy and Objectivity: A Crisis in the Professionalization of American Social Science, 1865–1905* (Lexington: University Press of Kentucky, 1975).

2. Many middle-class women's clubs of the turn of the century, for example, pursued programs of study in the "social and political sciences" that examined such problems as philanthropy, public health, immigration, and social reform. See William Howe Tolman, *Municipal Reform Movements in the United States* (New York: Fleming H. Revell Co., 1895), pt. 4; Marion Talbot and Lois Kimball Mathews Rosenberry, *The History of the American Association of University Women, 1881–1931* (Boston: Houghton Mifflin Co., 1931), 98–99, 102–3.

3. William Leach, *True Love and Perfect Union: The Feminist Reform of Sex and Society* (New York: Basic Books, 1980), 314.

4. The most extensive history of the ASSA (which, however, overlooks women and gender) can be found in Thomas L. Haskell, *The Emergence of Professional Social Science: The American Social Science Association and the Nineteenth Century Crisis of Authority* (Urbana: University of Illinois Press, 1977). The membership figures are from Rosalind Rosenberg, *Beyond Separate Spheres: Intellectual Roots of Modern Feminism* (New Haven: Yale University Press, 1982), 25.

5. On the ASSA's opposition to narrow specialization and the compartmentalization of knowledge, see Furner, *Advocacy and Objectivity*, chap. 13, and Leach, *True Love and Perfect Union*, chap. 12.

6. The affinities between the new empiricism and nineteenth-century feminism are discussed extensively in Leach, *True Love and Perfect Union*, chaps. 11–12.

28 SILVERBERG

7. For the history of the movement to open higher education to women, see Mabel Newcomer, *A Century of Higher Education for Women* (New York: Harper, 1959); Barbara Miller Solomon, *In the Company of Educated Women* (New Haven: Yale University Press, 1985), chap. 4. For the experience of women college students during these years, see Lynn Gordon, *Gender and Higher Education in the Progressive Era* (New Haven: Yale University Press, 1990).

8. Newcomer, *A Century of Higher Education*, 46. To be sure, only a small number of women had access to a college education at this time. In 1920, women enrolled in institutions of higher learning represented only 7.6 percent of all women aged eighteen to twenty-one.

9. Solomon (*In the Company of Educated Women*) notes that the desire among college-educated women for employment other than teaching helped foster efforts to professionalize nursing, social work, and, of course, education.

10. This is the argument of Furner, *Advocacy and Objectivity*.

11. On the National Consumers' League, see Maud Nathan, *The Story of an Epoch-Making Movement* (New York: Doubleday, Page, 1926). On the settlements, see Kathryn Kish Sklar, "Who Funded Hull House?" in *Lady Bountiful Revisited: Women, Philanthropy, and Power*, ed. Kathleen McCarthy (New Brunswick, N.J.: Rutgers University Press, 1990), and Sklar, "*Hull-House Maps and Papers*" in this volume. For an excellent discussion of the vibrant communities that flourished at women's colleges, see Patricia A. Palmieri, *In Adamless Eden: The Community of Women Faculty at Wellesley* (New Haven: Yale University Press, 1995).

12. The ACA's study is discussed in Talbot and Rosenberry, *History*, chap. 5. See also Rosenberg, *Beyond Separate Spheres*, 18–24.

13. The classic general studies of this period are Dorothy Ross, "The Development of the Social Sciences," in *The Organization of Knowledge in Modern America, 1860–1920*, ed. Alexandra Oleson and John Voss (Baltimore: Johns Hopkins University Press, 1979), chap. 3, and Dorothy Ross, *The Origins of American Social Science* (Cambridge: Cambridge University Press, 1991). For good historical overviews of the individual disciplines, see Kurt Danziger, *Constructing the Subject: Historical Origins of Psychological Research* (Cambridge: Cambridge University Press, 1990); Albert Somit and Joseph Tannenhaus, *The Development of American Political Science* (Boston: Allyn and Bacon, 1967); Anthony Oberschall, *The Establishment of Empirical Sociology* (New York: Harper and Row, 1972); George W. Stocking, *Race, Culture, and Evolution* (New York: Free Press, 1968); Joseph Dorfman, *The Economic Mind in American Civilization* (New York: Viking Press, 1959).

14. Rosenberg, *Beyond Separate Spheres*, 81–82.

15. Susan Carter, "Academic Women Revisited: An Empirical Study of Changing Patterns in Women's Employment as College and University Faculty, 1890–1963," *Journal of Social History* 14, no. 4 (Summer 1987): 675–99; Margaret W. Rossiter, *Women Scientists in America: Struggles and Strategies to 1940* (Baltimore: Johns Hopkins University Press, 1982), chap. 1.

16. On the importance of language to the creation of professional authority, though without attention to gender, see JoAnne Brown, *The Definition of a Profession: The Authority of Metaphor in the History of Intelligence Testing, 1890–1930* (Princeton: Princeton University Press, 1992).

17. Cited in ibid., 62.

18. On Ogburn and more generally on this topic, see Barbara Laslett, "Unfeeling Knowledge: Emotion and Objectivity in the History of Sociology," *Sociological Forum*

5 (1990): 413–33, and idem, "Gender in/and Social Science History," *Social Science History* 16, no. 2 (Summer 1992): 177–95 (quotation on 182); on Bernard, see Robert Bannister, *Sociology and Scientism: The American Quest for Objectivity, 1880–1940* (Chapel Hill: University of North Carolina Press, 1987), chap. 9; on Hall, see Dorothy Ross, *G. Stanley Ross: The Psychologist as Prophet* (Chicago: University of Chicago Press, 1972), chap. 5; on Cattell, see E. Anthony Rotundo, *American Manhood: Transformations in Masculinity from the Revolution to the Modern Era* (New York: Basic Books, 1993), 223, 232, 267.

19. For a good gender analysis of Thomas's work, see Rosenberg, *Beyond Separate Spheres*, 120–31.

20. Quoted in John P. Diggins, *The Bard of Savagery: Thorstein Veblen and Modern Social Theory* (New York: The Seabury Press, 1978), 147.

21. Thomas and Veblen's truncated academic careers, for reasons directly related to unconventional sexual activities, no doubt warned others away from such open discussion of these matters in their scholarly work.

22. Gordon, *Gender and Higher Education*, chap. 1; Rossiter, *Women Scientists*, chap. 2; Solomon, *In the Company of Educated Women*, 133–38. Prior to the 1890s, women either attended European graduate schools (this was the route taken by Florence Kelley) or pursued graduate study in the United States but were not awarded the doctoral degree—as in the case of the psychologist Mary Whiton Calkins.

23. W. Norman Brown, *Johns Hopkins Half-Century Directory* (Baltimore: Johns Hopkins University Press, 1926), 411–12. By the time the American Psychological Association celebrated its twenty-fifth anniversary in 1917, the APA could boast of having had two women presidents and a membership that was 13 percent female. Laurel Furumoto, "On the Margins: Women and the Professionalization of Psychology, 1890–1940," in *Psychology in Twentieth-Century Thought and Society*, ed. Mitchell G. Ash and William R. Woodward (New York: Cambridge University Press, 1987), 97. In political science, the numbers were far lower: only 12 of the 163 dissertations in progress in 1912 were being written by women, and the numbers reached only about 12 percent during the 1920s. See *American Political Science Review* 6 (1912): 464–71; 14 (1920): 155–58; 16 (1922): 497–99; 19. Similarly, 29.9 percent of Ph.D.'s awarded in anthropology between 1923 and 1938 were awarded to women. Rossiter, *Women Scientists*, 157.

24. Rosenberg, *Beyond Separate Spheres*, chaps. 3–5.

25. Several recent books explore Abbott's life and work. See Lela B. Costin, *Two Sisters for Social Justice: A Biography of Grace and Edith Abbott* (Urbana: University of Illinois Press, 1983); Ellen Fitzpatrick, *Endless Crusade: Women Social Scientists and Progressive Reform* (New York: Oxford University Press, 1990).

26. This is, in part, the argument of Rosenberg, *Beyond Separate Spheres*. Quotation on 83.

27. Palmieri, *In Adamless Eden*, chap. 6. Rossiter also makes this same point about women scientists at the women's colleges during these years. Rossiter, *Women Scientists*, chap. 1.

28. Estelle Freedman, "Separatism Revisited: Women's Institutions, Social Reform, and the Career of Miriam van Waters," in *U.S. History as Women's History: New Feminist Essays*, ed. Linda Kerber, Alice Kessler-Harris, and Kathryn Kish Sklar (Chapel Hill: University of North Carolina Press, 1995), chap. 8. On Davis, see Fitzpatrick, *Endless Crusade*; on Kellor, see "Frances Kellor," in Mary Jo Deegan, *Women in Sociology: A Bio-Bibliographical Sourcebook* (New York: Greenwood, 1991).

29. Peixotto chaired the Heller Committee for Research in Social Economics at Berkeley for many years. Kingsbury directed the Carola Woerishoffer graduate department of social economy and social research at Bryn Mawr College. The histories of social economics, sanitary science, and domestic science have yet to be written, though something of their history can be gleaned from biographical material on their practitioners. See "Susan Kingsbury," in Deegan, *Bio-Bibliography of Women in Sociology*, 217–23; "Susan Kingsbury," *Notable American Women*, ed. Edward T. James, Janet Wilson James, and Paul S. Boyer (Cambridge: Harvard University Press, 1971) 2:335–36; "Jessica Blanche Peixotto," *Notable American Women*, 3:42–43; *Essays in Social Economics: In Honor of Jessica Blanche Peixotto* (1935; reprint, Freeport, N.Y.: Books for Libraries Press, 1967). Social economics, for example, was not exclusively a female domain. Edward T. Devine, director of the New York School of Philanthropy, held the title of Schiff Professor of Social Economy at Columbia School of Political Science from 1905 to 1919. Nevertheless, at Columbia (as elsewhere) the field was associated with social work and social reform; Devine's main qualification for the position seems to have been his experience in social work. See R. Gordon Hoxie, *A History of the Faculty of Political Science, Columbia University* (New York: Columbia University Press, 1955), 78–79. Moreover, he did not hold an advanced degree, unlike both Peixotto and Kingsbury.

30. Rossiter touches on this matter for the natural sciences, though she treats it primarily as a labor market issue, that is, in terms of the emergence of occupational segregation by sex, and not as a question of the reorganization and institutionalization of social knowledge. See Rossiter, *Women Scientists*, chap. 3.

31. Rosenberg, *Beyond Separate Spheres*, 35, 49.

32. Costin, *Two Sisters*, 58–67; Fitzpatrick, *Endless Crusade*; Robyn Muncy, *Creating a New Female Dominion in American Reform, 1890–1935* (New York: Oxford University Press, 1991), chap. 3.

33. See Michael J. Lacey and Mary O. Furner, "Social Investigation, Social Knowledge, and the State: An Introduction," in *The State and Social Investigation in Britain and the United States*, ed. Lacey and Furner (Cambridge: Cambridge University Press, 1993), chap. 1.

34. The role of these women as "policy experts" in the development of the American welfare state is extensively explored in Theda Skocpol, *Protecting Soldiers and Mothers: The Political Origins of Social Policy in the United States* (Cambridge: Harvard University Press, 1992), esp. pt. 3, and Kathryn Kish Sklar, "The Historical Foundations of Women's Power in the Creation of the American Welfare State, 1830–1930," in *Mothers of a New World: Maternalist Politics and the Origins of Welfare States*, ed. Seth Koven and Sonya Michel (New York: Routledge, 1993), chap. 1. On some of the female-dominated institutions that supported social investigation, though sometimes with an emphasis on activities other than research, see Sklar, "*Hull-House Maps and Papers*," in this volume; and idem, *Florence Kelley and the Nation's Work* (New Haven: Yale University Press, 1996); John M. Glenn, Lillian Brandt, and F. Emerson Andrews, *Russell Sage Foundation, 1907–1946* (New York: Russell Sage Foundation, 1947); Robert A. Woods and Albert J. Kennedy, eds., *Handbook of Settlements* (New York: Charity Publications Committee, 1911); Eileen Boris, *Home to Work: Motherhood and the Politics of Industrial Homework in the United States* (New York: Cambridge University Press, 1994), chap. 3; Sarah Deutch, "Learning to Talk More Like a Man: Boston Women's Class-Bridging Organizations, 1870–1940," *American Historical Review* (April 1992).

35. For the larger context of the legal brief, including its relationship to new legal approaches, see Nancy Woloch, *Muller v. Oregon: A Brief History with Documents* (New York: St. Martin's Press, 1996).

36. Glenn, Brandt, and Andrews, *Russell Sage Foundation*, 154.

37. See Dorothy Ross's essay in this volume.

38. Though the early legal briefs were worked out, in part, with Louis Brandeis. See Vivian Hart, *Bound by Our Constitution: Women, Workers, and the Minimum Wage* (Princeton: Princeton University Press, 1994), chap. 5.

39. Ross, *Origins*, 226–27; Woloch, *Muller v. Oregon*, 26–27; Hart, *Bound by Our Constitution*, 110–11.

40. On the Chicago School, see Costin, *Two Sisters*, 59–62 (quotation on 194), and Muncy, *Creating a New Female Dominion*, chap 3 (quotation on 76). On the New York School, see Elizabeth G. Meier, *A History of the New York School of Social Work* (New York: Columbia University Press, 1954). See also Roy Lubove, *The Professional Altruist: The Emergence of Social Work as a Career, 1880–1930* (Cambridge: Harvard University Press, 1965), 137–48.

41. Kriste Lindenmeyer, *"A Right to Childhood": The U.S. Children's Bureau and Child Welfare, 1912–46* (Urbana: University of Illinois Press, 1997), chap. 2, and Muncy, *Creating a New Female Dominion*, chap. 2, esp. 50–52.

42. On the Bureau of Home Economics, see Rossiter, *Women Scientists*, 229. On the Women's Bureau, see Judith Sealander, *As Minority Becomes Majority: Federal Reaction to the Phenomenon of Women in the Workforce, 1920–1963* (Westport, Conn.: Greenwood Press, 1983), 28, 40–44.

43. Ross, *Origins*, chap. 10; Donald T. Critchlow, *The Brookings Institution, 1916–1952* (De Kalb: Northern Illinois University Press, 1985); David Grossman, "Philanthropy and Social Science Research: The Rockefeller Foundation and Economics, 1913–1929," *Minerva* 20 (Summer 1982): 59–82; Barry D. Karl and Stanley N. Katz, "The American Private Philanthropic Foundation and the Public Sphere, 1890–1930," *Minerva* 19 (Summer 1981): 251–57.

44. Martin Bulmer, *The Chicago School of Sociology: Institutionalization, Diversity, and the Rise of Sociological Research* (Chicago: University of Chicago Press, 1984), 164–70 and chap. 11; Barry Karl, *Charles E. Merriam and the Study of Politics* (Chicago: University of Chicago Press, 1974), chap. 8; and Rossiter, *Women Scientists*, 36, 159, 185.

45. Arthur Burns, ed., "Introductory Sketch," in *Wesley Clair Mitchell: The Economic Scientist* (New York: National Bureau of Economic Research, 1952); Critchlow, *The Brookings Institution*, chap. 4.

46. Stuart A. Rice, ed., *Methods in Social Science: A Case Book* (Chicago: University of Chicago Press, 1931).

47. Rossiter, *Women Scientists*, 119.

48. J. Stanley Lemons, *The Woman Citizens: Social Feminism in the 1920s* (1973; reprint, Charlottesville: University Press of Virginia, 1990), chap. 8; Mary Jo Deegan, "Sociology at Wellesley: 1900–1919," *Journal of the History of Sociology* 5, no. 1 (Spring 1983): 91–115. Wartime reaction also forced the resignation of several male social scientists, most prominently Charles Beard, but there were simply fewer active reformers among the men. The academic trials had already removed or subdued them.

49. Hart, *Bound by Our Constitution*, chap 7; Lubove, *The Professional Altruist*, chap. 3; Judith Ann Trolander, *Settlement Houses and the Great Depression* (Detroit: Wayne State University Press, 1975), chap. 3; Allen F. Davis, *Spearheads for Reform: The Social*

Settlements and the Progressive Movement (New York: Oxford University Press, 1967), chap. 11.

50. On the School of Social Service Administration, see Costin, *Two Sisters*, 63–67, and Muncy, *Creating a New Female Dominion*, 79–92. On the child welfare institutes, see Furumoto, "On the Margins," chap. 4; Nancy Felipe Russo, "Psychology's Foremothers: Their Achievements in Context," in *Models of Achievement: Reflections of Eminent Women in Psychology*, ed. Agnes N. O'Connell and Nancy Felipe Russo (New York: Columbia University Press, 1983), 18; Bulmer, *The Chicago School of Sociology*, 68.

51. Furner, *Advocacy and Objectivity*; Haskell, *The Emergence of Professional Social Science*; Ross, *Origins*.

52. Furner specifically noted the invidious distinctions implied by these terms and recommended that the word *amateur* be rehabilitated to imply only different (rather than inferior) institutional affiliations, motives, and work routines.

53. Marcia Millman and Rosabeth Moss Kanter, eds., *Another Voice: Feminist Perspectives on Social Life and Social Science* (New York: Anchor Books, 1975). The anthology's publication by a trade press suggests the wide audience for feminist critiques of the social sciences at that time.

54. This literature is now very large. Collections that cover most of the social sciences include Christine Farnham, ed., *The Impact of Feminist Research in the Academy* (Bloomington: Indiana University Press, 1987), and Sue Rosenberg Zalk and Janice Gordon-Kelter, eds., *Revolutions in Knowledge: Feminism in the Social Sciences* (Boulder: Westview Press, 1992). Excellent discipline-specific studies include Marianne A. Ferber and Julie A. Nelson, eds., *Beyond Economic Man: Feminist Theory and Economics* (Chicago: University of Chicago Press, 1993); Micaela de Leonardo, ed., *Gender at the Crossroads of Knowledge: Feminist Anthropology in the Postmodern Era* (Berkeley and Los Angeles: University of California Press, 1991).

55. In psychology, see O'Connell and Russo, *Models of Achievement*, and Laurel Furumoto and Elizabeth Scarborough, *Untold Lives* (New York: Columbia University Press, 1987); in anthropology, see Nancy Parezo, ed., *Hidden Scholars: Women Anthropologists and the Native American Southwest* (Albuquerque: University of New Mexico Press, 1993), and Ute Gacs, Aisha Khan, Jerrie McIntyre, and Ruth Weinberg, eds., *Women Anthropologists: A Biographical Dictionary* (Westport, Conn.: Greenwood Press, 1988); in sociology, see Deegan, *Women in Sociology*; idem, "Women in Sociology: 1890–1930," *Journal of the History of Sociology* 1 (Fall 1978): 11–34. Among the best later studies are Rosenberg, *Beyond Separate Spheres*; Sklar, *Florence Kelley*; Costin, *Two Sisters*; Fitzpatrick, *Endless Crusade*.

56. The classic statement of this perspective is Joan Scott, "Gender: A Useful Category of Analysis," in her *Gender and the Politics of History* (New York: Columbia University Press, 1988).

PART ONE

Discourses of Gender in the Social Sciences

The "Sphere of Women" in Early-Twentieth-Century Economics

NANCY FOLBRE

IN THE 1930s, toward the end of her career, the economist and social reformer Edith Abbott spoke confidently of the direction her life had taken:

> Some of our social science friends are afraid that we cannot be scientific because we really care about what we are doing and we are even charged with being senti-mental. . . . This does not frighten me [either], for I know that a great physician also cares about the human beings he is taking care of and, like him, we can be kind with-out being sentimental.[1]

This point of view was not shared by most economists of Abbott's day. As many scholars have noted, women academics of the Progressive Era were more likely than their male counterparts to focus on social policy issues and to embrace an unabashedly reformist stance.[2] The men who came to dominate the social sci-ences distanced themselves from reformist efforts and defined objectivity as a desirable (and masculine) trait. They also channeled women scholars into sepa-rate specialties and disciplines.

The professionalization of the social sciences in the early twentieth century has been described as a contest in which objectivity superseded advocacy and science transcended reformism.[3] But while "objectivity" and "science" became central to the discourse of economics during this period, they were defined in highly gendered terms that undermined their own intent.[4] Economists took the metaphor of separate spheres to extremes, questioning not only the possi-bility but the very desirability of female objectivity.[5] Many insisted that women's sphere—defined by morality and sentiment—could not and should not be analyzed in economic terms. The notion that women, unlike men, should not pursue their own self-interest provided a convenient justification for their exclusion from skilled employment in the academy as well as in the economy as a whole.

The concept of women's sphere also had important consequences for the content of economic research, manifested in a widespread reluctance to con-sider women, children, or the family appropriate subjects of economic analysis. Both neoclassical and institutionalist economists considered women's unpaid labor in the home morally important but economically unproductive. A certain taboo against studying women and children extended even to their participa-tion in market work. Between 1886 and 1920, the overwhelming majority of scholarly publications on this topic were authored by women. In fact, women economists' major contribution lay in their careful and critical analysis of women's and children's economic position.

In this paper I explore the relationships among economic theory, discrimination against women scholars, and the treatment of "women's topics" both in the discipline as a whole and at the University of Chicago, where Edith Abbott and Sophonisba Breckinridge were at least partially successful at creating a new space for themselves and their research. I emphasize the mutually reinforcing character of the force fields defining gender segregation. Conventional economic theory provided an explicit rationale for discrimination, which discouraged the kinds of research that could effectively challenge theoretical assumptions, which in turn reinforced discrimination. The cumulative effect circumscribed both the composition of the profession and the content of the discipline. Neither the practical nor the theoretical boundaries were impermeable. But the very strategies that successful women economists used to infiltrate them suggest an awareness of their interconnectedness.

The starting point of this story is a summary of the ways economists conceptualized gender, showing how the rhetoric of objectivity concealed an uncritical acceptance of prevailing social norms. Academic economists actively promoted the concept of a family wage for men. Because female entrance into wage employment could lower male wages, it threatened not only the family but the very moral basis of society. The second section examines some practical consequences of this assumption. Women could be encouraged to study but not to compete for jobs. As a result, most of those who earned Ph.D.'s—even Edith Abbott, who published extensively in one of the best-known economics journals—were denied positions within the economics discipline. Modest successes for women at the University of Chicago resulted from a combination of unusual circumstances, exceptional faculty, and carefully planned collective action.

In the long run, their institutional victories may have been less significant than their intellectual accomplishments. The third section presents an empirical analysis of the content of research published in economic journals. The exception illustrates the rule: only one major journal editor, J. Laurence Laughlin, proved sympathetic to research on women's work, probably because it was authored by women who had been among his best students at the University of Chicago. As soon as Edith Abbott and Sophonisba Breckinridge got a foot in the door, they began to develop an analysis of women's work that revealed the unscientific and ideological character of the separate spheres approach.

THE FAMILY WAGE

Women's rights were hotly debated in the nineteenth century, and at least one influential economist, John Stuart Mill, was a feminist partisan.[6] By 1900, however, economists had established a paradigmatic consensus very much in keeping with the Victorian notion of separate spheres. Most were convinced that women's place was in the home, not in the market (and certainly not at the front of a university classroom). Some expressed this view directly. But the discourse of gender in political economy was defined more by its absence than by its presence. Male economists largely avoided issues concerning women's work, especially in the United States.[7] The bulk of important research on this topic was conducted by government agencies, women's groups, and journalists.

The most famous founding fathers of political economy, Adam Smith and Thomas Robert Malthus, pictured men as rational, self-interested agents, women as essentially moral and altruistic creatures.[8] Neoclassical theory refined this approach with a new emphasis on market exchange that treated women's nonmarket work as economically unproductive but morally crucial. As a result, many economists who believed in free choice for men strongly believed in the regulation of women's roles. In 1882, Stanley Jevons, otherwise a proponent of the glories of laissez-faire, became so distressed at growing levels of employment among married women that he called for the "complete exclusion of mothers of children under the age of three years from factories and workshops."[9] In 1890, Alfred Marshall expressed concern that higher market wages for women might tempt them to neglect their sacred duties as wives and mothers.[10]

The tension between a view of the world that emphasized individual competition and one that held family values sacred was partially resolved by the concept of the family wage, based on the presumption that men should earn sufficient wages to support a dependent wife and children. The concept originated within the U.S. trade union movement as an argument for paying men more money and for protecting them from the wage competition of young women who did not "need" to support a family.[11] Many economists supported the concept despite its lack of conformity with their theoretical emphasis on the virtues of the free market because they believed it crucial to the future of the race.

In the United States, the boldest case for the family wage was made by Father John Ryan, a faculty member at the Catholic University of America, who preached that male dignity itself dictated higher wages for men. In *Living Wage*, first published in 1906, Ryan wrote that "The welfare of the whole family, and that of society likewise, renders it imperative that the wife and mother should not engage in any labor except that of the household."[12] In England, similar arguments were made in a more empirical vein by Seebowm Rowntree, a tireless collector of data on family budgets.[13] Even more influential were the opinions of F. Y. Edgeworth, editor of the prestigious *Economic Journal*, who explained in 1922 that "If the bulk of working men support families, and the bulk of working women do not, it seems not unreasonable that the men should have some advantage in the labour market."[14]

Widespread agreement that housewives and mothers were fulfilling moral duties rather than performing economic labor was crucial to the formulation of a family wage that would allow a man to support his "dependents"—thus including a woman typically engaged in activities such as cooking, cleaning, and child care in the same category as helpless infants. The conviction that the traditional division of labor was efficient and appropriate implied that adult women really should not engage in wage employment, except as a temporary expedient. Even when its permanence became manifest, it was often assumed that women's motives were entirely different from those of men.[15]

The reluctance to view women's nonmarket work as productive was partially overcome, though closely contained, by the emergence of the discipline of home economics in the late nineteenth century. But it continued to exercise considerable influence within political economy itself, eventually surfacing in discussions of the minimum wage for women, which were heavily influenced by family wage logic. Marxists argued that a capitalist system based on individual wages failed to provide for the costs of rearing the next generation of workers. Socialists like Sidney and Beatrice Webb suggested that employers of young women were paying them less than the cost of their subsistence and therefore "parasitizing" the families that supported them.[16]

Academic economists in the United States, less influenced by the socialist tradition, largely avoided this issue. Frank Taussig of Harvard University, however, wrote at least one article insisting not only that a minimum wage for women would throw many out of work, but also that they did not need to earn enough to live on their own—they could live at home and take advantage of "expense-reducing cooperation."[17] Not until the early 1920s did women economists like Dorothy Douglas and Sophonisba Breckinridge articulate the view that all the wage earners in a family should earn enough to help remunerate the mothers and sisters who provided them with domestic services in the home.[18]

What economists said about such matters, however, is less interesting than how little they said. One can pore through early economics textbooks and most issues of professional journals without finding any mention of women workers. This seems surprising, given that women were entering the paid labor force in large numbers between 1880 and 1920, and that popular controversies over women's entrance into paid employment were raging. In the United States, the economic slump of the 1890s fanned the flames of male apprehension about joblessness, and Congress instructed the Bureau of Labor to ascertain the effect that women's and children's entrance into factories was having upon the wages and employment of men. The results of an extensive survey of employers were quite clear: "Females are to some extent entering into places at the expense of males."[19]

Anxiety about changing gender roles pushed government agencies into the vanguard of research on women's work. Carroll Wright, director of the Massachusetts Bureau of Labor, the 1890 U.S. Census, and later commissioner of the federal Bureau of Labor Statistics, was far more interested in women's work than any of his university-centered colleagues. He was also far more sympathetic to feminist concerns and often provided women academics with opportunities to contribute to government-sponsored research.[20] Wright hired many women agents to help conduct surveys, and by his own account, at least, he paid them the same as men.[21]

Organized political pressure helped motivate research on issues that the academic establishment largely ignored. In 1906, Jane Addams, Edith Abbott, Sophonisba Breckinridge, and others enlisted the help of the Women's Trade Union League, the National Federation of Women's Clubs, and the American Federation of Labor to persuade President Roosevelt to recommend a national study of women and children in the labor force.[22] Congress approved, and the result was a massive Bureau of Labor Statistics survey published in nineteen volumes, the *Investigation of Woman and Child Wage Earners.*[23] Distinctive in its emphasis on the collection of quantitative data and survey of state regulations, the study epitomized the genre of Progressive Era government reports.

Much of the energy behind such reports sprang from the conviction that a thorough list of social ills would prompt a general cleanup. Further responsibility was cheerfully assumed by a kind of Ladies' Auxiliary of Political Economy that operated outside the academy. Groups like the Boston Women's Educational and Industrial Union systematically promoted and published research. The federal Children's Bureau, established in 1912, became a beachhead for reformers, who used it as a vehicle for researching and publicizing children's issues. The Bureau of Labor Statistics was persuaded to inaugurate a "Women in Industry" series, and in 1921 a separate Women's Bureau was set up within the Department of Labor. Even without the right to vote in federal elections, women found it easier to influence the democracy than the so-called meritocracy of academia.[24]

The number of articles, reports, and books treating economic dimensions of "the woman question" increased dramatically. Between 1911 and 1920, the *American Economic Review* (*AER*), which devoted particular attention to policy-related reports and books, published reviews of thirty-three publications on women. About half were published by government agencies (such as factory investigation commissions), political groups (such as the Women's Educational and Industrial Union of Boston), or philanthropic organizations (such as the Russell Sage Foundation). Relatively few books on women in the economy were written by authors holding academic jobs, and, as later discussion will show, only one academic political economy journal consistently published articles on women, children, or the family.

The general reading public was not unreceptive. Charlotte Perkins Gilman's *Women and Economics*, published in 1898, went through seven printings over a twenty-five-year period and was translated into at least six languages.[25] The book argued enthusiastically that the advancing forces of technical and social change would inevitably pull women outside the domestic sphere, with healthy consequences for society as a whole. It was not reviewed in either the *Quarterly Journal of Economics* (*QJE*) or the *Journal of Political Economy* (*JPE*), the two major political economy journals of the day.

Gilman's arguments were at least partially echoed by Thorstein Veblen, who published an article entitled "The Barbarian Status of Women" in the *Journal of Political Economy* in 1899, which formed the basis for a chapter in his famous *Theory of the Leisure Class.* Veblen asserted that women had become a vehicle for the expression of their husbands' class status.[26] Much of the so-called work they did in the home merely aimed to increase conspicuous consumption. Unlike Gilman, however, Veblen did not welcome women's entrance into the world outside the home. He was far more concerned with the meaning of class than the significance of gender, and said little in defense of women's political rights or economic capacities.

Why were academics so uninterested in issues that were of momentous concern to social reformers, policymakers, and many citizens in general? A. W. Coats explains that the consolidation of economics as a profession partly reflected "economists' yearning for scientific status and prestige."[27] Research on women and the family, tinged with moral hues, probably seemed uninviting to men reaching for scientific certainty. More important, it was considered a "feminine topic" inappropriate for men. The emergence of a separate discipline of home economics helped ease this tension, allowing economists to accommodate new concerns while resisting the "feminization" of their own profession.[28] But within the economics profession itself, a separate, internal process of segregation emerged.

WOMEN AND THE ECONOMICS PROFESSION

Discrimination is hard to prove. It cannot simply be inferred from outcomes, and it is always easier to find a smoking gun than to discern who actually fired it. At the turn of the century, many women not only embraced the doctrine of separate spheres but used it to their advantage in developing their own niche within the newly feminized professions. Home economics, after all, employed more women Ph.D.'s than any other academic discipline in the early twentieth century.[29] The very attractiveness of this career track suggests that women who obtained advanced degrees in political economy were pursuing a different strategy and hoping to penetrate the male sphere.

Their success was extremely limited. Access to graduate training proved far easier for women to obtain than faculty positions. Most female Ph.D.'s simply disappeared into obscurity, and many highly qualified women who persisted with academic job searches never succeeded. Reformists like Richard Ely and John R. Commons did little to enhance their opportunities. Indeed, women economists fared best at an institution with a relatively conservative economics department—the University of Chicago. Although Edith Abbott and Sophonisba Breckinridge never obtained formal appointments in that department, they gradually consolidated enough institutional power to create a position for a member of the younger generation.

General Patterns

Evidence that women actively sought to enter the profession comes from records of those who completed the requirements for a Ph.D. In the period before 1900, women wrote about 6 percent of all dissertations in political economy (five compared to men's eighty-four).[30] This percentage increased significantly between 1906 and 1920, when women accounted for about 10 percent of all dissertations in progress.[31] Barbara Libby attempted an assessment of women's professional trajectories but was unable to track these with much accuracy.[32] Only a small number found academic jobs before 1920, mostly at private women's colleges or in the more remote branches of the land-grant university system. They probably never constituted more than 2 percent of all faculty members in economics.[33]

The available numbers tell us less than do more informal qualitative sources. Claire Hammond has traced the careers of the first three women to win the Ph.D. in political economy: Helen Frances Page Bates (University of Wisconsin, 1896), Sarah Scovill Whittelsey (Yale University, 1898), and Hannah Robie Sewall (University of Minnesota, 1898).[34] Bates spent eighteen years as librarian to the Department of Economics at the University of California. After a short stint teaching at Wellesley College, Whittelsey married, an act that disqualified her from an academic appointment. Sewall, who published a book on value theory that was well received (and is still highly regarded), was hired by Carroll Wright at the U.S. Bureau of Labor. Her subsequent research on child labor legislation, published in 1904, was the first systematic study of the subject.

Reformers like Richard Ely, Thorstein Veblen, and John R. Commons were somewhat ambivalent about women's issues. Their concerns about the contest between Capital and Labor, or the power of the "vested interests," did not necessarily extend to other dimensions of economic inequality. The general principles of class solidarity, as well as the specific legacy of the Marxian tradition, dictated a distinct conceptual subordination of gender and race.[35] The upstarts who framed the constitution of the American Economics Association (AEA) in 1885 pronounced the doctrine of laissez-faire "unsafe in politics and unsound in morals."[36] But since economists had never been willing to apply laissez-faire to women, the renunciation of it did not have overwhelming implications for the analysis of gender.

Ely's assault on orthodoxy did open a tiny crack in the door. An early AEA resolution listed the employment of women in factories as one of ten "proper subjects for reports."[37] One of the early annual meetings was attended by a number of eminent women including Florence Kelley and M. Carey Thomas, president of Bryn Mawr. But it was not an auspicious beginning. Social events accompanying professional meetings had long excluded women, and even the upstart AEA was conventional in this respect.[38] As Ely himself recounts in his autobiography, Dr. Stuart Wood planned a reception, but, according to the "inflexible social code of Philadelphia, he did not see how he could receive women and men both in his home."[39] His sister agreed, at the last minute, to hold a separate reception for the ladies, who chose to boycott it.

More genuine encouragement came from sympathetic women of means, such as Mrs. John Armstrong Chanler, who established an award of one hundred dollars for the best essay on women wage earners.[40] Even this prize, generous for its day, failed to elicit exactly the desired result. The first winner,

Clare de Graffenried, wrote primarily on child labor. The next winner, however, was Helen Campbell, a journalist and friend of Charlotte Perkins Gilman's who had published two well-received popular books on poverty. Her monograph on women wage earners was published in 1893, with an introduction by Richard Ely.

Campbell dressed her arguments up with references to Adam Smith and classical debates over the remuneration of unskilled labor. But the body of her book was indisputably feminist, with a somewhat indignant emphasis on the ways that men had combined to exclude women from access to education and skilled labor. Ely was careful to distance himself from her claims, noting that women's entrance into paid employment was reducing male wages and breaking up the home. Not that he wanted to go "backward," he explained, but there was a pressing need for reform. He was drawn to the women's movement primarily as a potential ally in the assault on laissez-faire.[41]

Ely did make some effort to promote Campbell's work. As a professor at the University of Wisconsin, he garnered an invitation for her to present twelve lectures on household economics in 1895.[42] In 1897, he recommended her for a teaching position in home economics at Kansas State Agricultural College, where a group of Populists was eagerly hiring East Coast reformers. This was hardly an attractive position for a woman who had published three books, and, after a short stay there, she resumed her career as a journalist.[43]

It seems likely that Ely's interest in both women economists and women's work declined as feminist concerns increasingly diverged from the pro-union agenda. In his 1886 classic, *The Labor Movement in America*, Ely praised the Knights of Labor for their efforts on behalf of women and Negroes. His own Socialistic Labor Party program called for "Equalization by law of women's wages with those of men where equal service is performed."[44] But Ely subsequently became a strong supporter of the American Federation of Labor, an organization fervently opposed to women's participation in wage employment. Its leader, Samuel Gompers (along with Mrs. Gompers), denounced women for undercutting men's wages. In 1906, Ely wrote an enthusiastic introduction to Father John Ryan's passionate defense of the male family wage.

Ely enjoyed sufficient professional influence to create a "school" of his own at the University of Wisconsin, where he hired John R. Commons, a prominent institutionalist reformer.[45] Commons's self-described "Gomperism" led him toward the articulation of extremely anti-immigrant and openly racist views.[46] He was interested in women workers, insofar as they were involved in unionization efforts.[47] His edited volume, *Trade Unionism and Labor Problems*, published in 1905, included several articles on this subject, including an essay by Margaret Hammond that boldly criticized the claim that women were paid less because their work was inferior.[48]

Wisconsin became an early center of labor economics, and the graduate program there attracted, among others, a young woman named Helen Sumner who came to study with Ely, became his secretary, and was awarded a fellowship in 1904. Sumner proved a good student and a prolific writer, and coauthored an undergraduate textbook with Thomas Adams (another Ely man) as well as contributing chapters to Commons's *Trade Unionism and Labor Problems*. At least initially, she reaffirmed the trade-unionist position that the increased employment of women and children would necessarily reduce the salaries of husbands and fathers.[49] But Sumner was clearly a feminist in political orientation. She took a fifteen-month leave of absence to conduct an investigation of women's suffrage in Colorado in 1906 before returning to complete a dissertation on the early labor movement that was later incorporated into Commons's *History of Industry in the United States*. She also wrote a major monograph on women in industry, published in 1910 as part of the massive Bureau of Labor Statistics *Report on the Condition of Woman and Child Wage-Earners in the United States*. Despite her accomplishments, she was apparently never offered a job at the University of Wisconsin, or any other academic institution, after graduation. She wrote to Commons reiterating her desire to "be an author" but finally moved to Washington to live with her widowed mother and engage in contract research for government agencies such as the Children's Bureau.[50]

Women complained of discrimination. Marion Talbot, dean of Women at the University of Chicago, was particularly outspoken. "Even allowing for alleged differences in capacity and availability," she wrote in her 1910 book, *The Education of Women*, "the discrepancy in academic treatment is unjustifiable."[51] Susan Kingsbury, of Simmons College, conducted empirical research on the small representation and low rank of women on college faculties.[52] These protests failed to attract the intellectual, much less the political, interest of their male colleagues. The early years of the profession witnessed many controversies over academic freedom, such as the firing of Edward Bemis from the University of Chicago for allegedly offending the Rockefellers. Sex discrimination was not, however, considered an important issue.[53]

The only woman who received a Ph.D. before 1910 and managed to hold a faculty position in economics at a major research institution before 1920 was Jessica Blanche Peixotto, who earned a Ph.D. at the University of California at Berkeley in 1900. Staying on to teach at her alma mater, she eventually became a full professor in the economics department in 1918 and a vice president of the AEA in 1928.[54] Her success is partly attributable to the fact that Berkeley had established a subfield of "social economics" that defined a distinctly feminine niche for her within the department.[55]

The term "social economy" was first used by John Stuart Mill to designate a broader field of study than political economy, one that could encompass ethical concerns as well as the pursuit of wealth. Franklin Sanborn, the founder and mainstay of the late-nineteenth-century American Social Science Association, specifically described it as "the feminine gender of Political Economy, and so, very receptive of particulars, but little capable of general and aggregate matters. . . ."[56] Thus stigmatized, social economy did not acquire a secure place in university curricula. Among major universities surveyed in 1892, only one other than the University of California—the University of Chicago—even listed a course on the subject.[57]

But "social economy" did become a field of employment for both the government and women's colleges, where a Ph.D. in economics was not a necessary credential. Susan Kingsbury received her doctorate in American colonial history from Columbia in 1905 before she taught economics at Simmons College and began to conduct research on women's underrepresentation in the academy. She then served as research director of the Women's Educational and Industrial Union of Boston, went to Bryn Mawr as professor of social economy in 1915, and was elected a vice president of the American Economics Association in 1919.[58]

The laurels of full professorship in social economy were eventually bestowed on two other women economists who never enjoyed regular faculty appointments in an economics department: Edith Abbott and Sophonisba Breckinridge. Many dimensions of their careers recapitulate in microcosm the history of their cohort of female graduate students. Their history, closely intertwined with that of the University of Chicago, provides further evidence of a process of exclusion that was only gradually overcome.

The Chicago Case

Founded in 1886, the University of Chicago originally modeled itself as an unconventional institution, a bold coeducational challenge to the East Coast academic establishment. President William Harper hired a prominent home economist, Marion Talbot of Wellesley College, as dean of women. He tried to hire Richard Ely away from Johns Hopkins but was unsuccessful. He decided to put the political economy program in the hands of J. Laurence Laughlin, a man with conservative opinions on issues of labor and reform, but a strong commitment to coeducation on the graduate as well as undergraduate level.[59]

Women flocked to the university in such numbers that they provoked fears of feminization, and in 1902 the Faculty Senate voted to institute separate classes for men and women, a plan approved by the Board of Trustees despite the eloquent opposition of Marion Talbot and, among others, John Dewey. But segregation proved difficult to implement, and after a couple of years the issue seemed to fade away.[60] The Chicago graduate program in political economy started out quite small, with far fewer students than Columbia, Harvard, Yale, or Wisconsin until 1909.[61] The difficulty in attracting students to a new program may have increased faculty willingness to admit women, and they came to be better represented than at any other university, writing almost 12 percent of all dissertations between 1908 and 1920.

Marion Talbot had studied sanitary engineering with Ellen Richards at MIT before moving to Wellesley College. She brought to Chicago her strong feminist convictions, a definite flair for university politics, and a young protégée who had recently graduated from Wellesley. Sophonisba Breckinridge, daughter of a prominent Kentucky congressman, had considered a career in law but decided instead to pursue graduate studies. While serving as a secretary to

Talbot she also enrolled in an ambitious program of graduate study in the departments of political science, political economy, and law, becoming the first woman to secure a Ph.D. in this combined area, as well as the first to secure a doctorate in jurisprudence.

She studied under Laughlin's tutelage, writing a dissertation on the history of the legal tender doctrine, and gratefully acknowledging his support.[62] Marion Talbot encouraged her to pursue her interests in the social and political aspects of women's position, and soon arranged an appointment for her as assistant professor of social economy. Originally Talbot and Breckinridge both taught classes under the auspices of the Department of Anthropology and Sociology, but this apparently caused some discomfort. In 1904 President Harper decided that their work "could be conducted more profitably to the University if separated from its classification with these departments."[63] The trustees, in response, established the Department of Household Administration. On the local as well as the national level, the distinction between economics and home economics safely demarcated masculine from feminine pursuits.[64]

Another bright young student of political economy was Edith Abbott, who came to the university in 1898, enjoyed a graduate fellowship in 1903–4, and finished her dissertation in 1905 under Laughlin's supervision. Talbot watched over her from the outset. Breckinridge became her best friend and eventually her coauthor. Abbott was openly grateful to Laughlin, describing him as "extremely generous about helping women students, at a time when women students were not particularly welcome in many Departments of Economics."[65] In addition to this academic support, Abbott was also well connected, through her sister Grace, with the social reform community associated with Jane Addams's Hull House.[66]

With these formidable allies, she seemed destined to break through any barriers in her path toward a career in economics. Upon completion of her Ph.D., she was immediately offered a part-time position researching women's employment for an industrial history of the United States, conducted by Carroll Wright and the American Economic Association with support from the Carnegie Foundation.[67] She then won a fellowship from the same foundation to spend 1906 at the London School of Economics, where she studied with Sidney and Beatrice Webb. After teaching a semester at Wellesley College, she returned to Chicago to join her sister Grace at Hull House. A short stint as a "special lecturer" at the Department of Political Economy failed to lead to a regular appointment. Abbott eventually found employment at a local institution for training social workers, the School of Civics and Philanthropy. It seems likely that she regarded this as a second-best arrangement.

Certainly, political economy continued to claim her intellectual energy. Between 1904 and 1913, when she still had reason to hope for a permanent academic appointment in the field, she published seven articles in the *Journal of Political Economy* on women's employment and wages (two coauthored with Breckinridge) and an article in the *American Journal of Sociology*. These articles provided the basis for her landmark work, *Women in Industry: A Study of American Economic History*, published in 1910. The book was well-received, enjoying favorable reviews not only in the *JPE* but also in the *Quarterly Journal of Economics*.[68] Abbott became the recognized expert on women's work.

She could hardly have accomplished this without Laughlin's support as the editor of the *Journal of Political Economy*. No economics journals of the day utilized the formal review processes, such as double-blind reviewing, that became typical in later years. All were edited for long periods of time by powerful individuals. As Chicago's Laughlin was to the *JPE*, Harvard's Frank Taussig was to the *QJE* and MIT's Davis Dewey to the *AER*.[69] Institutional pressures may also have been significant: Chicago, unlike Harvard, was strongly identified with coeducation. Laughlin was a traditionalist in the sense that he did not approve of the new marginalist school, with its emphasis on abstract theory.[70] But he was no traditionalist where women were concerned. In addition to publishing a large number of articles by Abbott, he often placed them in the prestigious first position, ran them in several lengthy parts, and published both critical comments and her rejoinders to them.[71]

Laughlin was not, however, powerful enough to get her a university appointment. Slowly but surely Abbott became disenchanted with her discipline. In 1916, she wrote a highly critical review of the *Summary of the Report on the Condition of Woman and Child Wage Earners in the United States*, the culmination of the congressional study she had helped agitate for in 1906. She complained that the report gathered too many uninteresting facts and failed to make any recommendations for reform.[72] Similarly, a 1917 article on women's work in England ended with bitter comments on poor levels of protection for women workers in the United States.[73] Her impatience with reform was surely heightened by the obstacles that she herself faced.

Breckinridge continued to hold her academic post within the Department of Household Administration at the University of Chicago but was not entirely happy there. A more prominent activist than Abbott, with a less ambitious research agenda, she nonetheless wanted to strengthen her academic base.[74] Together, the two women persuaded the University of Chicago to take over and incorporate the School of Civics and Philanthropy, where Abbott was employed, as a step toward creating a new school of social work. The university was impressed by the outside funding Abbott and Breckinridge were able to guarantee, thanks to potential women donors like Laura Spelman Rockefeller.

One immediate result was a new appointment for Abbott as associate professor of social economy at the University of Chicago. Her activities were not limited to the new School of Social Work, but while she was listed as a lecturer in sociology, she enjoyed no such listing with the Department of Political Economy. In 1924, the Board of Trustees declared the semiofficial merger a success, officially announced the formation of the Graduate School of Social Service Administration, and appointed Abbott dean.

Breckinridge also enjoyed some tangible improvement in her professional position. She had taught for eighteen years before being promoted from assistant to associate professor of household administration in 1920 and must have felt rather out of place in a department that was beginning to fill with specialists on the techniques of household production. Katherine Blunt, who succeeded Marion Talbot as chairperson in 1925 and changed the official name of the department to Home Economics and Household Administration, routinely published articles such as "A Comparison of Evaporated with Pasteurized Milk as a Source of Calcium, Phosphorus and Nitrogen," in the *Journal of Biological Chemistry*. Another notable example of the new "practical" emphasis was an article titled "The Human Energy Cost of Operating a Vacuum Cleaner at Different Speeds."[75] Home economics, like political economy, had learned to delegate its social concerns to other, less established disciplines.

The new Graduate School of Social Work must have been a welcome change, and Abbott and Breckinridge devoted themselves to the new journal they founded in 1927, the *Social Service Review*. They published there, rather than in economics journals (on topics such as crime, family policy, and poor relief), enjoying more influence than they would have been able to exercise within a conventional economics department. But they were by no means completely satisfied with their working conditions. Marion Talbot, their long-standing champion, had served the university many years as dean of women. Her annual report to the president normally included discussion of such mundane issues as overcrowding in the women's dining areas and problems with "secret societies." In 1924, however, she condemned the mistreatment of women graduate students, protesting that women received only 20 percent of the university fellowships for graduate study though they constituted 45 percent of the graduate students. She also documented the persistence and professional success of those women who received fellowships.[76]

This was only the first volley in a well-organized protest against university policies. In December of 1924, three women who held full professorships at the University of Chicago addressed a letter to the presidents of the university and the Board of Trustees expanding on Talbot's complaints. They noted that there were some women faculty members who remained at the associate rank although they had received their Ph.D.'s before 1907 and held (unlike any of the men who had been more quickly promoted) an additional doctor of laws degree.[77] Sophonisba Breckinridge was the most prominent of these.

A special committee was appointed to determine whether the women faculty had their facts straight. They did, and they gained enough support from the university community to force major concessions from the Board of Trustees. In the next round of promotions, Edith Abbott, Katherine Blunt, and Sophonisba Breckinridge were named full professors. Further, the dean of the School of Commerce and Administration began negotiating with Hazel Kyrk, a young Chicago Ph.D. teaching at Iowa State University. The tone of Kyrk's correspondence with Dean Leon Marshall, who was also serving as the chair of economics, suggests that she was in a relatively strong bargaining position. She held a tenured post as professor of household administration in the Department of Economics, History and Sociology at Iowa State, and she knew that Chicago was under pressure to hire a woman.[78] She stipulated that she would not accept the job without formal recognition from the Department of Economics (which had just changed its name from "Political Economy" to the more modern term). Marshall assured her a joint appointment in both economics and home economics. He insisted that his department had no objections, but it took him a surprisingly long time to deliver on his promise. Kyrk was hired in 1925; however, she was listed only as associate professor of home economics in official university publications. Marshall's papers of 1928 include a penciled note to himself: "Hazel's joint appt.—what came of it?" Finally, something did come of it, the culmination of many years of political and intellectual effort, shrewd bargaining, and bureaucratic persistence. In 1929–30, Hazel Kyrk was officially listed as a member of the University of Chicago economics department.

The experience of Edith Abbott and Sophonisba Breckinridge strongly suggests that academic achievement was insufficient to overcome discrimination, even when combined with a strong male mentor and powerful political contacts outside the university. Criteria for hiring and promoting faculty were overtly gender-biased. They were overhauled only by a lengthy, sustained process of institution building and carefully calculated protest. Still, the University of Chicago in general, and Laughlin in particular, deserve credit for a rare openness to the new research agenda their women students and faculty were developing. This agenda ultimately proved far more subversive than any specific hire, because it struck at the assumptions on which all hiring decisions were based.

THE RESEARCHER AND THE RESEARCHED

One of the most important features of a scientific paradigm is the nature of the research program it generates, the kinds of questions it encourages scientists to ask. The paradigm of neoclassical economics drew a sharp distinction between markets and families, men and women. Men were considered economic creatures, properly motivated by self-interest, properly engaged in market work. Women were considered moral creatures, bound by the dictates of duty to family work. The very notion that economic reasoning could be applied to women and the family violated both the principle of separate spheres and the official boundaries of the discipline.

The seriousness of this violation varied according to circumstances. It was clearly more acceptable for women than for men to apply economics to women's sphere, especially if they did so from within the separate disciplinary sphere of home economics. Within political economy itself, it was clearly more acceptable for women than for men to study women. Even so, the topic itself was suspect. It violated the assumptions of the paradigm, especially if it examined the work of women in the labor market and asked why they were paid less than men. In this case, of course, the paradigmatic bias coincided with a more ideological bias: the resistance to new ideas described by Thomas Kuhn and others is even stronger when these new ideas threaten to worsen the economic position of those who espouse them. Women had more to gain than men from challenging the assumption of separate spheres and, not surprisingly, were rather more likely to do so.

General Patterns

Who does research can affect what kinds of research get done. Some counter-factual questions of the "what would have happened if . . . ?" variety are impossible to answer. However, one conspicuous pattern is relatively easy to quantify: gender significantly affected researchers' propensity to explore topics related to women, children, and the family. According to the American Economics Association's *Index of Economic Journals* for 1886–1924, women authors represented 7.2 percent of all authors with determinate gender but 63 percent of all authors of determinate gender who published in the category of "Women and Children" (a subheading of "Components of the Labor Force").[79]

In an effort to explore the relationship between gender and research topics in more detail, I performed a year-by-year analysis of the list of dissertations in progress from 1906 (the first year for which I could obtain a copy of the dissertations list) until 1920. I defined works on women, children, or the family as those that had either these or related words, such as "wives" or "birth-rate," in the title. I identified gender by the first name of the author, supplemented by biographical research.

Women wrote on a wide variety of topics but were more likely than men to focus their research on topics of special relevance to women. Overall, the percentage of all dissertations on subjects explicitly related to women, children, or the family was quite small, averaging only 2.5 percent. The percentage of dissertations written by women on these subjects was far higher, averaging 16.3 percent. Did a focus on women's issues help or hinder women's careers during this period? Without additional information on career trajectories, it is difficult to say. Abbott and Breckinridge probably benefited, but their very success within a niche of limited size may have crowded out other potential contributors.

An analysis of the table of contents of the three major professional journals of the day shows that only one published a significant number of articles on women's issues. Over the period 1893–1920, about 2.6 percent of all articles published in the *Journal of Political Economy* directly pertained to women, children, or the family. While this may seem low, it far exceeded the 0.7 percent average for the *Quarterly Journal of Economics* between its founding in 1887 and 1920, or the 0.2 percent average (over a far shorter period) for the *American Economic Review* between its founding in 1911 and 1920. The overwhelming majority of articles on such topics in the *JPE*, 81.1 percent, were written by women.[80] The journal's interest in these issues helps explain why women authors were relatively well represented there.

The differences among the three major journals are truly striking in this respect. On the basis of a lower-bound estimate (of individuals identifiable as women as a percentage of the total), women represented 5.5 percent of all authors published in the *JPE* between 1893 and 1920 but only 0.5 percent of all those published in the *QJE* between 1887 and 1920.[81] Women represented only 1.4 percent of all authors published in the *AER*, which began appearing regularly in 1911.[82] The performance of the *JPE* is due largely to the publication of articles by Abbott and Breckinridge. Did Laughlin publish them because he was interested in women's work, or vice versa? His respect for his students' work may have widened his intellectual curiosity and increased his tendency to accept related articles. If that was the case, lower representation of women in other graduate programs may have reinforced conventional thinking there.

The pattern of gender specialization was not limited to dissertations and journal articles. Virtually all of the significant books on women, children, and the family published between 1890 and 1920 were authored by women.[83] Even most of the signed reviews of such books that appeared in economics journals were written by women: 63.6 percent for the *JPE* and 41.4 percent (over a shorter period) for the *AER* (the *QJE* did not regularly publish book reviews before 1920). In the short run, widespread public interest in women's issues gave women economists a distinctive niche in which they could operate with less disapproval, or perhaps simply less competition, from their male colleagues. But this niche also served to segregate them, and to absolve male economists of any responsibility for studying gender inequality.

Men's reluctance to publish on topics related to women grew out of the same social code of separate spheres that prohibited mixed company at the early AEA reception. This conceptual segregation was far more specific than the acknowledged tendency for women to focus on "social problems" rather than theoretical issues. In this respect, they were allied with the institutionalists against the neoclassical marginalism promoted by J. B. Clark.[84] But not even the institutionalists were very interested in research on women beyond that which their own female graduate students could provide. If women were more committed than men to the cause of reform, it was perhaps because they had more grievances.

Research Content

A closer look at the content of the most influential research on women's work, published by Abbott and Breckinridge, reveals pointed and profound challenges to the basic assumption of separate spheres. In an ironic and self-consciously recursive way, these two women provided a historical and analytical picture of the very processes that were blocking their own advance. The profession as a whole had good reason to insist that what they were doing was not really "economics": their research both undermined the theory of the family wage and discredited the basic rationale for excluding women from well-paying jobs.

Their critique of discrimination took a long time to emerge from the chrysalis of prescribed graduate study. In her dissertation, Abbott utilized nineteenth-century census data to investigate the wages of unskilled labor. She largely excluded women's wages from consideration, acceding to the established view that they were determined by forces entirely different from those which affected men. Indeed, she rather primly reiterated the conventional wisdom, quoting an article by Mayo-Smith in the *Quarterly Journal of Economics*: "The wages of men, women, and children are entirely different quantities, and are as incapable of addition and averaging as a bushel of potatoes and a pound of butter."[85]

Once her Ph.D. was in hand, however, Abbott began to mash and blend. Her first article specifically on women, entitled "Harriet Martineau and the Employment of Women in 1836," was a bit tentative, using a discussion of Martineau's accounts of travel in the United States to emphasize that women had held a variety of employments in the early nineteenth century, and that accounts of their recent encroachment on men's jobs were exaggerated.[86] Her next piece, coauthored with Breckinridge, was more assertive, describing widespread opposition to women's participation in wage employment:

> For all these reasons, the system itself is on trial; and the right of women to a place in that system begins to be questioned by workingmen who, believing in the "lump of labor" theory, prefer not to see the opportunities to work shared by women; by well-meaning persons of other classes who, accepting the "sphere of woman" doctrine, would limit the activities of women of all classes to the bearing and rearing of children, and to making home comfortable under circumstances determined by the amount of the man's wages rather than by the woman's energy or peculiar ability.[87]

They went on to observe that the entrance of women into middle-class occupations was creating not only controversy but emotional turmoil.[88] The remedy that they proposed was scientific method: attention to facts and figures. Nine months later, the next installment on this topic appeared in the *Journal of Political Economy*, authored by Abbott alone. This was a more systematic historical account of trends in women's employment over the course of the nineteenth century, and the conclusion drawn seemed intended to allay emotional concerns about women's entrance into the paid labor force by claiming that women had actually been more economically active, relative to men, in the past.[89]

Abbott oversimplified her case somewhat by comparing 1900 with 1850, rather than looking at trends from, say, 1870 to 1900, which showed a steady increase in women's wage employment relative to men's. But she was prescient in her emphasis on the fact that many forms of female participation in the market had been obscured by reliance on conventional census categories.[90] Subsequent articles focused in more detail on specific industries, such as cotton manufacture, cigar making, and printing. Breckinridge collaborated with Abbott on a study of the Chicago stockyards, examining the movement of women into traditionally male jobs and combining the methods of historical research with actual observation and investigation of a local meat-processing plant.[91]

Many of the *JPE* articles were essentially republished as chapters of Abbott's *Women in Industry*, which emphasized that women were not "taking men's jobs." She based this argument on historical precedent: women had always contributed to family income. Further, she insisted, well-paying jobs were not inherently or intrinsically male. Rather, they came to be defined that way under contingent historical circumstances that often included well-organized efforts to exclude women. Both Abbott and Breckinridge were so focused on contesting the norm of female domesticity that they hesitated to make the more radical argument that women were unfairly paid less than men. Though they clearly believed this to be the case, they seemed almost anxious to concede that women themselves were partly at fault. For instance, Breckinridge noted, in the introduction to Abbott's book, that women were "poor bargainers," who "have never accepted the ideal of giving as little and getting as much as they can."[92] This was a clear allusion to the socialist notion that competition itself placed women at a disadvantage, qualified by Breckinridge's suggestion that women simply needed more practice.

One of the major obstacles to a focus on women's pay was the fact that leading socialist, as well as neoclassical, economists refused to seriously consider the possibility that lower pay for women was unjustified. In the conclusion to her book, Abbott actually deferred to the conventional wisdom by noting that her research was consistent with Sidney Webb's theory that women were poorly paid because they were inefficient and were doing less-skilled work than men. As in her dissertation, she took pains to display her allegiance to the profession, even as she criticized it. But in a classic academic trope, she went on to subtly undermine Webb's argument by suggesting that it was susceptible to future criticism:

> To discuss the causes which lie back of the woman's lack of efficiency—how far it is due to her exclusion from the occupations which demand higher skill and in turn offer larger remuneration, or to a restriction of opportunity by which she is denied proper training for her trade—would be of interest, but such an inquiry is clearly beyond the scope of this study.[93]

In other words, differences in men's and women's ability were probably attributable to earlier discrimination.

Intellectually, Breckinridge was usually at her best as a collaborator, either with Abbott or with Talbot. Several short notes she published in the *Journal of Political Economy* on her own had a dry factual tone, though they were all oriented toward important feminist issues. In a short note published in that journal in 1906, she not only summarized the extent of protective legislation in force at the time but emphasized that it imposed unfortunate costs on women.[94] Similarly, in 1915, she documented the legal barriers against women's entrance to the bar in England and several states within the United States.[95]

None of these represented a substantial theoretical contribution. But in 1923, exercised perhaps by years of frustrating debate over the issue of mini-

mum wages for women, Breckinridge published a brilliant article entitled "The
Home Responsibilities of Women Workers and the 'Equal Wage.'" Utilizing
both her legal skills and a facility for analysis of survey data honed by years of
collaboration with Abbott, she decisively rebutted the argument that women
need not earn as much as men because they had fewer "dependents."[96] For empirical evidence, she cited a Women's Bureau survey of women's contributions
to family support, published that same year.[97] The short-run political effect was
nil; the minimum wage issue had already lost its momentum, and the Supreme
Court declared minimum wages unconstitutional in 1923.

Nor did Breckinridge's article have an immediate impact within the academic community. Even the *JPE* lost interest in social and political issues after
about 1925. A long intellectual drought followed. But when the issue of the
minimum wage resurfaced within both political and academic discourse in the
1940s, it was no longer couched in the old family wage rhetoric. Similarly, the
later equal pay debate focused more narrowly on the relative productivity,
rather than the relative "needs," of men and women workers. For this, both
Breckinridge and Abbott deserve considerable credit.

In a sense, the "Home Responsibilities" article was Breckinridge's (and probably by extension, Abbott's) parting shot at the economics profession. In 1933,
Breckinridge published a book with the sweeping title *Women in the Twentieth
Century: A Study of Their Political, Social, and Economic Activities*. She summarized the early efforts of the women's movement and cataloged its successes
and defeats. Women had gained access to many jobs, but "the question of
women's having the right to combine marriage and wage earning is by no
means settled. . . . Not infrequently married women are barred from admission
to certain employments."[98] On the one hand, the principle of equal pay for
equal work was now widely accepted. On the other hand, women's average
wages remained about 54 percent of men's, unchanged since 1900.[99]

Abbott and Breckinridge did more than merely conduct research on
women's work. Despite their exclusion from the mainstream of the profession—perhaps, in part, because of it—they carefully documented male efforts
to exclude women from competition in the paid labor force as a whole. Accused
of "sentimentality," they persisted in efforts both to promote social reform and
to understand the mechanics of social change. In the process, they also challenged the core assumptions of neoclassical economic theory.

CONCLUSION

In a well-known article looking back at methodology in his discipline a hundred
years ago, William Baumol noted that women economists "predominantly specialized in 'women's issues,' of considerable interest in themselves, but unrelated to the subjects that were attracting the bulk of the profession."[100] He did
not ask why the bulk was not attracted to such issues, or, for that matter, why
he himself was not. This essay has addressed that question, exploring a complex
interaction between the concepts and the practices of social science. Prevailing

theories of political economy provided a rationale for discouraging women's entrance into the profession.

At the same time, the composition of the profession clearly shaped the content of its collective research. The exclusion of women affected not only the
economics profession but economics itself. What would have happened if more
women graduate students had found academic jobs, or if Edith Abbott and Sophonisba Breckinridge had received academic appointments in political economy? It seems likely that research on women in general, and gender inequality
in particular, would have proceeded further and faster than it did.

As philosopher of science Sandra Harding points out, objectivity does not
necessarily require neutrality: a claim may be valid or true, regardless of the
motives that underlie its articulation. A medical researcher motivated by a desire to cure cancer is no less likely to be scientific than one who is not.[101] The
experience of the early economics profession supports Harding's argument: the
moral and political concerns expressed by Abbott, Breckinridge, and other
women economists energized excellent scholarly research. On the other hand,
many economists putatively committed to objective analysis actively defended
the concept of a male family wage and helped preserve a male monopoly within
their own discipline.

Some scholars suggest that the increased emphasis on theory and diminished
concern for social reform within the economics profession constricted the space
available for women economists.[102] However, it seems equally likely that the
threatened "feminization" of the profession motivated a defensive response
that included a narrowing of the scope and method of political economy to
focus, at least initially, on more "masculine" topics. Not until the 1970s did
women and the family again receive the attention they had received in the early
years of the century. Not incidentally, new interest in these topics went hand
in hand with women's increased access to university positions.

Certainly, there is an urgent need for further research on the relationship between who does economics and what economics does. Gender was only one of
many aspects of social identity that shaped the early evolution of social science.
Even among women economists, only a small minority pursued research on
women, children, and the family before 1920. Yet it was a particularly significant minority, because it challenged the assumption that men's and women's
work were incommensurable. Women like Abbott and Breckinridge entered a
masculine realm in order to pursue what were considered feminine interests.
In the process, they altered both economic theory and social policy.

NOTES

I am grateful to Helene Silverberg and Desley Deacon for comments and criticisms.
This is an expanded version of a paper presented at the meetings of the History of
Economics Society, June 11, 1994. Thanks to A. W. Coats, Zoreh Emani, and War-
ren Samuels for suggestions made at that venue, and to Margo Anderson, Linda Bar-

rington, Daniel Fusfeld, Margaret Levenstein, and Martha Olney for suggestions made at presentations at the Social Science History Association and the University of Michigan.

1. Cited in Ellen Fitzpatrick, *Endless Crusade: Women Social Scientists and Progressive Reform* (New York: Oxford University Press, 1990), 200.

2. Mary O. Furner, *Advocacy and Objectivity: A Crisis in the Professionalization of American Social Science, 1865–1905* (Lexington: University Press of Kentucky, 1975); Penina Mignal Glazer and Miriam Slater, *Unequal Colleagues: The Entrance of Women into the Professions, 1890–1940* (New Brunswick, N.J.: Rutgers University Press, 1987).

3. Furner, *Advocacy and Objectivity*.

4. For a discussion of the philosophical issues at stake here, see Marianne Ferber and Julie Nelson, "Introduction: The Social Construction of Economics and the Social Construction of Gender," in *Beyond Economic Man: Feminist Theory and Economics*, ed. Marianne Ferber and Julie Nelson (Chicago: University of Chicago Press, 1993), 1–22, and Julie Nelson, *Feminism, Economics, and Objectivity* (New York: Routledge, 1996).

5. For a description of the greater openness of sociology and anthropology, see Rosalind Rosenberg, *Beyond Separate Spheres: Intellectual Roots of Modern Feminism* (New Haven: Yale University Press, 1982).

6. Nancy Folbre, "The Unproductive Housewife: Her Evolution in Nineteenth Century Economic Thought," *Signs: Journal of Women in Culture and Society* 16, no. 3 (1991): 463–84.

7. On the English case, see Michele Pujol, *Feminism and Anti-Feminism in Early Economic Thought* (Aldershot: Edward Elgar, 1992), and Peter Groenewegen, ed., *Feminism and Political Economy in Victorian England* (New York: Edward Elgar, 1994).

8. Nancy Folbre and Heidi Hartmann, "The Rhetoric of Self Interest and the Ideology of Gender," in *The Consequences of Economic Rhetoric*, ed. Arjo Klamer, Donald McCloskey, and Robert Solow (Cambridge: Cambridge University Press, 1988), 184–206.

9. Stanley Jevons, "Married Women in Factories," in *Methods of Social Reform and Other Papers* (London: Macmillan and Company, 1883), 172.

10. Alfred Marshall, *Principles of Economics*, 8th ed., reprinted (London: Macmillan, 1930), 685, 718. See also Pujol, *Feminism and Anti-Feminism*.

11. Martha May, "The Historical Problem of the Family Wage: The Ford Motor Company and the Five Dollar Day," *Feminist Studies* 8, no. 2 (Summer 1982): 399–424; idem, "Bread before Roses: American Workingmen, Labor Unions and the Family Wage," in *Women, Work and Protest: A Century of U.S. Women's Labor History*, ed. Ruth Milkman (Boston: Routledge and Kegan Paul, 1985); Alice Kessler-Harris, *A Woman's Wage: Historical Meanings and Social Consequences* (Lexington: University Press of Kentucky, 1990).

12. John A. Ryan, *Living Wage* (New York: The Macmillan Company, 1920), 101.

13. B. Seebowm Rowntree, *Poverty, a Study of Town Life* (New York: Longmans, Green and Co., 1922); idem, *Poverty and Progress: A Second Social Survey of York* (New York: Longmans, Green and Co., 1941).

14. Francis Y. Edgeworth, "Equal Pay to Men and Women for Equal Work," *Economic Journal* 32, no. 128 (December 1922): 444; idem, "Women's Wages in Relation to Economic Welfare," *Economic Journal* 33, no. 132 (December 1923): 487–95.

15. Kessler-Harris, *A Woman's Wage*.

16. See "Women's Wages" in Sidney Webb and Beatrice Webb, *Problems of Modern Industry*, new ed. (New York: Longmans, Green and Co., 1902).

17. Frank Taussig, "Minimum Wages for Women," *Quarterly Journal of Economics*, May 1916, 411–42.

18. Dorothy Douglas, "The Cost of Living for Working Women: A Criticism of Current Theories," *Quarterly Journal of Economics*, February 1920, 235; Sophonisba Breckinridge, "The Home Responsibilities of Women Workers and the 'Equal Wage,'" *Journal of Political Economy* 31, no. 4 (1923): 521–43.

19. U.S. Bureau of Labor, "Work and Wages of Men, Women, and Children, 1895–96," Annual Report 11, 54th Cong., 2d sess., H. R. 341, 21.

20. Wright was an innovator with respect to studies on race as well as gender, providing indispensable support for W.E.B. Du Bois and other black sociologists for early statistical studies of the African-American population. See Joseph Goldberg and William T. Moye, *The First Hundred Years of the Bureau of Labor Statistics* (Washington, D.C.: U.S. Government Printing Office, 1985), 33, and David Lewis, *W.E.B. DuBois: Biography of a Race, 1868–1963* (New York: H. Holt, 1993).

21. Goldberg and Moye, *The First Hundred Years*, 29.

22. Allen F. Davis, *Spearheads for Reform: The Social Settlements and the Progressive Movement, 1890-1914* (New York: Oxford University Press, 1967), 133.

23. Fitzpatrick, *Endless Crusade*; Lela Costin, *Two Sisters for Social Justice* (Urbana: University of Illinois Press, 1983), 101; Mary McDowell, "The Need for a National Investigation into Women's Work," *Charities and the Commons* 17 (October 1907): 634–36.

24. On women's political influence, see Theda Skocpol, *Protecting Soldiers and Mothers: The Politics of Social Provision in the United States, 1870s–1920s* (Boston: Harvard University Press, 1993).

25. Mary A. Hill, *The Making of a Radical Feminist, 1860–1896* (Philadelphia: Temple University Press, 1980).

26. Thorstein Veblen, *The Theory of the Leisure Class: An Economic Study of Institutions* (New York: The Modern Library, 1934).

27. A. W. Coats, "The AEA and the Economics Profession," *American Economic Review* 50 (September 1960): 566; see also Furner, *Advocacy and Objectivity*.

28. Home economics was a broadly defined field that encompassed concerns with women, work, and the family until about 1910, the year when the American Home Economics Association was founded. The field then began to focus more narrowly on topics such as nutrition and household budgeting. In 1914, new land-grant legislation encouraged an even more practical emphasis.

29. Margaret W. Rossiter, *Women Scientists in America: Struggles and Strategies to 1940* (Baltimore: Johns Hopkins University Press, 1982).

30. Walter Crosby Eels, "Earned Doctorates for Women in the Nineteenth Century," *American Association of University Professors Bulletin* 42 (Winter 1956): 658; Claire H. Hammond, "American Women and the Professionalization of Economics," *Review of Social Economy* 51, no. 3 (Fall 1993): 358.

31. The percentage figures are approximate because of the difficulty of identifying the gender of some authors.

32. Barbara Libby, "A Statistical Analysis of Women in the Economics Profession," in *Selected Papers from the Economic and Business Historical Society*, ed. Edwin J. Perkins (Published by the History Department, University of Southern California, for the Economic and Business Historical Society, 1987), 179–202.

33. See Hammond, "American Women," and Rossiter, *Women Scientists*. The "Notes" section of the *American Economic Review* between 1911 and 1920 often in-

cluded announcements of appointments and promotions. It is impossible to tell how complete these were, but there is no mention of the appointment of a woman to a major research university. The women's colleges (particularly Wellesley, Bryn Mawr, Vassar, and Mount Holyoke) are often mentioned in connection with women Ph.D.'s, and at least one mention is made of women's appointments at Oberlin College, Ohio State University, the University of Nebraska, the University of Washington, and Tufts.

34. For a more detailed description of these three women, see Hammond, "American Women."

35. Nancy Folbre, "Socialism, Feminist or Scientific?" in Ferber and Nelson, *Beyond Economic Man*, 94–110.

36. Richard Ely, *Ground under Our Feet: An Autobiography* (New York: The Macmillan Company, 1938), 24.

37. Cited in Randy Albelda, "Feminism and Economics: On the Margin" (manuscript, Department of Economics, University of Massachusetts at Boston, 1996), 23.

38. Rossiter, *Women Scientists*, 91.

39. Ely, *Ground under Our Feet*, 147.

40. Albelda, "Feminism and Economics," 23.

41. Helen Campbell, *Women Wage-Earners: Their Past, Their Present, and Their Future*, with an introduction by Richard Ely (Boston: Roberts Brothers, 1893).

42. Helen Campbell, *Household Economics: A Course of Lectures in the School of Economics at the University of Wisconsin* (New York: G. P. Putnam's Sons, 1898).

43. See biographical entry in *Notable American Women 1607–1950: A Biographical Dictionary*, ed. Edward T. James, 3 vols. (Cambridge: Harvard University Press, Belknap Press, 1971), 1:280–81.

44. Richard Ely, *The Labor Movement in America* (New York: Thomas Y. Crowell and Co., 1886), 82–83, 369.

45. Benjamin Rader, *Academic Mind and Reform: The Influence of Richard T. Ely in American Life* (Lexington: University of Kentucky Press, 1966), 167.

46. On attitudes toward immigrants and African Americans, see John R. Commons, *Races and Immigrants in America* (New York: The Macmillan Company, 1927); on Gomperism, see idem, *Myself: The Autobiography of John R. Commons* (Madison: University of Wisconsin Press, 1963).

47. See, for instance, John R. Commons, "Labor Conditions in Slaughtering and Meat Packing," *Quarterly Journal of Economics* 19 (1904): 1–32.

48. Margaret L. Hammond, "Women's Wages in Manual Work," in *Trade Unionism and Labor Problems*, ed. with an introduction by John R. Commons (Boston: Ginn and Co., 1905), 396–422.

49. Thomas S. Adams and Helen L. Sumner, *Labor Problems: A Text Book* (New York: Macmillan, 1905).

50. James, *Notable American Women*, 3:42–43.

51. Cited in Rossiter, *Women Scientists*, 108.

52. Ibid., 110.

53. Nor is there any significant discussion of these forms of discrimination in the best-known secondary literature on this period, which includes Rader, *Academic Mind and Reform*; Furner, *Advocacy and Objectivity*; Thomas L. Haskell, *The Emergence of Professional Social Science: The American Social Science Association and the Nineteenth-Century Crisis of Authority* (Chicago: University of Illinois Press, 1977); Joseph Dorfman, *The Economic Mind in American Civilization* (New York: Augustus Kelley, 1969). For a recent treatment of racial discrimination, see Lewis, *W.E.B. DuBois*.

54. James, *Notable American Women*.

55. See Mary E. Cookingham, "Social Economists and Reform: Berkeley, 1906–1961," *History of Political Economy* 19, no. 1 (1987): 47–63.

56. Cited in Haskell, *The Emergence of Professional Social Science*, 137.

57. See appendix to vol. 1, *Journal of Political Economy*, "Courses of Political Economy in the U.S. in 1876 and in 1892–93."

58. James, *Notable American Women*, 2:335–36.

59. In her autobiographical notes, Sophonisba Breckinridge mentions Laughlin as well as Talbot as individuals whom she benefited from being in contact with (Breckinridge Papers, Folder 11), Regenstein Library, University of Chicago.

60. Lynn Gordon, *Gender and Higher Education in the Progressive Era* (New Haven: Yale University Press, 1990), 115.

61. Lewis Froman, "Graduate Students in Economics, 1904–1928," *American Economic Review* 20 (June 1930): 235.

62. Fitzpatrick, *Endless Crusade*, 47.

63. University of Chicago, Board of Trustees Minutes, March 22, 1904.

64. Rossiter, *Women Scientists*.

65. Cited in Fitzpatrick, *Endless Crusade*, 49.

66. Costin, *Two Sisters*; Mary Jo Deegan, "Women and Sociology: 1890–1930," *Journal of the History of Sociology* 1, no. 1 (Fall 1978): 22.

67. Costin, *Two Sisters*, 29.

68. Ernest Bogart, "Review of Women in Industry," *Journal of Political Economy* 18, no. 4 (April 1910): 317–19; Warren M. Persons, "Recent Publications on Women in Industry," *Quarterly Journal of Economics*, May 1911, 594–612.

69. Laughlin edited the *JPE* from its inception through 1916; Taussig edited the *QJE* from 1896 to 1936; Dewey edited the *AER* from 1911 to after 1930.

70. Dorothy Ross, *The Origins of American Social Science* (Cambridge: Cambridge University Press, 1991), 175. Note that the *Journal of Political Economy* published both Thorstein Veblen's famous article "The Limitations of Marginal Utility" in 1909 and another article by E. H. Downey expressing similar sentiments the following year.

71. Isaac Rubinow, "Women in Manufactures: A Criticism," *Journal of Political Economy* 15 (January 1907): 41–47; Edith Abbott, "Employment of Women in Industries: Cigar-Making—Its History and Present Tendencies," *Journal of Political Economy* 15 (January 1907): 1–25; idem, "Municipal Employment of Unemployed Women in London," *Journal of Political Economy* 14 (November 1907): 513–30; idem, "Women in Manufactures, Supplementary Notes," *Journal of Political Economy* 15 (November 1907): 619–24; Frank Sargent, "Census Statistics of Employment of Children in Manufactures," *Journal of Political Economy* 16 (October 1910): 628–33.

72. Edith Abbott, "Review of Summary of the Report on Condition of Woman and Child Wage Earners in the U.S.," *American Economic Review* 6, no. 3 (September 1916): 662–64.

73. Edith Abbott, "The War and Women's Work in England," *Journal of Political Economy* 25, no. 7 (July 1917): 641–78.

74. Edith Abbott, "Sophonisba P. Breckinridge: Over the Years," *Social Service Review* 22 (December 1948): 417–23.

75. President's Report, University of Chicago, 1927–28.

76. There is at least some evidence that women fellows were also paid less than their male counterparts. In August of 1926, two individuals who were recommended as re-

search assistants for exactly the same term, with exactly the same listed qualifications, were offered contracts for quite different amounts—Miss Mabel Magee, $500; Ross A. McReynolds, $1,200. See President's Papers, Economics Department Appointments and Budget, 1925–1927, Regenstein Library, University of Chicago.

77. Marion Talbot, *More Than Lore: Reminiscences of Marion Talbot, Dean of Women, the University of Chicago 1892–1925* (Chicago: University of Chicago Press, 1936), 138.

78. See Economics Department Records Box 4, File 23, the correspondence of Chairman Marshall, Special Collections, Regenstein Library, University of Chicago.

79. A total of 2,126 authors are cited. The gender of 1,808 of these can be determined by first names. A total of 44 articles on the subject of women and children are cited, and the author's gender can be determined in all but 3 cases. Women authored 26 articles on this subject during the period, or 63 percent of the total of articles by authors of determinate gender. If we assume that all those of indeterminate gender were men, which is not unlikely, women wrote 59 percent of the total.

80. The tables on which these calculations are based are available from the author on request.

81. The percentage of authors whose gender could be decisively identified is much lower for the *Quarterly Journal of Economics* because the journal went through several periods of listing only the authors' first initials.

82. If we employ an upper-bound estimate, of identifiable women as a percentage of those of definite gender, the comparisons are slightly muted, because the *QJE* often made it a practice of using the author's initials, rather than first name: 7.1 percent for *JPE*, 2.6 percent for *QJE*, and 1.9 percent for *AER*. It is very unlikely that many of those of "unknown gender" were women. For journals and dissertations alike, the lower-bound estimate is far more plausible than the upper-bound.

83. A data appendix listing the best-known books and book chapters on women's work between 1890 and 1920 is available from the author upon request.

84. On women's interest in social problems, see Libby, "A Statistical Analysis." On the impact of marginalism, see Rossiter, *Women Scientists*, 173.

85. Cited in Edith Abbott, "The Wages of Unskilled Labor in the U.S., 1850–1900" (Ph.D. diss., Department of Political Economy, University of Chicago), published in the *Journal of Political Economy* 13 (June 1905): 348.

86. Edith Abbott, "Harriet Martineau and the Employment of Women in 1836," *Journal of Political Economy* 14 (December 1906): 614–26.

87. Edith Abbott and Sophonisba Breckinridge, "Employment of Women in Industries: Twelfth Census Statistics," *Journal of Political Economy* 14 (January 1906): 16.

88. Ibid.

89. Edith Abbott, "The History of Industrial Employment of Women in the United States: An Introductory Study." *Journal of Political Economy* 14 (October 1906): 461–501.

90. Nancy Folbre and Marjorie Abel, "Women's Work and Women's Households: Gender Bias in the U.S. Census," *Social Research* 56, no. 3 (1989): 545–70.

91. Sophonisba Breckinridge and Edith Abbott, "Women in Industry: The Chicago Stockyards," *Journal of Political Economy* 19, no. 8 (1911): 632–54.

92. Sophonisba Breckinridge, "Introductory Note" to Edith Abbott, *Women in Industry: A Study in American Economic History* (New York: D. Appleton and Company, 1924).

93. Abbott, *Women in Industry*, 315.

94. Sophonisba Breckinridge, "Legislative Control of Women's Work," *Journal of Political Economy* 14 (January 1906): 107–18.

95. Sophonisba Breckinridge, "A Recent English Case on Women and the Legal Profession," *Journal of Political Economy* 23, no. 1 (January 1915): 64–71.

96. Breckinridge, "Home Responsibilities."

97. Women's Bureau, "The Share of Wage Earning Women in Family Support," Bulletin No. 30, U.S. Department of Labor (Washington, D.C.: Government Printing Office, 1923).

98. Sophonisba Breckinridge, *Women in the Twentieth Century: A Study of Their Political, Social, and Economic Activities* (New York: McGraw-Hill, 1933), 118.

99. Ibid., 219, 225.

100. William Baumol, "On Method in U.S. Economics a Century Earlier," *American Economic Review* 75, no. 6 (December 1985): 10.

101. Sandra Harding, "After the Neutrality Ideal: Science, Politics, and 'Strong Objectivity,'" *Social Research* 59, no. 3 (Fall 1992): 567–87.

102. Peter D. Groenewegen and Susan King, "Women as Producers of Economics Articles: A Statistical Assessment of the Nature and the Extent of Female Participation in Five British and North American Journals 1900–39," Working Papers in Economics, no. 201 (University of Sydney, Australia, June 1994), 23.

CHAPTER 3

"Politics Would Undoubtedly Unwoman Her": Gender, Suffrage, and American Political Science

MARY G. DIETZ AND JAMES FARR

> The faithful teacher of politics ought to be a manly
> and profound observer and construer.
>
> —Francis Lieber[1]

THE DISCIPLINE of political science made its entry onto the stage of American history in the middle of the nineteenth century. Flattering itself on an antique heritage traceable to Aristotle, it had more immediate origins in the New World and it certainly took sides in the great struggles of the day. Political science was for state, for nation, for union—and against the political rights of women. The "manly" teachers of this science of politics, to use Francis Lieber's striking adjective, undermined time-honored notions about the nature of rights; they argued against "woman suffrage"; and they called up the imaginative powers of gender to adorn and enforce their theories of citizen and state.

In observing and construing nineteenth-century political life, American political scientists, from Lieber at midcentury to Woodrow Wilson at century's end, succeeded, on their own terms, in a number of tasks. They transformed the study of politics from one branch of moral philosophy into an independent science of the state that was distinguished from the other social sciences and directed toward the education of young citizens. In taking the state as their principal theoretical object, they also advanced a dialogue with leading European and especially German political theorists while advocating the causes of nationalism, union, and civil service reform at home. But American political scientists were less successful, again on their own terms, in arguing convincingly against the political rights of women to vote, to hold office, or to emerge fully enfranchised into public life. The weakness of the argument was complemented by the ultimate incoherence of the masculine and feminine imagery brought to bear on citizen and state.

This, in brief, is the analysis we wish to give of the formative years of American political science mainly through a critical reading of originary texts. The interpretation of texts is of course only one avenue to the broader questions about gender, suffrage, and the origins of the social sciences. But it is a central avenue since such texts mark the social sciences as practices of literary and intellectual production; and the texts in question here are the most important products of nineteenth-century political science.[2] They are indispensable to an understanding of not only the theoretical teaching tools of the early discipline but the political world as the scientists of the state understood and engaged it. These texts gave voice to a discipline that thought of itself as educating young citizens for a modern republic in a new world amidst the increasing trials of modernity, including the demands by and for women to participate in the professions and in public life. This modern backdrop was influential on all the social sciences in the nineteenth century, as well as on the ostensibly "natural" sciences like biology and anatomy.[3] It was even more influential on political science, whose profession was to understand and explain political life. Indeed, the rise of disciplinary political science in the United States is contemporaneous with the early feminist movement before and after the Civil War, especially regarding "woman suffrage," and can be understood only in light of this fact. This was a period symbolized by the Seneca Falls Declaration of 1848, the formation of both the National Woman Suffrage Association and the American Woman Suffrage Association in 1869, as well as their merger in 1890, the enfranchisement of women in western states beginning in 1870, and the repeated introduction in Congress of a voting rights amendment to the Constitution from 1868 through the turn of the century (and on to 1920). Cognizant of the pressure exerted by and for women to vote, the nineteenth-century political scientists entered none too democratically into the debate over "the other Civil War."[4]

The arguments in the originary texts of political science figure in the background history of the fight over suffrage, and in the foreground history of gender in political science. Of the emerging social sciences, political science was the natural volunteer to take up arms in the other civil war. Consistent with the party line taken by other antisuffragist women and men, the political scientists offered not so much novel arguments as a broader configuration and theoretical grounding for them in their science of the state. In the context of the nineteenth century, this science of the state was not an insulated academic exercise; it was a contribution to American political thought and public opinion more broadly.[5] The theorists of this science, moreover, were university presidents and professors at elite institutions who had significant public standing. Some of them, most famously Woodrow Wilson, served in high public office; others, like Francis Lieber, had the ear of those who did. But most important, the political scientists occupied a unique position and took advantage of it to propagate antisuffragist arguments in the form of teachings to their students and, through them, to the broader public.

The antisuffragist arguments of political scientists dealt with gender as an object of inquiry (since the natural and familial qualifications of women and men as voters were under scrutiny). But gender was also at work in the very framework for inquiry (as an embedded template that symbolically constructed State and Citizen in masculine and feminine terms laden with differences of power). In both ways, gender marked the knowledge that political scientists produced. Analyzing gender in this way obviously differs from a focus on women in the discipline of political science,[6] not to mention a perspective that sticks upon or finds great significance in the undeniable fact that we are dealing here mainly with men. We share the spirit of a recent title, *Gender Is Not a Synonym for Women*—or men, for that matter.[7] Our understanding of gender analysis, especially in the second sense of gender above, shares much with that of other theorists and historians who work at the level of the text or of symbolic construction.[8]

Our general thesis is that one cannot understand nineteenth-century political science without understanding its resistance to "woman suffrage," and one cannot understand this resistance without attending to the ways in which State and Citizen were gender-constructed in the teaching texts that political scientists put before their students and a broader reading public. We intend this thesis to contribute to the literature on gender analysis, which previously has not taken on political or social science texts in the formative period. In this way, we hope to fill a lacuna at the intersection of two other literatures (on the history of political science[9] and on the history of women's suffrage)[10] that heretofore have been inattentive not only to each other but to each other's respective concerns. In what follows we substantiate our thesis by a critical reading of text, argument, and imagery. The first section introduces the principal texts, academic influence, and public presence of the founding scientists of the state. The second section sketches their basic conception of "the state," as well as its bearing on natural rights and suffrage in general. The third section unveils how gendered imagery was embedded in the framework of the science of the state, and then considers the arguments against "woman suffrage" that were drawn from it. The final section criticizes these arguments for their weakness, in context, and points out how the gendered imagery was none too coherent. While calling attention to weak arguments and incoherent imagery is an unavoidably critical stance with respect to the past, it proceeds by taking the past seriously in order to avoid the "enormous condescension of posterity" that afflicts many histories of the social sciences.[11]

SCIENTISTS OF THE STATE

When the members of Francis Lieber's initial audience heard the faithful teacher of politics characterized as "a manly . . . observer and construer," they were attending a public lecture that tells us quite a bit about the intellectual shape of political science as it emerged in the nineteenth century. That lecture was delivered in 1859 in New York, a city known for suffragist agitation, by Columbia's (indeed America's) first professor of history and political science. Known for the *Encyclopedia Americana* and other writings, Lieber was connected to the class of political elites and befriended by, among others, Charles Sumner, Henry Clay, Justice Joseph Story, Chancellor James Kent, and John

C. Calhoun (who read Lieber's treatise on statistics—literally "state-istics"—into the *Congressional Record*). The lecture in New York was entitled "The Ancient and Modern Teacher of Politics: An Introductory Discourse to a Course of Lectures on the State" (published in 1860). The subtitle regarding "the state" connected the address to his popular textbook, *Civil Liberty and Self-Government* (1853),[12] as well as his *Manual of Political Ethics* (1838), which Lieber thought of as his "book on the State" and which Story praised as containing "the fullest and most correct development of the true theory of what constitutes the State that I have ever seen."[13] These various antebellum works form the basis for Lieber's reputation as "the founder of systematic political studies in the United States."[14] In their immediate context, moreover, these works harbored argument and imagery directed against "woman suffrage" that were in print well before antisuffragist pamphlets like Horace Bushnell's *Woman Suffrage: The Reform against Nature* (1869) and Carlos White's *Ecce Femina* (1870). Lieber's texts were given renewed prominence when they were republished after the Civil War (when he produced unionist literature and a code of war for Lincoln and General Halleck). Lieber or those who edited his posthumous works judged that they continued to speak to the political problems that were to dominate the Gilded Age—including the question of suffrage. Lieber himself would repair to them when public occasion summoned some of his more arresting images. When addressing the conventioneers who would change the New York Constitution in 1867, for example, Lieber threw the full force of his rhetoric at the suffragists in attendance. "Woman" had her place in the divine order, he insisted, but not in the voting booth or in public office, for "politics would undoubtedly unwoman her, and her essential character . . . would be lost."[15]

Theodore Dwight Woolsey was principally responsible for republishing Lieber's works after the Civil War.[16] By that time Woolsey had been president of Yale for two decades and was the author of a proscriptive pamphlet, *Divorce and Divorce Legislation* (1868). In his capacity as president, Woolsey carried on the "old college" system of lecturing to the senior class on moral and political philosophy, using not only Lieber's texts but his own work that emphatically tied the identity of political science to the state, *Political Science: or, The State Theoretically and Practically Considered* (published in 1878). Other texts through the close of the century followed Woolsey and Lieber in developing a science of politics as a science of the state and would serve as textual ramparts against the movement to enfranchise women. Among them are *The State: Elements of Historical and Practical Politics* (1889) by Woodrow Wilson, future president of Princeton, governor of New Jersey, and president of the United States; *An Examination of the Nature of the State* (1896) and its didactic companion, *The Rights and Duties of American Citizenship* (1898), by Westel Woodbury Willoughby, professor at Johns Hopkins University, future president of the American Political Science Association, and adviser to the nationalist Chinese government.[17] They also include *Political Science and Comparative Con-*

stitutional Law (1891) by John W. Burgess, who succeeded Lieber at Columbia, founded the School of Political Science there in 1880, and counted Theodore Roosevelt among his students.

The science of the state had American provenance, but German *Staatswissenschaft* backed it. Lieber was himself a German émigré who brought with him a liberal nationalism and statist philosophy forged out of studies with Niebuhr, Schleiermacher, and von Humboldt. Many American postgraduates, including Burgess, studied in Germany under a range of post-Hegelian philosophers, among them Savigny, Treitschke, Gierke, Droysen, Waitz, Ranke, and von Gneist.[18] Even Americans who studied at the new American universities, like Wilson and Willoughby at Johns Hopkins, were influenced by German theorists. Of them all, Johann K. Bluntschli served, in the words of Daniel Rodgers, as "the master of their fledgling science."[19] Bluntschli's major treatise, *Allgemeine Staatslehre* (originally 1851), had been familiar to American political scientists well before its sixth edition was translated into English in 1885 as *The Theory of the State*.[20] Bluntschli and Lieber were frequent correspondents and mutually indebted to one another, especially in matters of international law, for which each gained considerable public fame. Lieber thought that he and Bluntschli (as well as Edouard de Laboulaye) formed a transcontinental "scientific clover-leaf."[21] Bluntschli's influence on the later-nineteenth-century political scientists was felt most profoundly thanks to scholars at Johns Hopkins. Daniel Coit Gilman, founding president of the university, as well as one-time president of the American Social Science Association and editor of Lieber's *Miscellaneous Writings*, successfully secured Bluntschli's library for Hopkins (and, later, Lieber's for the University of California). Herbert Baxter Adams, who established the Johns Hopkins University *Studies in Historical and Political Science*, had directly studied under Bluntschli at Heidelberg and passed on Bluntschli's teachings to his own graduate students, most notably Wilson and Willoughby. Wilson and Willoughby, as well as Burgess, all repaired to Bluntschli on several points regarding the theory of the state. Only the idea of "the Fatherland" would separate their imaginations, but not what Bluntschli called "The Position of Woman."[22]

The American scientists of the state were not mere ivory-tower intellectuals, cut apart from a broader public. Nineteenth-century professors, not to mention university presidents, were influential figures. All of them were participants in public venues where they aired their opinions, spoke to a broader community of citizens and social scientists, and tried to influence statesmen in the formation of public policy. In his various public offices, Wilson gave practical political form to his ideas on the state, including opposing suffrage as governor and dragging his feet as president in the run-up to the Nineteenth Amendment.[23] Besides university or public office, one of the most important political venues for the nineteenth-century political scientists was the American Social Science Association, founded in Boston in 1865 as a vehicle of reform via the propagation of social scientific knowledge. At different times, Lieber, Woolsey, and

Willoughby were leading members in various departments of the association: Lieber as the first head of the Department of Jurisprudence and the Amendment of Laws (under whose charge was the topic of the suffrage); Woolsey as the first head of the Department of Economy, Trade and Finance; and Willoughby as one of the last heads of the Department of Social Economy (whose domain the association's founder, Franklin Sanborn, called "the feminine gender of Political Economy").[24] The ASSA proved to be the *ur*-association for the later disciplinary associations, including the more self-consciously professional American Political Science Association, whose founding in 1903 signaled the demise of the ASSA. Aspirations toward scientific objectivity got the better of those for advocacy.[25]

Of relevance to women's rights and to this formative episode of political science, the ASSA was known for its large number of women members, its egalitarianism with respect to their participation, and the feminist sympathies of some of its men, including Sanborn. The women's rights activist Caroline Healey Dall was, like Lieber and Woolsey, a founding member who exerted much influence in and through the association.[26] But for all its reformism, including support of many legal rights of women, the ASSA never took a public stance on the extension of suffrage in national elections. If some members were advocates for suffrage, the likes of Lieber, Woolsey, and Willoughby (as well as other political scientists, like Simeon Baldwin, one of its last presidents) prove that others emphatically were not. The ASSA, as such, occupies a curious niche in the history of women's rights. The association's *Journal of Social Science* dedicated many articles to the education, working conditions, physical training, and even the "inebriety" of women.[27] But suffrage was headlined only in the first volume, in "The Protection of the Ballot in National Elections," and in the tenth, in "The Voting of Women in School Elections." The author of the first article, treasurer of the association and enthusiastic supporter of Lieber, Charles F. Adams, Jr., worried that universal suffrage would introduce "a large infusion of the more voluble, demonstrative, and impulsive female element into the arena of politics."[28] The founding political scientists not only shared these worries, they helped by their very membership to aggravate them in key sectors of the ASSA—and in their classrooms, as well. Social science reformism should move ahead, but on other fronts, especially civil service reform, for which the association was to gain its greatest notice. This was most appropriate in "the age of statistics," as the journal reported a speech before Congress by another friend of Lieber's, representative and future president James Garfield. For "statistics are State facts, facts for the consideration of statesmen."[29]

THE SIGNIFICANCE OF THE STATE

Statesmen, just like state facts, needed scientific theories to back them. This was precisely what the formative political scientists thought that they were articulating in their textbooks. All agreed with the spirit of Burgess's observation that "the national popular state alone furnishes the objective reality upon which political science can rest in the construction of a truly scientific political system."[30] Thus one cannot appreciate the meaning of gendered images or the force of inferences about suffrage without first understanding what constituted the "objective reality" that the scientists called "the state."

The state, according to the political scientists, was the highest and latest form of the political organization of society. Its origins could be traced back through feudal manors to ancient city-states to primitive tribes where it emerged out of the patriarchal family. Its "essence," as Willoughby put it in *The Nature of the State*, differed, however, from these earlier forms and certainly from the patriarchal family.[31] The state had progressed most completely in those northern European countries where the Teutonic, Aryan, or simply "our own white race" had proliferated.[32] Thus the nineteenth-century statists from Lieber to Wilson were historicists about tracing origins, and racialists about explaining progress in the development of the modern national state. Furthermore, they understood the fundamental concept of "the state" in juridical terms. The state was "a jural society." It expressed the sovereign legal power of a community of people, socially united as a nation, and living in a given country. A particular state was given identity not only by the country and nation to which it gave political expression, but especially by its "permanent law" or constitution. States, accordingly, differed as their legal and constitutional systems differed, and this provided the empirical premise for the investigations of "the comparative, historical method." Woodrow Wilson best captured the method: "The nature of each State, therefore, will be reflected in its law; . . . and in its law will it be possible to read its history."[33]

As no state could exist without law, so no state could act without government. However, the government was *not* to be equated with the state. Government was simply the principal agency or organ through which the state acted. Actual forms of government could vary, but the Americans predictably favored a representative form of government, justified along lines traceable to the old Federalists and Whigs. Representative government, in theory, allowed educated men to govern but also to represent all interests (including women's) in the state. Moreover, representative government could and should be limited in the scope of its activities, whereas the state was supreme. Fearful of the specter of "paternalistic" government's meddling too much in society and economy, the American statists nonetheless never denied that "assistance of the poor" and "support of those who cannot support themselves" were appropriate policies for government.[34] While hoping to keep such policies to a minimum, none shared the extreme social Darwinism found in Herbert Spencer's *The Man versus the State* (1884), a title whose implied antagonism they could scarcely comprehend.

The state, then, was a jural society of a particular nation in a given country whose organ was the government. Calling the government an organ was intentional, for jural society was itself an "organism." Neither machine nor artificial invention of atomized individuals, the state was a real living organism, although not a "natural" one like a plant or an animal. Rather, the state was a "moral and spiritual" organism best analogized, as Willoughby claimed, to "a person because it has a will of its own," as well as personality, character, and the capacity for self-directed growth. One rather simplified version of this organicist analogy viewed "the State . . . as an enormous Man."[35] This "person" or "enormous Man" gave identity to rather more life-size men in their capacities *as citizens*. Citing Aristotle, Lieber wrote that "Man to be fully man must be a citizen," that is, an "active member of the state." Citizens were individuated "members" of the state, organic parts of the overall organism. As members of the state, they were expected to foster virtues appropriate to their respective stations in life and to assume the duties and corresponding rights of the office of citizenship. As Lieber put it, "Right and Duty are correlative terms."[36]

Rights, to say nothing of duties, were not juridical powers or normative properties of individuals outside the state; nor did the state come into existence in order to protect any so-called natural rights. Political scientists rejected the notion of a "social contract" that explained the origin of government or backed allegations about so-called natural rights. Indeed, they broke dramatically with traditional theories of the nation's founding whether in Paine, Jefferson, or Madison. And they were fully aware of this. A. Lawrence Lowell, president of Harvard and future president of the American Political Science Association who was praised as an antisuffragist by the women antisuffragists of Massachusetts, discarded "the exploded doctrine of the natural rights of man."[37] Burgess found the doctrine of natural rights "pernicious" and insisted that the Bill of Rights was really a misnomer for a list of "immunities." Willoughby bluntly concluded that "there are in the individual no so-called innate or 'natural rights,' that is, such rights as exist independently of the State and beyond its control." The "permanent power" needed "to define and realize rights" was none other than the state, Woolsey insisted. If the phrase "natural rights" made any sense, it was only because "man's nature" was to be in the state.[38]

Denying "natural" rights in theory bore directly upon the practical question of who could vote, that paradigmatic act of citizenship.[39] In the half century after the Civil War, the time-honored language of "natural rights" was being invoked in many different contexts, including arguments by or on behalf of freed slaves, immigrants, and women that they be given the right to vote. Indeed, the theorists of the women's suffrage movement had leaned heavily on the notion, and nowhere was this clearer than in Elizabeth Cady Stanton's aptly titled work, *Suffrage, a Natural Right* (1894). Willoughby's reaction to "so-called . . . 'natural rights'" in 1896 comes across as if it were directed at Stanton:

> There are those who would go so far as to have us believe that the exercise of the suffrage is an inherent inalienable right of the free-born citizen. It does not need to be said that it is not. It is a political privilege, and is founded only on law. . . . The citizen is endowed with right of suffrage, in order that by its exercise the good of society may be maintained, and it is for society to determine to what extent, and by whom, and under what conditions this power is to be used.[40]

Willoughby's views about natural rights and voting were foreshadowed in the writings of Lieber and Woolsey and shared by his contemporaries, Burgess and Wilson. Their collective views were, in short, deep-seated and intransigent. Voting was nominally a "right," but better termed a privilege, and then only for the most active enfranchised members of the state. The members in question, by the broadest count allowable, were "all resident loyal male citizens, of mature age, suffering no civil disability," as Burgess defined them. Even a definition like this one (of "a suffrage very nearly universal") harbored evident hedges with regard to those male citizens of questionable "loyalty" and "civil disability."[41] This created lexical room for the expression of misgivings about any rapid expansion of manhood suffrage amid a tide of manumitted slaves and of new immigrants of various racial stocks and previous national loyalties.[42] But when it came to women—immigrant, ex-slave, or freeborn—no flexibility was necessary. Residency, loyalty, maturity, or civil ability notwithstanding, women simply were not male citizens.

However, the political scientists did not leave matters here. From the decade preceding the Seneca Falls Declaration to the turn of the century, they developed expansive antisuffragist arguments that placed them at the dead center of the forces against the enfranchisement of women. Unlike many pamphleteers and publicists, however, political scientists intended to provide the "scientific" framework from which logical inferences to women as voters could be drawn. But more than science and logic were at work, and more than real men and women at issue. For State and Citizen were also symbolically gendered and figuratively constructed in feminine and masculine terms. That is, political scientists applied their science of state and citizen to men and women as potential voters; but only after first representing State and Citizen as embodying masculine and feminine traits. Inevitably, these traits also marked distinctions of power.

Manly State and Woman Suffrage

Whatever made them "manly" teachers of politics, the scientists of the state displayed a tendency that was, as Lieber himself recognized, all too human. Humans frequently express themselves by "applying the *different grammatical genders*" to worldly objects, he noted, including "abstract principles of their own design."[43] A wide array of objects and principles were represented, that is, as "he or she," "manly or womanly," "masculine or feminine." The abstract principles of the all-too-human political scientists, Lieber's included, proved to be no exception to this rule.

When political scientists configured their object of study as a person, they did not think in gender-neutral terms or consistently employ generic language. When they wrote "man" they did not mean "man and woman." Thus the state when not "it" was "he," a manly figure of sovereign power. The Americans drew much of their imagery from Bluntschli's text. Willoughby, for example, ended a very long quotation with a favorite conceit of the German philosopher: "the State is humanity organised, but humanity as masculine, not as feminine: the State is the man." This man had the traits of self-determination, independence, willfulness, strength, spirit, and genius. When states did not fully display these masculine traits, they nonetheless were making progress toward realizing them. Modern nation-states, as Wilson wrote admiringly, are at last "growing up into manhood."[44]

This symbolic foundation of the state as man allowed for further variations on the gendering of the political world. Bluntschli himself gendered the political world in two telling ways, reflecting the peculiarities of German political culture. First, he invoked "the whole great idea of Fatherland" in connection with the (German) state and thereby fused state *with* country (as land). The masculine figurations of fatherhood and paternalism captured both state *and* country. Second, Bluntschli contrasted the masculine character of the state with "the feminine character of the Church . . . because she [the Church] does not consciously rule herself like a man, and act freely in her external life."[45] On the other side of the Atlantic, the Americans resisted these particular tropes. But by no means did they expunge their works of equally evocative gendered images. They simply innovated in ways that helped constitute their own political culture. In the New World where no single organized church stood against the state, as woman to man, the symbolic feminine was assigned to a different entity, as Lieber made plain: "woman represents country." In Lieber's thinking, any particular country acted as "she" would, given "her laws." Hence one could speak of England in terms of the glorious consequences of "her revolution," and especially "her institutions of an organic character, her jury, her common law, her representative legislature, her local self-government, her justice of the peace, her sheriff, her coroner."[46] Willoughby, Wilson, and Lowell maternalized the image with the phrase "mother country" and infantilized "her" colonies as "children."[47] The mother country, to whom Americans owed loyalty, could not therefore also be cast in the contrary image of "father" or "fatherland." Indeed, the image of the father, and the ideas of paternalism and patriarchy more generally, posed peculiar problems for the Americans' symbolically gendered political world. These problems were not so much resolved as relocated to the horizon of the citizen, where a masculine, fraternal, and fatherly vocabulary played other roles.

The citizen, like the state, was a man, imbued with masculine traits and virtues, inhabiting a world of fellow citizens. "We are citizens because we are men," Lieber proclaimed in his *Manual*, describing "those virtues which form the common stock of man's morality—justice, honesty, and a pure family life" as those constitutive of the virtues of a citizen. Against "unmanly characters" that threaten the state, he united "perseverance, firmness, fortitude, constancy, courage, calmness, manfulness, dignity of mind, self-esteem and consistency" as "each the same in principle."[48] The adjective "manly" was a veritable mantra to the "manly" teachers of politics whom Lieber hailed. The citizen showed "manly calm" (Lieber), "manly independence" (Lieber), "manly self-control" (Willoughby), "manly spirit" (Bluntschli), and a "manly, liberal, harmonious, and dignified character" (Woolsey).[49] The emphasis in these locutions fell less on the virtues themselves than on their manliness. Although some features of these locutions can be traced back to the American Revolution, their emphatic manliness appears endemic to the later nineteenth century.[50] Thus the Gilded Age political scientists were not merely echoing the older republican discourse of the "manly citizen." They were celebrating citizens *as men.* As men, citizens were bound together in a fraternity of "fellow citizens." Their rights and duties were fraternalized, as well. As Lieber noted, "Right and Duty are twin brothers."[51]

In the gendered world of the nineteenth-century political scientists, the fraternal citizens had a mother (country) to whom they owed both loyalty and love. There was also a potential father figure in this world, not as state or fatherland, but as a certain kind of government. Lowell called this "the paternal system of government" that threatened to undermine "strong and healthy manhood." Referring to the same paternal system, Woolsey proclaimed: "If the individual leaves everything to the government, he remains a dependent, undeveloped citizen; he is not a freeman in his spirit."[52] The government, as the state's mere organ, should not become a father figure or paternal master to the citizen, upon pain of emasculation associated with the loss of liberty. American citizens, then, were men whose manhood was defined against fathers as well as against females. Their manhood made them candidates for civic involvement in the American system in the first place; and the system in turn helped ensure their manhood.

One can only imagine a century later what the American political scientists thought they were doing or gaining by using gendered symbolism in these ways. They certainly introduced problems, as we shall see. But at the very least it seems clear that these diverse gendered images provided a workaday hermeneutics or interpretive bridgehead that clarified the abstractions of the science of the state. Gendering the presumptive familiarities of everyday life helped to render accessible the more abstract and unfamiliar realm theorized by political scientists. Readers could make better sense of the world of states and citizens because they already had some pretheorized sense of the world of men and women, fathers and mothers, things manly and not. Moreover, and most significant, gendering the state and citizen in manly ways made the work of arguing against "woman suffrage" all the easier and heightened the possibility of moving the public toward antisuffragism.

"The State," thus claimed Bluntschli, "cannot afford to weaken its manly character by the admixture of feminine weakness and susceptibility."[53] The Americans endorsed and bolstered this claim with a series of arguments concerning (1) the nature of Woman; (2) the sphere of the family; (3) the representation of interests; and (4) women's desire to not vote. At the margins lurked (5) the corruption of morals and the unleashing of aggressive sexuality. These arguments meshed seamlessly with those being offered by antisuffragist pamphleteers.[54] They were meant to be decisive not only for the vote but for canvassing for election, joining electoral groups, engaging in public speech, and of course running for office. In short, they were designed as all-purpose arguments against women's participation in electoral politics.

Lest his students and readers miss the point, Lieber would summarize his views about the first of these arguments with an arresting image: "The woman who should go to the poll must have disrobed herself of her essential nature as woman."[55] In comparison to the manly citizen, "the woman" was by nature passive, weak, small, delicate, gentle, sensitive, sentimental, caring, timid, bashful, retiring, given to affection, and less amenable to the guidance of reason. As attributes of women's "duties and callings," these characteristics were unobjectionable in themselves; but they were ill-suited to voting and electoral politics. Worse still for the fate of public life, "the woman" could also be passionate, jealous, vengeful, cunning, deceiving and deceivable, given to intrigue.[56]

The second argument that bolstered the political scientists' antisuffragism held that engaging in electoral politics would exact too heavy a price on the family. The family constituted in Bluntschli's words "the proper sphere" and in Lieber's "the true sphere of woman's best and noblest activity." The familial relations of wife, mother, daughter, and sister gave identity to women, especially as educators of the young. The hierarchical relations of the family created no place for voting within the family, or for women's civic education in preparation for voting outside the family. As Woolsey noted in a typical passage, there existed in the family "a certain dominion on the part of the man. This is so far true that superior strength and knowledge of business fit him to manage family affairs, and there can, in most jural relations, be but one manager."[57] The family did not, then, prepare women for the exercise of the elective franchise, and voting would undermine the sanctity of the family. The family was in this sense private. But it was no less "political" for that, or irrelevant to the state. Rather, the family provided the sort of "political" life that women could expect as regards their contribution to the organic life of the state. As Lieber put it, "the most important calling of the woman respecting politics is, that, as wife, she identify herself with her husband," keeping alive in him her gift of "high-minded patriotism." In this way, as Bluntschli averred, "woman receives her true place in the organisation of the State, and is amply compensated for her exclusion from political rights."[58]

Endowing family life and domesticity with political meaning was not unique to the nineteenth-century scientists of the state. In some respects, they were continuing to work within a discursive context that went back to the eighteenth century and particularly to its image of the Republican Mother. Nurturer of nascent citizens, helpmate to republican husbands, the Republican Mother was an important piece of the iconography of the American Founding. Over the course of the century, this iconography transmogrified into the Maternal Commonwealth where woman's special "difference" as mother was put to various political uses.[59] Some, including the suffragists, argued that, as mothers, women were caring citizens whose fully enfranchised civic involvement would make for a more nurturing public life. Others, including the political scientists, seized upon these emblems of femininity and motherhood, as Mary P. Ryan notes, "to place women on the margins of the public domain."[60] The political scientists, however, were less interested in the Maternal Commonwealth as such than in defending the state and securing its organic wholeness. Women, as wives, mothers, and sisters, were political parts of the organic state, but not as voters. Their vote would violate the organic wholeness of the state. It would be a kind of abomination or, as Lieber concluded, "an inorganic suffrage."[61]

The political scientists' third argument against granting women the vote was linked to the notion that organic suffrage rested with the male voter alone. But in the context of this suffrage, the male voter, as head of family, represented and protected not only his own interests but the interests of women in the family as well. In Woolsey's terms, since those "excluded by sex . . . follow the condition of the families to which they belong, there can be *in general* for them no want of protection"—and therefore no need to cast a ballot.[62] Since the family, too, formed an organic whole, the influence of women through their counsel was already implicit in the formation of a husband's and father's interests. Since women's interests were thereby represented, as Willoughby argued, "giving women the right to vote will be tantamount to giving extra votes to their husbands or fathers, in accordance with whose wills most of them will be inclined to exercise their right."[63] Thus women did not need the vote because it was redundant; to give it to them would only add to the already established power of men.

A convenient addendum to this view made for a fourth argument. As Lieber put it in 1867, "We say boldly, that those women who truly know their calling, which lies far beyond politics, do not desire the vote." At the much later date of 1898, at a time of heightened antisuffragism on the part of women themselves, Willoughby could give the same point a flatly empirical rendering. "As a matter of fact, very few women as yet desire the privilege of voting."[64]

Desire of a more frankly sexual kind lurked in the imaginations and at the margins of the arguments deployed by the scientists of the state. Inhibitions of bashfulness and "sexual shame" would be destroyed were Woman to come into contact at the polling places with what Woolsey called the "coarse" and Willoughby the "rough elements which will tend to destroy her delicacy and charm." "The most gloomy consequences must follow," Lieber noted, for "it would be impossible for womankind to retain modesty and continency, and thus society would hasten to speedy dissolution." She would stand "disrobed" at the polls, "unwomaned" by politics.[65] When Victoria Woodhull announced her candidacy for president in 1872, just months before Lieber's death, the old professor proved even more forthcoming in a letter to Garfield when he noted a "manifest vein of lechery in the advanced women's rights women." Next would come communism and "promiscuous intercourse of the sexes." Lieber thus answered the rhetorical question that he himself had posed to the dele-

gates to the New York constitutional convention of 1867 when he publicly opposed "woman suffrage": "How would we like to have a female president, and
what would it lead to?"[66]

THE INCOHERENCES OF GENDER

For all of their rhetorical forcefulness in shoring up the theory of the state, the
political scientists' arguments against "woman suffrage" nonetheless betrayed
a number of serious problems and their imagery masked real incoherences.
With respect to the opening argument concerning the nature of woman, Lieber
was the first to admit that "there are, of course, women whose extraordinary
mental organization is such that they form exceptions." Exceptional women,
even if not all women, met the relevant criteria for participation in the active
affairs of state; their interests and (social) rights were at issue and could be
expressed and protected only by their personal enfranchisement. This was virtually conceded by Woolsey, who emphasized, in the passage quoted above,
that only *"in general"* were women's interests and "private rights" protected
"from invasion" insofar as their men's suffrages were intact and their votes
tallied.[67] Even Woolsey's dutiful students must have wondered: what, then,
about the exceptions, in particular?

Talk of exceptions, in any case, hides a more egregious problem. In politics,
arguments about "nature" are notoriously intractable and usually false. The
political scientists themselves were the first to point this out in the case of
so-called natural rights and the improper analogy of the state to a "natural"
(versus a spiritual) organism. The conventions that lay at the foundation of
alleged "natural" rights were no different in kind from the conventions that
defined and reinforced the alleged "natural" characteristics of women and men,
including the family. The argument from the family, moreover, suffered from
the same general liabilities as did the one from nature. "Exceptional" wives and
mothers upset the alleged order of family life and the convenient assignment of
women to its sphere of privacy.

Furthermore, the political scientists' arguments revealed a deep inconsistency regarding the family. They denied women the right to vote because of the
hierarchy of the family; but then they denied that the family, especially the
patriarchal family, was a model illuminating the rights between citizens which
made up the "essence" of the *modern* state.[68] The argument about the inclusion
of women's interests in those of their male family members also demonstrates
the theorists' disregard of this inconsistency. Lieber, for example, raised Kant-
ian objections to those who would pardon crimes committed by females on
account of their sex. "Is then woman not a moral and responsible being, and
shall we again disgrace her by holding her unaccountable. . . . The Chinese
wife is not morally emancipated to this day. They have a maxim to this day that
a 'married woman can commit no crime; the responsibility rests with the husband.' How degrading for the woman!"[69] One need only switch "American" for

"Chinese," replace "morally emancipated" by "enfranchised," and substitute "vote" for "crime" to appreciate the relevance of this passage to the issues of American women's suffrage.

The empirical-sounding argument that women did not as a "matter of fact" desire the vote had logical and evidentiary peculiarities, as well. First, it credited women with having individual opinions about interests independently of their men, and so with having a public opinion representable for the whole class of women. It was sort of a vote before the vote, one that paradoxically precluded the other. Even then, no anecdotal evidence was forthcoming, much less statistical information of the kind that political scientists boasted. In his address on the Constitution of New York, for example, Lieber could cite his own "paper on election statistics in the Appendix to *Civil Liberty*" in the very paragraph preceding his claim about women's lack of desire to vote, without thinking it at all incumbent upon him to offer even a few statistical facts about women's opinions in this connection.[70] There were indeed women who did not desire the vote, to judge by the Women's Anti-Suffrage Association of America and other organizations.[71] But whether or not "most women" wished forever to stand down from the suffrage remained an uninvestigated "matter of fact."

This failure to present any evidence was a particular instance of a more general fault exhibited by the American scientists of the state. They simply did not study women, despite their alleged commitment to the comparative, historical method. In *The State*, for example, Wilson mentioned the enfranchisement of women in the western territories of Wyoming, Washington, and Utah, and took note of their participation in school board elections in Minnesota, Massachusetts, and Colorado. But he showed no interest in probing these developments.[72] It is important to note that the most systematic studies of women's (including American women's) political rights were undertaken not by Americans but by Europeans. Indeed, serious American scholarship on American women's political activities would not begin until Sophonisba Breckinridge's study of 1933.[73] The European works included *Histoire de l'Amerique* (1859) by Edouard de Laboulaye, the third in the clover-leaf with Lieber and Bluntschli;[74] Moisei Ostrogorski's *The Rights of Women: A Comparative Study in History and Legislation* (translated into English from the French in 1893);[75] and, by far the most famous, *The American Commonwealth* by the Englishman James Bryce. In his chapter on "woman suffrage," Bryce covered many of the electoral developments in the American state, noting that the "ladies" with whom he spoke were generally opposed, but that "the suffragists have some grounds for the confidence of victory they express." Wryly and prophetically, Bryce concluded of the European observer, like himself, "If he sees no reason to expect an improvement in politics from the participation of women in elections and their admission to Congress and to high political office, neither does he find much cause for fear."[76]

Yet another European, John Stuart Mill, highlights the more generalized weakness of the Americans' arguments. Mill had raised and refuted the arguments at issue in *On Representative Government* (1861) and even more deci-

sively in *On the Subjection of Women* (1868), that "wonderful work" in Elizabeth Cady Stanton's estimation.[77] "What is now called the nature of women is
an eminently artificial thing," Mill famously concluded after a long list of comparative historical evidence. As a "school of despotism," the family contributed
to this artificiality and its contrived gender stereotypes. As for the alleged inclusion of women's interests in the votes of men, Mill observed that "the majority
of the women of any class are not likely to differ in political opinion from the
majority of the men in the same class, unless the question be one in which the
interests of women, as such, are in some way involved; and if they are so,
women require the suffrage. . . ."[78] If the Gilded Age political scientists failed
to cite and engage similar arguments by Stanton, Woodhull, Susan B. Anthony,
Lucretia Mott, Lucy Stone, Sojourner Truth, or Carrie Chapman Catt, they
could not and did not hide their familiarity with Mill's works. The weaknesses
of their own arguments about women, family, and interests were, in short, exposed by a political theorist whom they could not ignore.

Mill did not address the argument about the manly character of the state,
which might suggest that he did not think it actually was a proper argument,
and which might explain why Bluntschli placed so much emphasis on it when
singling out Mill as an adversary. In any case, there was nothing to the argument apart from the gendered imagery that the political scientists themselves
had plentifully assigned to state and citizen, as well as country, land, and government; and the imagery was not accountable to any standards of evidence.
Nevertheless its plenitude conspired to make the science of the state con-
fusingly overgendered. The dizzying array of gendered images—manly states,
mother countries, father lands, sister nations, paternal governments, fellow citizens—were bound to collide and to confuse.

Consider some of the confusions that resulted when state, country, and nation were gendered. Abstractly considered, the state was a jural society, constituted by law, incorporating the nation, in a given country. There could be no
state without a country, although there could be a country without a state,
because country was an aspect of the idea of the state. But once state was
gendered a man, and country a woman, the imagery undermined the abstraction. What sense survived the transposition? There could be no man without a
woman, although there could be a woman without a man, because woman was
an aspect of the idea of man? If "woman" becomes "mother," as in "mother
country," matters prove even more senseless. Having labored so hard to theo-
rize man's nature as distinct from woman's, precisely because suffrage was at
stake, the gendered imagery undermined the theory. Similar confusions
emerge when one tries to square the theoretical connection between state and
nation with their gendered imagery. "Manly" states incorporated their respective nations, which, in relation to one another, are "sister nations"?

The gendered assignments proved culturally arbitrary, and even diametri-
cally opposed, as well. The German Bluntschli and the American Willoughby,
for example, shared the same abstract principles and much of the same gender-

ing, including the notion that "the state is a man." But then they absolutely diverged when Bluntschli likened the land to a father and Willoughby the country to a mother. Arbitrary enough, the picture was more confusing still when gendered oppositions were respectively spelled out. Bluntschli's male Fatherland may have had as its Other a feminine Church. But Bluntschli also characterized Europe in female terms; and what sense was there to a world in which the German Fatherland was part of a larger female Europe?[79] As for Willoughby, who played the father figure husband to the mother country? There was no comparable Fatherland; and the government was denied a paternalistic role lest it threaten the "manhood" of citizens.

Nothing could threaten the manhood of citizens more, evidently, than the inclusion of women in civic life. Nothing could threaten women more, as well, to judge by Lieber's fevered images of woman "disrobed . . . of her essential nature" and "unwomaned" by politics. But such imagery, which abounded in the broader antisuffrage literature,[80] was ultimately as incoherent as that of a world of commingling manly states, sister nations, mother countries, and father lands. One falls into incredulous questioning. How could a woman "disrobe" herself of something as "essential" as a "nature"? How exactly would the "artificial" woman (as voter) undo the clothed (enrobed, girdled, tucked, pinned, and stayed) "natural" woman (as woman)? Didn't exceptional women and certainly queens show that politics would not "undoubtedly unwoman her"? Wasn't it merely tautological and question-begging to construct state and citizen as manly and then to turn around and allege that politics would "unwoman" woman? Even then, if politics were to "unwoman" woman, wouldn't "she" simply become the civic equivalent of a man capable of voting?

The scientists of the state made no attempt to answer such questions. Given their opposition to women's enfranchisement, perhaps they did not recognize them as valid questions, much less as the occasion for critical reflection on their arguments and images. But this only proves the circularity of their effort: voters should not be women because women should not be voters. Among the many accomplishments of formative political science cannot be numbered a coherent and convincing case why women should continue to be denied the vote or why the complex world of nation-states and democratic citizens was more perspicacious thanks to their constructions of gender.

CONCLUSION

"We smile now at Bluntschli's insistence that the state is a man." This was Jesse Reeves's reaction to the gendered constructions of the outmoded science of the state in his presidential address to the APSA in 1928.[81] The inevitable change of modernity had already visited Lieber's "manly" teachers of politics as much as it had states, citizens, and voters heading into the twentieth century. The discipline had already begun to distance itself from or simply to forget the antisuffragist arguments, gendered images, and public passions of its Founding Fathers. Two significant developments help close this formative chapter in the history of political science.

First, the discipline increasingly ceased to think of its identity in terms of "the state."[82] This cannot be attributed to the political insignificance of actual states, especially under the specter of world war. Indeed, some of it might be attributed to the identification of "the state" with Germany; the rest an abandonment of the philosophically ambitious program of the science of the state. As "the state" slipped away, so too did the urge to gender it or the political world associated with it. Political scientists started increasingly to think of "administration" or "actual government" as their defining object of study, and soon enough the language of "process" and "behavior" would set the stage for the two behavioral revolutions later in the century. With this theoretical shift came a second, more practical one: an increasing unwillingness to engage in outright political controversy. The concern with objectivity and new methods of science brought in train greater reserve about partisan or heated public disputation,[83] including that over "woman suffrage." When political scientists raised the topic, as, for example, they did in the 1910 *Proceedings of the American Political Science Association*, they disputed more guardedly and reservedly than had the earlier scientists of the state.

The two changes in play here—the displacement of the state as the theoretical focus of the discipline and a political reserve about discussing charged political issues like the voting rights of women—can be seen in Arthur F. Bentley's *The Process of Government*. Published in 1908 and heralded later as a classic of behavioral political science, Bentley's powerful study raised "process" and "interest groups" to dominant theoretical status, called for greater methodological rigor, and maligned the Germanic idea of the state as "among the intellectual amusements of the past." For example, "what Professor Burgess so admirably studied under the name of the 'state behind the government,' is from my point of view nothing else than government itself." Discussing "women-interest groups," Bentley would observe of suffrage, as if from a distance:

> Where women's interests push themselves out . . . as is sometimes the case with the conduct of the public schools . . . the women may break through to partial participation in the suffrage in that particular field. The more the family organization transforms itself and the more the women come to stand apart from the men, the more certain will be their speedy direct participation in the suffrage. This is not saying that there is any "reason" why they should not participate directly in the general suffrage now, or why they should. It is only pointing to an habitual suffrage system, grown out of earlier conditions, and lacking as yet any sufficient impetus to its transformation.[84]

Here was a snapshot of the discipline's future: detached scientifically, unattached to the science of the state. And, by 1920, political scientists were relieved of the whole question of whether they should be for or against "woman suffrage." The Nineteenth Amendment obviated it. Given the analysis of this study, it is ironic that it was one of the scientists of the state—Woodrow

Wilson—who presided over this constitutional sea change. The forces of anti-suffragism, including that which remained in the private sentiments of some political scientists, lapsed into history. The National American Woman Suffrage Association became the League of Women Voters and began its long career of informing and turning out the vote. The discipline of political science began its parallel career of investigating the causes and consequences of how informed and turned out the vote actually was.

The relation of political science to "woman suffrage" did not end here, though it was much transformed. Indeed, no sooner was "woman suffrage" a fact than political scientists had a new research agenda on their hands. As the classic study *Non-Voting* (1924) showed, political scientists had to reconsider "causes and methods of control" in the context of abstention from voting, since women *did not* turn out in great numbers and overall turnout had actually declined in Chicago's first elections after passage of the Nineteenth Amendment.[85] By 1928, this opened up yet another research agenda: explaining why "a pragmatic electorate" *need not* vote very often or in very great numbers anyway.[86] The political system as a whole contrived to represent interests and govern effectively (much as men had been alleged to do for women). Neither of these research agendas was short-lived; efforts to explain or explain away non-voting are very much alive. Moreover, neither of them can be properly or fully understood unless they are placed in a longer historical narrative that goes back through the "woman suffrage" amendment and begins with the scientists of the state, Lieber and Bluntschli, Willoughby and Wilson. The questions of why women do not, need not, or should not vote are thoroughly entangled in historical perspective.

As for gender, we too may "smile"—as Reeves did nearly seventy years ago—at the blatancy of Bluntschli and company's insistence that "the state is a man." But digging such images out from beneath layers of disciplinary forgetfulness might prompt us to analyze how, in many less blatant ways, constructions of gender continue to constitute the subject matter of political science and constrain its discourses.

NOTES

We are indebted to Ido Oren for his comments on an earlier draft of this essay, and to Beverly Cook and Sara Evans for advice. All errors of fact and interpretation are, of course, our own.

1. Quotation in title from "The Constitution of New York," reprinted in *Miscellaneous Writings*, 2 vols. (Philadelphia: J. B. Lippincott, 1881), 2:208. The epigraph is from "The Ancient and Modern Teacher of Politics," reprinted in *Miscellaneous Writings*, 1:381.

2. Anna Haddow, *Political Science in American Colleges and Universities, 1636–1900* (New York: Appleton Century, 1939), esp. 138 and 241 on "the most significant texts" by Lieber, Woolsey, Burgess, Willoughby, and Wilson. A broader study would have to attend to some lesser texts in political science, as well as any (if any) pedagogical differences regarding the teaching of politics and the science of the state at the women's

colleges. A much broader study would have to attend to other social scientists, including those very late-nineteenth- and early-twentieth-century figures, like Thorstein Veblen, W. I. Thomas, and Charles Beard, not to mention Jane Addams, Mary Beard, Mary van Kleeck, and Charlotte Perkins Gilman, who supported women's suffrage. Also, there are important disagreements among the political scientists on particular issues. However, they were remarkably aligned on the general theory of the state, as well as its application to suffrage. In what follows, then, we stress and critically engage the commonalities in the major originary texts of the central figures of formative political science.

3. See Dorothy Ross, *The Origins of American Social Science* (New York: Cambridge University Press, 1991), esp. chap. 1; and Cynthia Eagle Russett, *Sexual Science: The Victorian Construction of Womanhood* (Cambridge: Harvard University Press, 1989).

4. To borrow a striking phrase from Catherine Clinton, *The Other Civil War: American Women in the Nineteenth Century* (New York: Hill and Wang 1984). For the broader antidemocratic hesitations of political science during this period, see James Farr, "From Modern Republic to Administrative State: American Political Science in the Nineteenth Century," in *Regime and Discipline: Democracy and the Development of Political Science*, ed. David Easton, John G. Gunnell, and Michael B. Stein (Ann Arbor: University of Michigan Press, 1995), 131–68.

5. Charles E. Merriam, *A History of American Political Theories* (New York: Macmillan, 1924), chap. 8; Daniel T. Rodgers, *Contested Truths: Keywords in American Politics since Independence* (New York: Basic Books, 1987), chaps. 4–5; and John G. Gunnell, *The Descent of Political Theory: The Genealogy of an American Vocation* (Chicago: University of Chicago Press), chaps. 2–3.

6. For work in this area, see, among others, Jessie Barnard, *Academic Women* (University Park: Pennsylvania State University Press, 1964); Victoria Schuck, "Sexism and Scholarship: A Brief Overview of Women, Academia, and the Disciplines," *Social Science Quarterly* 55 (1974): 563–85; Mary L. Shanley and Victoria Schuck, "In Search of Political Woman," *Social Science Quarterly* 55 (1974): 632–44; Beverly B. Cook, "First Women in Political Science: No Home in the Discipline" (paper delivered at the American Political Science Association meetings, Chicago, 1983); and idem, "Support for Academic Women in Political Science, 1890–1945," *Women and Politics* 8 (1987): 75–104.

7. Terrell Carver, *Gender Is Not a Synonym for Women* (Boulder: L. Rienner, 1996).

8. We have in mind Joan Wallach Scott, *Gender and the Politics of History* (New York: Columbia University Press, 1988); Hanna Pitkin, *Fortune Is a Woman: Gender and Politics in the Thought of Niccolò Machiavelli* (Berkeley and Los Angeles: University of California Press, 1988); Carole Pateman, *The Sexual Contract* (Stanford: Stanford University Press, 1988); and Linda M. G. Zerrilli, *Signifying Woman: Culture and Chaos in Rousseau, Burke, and Mill* (Ithaca: Cornell University Press, 1994); as well as the works by Ruth Bloch, Sara Evans, Mark Kann, Linda Kerber, and Mary Ryan cited below. For a critical reading of the gender subtext of *The Human Condition*, see Mary G. Dietz, "Feminist Receptions of Hannah Arendt," in *Feminist Interpretations of Hannah Arendt*, ed. Bonnie Honig (University Park: Pennylvania State University Press, 1995), 17–50.

9. See Bernard Crick, *The American Science of Politics* (Berkeley and Los Angeles: University of California Press, 1959); Albert Somit and Joseph Tanenhaus, *The Development of American Political Science: From Burgess to Behavioralism* (Boston: Allyn and Bacon, 1967); David Ricci, *The Tragedy of Political Science: Politics, Scholarship, and Democracy* (New Haven: Yale University Press, 1984); Raymond Seidelman with Edward J. Harpham, *Disenchanted Realists: Political Science and the American Crisis,*

1884–1984 (Albany: State University of New York Press, 1985); Gunnell, *Descent of Political Theory*; and James Farr, John S. Dryzek, and Stephen T. Leonard, eds., *Political Science in History: Research Programs and Political Traditions* (New York: Cambridge University Press, 1995). Even Ross, *Origins*, touches upon suffrage only incidentally, for example, at 280, 309, and 457 f.

10. For example, Aileen S. Kraditor, *The Ideas of the Woman Suffrage Movement, 1890–1920* (New York: Columbia University Press, 1965); Eleanor Flexner, *Century of Struggle: The Woman's Rights Movement in the United States*, rev. ed. (Cambridge: Harvard University Press, Belknap Press, 1975); and Ellen Carol DuBois, *Feminism and Suffrage: The Emergence of an Independent Women's Movement in America, 1848–1869* (Ithaca: Cornell University Press, 1978); as well as the works on antisuffragism by Jane Jerome Camhi and Thomas J. Jablonsky cited below. For an important work located at the intersection of feminism and social science, more broadly, see William Leach, *True Love and Perfect Union: The Feminist Reform of Sex and Society* (New York: Basic Books, 1980).

11. Stefan Collini, Donald Winch, and John Burrow, *That Noble Science of Politics: A Study in Nineteenth-Century Intellectual History* (Cambridge: Cambridge University Press, 1984), 377.

12. Pagination throughout is taken from *Civil Liberty and Self-Government*, ed. Theodore Dwight Woolsey, 3d ed. rev. (Philadelphia: J. B. Lippincott, 1880; reprint, 1901).

13. Printed in the preface to the second (1874) and second revised (1911) editions of *Manual of Political Ethics*, ed. Theodore Dwight Woolsey, 2 vols., (Philadelphia: J. B. Lippincott), 1:3. Pagination throughout is from the second revised edition.

14. Gunnell, *Descent of Political Theory*, 25, where Lieber is also credited as "more deeply involved in public life than any academic of the century." More generally, see Frank Freidel, *Francis Lieber: Nineteenth Century Liberal* (Baton Rouge: Louisiana State University Press, 1947); and James Farr, "Francis Lieber and the Interpretation of American Political Science," *Journal of Politics* 52 (1990): 1027–49.

15. *Miscellaneous Writings*, 2:208.

16. Herbert Baxter Adams claimed that "the great northern and the great southern tributaries to American political science were brought together when Woolsey edited, in 1874, a revision of Lieber's *Civil Liberty and Self-Government*," in *The Study of History in American Colleges and Universities* (Washington, D.C.: Bureau of Education, 1887), 55.

17. Theodore Dwight Woolsey, *Political Science: or, The State Theoretically and Practically Considered*, 2 vols. (Philadelphia: J. B. Lippincott, 1878); Woodrow Wilson, *The State: Elements of Historical and Practical Politics* (Boston: D. C. Heath, 1889); W. W. Willoughby, *An Examination of the Nature of the State* (New York: Macmillan, 1896); and idem, *The Rights and Duties of American Citizenship* (New York: American Book Company, 1898).

18. Jürgen Herbst, *The German Historical School in American Scholarship: A Study in the Transfer of Culture* (Ithaca: Cornell University Press, 1965). German influence was considerable, but it is an exaggeration to say that the Americans "acquired the term State" from Germany (as Rodgers does in *Contested Truths*, 167) or that the concept was "alien to American experience and institutions" (as Crick does in *American Science of Politics*, 96).

19. Rodgers, *Contested Truths*, 167–68.

20. Pagination throughout from Johann K. Bluntschli, *The Theory of the State*, 2d ed. (Oxford: Clarendon Press, 1892).

21. From Bluntschli's introduction to Lieber, *Miscellaneous Writings*, 2:13, where he acknowledges his "intimate, personal connection" to Lieber.

22. Bluntschli, *Theory of the State*, bk. 2, chap. 20. While Bluntschli's influence was mainly on the American academic figures in this study, Freidel (*Francis Lieber*, 398–99) notes how secretary of state Hamilton Fish sought out and secured Bluntschli's assistance in 1869 as an international jurist and publicist to help mollify public clamors for reparations from Britain for that country's harboring of Confederate raiding ships like the *Alabama*. The work was published as a pamphlet by the U.S. government in 1871.

23. On Wilson and suffrage, see Flexner, *Century of Struggle*, 265–67, 278–80; and Thomas J. Jablonsky, *The Home, Heaven, and Mother Party: Female Anti-Suffragists in the United States, 1868–1920* (Brooklyn: Carlson, 1994), 93 ff.

24. Quoted in Thomas L. Haskell, *The Emergence of Professional Social Science: The American Social Science Association and the Nineteenth Century Crisis of Authority* (Urbana: University of Illinois Press, 1977), 137. We have relied on Haskell and Leach, *True Love and Perfect Union*, for a number of points.

25. To use the categories of Mary O. Furner, *Advocacy and Objectivity: A Crisis in the Professionalization of American Social Science, 1865–1905* (Lexington: University of Kentucky Press, 1975).

26. On Dall and the ASSA, see Leach, *True Love and Perfect Union*, chap. 10. Apart from Dall, Leach leaves the impression that the ASSA was a feminist organization, supportive of all women's rights and issues, including the suffrage. We think that this overstates matters. In any case, the antifeminism of the political scientists—especially Lieber, who is curiously described as "a common sense philosopher" (325)—is not mentioned.

27. *Journal of Social Science*, esp. vols. 3, 14, 18, 20, 21, 23, 25, 30, and 38.

28. *Journal of Social Science* 1 (1869): 106. On Adams and Lieber, see Freidel, *Francis Lieber*, 296.

29. "General Intelligence" report from *Journal of Social Science* 1 (1869): 167.

30. John W. Burgess, *Political Science and Comparative Constitutional Law*, 2 vols. (Boston: Ginn and Company, 1891), 1:58. Compare Woolsey's assertion that "*state* is the only scientific term proper for a treatise on politics," in *Political Science*, 1:142.

31. Willoughby, *Nature of the State*, 20. Cf. Lieber, *Manual of Political Ethics*, 1:145, on the "different character" of state and family.

32. Lieber, *Civil Liberty and Self-Government*, 261. While we cannot develop the point here, race, too, came engendered in this literature, as when Lieber praised "the virile branch of the Teutonic race" (*Miscellaneous Writings*, 2:232) and Bluntschli "the manly genius for politics" displayed by the "Aryan" versus the "Semitic" race (*Theory of the State*, 82, 84).

33. Lieber, *Manual of Political Ethics*, 1:152 ff.; Woolsey, *Political Science*, 1:140; and Wilson, *The State*, xxv, 610.

34. Woolsey, *Political Science*, 1:208; and Lieber, *Miscellaneous Writings*, 1:358.

35. Willoughby, *Nature of the State*, 134, 394. Cf. Bluntschli's short definition of "the State [as] the politically organised national person of a definite country," *Theory of the State*, 23.

36. Lieber, *Manual of Political Ethics*, 2:109.

37. A. Lawrence Lowell, *Essays on Government* (Boston: Houghton, Mifflin, and Company, 1889), 9; Mrs. Charles P. Strong, in *Anti-Suffrage Essays by Massachusetts Women*, ed. Ernest Birnbaum (Boston: Forum Publications, 1916), 75.

38. Burgess, *Political Science*, 1:185 ff.; Willoughby, *Nature of the State*, 181;

Woolsey, *Political Science*, 1:139, 24. The rejection of the social contract theory was entailed by the rejection of the very idea of natural rights, as in Wilson, *The State*, 13.

39. Lieber thought that this question was "one of vastest extent, and emphatically belongs to the science of politics and real statesmanship," in *Civil Liberty and Self-Government*, 174.

40. Willoughby, *Nature of the State*, 412–13. Cf. Woolsey on the rights of suffrage as justifiably "restricted in the freest societies" for "these rights are rather privileges involving duty," in *Political Science*, 1:27–28.

41. Burgess, *Political Science*, 2:110.

42. Even before the Civil War, Lieber argued in the second (1859) edition of *Civil Liberty and Self-Government* that "the staunchest abolitionist, who insists upon immediate manumission of all slaves, does not likewise insist upon an immediate admission of the whole manumitted population to a perfect political equality." Woolsey, his editor, noted in the third (1874) edition that "since Dr. Lieber published these words, in 1859, the system of slavery has disappeared, and perfect, or nearly perfect, political equality of all colors exists" (260n). Yet in his own works, Woolsey hardly pressed for "nearly perfect" equality regarding manhood suffrage. Burgess, for his part, quibbled about the Fifteenth Amendment, suggesting that it expressed "negative language and does not directly confer upon any one the privilege of suffrage" although it might do so "indirectly" (*Political Science*, 2:42). The racialism of the political scientists brokered their antislavery and their antisuffragism.

43. Lieber, *Manual of Political Ethics*, 2:121–22, emphasis added. In an intriguing footnote (122n), Lieber refers to the "masculo-feminine principle" in Eastern and Pythagorean philosophy that contrasts with later Western ideas. Lieber's own gendered science of the state might well have been different had he further investigated the implications of this principle.

44. Willoughby, *Nature of the State*, 407–8, citing Bluntschli, *Theory of the State*, 32 (cf. 207 on "the manly character of the state"); Wilson, *The State*, 608. Bluntschli also described parties as masculine (liberal and conservative) and feminine (radical and absolutist), 208n.

45. Bluntschli, *Theory of the State*, 22–23. Bluntschli also gendered the political world when he referred in feminine terms to Europe as having "already fixed her eye more firmly on [the] high aim" of a "universal state" than on any particular European state (26; cf. 32). We return to this below.

46. Lieber, *Manual of Political Ethics*, 2:413; idem, *Miscellaneous Writings*, 1:127; idem, *Civil Liberty and Self-Government*, 363. German by birth, Lieber looked upon the United States as his "wedded country" (*Miscellaneous Writings*, 1:386).

47. Willoughby, *Nature of the State*, 196; Wilson, *The State*, 458, 464; and Lowell, *Essays on Government*, 59n. Lieber would also refer to "the sister nations of our race" (*Miscellaneous Writings*, 1:267).

48. Lieber, *Manual of Political Ethics*, 2:163, 400, 413; cf. 2:407, 425.

49. Ibid., 337, 427; Willoughby, *Nature of the State*, 438; Bluntschli, *Theory of the State*, 27; and Woolsey, *Political Science*, 1:226.

50. For the revolutionary period, see especially Ruth H. Bloch, "The Gendered Meanings of Virtue in Revolutionary America," *Signs: Journal of Women in Culture and Society* 13 (1987): 37–58. For gendered developments before and after this period, see Mark E. Kann, *On the Man Question: Gender and Civic Virtue in America* (Philadelphia: Temple University Press, 1991).

51. Lieber, *Miscellaneous Writings*, 1:356.

52. Lowell, *Essays on Government*, 15; Woolsey, *Political Science*, 1:234. The specter of socialism and communism hovers over these gendered images, since this is the topic Lowell next takes up. See also Woolsey, *Communism and Socialism in Their History and Theory* (New York: Scribner's, 1880).

53. Bluntschli, *Theory of the State*, 207.

54. For these arguments, see Jane Jerome Camhi, *Women against Women: American Anti-Suffragism, 1880–1920* (Brooklyn: Carlson, 1994); and Kraditor, *Ideas of the Woman Suffrage Movement*, chap. 2.

55. Lieber, *Manual of Political Ethics*, 2:124, 126.

56. These adjectives have been faithfully compiled from the texts of the authors we have studied, although they are hardly surprising as stereotypes.

57. Bluntschli, *Theory of the State*, 207; Lieber, *Manual of Political Ethics*, 2:124; and Woolsey, *Political Science*, 1:99.

58. Lieber, *Manual of Political Ethics*, 2:130, 129; Bluntschli, *Theory of the State*, 208.

59. For the Republican Mother, see Linda K. Kerber, *Women of the Republic: Intellect and Ideology in Revolutionary America* (New York: Norton, 1986), esp. chap. 9; and on the Maternal Commonwealth, see Sara M. Evans, *Born for Liberty: A History of Women in America* (New York: Free Press, 1989), chap. 6 and the vast literature cited.

60. Mary P. Ryan, *Women in Public: Between Banners and Ballots, 1825–1880* (Baltimore: Johns Hopkins University Press, 1990), 134. Ryan notes more generally, however, that "women's presence became more visible if only through their symbolic representation as emblems of femininity" (135).

61. Lieber, *Civil Liberty and Self-Government*, 355.

62. Woolsey, *Political Science*, 1:301, emphasis in original.

63. Willoughby, *Rights and Duties*, 32, adding the corollary that "when [women] are not guided by the wishes of their husbands or other male relatives, inevitable dissension will be introduced into the family life where all should be harmonious."

64. Lieber, *Miscellaneous Writings*, 2:207; Willoughby, *Rights and Duties*, 31.

65. Woolsey, *Political Science*, 2:122; Willoughby, *Rights and Duties*, 31; Lieber, *Manual of Political Ethics*, 1:209–10; 2:126–27.

66. Quoted in Freidel, *Francis Lieber*, 416; Lieber, *Miscellaneous Writings*, 2:208–9. Charles Merriam noted these aspects of Lieber's work in his review of Freidel's biography, in *American Political Science Review* 42 (1948): 781.

67. Lieber, *Manual of Political Ethics*, 2:125; Woolsey, *Political Science*, 1:300–301. Exceptions to nature were also evident in the history of states successfully ruled by queens. In conceding their success, Bluntschli tried to be clever in *Theory of the State*: "they have been more ready than male rulers to accept the guidance of great statesmen" (206n). Even if the assertion is true, the argument proves no better. Arguably, it made matters worse if male, as opposed to female, rulers hesitated to accept guidance from great men of state!

68. Willoughby, *Nature of the State*, 20.

69. Lieber, *Manual of Political Ethics*, 2:398.

70. Lieber, *Miscellaneous Writings*, 2:206n.

71. See Camhi, *Women against Women*; Jablonsky, *The Home, Heaven, and Mother Party*; and Kraditor, *Ideas of the Woman Suffrage Movement*, chap. 2.

72. Wilson, *The State*, 507.

73. Sophonisba Breckinridge, *Women in the Twentieth Century: A Study of Their Political, Social, and Economic Activities* (New York: McGraw-Hill, 1933).

74. Cited in Bluntschli, *Theory of the State*, 205.

75. One of Ostrogorski's reviewers was laudatory of his "inductive" methods, as well as the consoling fact that he "finds no serious inclination to clothe her with political power." See *Political Science Quarterly* 8 (1893): 171.

76. James Bryce, *The American Commonwealth*, 2 vols. (New York: Macmillan, 1894), 2:562. On Bryce and his comparative method, see Collini, Winch, and Burrow, *That Noble Science of Politics*, chaps. 7 and 11.

77. In *History of Woman Suffrage*, ed. Elizabeth Cady Stanton, Susan B. Anthony, and Matilda Joslyn Gage, 6 vols. (Salem, Mass.: Ayer, 1886), 3:923.

78. John Stuart Mill, *On Liberty and Other Essays* (Oxford: Oxford University Press, 1991), 493, 518, 527. None of this suggests that Mill himself somehow escaped gendering politics, especially political economy, in other ways. See Zerilli, *Signifying Woman*, chap. 4.

79. See n. 45 above.

80. See Camhi, *Women against Women*, chap. 2; and fears about "these unsexed women," reported in DuBois, *Feminism and Suffrage*, 46–47. Caroline Healey Dall apparently wished she were "unsexed," as reported in Leach, *True Love and Perfect Union*.

81. Jesse Reeves, "Perspectives in Political Science," *American Political Science Review* 23 (1929): 6.

82. At least as conceived in the way the nineteenth-century political scientists had. The term "state" would continue to be present; so too would serious theorizing about "the pluralistic state" and "the democratic state." See Ross, *Origins*; Gunnell, *Descent of Political Theory*; and several contributors to Farr, Dryzek, and Leonard, *Political Science in History*.

83. This is different from the claim that political science proved value-free, or that it ceased to be interested in politics. On these themes, see works cited in n. 9.

84. Arthur F. Bentley, *The Process of Government* (1908; Cambridge: Harvard University Press, 1967), 263, 300, 425–26.

85. Charles E. Merriam and Harold F. Gosnell, *Non-Voting: The Causes and Methods of Control* (Chicago: University of Chicago Press, 1924).

86. Francis G. Wilson, "The Pragmatic Electorate," *American Political Science Review* 22 (1928): 16–37, which may be seen as instantiating if not inaugurating a longer tradition of "empirical democratic theory" in American political science, especially regarding democratic elites.

"Wild West" Anthropology and the Disciplining of Gender

KAMALA VISWESWARAN

> While we were in Boston in 1879, a lady told me that after studying ethnology
> for years in books and museums she now wished to visit Indian tribes in their
> own lodges, living as they lived and observing their daily customs herself—
> especially the women's and children's ways.
> "Did you ever camp out?" I asked.
> "No, never."
> I found it hard to take her plan seriously. She, a thorough product of city life,
> was evidently nearing her forties. I could not imagine her leaving all her home
> comforts to go out to the far frontier and live among the Indians in an Indian
> lodge. Still, she was so earnest that I reluctantly agreed to take her someday with
> our group for the trip she wished. But I gave her fair warning:
> "You can't stand such a trip. You'll have to sleep on the cold ground. The food
> will be strange to you. You'll meet storms on the open prairies and be wet to the
> skin. Burning sun and wind will blister your face and hands. Long days
> of travelling will exhaust you. You'll have no privacy night or day.
> I'm sure you can never endure it."
> "Yes I can!" she insisted.[1]

THE IMAGE of tender womanhood scourged by the wilderness of the western
frontier was perhaps one of the most potent underlying the ideological structure of "manifest destiny." Stereotypes of the "courageous" frontier woman notwithstanding, the idea that the West was "no place for a woman" defined the
skepticism "pioneer" anthropologists like Alice Fletcher faced from more experienced field companions like Henry Tibbles, as illustrated in his account
above. Yet the first generation of women anthropologists contributed much to
destabilizing the trope of "white woman in peril," even as its persistence enabled the popularization of their writing and established their reputations as
professionals. If strands of Progressivist feminism promulgated by the
Women's Christian Temperance Union (WCTU) were defined by the mission
of "taming" unruly frontier masculinity through appeals to Christian notions of
domesticity and familial responsibility, early women anthropologists also par-

ticipated in the ideology of the western frontier by characterizing native cultures as "wild" and "untamed" by civilization—a kind of feminine counterpart to Rooseveltian "rough-riderism."[2]

Anthropology has been called "the welcoming science" because of the numbers of women in its early ranks.[3] Yet while the presence of women like Erminnie Platt Smith (1836–1886), Alice Fletcher (1838–1923), Sara Yorke Stevenson (1847–1921), Matilda Cox Stevenson (1849–1915), Zelia Nuttal (1857–1933), Frances Densmore (1867–1957), and Elsie Clews Parsons (1874–1941) in anthropology has often been remarked, their significance for the emergence of the discipline has been less well understood.[4]

Platt Smith, Fletcher, Yorke Stevenson, Parsons, and Densmore were all known as engaging and popular public speakers.[5] Platt Smith's parlor lectures on geology and on literary and aesthetic topics led to the founding of the Daughters of Aesthetics in Jersey City in 1879, and she served as its president from 1879 to 1886. The *New York Times* of August 29, 1880, reporting on one of her Iroquois lectures, noted, "Mrs. Smith is not only a good writer, well-known in literary and scientific circles in New York, Boston, and other cities[,] but also an eloquent speaker . . . and is deeply interested in the results of scientific investigation." Fletcher's work with the Omaha began in 1879 when she met long-term collaborator Francis La Flesche at a meeting of the Boston Literary Society. After years of philanthropical work, Fletcher began her professional career as an independent lecturer in order to earn money, speaking on such popular topics as "The Lost Peoples of America." By 1879 she had received attention as the "noted lecturess of New York City" who "tells a wonderful story and tells it well" with a "pleasing voice and attractive manner."[6] She drew the attention of Frederick Putnam, and by 1880 he was inviting her audiences to tour the Peabody Museum at Harvard University. Women, then, were instrumental in bringing anthropology into the public sphere.[7]

The 1880s thus also witnessed marked redefinition of avenues of public participation for women, of which anthropology was but one.[8] The liberal evolutionist Edward Tylor, addressing the Anthropological Society of Washington in 1884, had similarly argued that "the man of the house, though he can do a great deal, cannot do it all. If his wife sympathizes with his work, and is able to do it, really half the work of investigation seems to me to fall to her, so much is to be learned through the women of the tribe, which the men will not readily disclose." Speaking in particular of Matilda Cox Stevenson's collaboration with her husband, Tylor concluded that it was a lesson "not to sound the 'bullroarer,' and warn the ladies off from their proceedings, but rather to avail themselves thankfully of their help."[9]

Tylor's advice to the Anthropological Society of Washington was not immediately heeded, however. Thus in 1885 Cox Stevenson established the Women's Anthropological Society, with Fletcher and Zelia Nuttal among its first members. The Women's Anthropological Society concerned itself with social reform issues such as slum sanitation and the "Negro Problem."[10] Fletcher served as the society's vice president in 1885, and as its president from 1893 to 1898. The Anthropological Society of Washington finally admitted women to its membership in 1899, and after that date women seem to have been fully integrated into anthropological organizations, for there is no further mention of the Women's Anthropological Society.[11] Fletcher became president of the Anthropological Society of Washington in 1903, a year after she had been the only woman among the forty founding members of the American Anthropological Association.

Despite an early record of exclusion from organizations like the Anthropological Society of Washington, women like Fletcher were also prominent members and officers of the leading scientific organizations of the era,[12] and central to institution building within the discipline. Platt Smith, Nuttal, Yorke Stevenson, and Parsons were independently wealthy and able to fund their own work, but they were also major patrons of early anthropological research.[13] Although only two of these women possessed doctorates, and none were formally trained as anthropologists in an era still dominated by amateurs,[14] they were prominent women and advanced the professionalization of the discipline in important ways. Fletcher, Nuttal, and Yorke Stevenson founded archaeological institutes that still exist today;[15] while Platt Smith, Fletcher, and Cox Stevenson established participant observation as anthropological method contemporaneously with Franz Boas's and Frank Cushing's own interventions on the subject.

In rehearsing such details, I hope to dispel a common set of assumptions about the marginality of this group of women in the discipline. Anthropology as a discipline is properly the child of Progressive Era politics. To the extent that women were empowered by this set of politics as clubwomen or suffragists, they were also influential in defining what came to be known as the "reformer's science." Women for many years afterward were not to have as much say in the actual founding and funding of anthropological institutions as they had between 1880 and 1920.

It is commonly advanced that Franz Boas was responsible for bringing women into anthropology; however, Frederick Putnam also mentored a number of women.[16] Yet to reduce the question of women's participation in the field to either Putnam's goodwill or Boas's experience of anti-Semitism[17] is to lose sight of the transformative effects of feminism in the nineteenth century. Equally problematic is the assumption that the early participation of women in the discipline led inevitably to the emergence of gender as an analytical category within anthropology; this is to lose sight of the limitations of feminism at this historical moment. Although Progressive Era women in anthropology formed close professional and personal ties to one another,[18] the structure of male patronage meant that they did not usually advance theoretical perspectives distinct from those of their mentors,[19] with the result that they remained complicit with dominant discourses of civilization.

Though some feminist scholars understand "gender" to be a late-twentieth-century category of analysis, the terms by which we understand its modern usage were emergent during the Progressive Era. In referring to the "disciplining of gender," then, I point both to the ways in which gender has been schooled out of the discipline's telling of its own history, and to the ways gender shaped Progressive Era anthropology. A particular late-nineteenth-century gender politics impacted upon the production of the central defining feature of a professionalizing anthropology: the relativist notion of culture. I therefore attempt to understand the submergence of gender as central to the disciplinization of anthropology, and as paradoxically coeval with its emergence as a generative (rather than additive) category of analysis within the discipline. I suggest that an account of the emergence of gender as a category of analysis within the discipline has important consequences for how we understand the rise of cultural relativism in anthropology.

I take the emergence of gender as a category of analysis within anthropology to be marked by two broad propositions, which, while linked, are not reducible to one another. First, gender indicates the cultural construction of sex roles, or the "social creation of ideas about appropriate roles for men and women"; and second, the "description of social relations between the sexes," or the marking of asymmetrical power relations between the sexes.[20]

I argue that gender consciousness, understood as awareness of inequality between the sexes, was indicated both by the contradictions posed to Victorian society by evolutionary theory and by nineteenth-century feminism's engagement with Victorian social anthropology over "the woman question," which indexed a series of debates about the nature of women's role in society. During this era, biological sex was seen to determine the social roles of men and women. As Elizabeth Fee has demonstrated, however, the evolutionist debates on the question of matriarchal and matrilineal societies provided a challenge to the notion that men's and women's roles were "natural."[21] In response to this challenge, progressive evolutionary theory reconfirmed the high status of Victorian society; however, it did so by suggesting that its sex roles were not natural but rather the achievement of civilization.

At the same time, as Gail Bederman has shown, the notion of civilization itself was increasingly challenged by various forms of feminist and African-American activism, leading to its reconsolidation as the exclusive achievement of white manhood. Women could contribute to civilization only as wives and mothers, and civilization could advance only if the doctrine of separate spheres was maintained. But if the elevated status of women had been seen as the effect of civilization, some women sought to show that they were also its cause: they were its agents not only as wives and mothers in the domestic sphere, but variously as the reformers of savage peoples or inventors of technology. On the other hand, prominent feminist Charlotte Perkins Gilman (inspired by the work of Edward Tylor and John Lubbock), sought to reverse the equation of civilizational advancement with extreme sex differentiation by arguing that women and men alike were partners in the racial advancement of civilization.[22]

Thus while the revisionist idea that Victorian sex roles emerged with "civilization" pointed to a notion of gender as culturally constructed, it did not necessarily entail a feminist refusal of evolutionary racism. Rather, the racial identity of early women anthropologists could not be separated from their positioning in the field (something they themselves frequently evoked), which alternately gendered them as maternal or masculine (or, more accurately, as brokers of the masculine). White women's unchallenged racial positioning and their participation in late American settler ideology thus worked against the identification of white women with native women, and therefore against an understanding of women's oppression as being singly or multiply derived from a transcultural Patriarchy.

Here, the lack of something like "gender identification" qualifies the emergence of "woman" as a universal category.[23] For the more civilized a society, the more highly sex differentiated it was. "Primitive" societies were thus seen to lack sex differentiation altogether, or to possess it in mere rudimentary form, prohibiting the admission of Native-American and African-American women into the very category of womanhood. As a result, the second proposition of gender—as an analysis of unequal relations between the sexes, shared across cultures—does not fully emerge as an epistemological category in Progressive Era anthropology. Its seeds are found in the work of Victorian women anthropologists, but it is most present in the early writings of Elsie Clews Parsons, which she characterized as "propaganda by the ethnographic method" but which actually predate her entry into empirical anthropology around 1915.[24]

.   .   .

Nineteenth-century popular anthropology is frequently portrayed as the result of amateur participation, from which natural scientists like Franz Boas sought to distance themselves in order to professionalize the discipline.[25] A more careful look at the emergence of the discipline in the late nineteenth century shows that popularization and professionalization were two sides of the same coin, not a case of the former's existing as a stage to be superseded by the latter. Ethnological pamphlets produced at the world's fairs and articles written for the popular press were normative rather than unique, and analysis of the writings of early women anthropologists proves it difficult to distinguish the articles that appeared in the *American Anthropologist* or the *Journal of American Folklore* from those appearing in more popular fora. I therefore want to explore how the nineteenth-century "woman question" and women's participation at the fairs might illumine the importance of popular anthropology in ways obscured by conventional disciplinary history, which portrays the participation of Putnam, Boas, and others in the world's fairs as a necessary evil, rather than as symptomatic of the period.[26] For this reason, the paper also explores overlapping zones of popular and scientific influence for the production of Progressive Era anthropology.

I first examine the gendering of the fieldwork ethic as a means of describing the relationship of a particular kind of Wild West ethic to Progressive Era feminism and its relationship to "evangelical ethnology." I next explore feminist participation in the "midway ethnology" of the world's fairs. If the world's

fairs earned mass exposure for the suffragist cause, they also reaffirmed feminist participation in the imperial subtext of the expositions. The elaboration of
the "woman question" in the context of the world's fairs also set the stage for
feminist engagement with the "matrilineal conundrum of evolutionary theory."
I conclude with some observations about Elsie Clews Parsons's break from this
milieu, which underscores her contribution to the emergence of gender as an
analytical category in the discipline.

Turning "the Century": The Emergence of Popular Ethnography

During the late nineteenth and early twentieth centuries, newspapers and
journals like the *Southern Workman* or *Century Magazine* provided a mass
medium whereby emerging ethnography was popularized by women anthropologists in the context of westward expansion and white settler ideology. Beginning in 1882, the *Century Magazine* ran a series of articles on the "New
Northwest" and "Indian Country," reports on various expositions,[27] and writings of anthropologists such as Frank Cushing, Frederick Putnam, and Alice
Fletcher.[28] Sara Yorke Stevenson's series of five articles on the French Intervention in Mexico also appeared in the *Century Magazine* in 1897 and was the
basis of her book-length memoir, *Maximillian in Mexico* (1899).

Cushing's three-part *Century Magazine* serial, "My Adventures in Zuni," and
Fletcher's series of articles under the heading "Personal Studies of Indian
Life," which ran over a period of four years, are arguably some of the first
documents that establish participant observation as anthropological method,
contemporaneously with Boas's own writings on the subject. Indeed, it is perhaps Cushing's escapades that Boas had in mind when he began his 1887 article "A Year among the Eskimo" with the disclaimer, "If I undertake to describe
some of my arctic experiences, I cannot entertain you with exciting adventures,
such as shipwrecks and narrow escapes, for such were not my share. My narrative must be that of the daily life of the inhabitants of these ice-bound coasts,
the Eskimo."[29] Boas's insistence on sticking to descriptions of daily life was not
lost on Fletcher, who excelled in the ethnographic particular, even as her first
accounts seem sensationalized in retrospect. And yet her narrative of the
fieldwork scene that established the grounding of modern ethnographic consciousness is arguably the most classic account of transforming savage images
into human ones, working to establish cultural relativism as humanist credo for
anthropology.[30] Describing her first encounter with Indian ceremonial performance, she wrote:

> As I entered [the tent] I was startled by a sudden, mighty beating of the drum, with
> such deafening yells and shouts that I feared my ears would burst; but following the
> dictates of Indian etiquette, I took no notice of this extraordinary welcome, and
> passed as calmly as I could to the back of the tent, where I sat down in the middle of
> an unoccupied space, close to the edge of the covering.

As I looked about me, I felt a foreignness that grew into a sense of isolation. On each side were lines of silent, motionless figures, their robes so closely wrapped about them that, in the fading light, I could scarcely realize that they were living beings. There was not a touch of color within the tent, except upon the few women who sat near the drum. Their glossy black braids fell in heavy loops upon their red and green tunics, the russet hue of their faces was heightened by touches of vermillion on their cheeks, their ear-ornaments of white shell hung nearly to their waists, and their arms were encircled with shining brass bangles. These glints of brightness only added to the weirdness of the place, and my eyes gladly looked beyond, where, framed by the opening of the tent against the pale primrose of the twilight sky, I saw the contrasting picture of gaily dressed and painted men and women, chatting or laughing, and showing their small, white, teeth.

As the passage continues, Fletcher's sense of "foreignness" and "strangeness" precludes any "starting point of sympathy." Fletcher presents herself, "distressed," and "distraught," a white woman imperiled as much by the "wild movements of advancing and retreating forms," "violently shaken feathers," and "arms brandishing war clubs," as by the accounts of Indian atrocities "crowding upon her memory."

The whole scene was utterly unlike any I had ever beheld. I was oppressed by its strangeness, and before I could find any starting point of sympathy with my surroundings, there was a slight stir in the vicinity of the drum, and suddenly half a dozen arms rose and fell upon the drum with such force as to make it rebound upon its fastenings; a solitary voice, pitched high and shrill, uttered a few wavering notes, followed on the next drum beat by the whole company of singers, each one apparently striving to outsing all the rest. It was nothing but tumult and din to me; the sharply accented drum set my heart to beating painfully and jarred every nerve. I was distressed and perplexed, my head was ringing, and I was fast becoming mentally distraught, when, as if by magic, a dozen of the silent, mysterious figures sprang high into the air, their robes falling into a heap, as with bended arms and knees they leaped toward the center of the tent, each man in full undress, save for the breech-cloth, paint, and feathers. The sudden appearance, the wild movements of the advancing and retreating forms, the outlines of the violently shaken head feathers, the out-stretched arms brandishing the war clubs, and the thud of the bare feet upon the ground, called up before me every picture of savages I had ever seen; while every account of Indian atrocities I had ever heard crowded upon my memory, and gave a horrible interpretation to the scene before me.

As the passage builds to a climax, Fletcher effectively plays upon images of Indian savagery and the trope of the "white woman in peril" in order to dismiss them as the result of popular misconceptions conquered by scientific temperament.

I would have escaped if I could, but between me and the opening were these terrible creatures, and even if it were possible to elude their grasp, it would only be to fall into the hands of hundreds more outside; those "treacherous," gaily dressed, and laughing people were "Indians" who even now might be transforming into similar fiends. The ground was cold and solid beneath me, and the tent was pegged tight to it, with no crack to crawl through. My suffering grew intense in the few moments before I was able to come to myself, and to remember that I was there present by my own deliberate purpose to study this very performance then going on around me.

Here, Fletcher's reflection upon her suffering and desperation establishes the emotional contrast necessary to enable her to arrive at scientific rationality, transforming her desire for escape into escapade:

I have since had many a laugh with my red friends over this my first and only fright, caused, as I now know, by the unconscious influence of the popular idea of "Injuns"; but it was long after this initiation before my ears were able to hear in Indian music little besides a screaming downward movement that was gashed and torn by the vehemently beaten drum. However, as the weeks wore on, and I observed the pleasure the Indians took in their own singing, I was convinced that there existed something which was eluding my ears. I therefore began to listen below this noise, much as one must listen to the phonograph, ignoring the sound of the machinery in order to catch the registered tones of the voice.[31]

Though Fletcher was not the first to reflect on the transformational nature of "fieldwork," her *Century Magazine* writing helped expose anthropology to a larger audience. Significantly, the phrase "listening below the noise" recurred in different forms throughout Fletcher's lifelong study of Native-American music.[32] "Listening below the noise" not only exemplified the credo of an emerging form of cultural relativism[33] and its peculiar gendering but also provided Fletcher's solution to the "Indian problem": through patience and proper understanding, Native Americans could be brought to civilization.

Engendering the West in the Colonial Encounter

The first generation of women ethnographers all worked in (or had personal experience of) areas marked by recent and ongoing colonial intervention. Nuttal, Yorke Stevenson, and later Parsons wrote extensively on the impact of Spanish conquest on Mexico. Yorke Stevenson also produced a popularly written "Woman's Reminiscences of the French Intervention" in Mexico between 1862 and 1867.[34]

Yet while Yorke Stevenson sympathized with the "ill-fated" intervention, and recounted the "last heroic hours of the Empire" by reproducing stereotypes of Mexican banditry, Nuttal argued forcefully against stereotypes of Mexico's native peoples. In 1897, the same year Yorke Stevenson's work was serialized in the *Century Magazine*, Nuttal appealed to an audience of folklorists to guard against "unscrupulous exhibitions" by showmen who claimed to feature "the last living representatives of the Aztec race."

The erroneous idea that the Aztec race was a hideous one and is now extinct, has been widely disseminated, and become deeply rooted in the public mind, where it flourishes with the remarkable persistency that has long been recognized as the special characteristic of scientific errors. Thus, it is not surprising to find in George du Maurier's last novel, "The Martian," an individual being spoken of as being, 'as hideous as an Esquimaux or Aztec,' and this combination of ideas is likely to linger on indefinitely in European countries although the fraudulency of the showman's announcement has been exposed by leading anthropologists.[35]

But in Nuttal's view, it was ultimately Spanish conquest narratives about human sacrifice that were responsible for stereotypes about Aztecs as "ugly, dwarfish, and bloodthirsty savages, having nothing in common with civilized humanity." She argued that "to the extent it was practiced, it has long been recognized by students of ancient Mexico that the current accounts, based on the reports of certain Spanish writers, are grossly exaggerated, some say purposely, in order to justify, in the eyes of the civilized world, the cruel extermination of the native civilization."[36]

Unfortunately, Nuttal's consciousness about the relationship between conquest and ethnic stereotype, along with her criticism of "unscrupulous exhibitions," is almost singular among early anthropologists.[37] Too often their ethnographies were silent about the effects of conquest and westward expansion upon the people they studied, and when they did note such effects, they were concerned more with the salvage of custom than with the disappearance of its bearers. For example, Cox Stevenson began her monograph on the Sia by noting:

> All that remains of the once populous pueblo of Sia is a small group of houses and a mere handful of people in the midst of one of the most extensive ruins of the Southwest, the living relic of an almost extinct people and a pathetic tale of the ravages of warfare and pestilence. This picture is even more touching than the infant's cradle or the tiny sandal found buried in the cliff in the canyon walls. The Sia of today is in much the same condition as that of the ancient cave and cliff-dweller as we restore their villages in the imagination.[38]

Implied here is a nostalgic evolutionary view of the Sia as near extinct, unchanged relics of a distant past—an example of what Fletcher called the "fossil bed" of human society and its institutions.[39] "Thus the railroad, the merchant, and the cowboy, without this purpose in view, are effecting a change which is slowly closing, leaf by leaf, the record of the religious beliefs of the pueblo Indian. With the Sia this record book is being more rapidly closed . . . ," leading Cox Stevenson to conclude dispassionately, "Each shadow on the dial brings nearer to a close the lives of those upon whose minds are graven the traditions, mythology, and folklore as indelibly as are the pictographs and monochromes upon the rocky walls."[40] The view that the "past life of the Indian was a closed book" was echoed by Alice Fletcher,[41] bringing reform projects designed to "civilize" Native Americans in line with Boasian salvage ethnography.

Fletcher was, in fact, a key architect of Bureau of Indian Affairs (BIA) land distribution policy: when the Omaha Severalty Act was passed in 1882, she was sent to implement it. Her work for the Omaha reallotment scheme was so meticulous that she was hired to complete a nationwide survey of all reservations and the history of treaties between Indian nations and the U.S. government with the aim of helping Indians move toward "civilization." Fletcher's early report titled "Indian Education and Civilization," prepared in "Answer to Senate Resolution of February 23, 1885," established her as one of the foremost authorities on Native Americans in the United States,[42] while her participation in the Lake Mohank Conferences of the Friends of the Indian also resulted in passage of the Dawes Act of 1887, which extended allotment and the breaking up of Indian reservations to other tribes. It was thus that she came to do allotment work among the Winnebago from 1887 to 1889, and among the Nez Perce from 1890 to 1893.[43]

By 1897, Fletcher apparently realized the debilitating, irreversible effects of allotment upon Native-American life,[44] but one would not know that from reading her 1905 coauthored monograph, where she reaffirms its benefits for the Omaha, mystifying the colonial processes that had alienated Native Americans from their land and former ways of life by noting only that "Contact with the white race was increasing daily and beginning to press on the people. The environment was changing rapidly, and the changes brought confusion of mind to the people as well as to many in mature life." Describing the "great unrest and anxiety" that had come to the Omahas through "force of a power" they could not understand, she sympathized, ". . . the trouble of mind everywhere manifest in the tribe can hardly be pictured, nor can the relief that came to the people when, in 1882, their lands were assured to them by an act of Congress."[45] Thus not only did Fletcher portray Native Americans as subjects of her own rescue narrative, but she represented an act that would actually reduce the amount of their lands as a form of relief, evidence of her inability to break from or criticize U.S. Indian policy.

The identification of early women anthropologists with the U.S. government meant that they were sometimes racially positioned as brokers of Indian masculinity. For example, in Fletcher's first meeting with the Nez Perce, her companion Jane Gay recounted resistance to Fletcher's efforts to propound allotment and the meaning of citizenship: "A little stir arose among the people, two or three whispered together, and at length one man stood up, a tall broad-shouldered fellow with a deep voice, and an air of authority about him. . . . He said, 'We do not want our land cut up in little pieces, we have not told you to do it.'"[46] Gay comments sardonically that "They could scarcely be blamed for their incredulity; that reasonable human beings, thought worthy of having citizenship thrust upon them, should have no voice what ever in matters which so exclusively concerned themselves, was an idea too difficult for the untutored mind to grasp."[47] But Fletcher carried on, telling the Indians that "she has come to bring them manhood, that they may stand up beside the white man in equality before the law."[48] In this formulation, white women reformers sought to bestow citizenship upon Native-American men, but the act of identification that might have envisioned suffrage for white women and Native-American women is never made.

Other evidence similarly suggests the inseparability of gender from racial positioning, preventing identification across cultures as "women." Writing of her efforts to collect Mide'wiwin mystical knowledge among the Chippewa, Frances Densmore reported pursuing a reluctant woman until she agreed to sing a "love-charm song" in a secluded place where no one could hear her. "She was a woman of about 60 years of age, and the most dirty and unattractive woman with whom the writer has come in contact. In a thin nasal tone she sang the song. . . . With coy shyness she said the song meant she was as beautiful as the roses."[49] Densmore's incredulity that the song's performance could ever transform the "dirty and unattractive woman" before her suggests that gender as a category of analysis which marked women's shared oppression across cultures could not emerge when even sympathy of women reformers for their female subjects was lacking.

In a later article, Densmore recounted an incident from fieldwork in 1920 that similarly underscored not her gender status but her racial membership:

> The Papago were dancing by the light of a full moon, on Christmas eve in 1920. My sister and I were the only white persons present, and we watched them until midnight. Later I was told that only a few women could sing this drone, which was considered an embellishment to the music. A few weeks later I attended the Morning Star ceremony of the Pawnee. It was said that only one other white person had ever entered the tent during this ceremony.[50]

Although Densmore might have argued, like Tylor or Parsons, that the fact of her being a woman gave her an access to Papago and Pawnee performances that male ethnographers did not have, she was instead at pains to claim status as one of the first whites to have viewed them.

The idea that the first women anthropologists, in reaffirming their racial membership, might be seen either literally or symbolically to occupy male roles is illustrated when Fletcher faced off with white ranchers and farmers who saw allotment as a way to increase their own land holdings. Jane Gay, Fletcher's traveling companion for the Nez Perce allotment party, recorded Fletcher's first meeting with this interest group in her popular, tongue-in-cheek letters:

> Her Majesty read her instructions to the delegation and explained that it was her sworn duty to place the Indians upon their best lands and in the localities where they must rapidly become self-supporting and valuable citizens, not so to dispose of them that they must be paupers and a charge upon the white population of the territory. The men are evidently non-plussed, for, as they mounted their horses, the Photographer heard one mutter, "Why in Thunder did the Government send a woman to do this work? We could've got a holt on a man." They "sound" the Surveyor before they ride away and he tells them he does not yet know anything of their prospects, but he

rather thinks "from looks of the Allotting Agent's eye, that everything will have to be done on the square." The introduction of the square idea has a depressing effect, for hitherto they have worked only in rings, but I dare say they really have no faith in anybody being able to square their circle.[51]

Here a scene in which Fletcher's authority might have been challenged because she was a woman is deflected by her claim to a superior morality *as a woman*, the assumption that things will be done "on the square."

However, racial membership and gender positioning could also be transmuted into a womanist frontier machismo, where white women were seen to neutralize not only white men but Indian men as well. In 1886, newspaper coverage of an incident in which Matilda Cox Stevenson and her husband were held prisoner for intruding upon a Hopi Kiva ceremony portrayed Matilda as the hero of the story. Although they were both later rescued by a trader, the newspaper headline crowed: "COWED BY A WOMAN. A CRAVEN RED DEVIL WEAKENS IN THE FACE OF A WHITE HEROINE—EXCITING ADVENTURE IN AN INDIAN VILLAGE IN ARIZONA."[52]

Cox Stevenson also had legendary fights with Major John Wesley Powell, over (among other things) itemizing expenses. On one occasion, asking reimbursement for informant expenses, she wrote in a decidedly provocative manner: "One man, one night, one dollar." On still another occasion:

> She included a case of Scotch in her expense account, which of course was turned down. She insisted that it was necessary in her work, since nothing else would induce the Indians to give out their more secret information. It was pointed out to her that it was illegal to give whiskey to the Indians. She replied that it was only illegal to *sell* it to them. The item became a matter of pride and principle to her, and she insisted she would fight it through.[53]

This stands in marked contrast to Cox Stevenson's description of the devastating effects of alcohol upon the Zuni Sha'lako festival: in her 1904 monograph, she wrote of "lawbreaking" Indians with little sympathy, "Every man in Zuni spends what money he can obtain on whiskey, not only for his own use and that of his friends, but to dispose to the Navahos, who come in large numbers to the dances." Cox Stevenson reported that in 1879 whiskey was rarely used by the Zunis, "but with the advance of civilization, intoxicants are producing demoralizing effects," and though there was a law forbidding the sale of liquor to Indians, it had not been enforced up to 1896. She observed harshly, "The Navaho is a close trader, but the Zuni is closer."

> The writer has observed many trades in which the Zunis come out the better. One Navaho, crazy for liquor, trades a fine pony for a gill of liquor. . . . While the younger men of Zuni drink as much as the Navahos, the older men and more clever traders keep their heads clear enough to get the best of the bargain. This trading of liquor goes on in inner rooms, which are supposed, as has been stated, to be for the use of the elect; but the Zunis, being no exception to those who are demoralized by the liquor traffic, indulge their love of gain at any cost.[54]

Cox Stevenson's contradictory position on alcohol,[55] her simultaneously arguing its necessity for work with the Indians and against its abuse among the Zuni
and Navaho, may also indicate the conflictual gender positionings she and
Fletcher occupied: pressure to deal "like a man" on the one hand, and to reform
like a woman on the other.

EVANGELICAL ETHNOGRAPHY

Victorian ideas of feminine purity enabled nineteenth-century women anthropologists to work independent of men on the frontier because they were considered morally superior and thus desexualized. As Ann Ardis put it, "So long
as women were assumed to be without sexual appetite, they could be recognized as autonomous moral agents in middle class Victorian culture . . . credited with having minds that were not controlled by their animal passions."[56]
The social work orientation of the Women's Anthropological Society, informed
by the assumption that "The highly organized religious nature of woman gives
her special adaptation for the study of the sublime differentia, by reason of
which man alone sins, sacrifices, worships,"[57] supports Ardis's claim that the
development of women's philanthropical organizations and new categories of
women's work did not threaten established male professions or institutions because in entering the public sphere they were supplementing existing services,
and "mothering the public."[58]

The existing photos of Platt Smith, Fletcher, Densmore, and Cox Stevenson
show somber-faced, darkly clad, proper Victorian women, often incongruously
appearing against scenes of tranquil wilderness. Victorian maternalism was also
literally mapped onto Fletcher's physiognomy, prompting her friends to compare her with Queen Victoria and to address her as "Her Majesty."[59] When
Fletcher was elected vice president of Section H (Anthropology) of the American Association for the Advancement of Science (AAAS) in 1895, her friends in
the Association for the Advancement of Women toasted her by singing "God
Save the Queen."[60]

Historians have suggested that the social reform influence of Victorian
evangelicalism resulted in both the "feminization of religion" and the emergence of "evangelical ethnology" in the late nineteenth century.[61] Missionary
work attracted women because it combined a gender specific, Christian way of
life with degrees of freedom denied to women in traditional urban spheres.
While Victorian ideology stressed domesticity, it paradoxically also encouraged
women to move away from the home, for woman's moral superiority or spiritu-
ality, the very qualities that made her custodian of the home, also qualified her
as a social and religious reformer.[62] Thus while the "field" afforded some escape
from urban gender roles for early women anthropologists, they entered the
field enabled by those very gender roles.

Whether unmarried or freed from household duties by technological change
and increasing affluence, women like Jane Addams and her Hull House volun-

teers redefined the public sphere of late-nineteenth-century North America.[63] For this reason, it was the settlement house women who were seen to be the heroines of reform in the early twentieth century, not the women like Alice Fletcher or Matilda Cox Stevenson who had applied themselves to the "Indian Question."[64]

While there is some evidence that Alice Fletcher's early participation in the clubwomen's movement[65] led her to anthropology where she "hop[ed] to add to the historical solution of the woman question,"[66] she devoted herself to the resolution of the "Indian question" through a form of evangelical ethnology. Jane Gay provides a troubling account of how missionization and government work were tied together in Fletcher's use of local churches to hold informational sessions on allotment.

> She stood looking straight before her a few minutes until there was absolute silence in the room, and then she said, "My friends, this is God's house and what we are to talk about is a serious matter, affecting the lives and happiness of all. . . . It is right to ask God's blessing here in this house, that all we do may please Him."[67]

Yet it is also true that the conversion scenes rendered in the ethnographies written by the discipline's first women carried parodic undertones when Indian men had to school white women in their chores. One such scene occurs when Cox Stevenson acknowledged that it was her own ineptitude in introducing "sanitary measures" among the Zuni which ultimately led to her success:

> Soap was introduced in 1879 in the hope that the Zuni would wash their cotton clothes, and the writer undertook the task of instruction. She selected as a pupil a man who had adopted woman's dress and who was known to be the strongest, most active, and most progressive Indian in the tribe; but he was averse to the work, and at first refused to wash. He looked on in silence for a while as the writer worked. Never having had any experience in that work herself, she soon had most of the water from the tub on the floor and was drenched to the skin. The pupil exclaimed: "You do not understand that which you would teach. You do not understand as much as the missionary's wife; she keeps the water in the tub, and does not make a river on the floor. Let me take your place."[68]

The Zuni's reference to the missionary's wife, and Cox Stevenson's and Fletcher's own Christian views, lend support to the idea that their "evangelical ethnography" was enabled by a form of "Victorian maternalism,"[69] even as they were often structurally positioned as males, that is, as whites with power over their subjects. Fletcher's biographer refers to her as "Mother of the Indians," and although Cox Stevenson often incurred the wrath of the Zuni for intruding upon ritual performances, they also called her "Washington Mother,"[70] while she, in turn, described them as children. After a typical expedition to remove and photograph Zuni sacred objects, Cox Stevenson observed:

> The party was discovered when descending the mountain, and the information was carried to the village, so that upon the return of the writer and her companions there

was great excitement. Had the people in general known of the removal of the images of Pa'yatamu their wrath would have known no bounds; but these children of nature are like civilized beings of tender years, and can be controlled through kindness or firmness, as occasion requires, by those for whom they entertain profound respect.[71]

She concluded, "Primitive man must be approached according to his understanding; thus the prime requisite for improving the conditions of the Indian is familiarity with Indian thought and customs. Those possessing superior intelligence and a love for humanity, and only such may lead our Indians from darkness to light."[72]

Fletcher, on the other hand, did not immediately see Native Americans as children. Rather, in their "old life" they were adults teaching the ways of their vanishing cultures to concerned whites. But as she became more involved in allotment and urged Native Americans to take on white ways, she increasingly saw them as children.[73] Thus "Fletcher was to pride herself on doing science like a man. But she did her philanthropy with the special claims of a woman, one who had suffered for, and who knew what was best for her children."[74]

The view that Indians were wild children seeking tenderness and understanding was echoed by Frances Densmore in a two-page popular pamphlet she wrote at the turn of the century, *The Plea of Our Brown Brother*. Commissioner of Indian Affairs Francis Leupp, contributing the pamphlet's preface, averred that the "Indian problem is, after all, less a race problem than a human problem," the solution of which was sympathy.[75]

In Densmore's pamphlet, Indian life as the childhood of the white race was portrayed in mythological terms that recalled Rousseau's "noble savage" and reaffirmed the inseparability of Native Americans from nature:

> Long ago, when the world was new, a little Brown Brother of Mankind strayed away and was forgotten. The animals welcomed the child, leading him far up the mountains, where they hid him in the deep of the canyons and the quiet of the pine forest. There they told him strange stories of the winds and the clouds; there too, he learned the history of every beast and bird.
>
> Soon he forgot his ancestry and believed that he descended from an animal. When he played at war he cried, "I am from the bears," or "I am of the turtles." For this reason he never killed an animal except for necessary food. On the walls of the canyons he drew strange pictures, and when he roamed the prairie he drew pictures on the skins that framed his dwelling. He knew the meaning of his pictures and his magic. He loved the sound of his own singing, though it often sounded like the cry of his wolf-friends.
>
> Time passed, and the White Race in the pride of manhood came face to face with its Brown Brother. It saw the pictures and they brought a memory of its own half-forgotten childhood, but when it heard the wild songs, mingled with shrill whistles and pounding drums, it turned aside. Too many centuries had passed since, by the shore of the forgotten sea, it played with bits of broken shell and whispering reed, calling it music.

The Mowgli of North America was still a child and with the trustfulness of child-hood he welcomed the stranger, calling him Brother.

He offered him freely of the spoils of the chase, told of his visions, sang his songs and exhibited his magic, but there was no answer of understanding on the face of his Brother, who mocked and cheated him. Then the child grew suddenly to be a man. Wrapping himself in his robe of buffalo-skin he hid his heart in a grim silence, but under the buffalo robe he held the poisoned arrow, and beneath the silence lay a deadly treachery. So the Indian became the problem of the New World.[76]

Densmore continues her parable, compressing time and entire histories of con-quest and genocide:

For five centuries there has been a struggle. Spanish adventurers, French priests, English soldiers and American civilization tried to bring the American Mowgli back to man and he defied them. Cheated and deceived, he kept the haughty dignity that is his by right of inheritance; beaten back step by step he flung out his defiance, and bore his defeat with proud stoicism.

But a change has come. Today he returns to his white brother led by something within himself that he does not understand. He no longer teaches his children the weird jungle songs, but he sings them to himself when the night is full of the witchery that the wild creatures know. He comes at last—ignorant of the ethics of clothes, with the pitiful childish decorations in his hair, but in his heart the strength of Nature's noblemen.

He comes at last of his own accord to us who do not understand him, and the tragedy of the past, the sadness of the present and the hope of the future are in his plea that his children be given an education and taught the White Man's Way.

He comes:—What shall be his Welcome?[77]

In sum, Densmore, like Cox Stevenson and Fletcher before her, romanti-cized Native-American life in a field of discourse that displaced questions of genocide and survival into talk of "change" and "passing ways of life." In this discursive field, Native Americans were noble but "vanishing," a case study of failed assimilation scored by dignity, defiance, and defeat—"the problem of the New World." Densmore's recourse to the civilizing mission of Kipling's *Jungle Book*, along with her description of the "American Mowgli" who emerges from the jungle, functions as a cross-validation of British and American imperialisms even as it obliterates the specific material effects of westward expansion and "manifest destiny."

Expository Feminism, Midway Ethnology

By the end of the nineteenth century, in part owing to the contributions of Boas, Cushing, Cox Stevenson, and Fletcher, the model of experientially gained knowledge of other cultures was displacing "armchair anthropology." Yet "fieldwork" was conducted not only in the "wilds" but in the showcases of civilization as well. The century-end expositions and world's fairs were both major sites for anthropological research and proof of how the West had been tamed for civilization.

In the Dakota state display at the New Orleans Industrial Exhibition of 1884–85, "pitches the wigwam of a Sioux war-chief, with wife and child to be stared at by the passing multitude," wrote an essayist for the *Century Magazine*.[78] But as the BIA was still reeling from the charges leveled by Helen Hunt Jackson's *A Century of Dishonor* (1881), it was to Alice Fletcher that the Committee on Education turned, asking her to prepare an exhibit on Indian education that would demonstrate government efforts to help Native Americans. In part owing to lack of funds, and to Putnam's unwillingness to loan objects from the Peabody, Fletcher was able to mount only a display of sixteen photographs and two drawings, accompanied by an explanatory pamphlet, *Historical Sketch of the Omaha Tribe of Indians in Nebraska*. The concluding paragraph of the pamphlet speaks to Fletcher's view that exhibitions should show "what has been actually accomplished in bringing a people from barbarism to civilized life," demonstrating that "civilization is no fanciful theory. . . . for here is a tribe which works, is educated, and is self-sustaining, having, within 25 years passed from Indian modes of life to farming upon their lands in severalty, independent of Government support."[79]

Fletcher's emphasis on Native-American capacity for civilization, while missionary, stood in marked contrast to the dominant theme of the expositions that sought to emphasize their savagery. Still, Fletcher's exhibit was one of the most popular at the fair. Julia Ward Howe, as director of the Woman's Building, drew most of the early press; one commentator noted that "Mrs. Julia Ward Howe and her zealous assistants have made this Department a pleasing and successful feature of the Exposition," though it is "of necessity inadequate to present a view of the attainments of women . . . and their share in carrying forward the world's civilization."[80] Yet Fletcher's tireless presence at the exhibit, and her celebrated noon talks on "Indian Custom" or "Dark and Bright Sides of Indian Life," drew crowds rivaling Howe's.[81]

Fletcher was also present at the 1893 Chicago World's Fair with Nuttal, Cox Stevenson, and Yorke Stevenson. Yorke Stevenson's role in the University of Pennsylvania's Middle East expedition led to her being appointed to the Jury of Awards for Ethnology at the exposition. A special act of Congress had been required to permit women to serve on such juries, and after it passed, Yorke Stevenson was elected jury vice president. The international jury of the World's Fair applauded "the wisdom of Congress in passing an act which has enabled scientific women to take their place on the highest planes of science, co-equal with men" in a resolution passed at its final meeting.[82] However, it was Zelia Nuttal who emerged as one of the fair's sensations, receiving much publicity for the discovery of a codex subsequently named after her, and becoming one of the few women whose own work was cataloged by both the Science and Ethnology Committees.[83]

By the time of the 1893 World's Fair, Fletcher hoped that her earlier success in New Orleans and Putnam's confidence in her abilities would lead him to appoint her as his chief assistant. Instead the position went to Boas. Fletcher's disappointment was not leavened by her being named an honorary corresponding member of the Women's Branch of the World's Congress Auxiliary of the Columbian Exposition. She wrote fretfully to Putnam, "I have accepted, but I can't see anything to do. I don't believe in trying to disentangle work according to sex, but many do."[84]

However, the Board of Lady Managers for the Woman's Building exhibit took the task of disentangling work according to sex quite seriously and, in their 1891 statement about the nature of the project, proclaimed, "The footsteps of women will be traced from prehistoric times to the present, and their intimate connection shown with all that has tended to promote the development of the race, even though they have worked under the most disadvantageous conditions."[85] To this end, the "Lady Managers" had also planned to place placards through the exposition's "White City" Building proclaiming which exhibits had been produced by women's labor.[86]

Otis Mason, one of Boas's major rivals, lauded the notion of tracing the footsteps of women through time and was to play a major role in bringing the much coveted Smithsonian exhibits to the Woman's Building. With his intervention, the Smithsonian—having intended its full collection to go to the Ethnology section of the fair—finally relented and contributed an eighty-case exhibit titled "Women's Work in Savagery," which was focused in large part on the material culture of Native Americans. In one exhibit, "Lady Managers from Colorado were given the landing of the southwest staircase for their 'Indian Alcove. Against a backdrop of Navaho blankets, a Navaho weaver worked her loom; a reed shuttle flew back and forth in her fingers.'"[87]

While Fletcher continued to focus her exhibits on the positive effects missionization had upon Native-American capacity for self-support, the Woman's Building exhibit transformed the lantern slide lectures of evangelical ethnography's "teaching by showing" into a kind of "expository feminism." This new "show-and-tell" stage of Victorian feminism was due, in part, to the successes of the first generation of professional and social reform women. The exhibitions and fairgrounds of the nineteenth century provided avenues for the leisured middle classes to view the hierarchically ranked achievements of women such that the progress from savagery to civilization was confirmed. While some historians suggest that the world's fairs moved away from a conception of culture as the function of time, and toward a notion of culture as a function of place through the display of ethnological villages,[88] I would argue that the latter actually consolidated an evolutionist, "time-centered" view of culture that was itself deeply gendered.

The Board of Lady Managers at the Chicago World's Fair faced a number of other issues besides questions of arranging and procuring exhibits. It was during the first Congress of Representative Women that its organizers managed, after protracted struggle with the more conservative women's club movement, to have women's suffrage placed on the speaker's agenda. As if in vindication of the suffragist cause, Susan B. Anthony was heralded as one of the heroines of the fair. The WCTU organ, the *Union Signal*, wrote of the "electric thrill of sympathy" that "noble women of all lands" must have felt with "these 'representative' women of the world who assisted to register an event in history as new as the creation—the consecration of a building, planned and decorated by women, to the arts, industries and literature of women; and greater still to chronicle the first setting of its women by a government, in a great national enterprise, in a position independent of and coordinate with the men of the nation."[89] African-American women, however, who were disenfranchised by a number of the prominent suffragist organizations of the time, waged another battle merely to earn representation at the congress.[90] Ida B. Wells coauthored a pamphlet with Frederick Douglass, *The Reason Why: The Colored American Is Not in the World's Columbian Exposition*, arguing that if African Americans had contributed productively to American civilization, but had been denied representation at the exposition, white Americans had "embraced barbarism and race hate" rather than civilization. Though white women organizers initially protested the creation of a separate Woman's Building, and the exclusion of their exhibits from the White City's display of the achievements of civilization, in the end they were no more inclusive than the male architects of the exposition.[91]

Feminists of the 1890s were increasingly a part of the "nativism" that was sweeping U.S. politics. During this period, few attempts were made to show that women, regardless of race or culture, shared something in common as "women." Rather, the overwhelming tendency of feminists at this time was to point to racial distinctions. Thus Carrie Chapman Catt and Anna Howard Shaw were both "fulminating at the humiliation suffered by American women, by which they meant native-born white middle-class women, at being ruled by all races and nationalities[, and]. . . . many suffragists argued that only the votes of women would enable white Protestant native Americans to outvote new immigrants in the North and blacks in the South."[92]

The fact that scientists like Fletcher or Nuttal and suffragists like Julia Ward Howe or Susan B. Anthony emerged as popular symbols of the 1885 and 1893 fairs says something not only about the relationship of feminism to domestic politics but about the question of colonial empire as well. Nowhere was the question of empire posed more clearly at the fair than in the circuslike atmosphere of the fair's Midway, an extended mile-long strip of land between Fifty-ninth and Sixtieth Streets, where native peoples of the world were placed on display in sordid conditions.

The only person who protested the treatment of Native Americans at Chicago was Emma Sickles, a member of Putnam's staff who said what Fletcher probably thought: that the display was used to "work up sentiment against the Indian by showing that he is either savage or can be educated only by government agencies. . . . Every means was used to keep the self-civilized Indian out of the Fair."[93] Sickles was, of course, right but lost her job. Wounded Knee was still a recent event, and Indian images of savagery were augmented by Wild Bill's Congress of Rough Riders performing just blocks from the fair.[94]

The internment of Native Americans in ethnographic villages at the world's fairs did not end in Chicago. At the 1895 Atlanta Cotton States and International Exposition, the chief attraction at the fair's Midway Heights was the Sioux on display who had been involved in the Ghost Dance Movement, and who had escaped massacre by U.S. troops.[95] Robert Rydell reports that the same lodges which had been riddled with gunfire had been transported to the Midway Heights for the Sioux to live in. Present were a young woman and her son who had been shot while asleep in their lodge. The director of publicity claimed, "This boy, known as 'Little Wound,' seems to be no worse physically for his early taste of war, and during the Exposition, showed all the lively and mischievous tendencies of a robust urchin."[96]

Fletcher was not in Atlanta to witness the cruel display of the Sioux, but at the Trans-Mississippi and International Exposition in 1898 she arranged for several Omaha Indians to sing for the audience of the Congress of Musicians. In the later edited collection of those songs for a popular audience, Fletcher argued that "Aside from its scientific value, this music possesses a charm and spontaneity that cannot fail to please those who would come near to nature. . . . These songs are like the wild flowers that have not yet come under the transforming hand of the gardener."[97]

While Fletcher deployed the same trope of wildness that was increasingly attached to Native Americans to mark their distance from civilization, she did object to the "glaring crudities" of the "Indian Congress" at Omaha,[98] which though immensely popular did not present the "true story" of Indian mental capacity, while her own "unheralded space of fifteen by forty feet in the Government Building at this same Exposition" displayed "the fine things that the Indian mind was capable of."[99]

The completion of westward expansion and the acquisition of new territory in the wake of a "trail of broken treaties" were celebrated by the Louisiana Purchase Exposition of 1904. As one *Century* columnist noted, "The widespread territory of the United States is illustrated by exhibits from such remote corners of the earth as Luzon, Porto Rico, Guam, Hawaii, and Alaska. A million dollars has been spent to show the wonderful present in the Philippines."[100] It was thus that the Louisiana Purchase Exposition held in St. Louis contained the largest ethnological display ever—nearly 1,200 Filipinos on display in a reservation—*and* the largest Anthropology Department of any fair, headed by W. J. McGee.[101] The presence of the Filipino and Native-American villages once again "underlined the continuities with America's expansionist past and with the national experience of subduing 'savage' populations."[102] The *Century* columnist concluded that North American Indians, "as they yet survived" would be "permanent memorials of the fair, extremes of American life and civilization in close juxtaposition."[103]

Fletcher was also present at this fair. Cox Stevenson had been given the responsibility of collecting display specimens, while Nuttal again served in an official capacity and Frances Densmore also participated.[104] Densmore, working with the Igorot peoples on the exposition reservation, confided, "For many years I have been a student of Indian music and expected to find some similarity between the music of the two races, but a few hours among the Filipinos showed that their music belongs to a period of development more primitive than that of the American Indian, and that it lies very near the beginning of musical expression."[105] She concluded her *American Anthropologist* article on her exposition observations by noting:

> The native music of the Filipinos will soon pass away. Beyond the bamboo paling of the Igorot village were the white tents of the Philippine constabulary, and there at set of sun a band of Filipinos played our own national anthem, while hundreds of Filipinos in khaki saluted the American flag as it was slowly lowered. So the sunset gun is measuring the days until all the Filipino music shall be merged at last in the Star Spangled Banner.[106]

If a generation of women contributed to the professionalization of ethnology, "objective description" had not yet been established as its dominant mode; as a result, popular and professional journals alike were media for the expression of imperial sympathies.[107]

THE MATRILINEAL CONUNDRUM

In the late nineteenth century, (liberal, contract-theorist) social anthropologists like Johann Bachofen, John McLennan, John Lubbock, Lewis Henry Morgan, Herbert Spencer, and Edward Tylor had questioned the seventeenth- and eighteenth-century notion of patriarchy (the rule of the father extended from family to government) as divine and natural, instead arguing that because it was the highest form of social fashioning, patriarchal civilization was the goal of evolution.[108]

If Bachofen's theory of an Amazonian matriarchy appeared to establish a women's golden age, other evolutionists went to considerable effort to show that women had in no time or place wielded political power.[109] Yet the evidence of Native-American and South Indian polyandrous and/or matrilineal societies, where rights to property were traced through the female line, was mounting. Fletcher, for example, wrote that "In most of the tribes of this country descent was traced through the mother" so "children inherited nothing from their father"; and "Where father right prevailed, the mother's heirs were her brothers and sisters and their children." However, "In the tribes where descent was by the father, where the child belonged to the gens of the father and not to that of its mother, the woman did not, as with the ancient Greeks and Romans, lose her place in her gens and become absorbed in that of her husband. The Indian woman when she married neither changed her name nor relinquished any of her gentile or clan rights."[110]

Thus the evolutionists were forced to reexamine the relations of paternity, patriarchy, and property to one another. John McLennan's *Primitive Marriage* (1865), the basis for his later work, *The Patriarchal Theory* (1885), provided at once an account of how the idea of fatherhood emerged, and an analysis of woman's position in society:

> If they had lost the sexual freedom of the "early world," and the power that sometimes accompanied polyandry, they were protected by the progress of "refinement" from the violent sexuality of the primitive male. Polyandry—the earliest form of the marriage "contract"—had been a kind of training ground for men, giving them both the "idea of a wife" and "obligations in matters of sex." The relationships thus established were the ultimate basis for the Roman concept of the permanent consortship of one man and one woman, "with interests the same in all things civil and religious"—the idea which "despite all woman's rights movements to the contrary," was "that destined to prevail in the world."[111]

Herbert Spencer concurred with McLennan's sentiment. In comparing the position of women among savage and civilized nations, he justified limiting political rights of the "screaming sisterhood" by arguing that women's mental traits were less developed.[112]

Otis Mason's interest in the Woman's Building exhibit can now be better understood in the context of the liberal reformulation of evolutionist thought. In his 1884 book, *Woman's Share of Primitive Culture*, he, too, reaffirmed the progress of civilization in the transition from polygamy to monogamy:

> It is said that woman was first the wife of any, then the wife of many, and then one of many wives. . . . Matrimony in all ages is an attempt to secure the identity of the father. So the poor female, always the mother well-known, has had curious ups and downs with regards her spouse. The evolution of the husband then, is the history of matrimony. The motives of this evolution will appear as the various standings of woman in this regard are unfolded.[113]

What further distinguished primitive women from Victorian women was his assertion that "If there is in savagery, any operation in which the women have always 'trodden . . . alone' it is in the supreme moment of motherhood."[114]

Unlike McLennan, Spencer, and Mason, Lewis Henry Morgan was sympathetic to women's emancipation; he believed that greater sexual equality and more perfect monogamy were possible, and that the transition to patrilineality had a damaging effect on the position of women. (It was from this view that Engels derived the "world historical defeat of the female sex.") Nevertheless, the position Morgan took in his *Systems of Consanguinity* (1871) and *Ancient Society* (1878) was disdainful of polyandry and also assumed that women had no productive function in society.[115] One would therefore be mistaken to conclude that in establishing the nondivine or contingent nature of patriarchy, these thinkers were somehow "revolutionary."[116] Though differing in emphasis, all of them upheld monogamous marriage and Victorian domesticity as the pinnacle of civilization. It was, rather, the inability of evolutionist thought to successfully contain the contradiction posed by matrilineal societies that provided a revolutionary opening for feminist contestation of the "woman question."

Thus the 1891 statement of the Board of Directors for the Woman's Building exhibit at Chicago reaffirmed that which the evolutionists had such a hard time explaining away: "It will be shown that women, among all the primitive peoples, were the originators of most of the industrial arts, and that it was not until these became lucrative that they were appropriated by men, and women pushed aside."[117] Here women in search of a common past emerges as a universal category that transcends cultural difference, even as Mason's notion that women were to be recognized only by their achievement of motherhood was rejected through an appropriation of that which had most commonly been seen as male prerogative: the invention of technology. The theme that "Woman's work has been taken from her by man, and with each appropriation she has been bereft of importance in the community," was echoed by Fletcher[118] and became the flash point of Victorian feminism's confrontation with evolutionary theory.

By 1895, the matrilineal conundrum had also worked its way into the *Century Magazine*. "We are not warranted in supposing the early condition of woman was one of bondage," wrote Helen Watterson. "In the earliest historical records we find that it was the woman, and not the man, who was head of the family; from her descent was reckoned, from her honors and inheritance came." "But," she continued, "as civilization advanced, and refined away the primitive rude strength of the race, woman was seen to weaken more rapidly than man. One day she failed to meet man's might with equal might. Then was born the 'woman question.'"[119]

The work of early women anthropologists, and their efforts to introduce it to the public sphere, thus fomented a nascent critique of civilization. Along with Fletcher's explications of Native-American matrilineal forms, Cox Stevenson's 1894 and 1904 accounts of childbirth among the Sia and Zuni pueblos show extensive ceremonial elaboration and family support around women's pregnancy and childbirth—a reinscription of "primitive" motherhood that contested Mason's evolutionist assertion of blissful maternity as the exclusive achievement of the white race. Erminnie Platt Smith's early work had furthermore documented social and mythological spheres of influence for Iroquois women,[120] and by 1910 Frances Densmore had also demonstrated that Chippewa women were not denied access to sacred ritual knowledge.[121] While early women anthropologists pointed to the contradiction between "primitive" but independent women and highly positioned "dependent" women, it must be remembered that with the exception of Parsons, they were not only unable to break with the conventions of Victorian society but were to a certain extent enabled by its gender ideology. Indeed, with the exception of Parsons again, the following statements are virtually all these women have to say about the question in a rather large body of work.

Cox Stevenson wrote that "The domestic life of the Zunis might well serve as an example for the civilized world";[122] and Parsons was to proclaim, "Few women are institutionally as independent as Pueblo Indian women . . . particularly [. . .] Zuni women [who] marry and divorce more or less at pleasure. They own their houses and their gardens. Their offspring are reckoned of their clan. Their husbands come to live with them in their family group."[123] Fletcher also acknowledged that "civilization" for the Indian woman was not without its drawbacks. "Their status is one of Independence in many ways, particularly as to property. Once when our laws respecting married women were being explained to them, an Indian matron exclaimed, 'I'm glad I'm not a white woman!'"[124] In a later article, "The Indian Woman and Her Problems," Fletcher expanded:

> Under the old tribal regime, woman's industries were essential to the very life of the people, and their value was publicly recognized. While she suffered many hardships and labored early and late, her work was exalted ceremonially and she had a part in tribal functions. Her influence in the growth and development of tribal government, tribal ceremonies, and tribal power shows that her position had always been one of honor rather than one of slavery and degradation.[125]

The central contradictions of Victorian evolutionism can then be simply stated: if the status of women was seen to be the measure of a civilization, why was it that white women were denied the vote, rights to property, and independence in a range of social activities, when "primitive" Native-American women might have rights to property, a say in ritual practice, and considerable social freedom? If "primitive" women were not degraded objects of pity as commonly supposed, what sense could be made of the claims to white women's unique sex superiority? If the apparent lack of sex differentiation in primitive societies resulted in women's labor, but was a sign of savage exploitation, why did middle-class Victorian women lack the freedoms of their less evolved sisters? Had white women traded the relative egalitarianism of simpler societies for the highly unequal and suffocating sex differentiation of Civilization? Was Civilization somehow responsible for women's plight? Native-American women thus became a foil against which the progress of white women could be judged, an idealized symbol of what Victorian women did not yet fully enjoy: independence.

Yet the question of political rights for Native-American women was never raised. Platt Smith and Fletcher, as "club movement" women, advocated women's independence but stopped short of suffrage. Perhaps for this reason, the question of enfranchising Native-American women never arose for Fletcher, who campaigned extensively for Native-American citizenship, but affirmed its masculine basis even as she sought to deracialize it. Thus the question of enfranchising Native-American women never arose for Fletcher. Describing a council of the Omaha tribe, she recounted: "In the speeches that were made, some used the English word 'citizen,' some the Indian word meaning 'white man,' to represent their present status. I explained to them . . . that one was a race word, and the other indicated a legal privilege irrespective of race. Thus, 'I feel more like a man for these words of our friend,' said one huge fellow." Fletcher concluded that the Indian "must be inducted into his rights of manly estate,"[126] but failed to recognize that the allotment of individual properties to *men* as a basis of enfranchisement under the Dawes Act was radically altering women's role in transmitting inheritance rights within matrilineal societies.

Parsons and Yorke Stevenson, on the other hand, were active in feminist politics of the period, the former writing several popular feminist tracts and the latter a founder of the Equal Franchise Society of Pennsylvania, and there is no evidence that early women anthropologists thought about the exclusion of other groups of women from the American suffrage movement. "Only twice through my association with the Pueblo Indians has it occurred to me to be a feminist," wrote Parsons in 1919.[127] Indeed, it may well have been the somewhat idealized perception of native women's rights that precluded Parsons and others from acknowledging native women's lack of rights both as women and as Native Americans *outside* their communities.

In arguing for their own independence, then, early women anthropologists did not argue for an end to the process that subjugated Native-American women as *women*. In fact, the perceived "independence" of Native-American women in spite of the allotment system, forced removal, and genocide may have worked as an ideological cloaking device in much the same way that white women were not seen to be subjugated as women because they were white.

Thus the "woman question" destabilized but did not sunder the logic of Victorian evolutionism. While women were unequal, they were not inferior. High Victorianism held that women were superior owing to their innate spiritual natures, cloaking their subordination in the glories of maternal duty. Yet it had also become increasingly difficult for Victorian evolutionary theory to explain away the results of emerging field-based ethnology, and this gender strain certainly contributed to its demise.

The confrontation of Victorian feminism with evolutionism created the conditions necessary for the articulation of "woman" as a universal category across cultures. Yet just at the moment women might have theorized a common history through a notion of shared "sex," in spite of cultural difference, the prevailing evolutionism of the day worked to prohibit gender identification.

It thus is difficult to offer easy generalizations about the emergence of gender as an analytical category in anthropology, for the ethnographers who most contributed to its emergence occupied highly contradictory positions. They were clearly enabled by Victorian gender ideology, but the "evangelical ethnology" Fletcher and Cox Stevenson produced was not entirely consistent with its terms and produced tensions within Victorian evolutionary thought.

Although they viewed their anthropology as a means to civilize the "Wild West," the ethnology of the first women anthropologists contributed to the analytical conundrum empirical fieldwork posed to nineteenth-century evolutionary theory.

By challenging the notion that women's status was an accurate marker of "civilization," the ethnographers of Native-American matriliny helped establish the importance of cultural relativism. The question of sex differentiation—the idea that gender roles were not naturally given but socially constituted—led ultimately to the question of legitimate cultural difference. The emergence of gender as a category of analysis, then, enabled and is entailed by the ascendance of cultural relativism.

But if evolutionism highlighted the "woman question," the consolidation by a newly professionalized anthropology of cultural relativism as opposite to evolutionism also obscured the ways in which cultural relativism was inflected by the question of sex difference in history: the search for a shared woman's past. This explains, in part, the submerged but foundational role gender has played in the shaping of the discipline.

Although the ethnologists discussed in this essay reproduced evolutionary themes in their work and were all too complicit with white settler ideology and imperialist projects, they also argued against racial and gender stereotypes, shaping a fieldwork ethic of cultural relativism that helped to dislodge the evolutionary paradigm. Though they were largely uncritical of the treatment accorded native peoples at the world's fairs, their work nonetheless enabled feminist challenge of evolutionist patriarchy. Through their writing for nonprofessional journals and their participation in the public sphere of lecture circuits and the world's fairs, they contributed to anthropology's role in the reinscription of the woman question.

CONCLUSION: THE EMERGENCE OF GENDER AS A CRITIQUE OF INEQUALITY BETWEEN THE SEXES

As we have seen, feminist currents shaped the emergence of anthropology; but so, too, did anthropology sculpt the form of modern feminism. This juncture is most clearly marked in Parsons's work. Much has already been written of Parsons's contribution to the notion that gender is culturally constructed, particularly with respect to her ethnographic writings on women and children after 1915.[128] I would, however, argue that the writings which precede her entry into the field supply a missing piece of the story about her contribution to the emergence of gender as a category of analysis, and her debts to the Victorian-era women.

In her work before 1915, Parsons often emphasized the positive characteristics women shared in common. Such shared positive characteristics also indicated the equivalence Parsons established between women's acts of resistance to patriarchy across cultures. She once asserted that "royal ladies of the African west coast and the queens of medieval Europe fought similar battles to establish their independence: All these queens, nuns, and femmes de joie were the celibate or grass widow pioneers of woman's rights, the ancestresses of the modern emancipated woman."[129]

Four years later, in *The Old Fashioned Woman*, Parsons had formulated ethnographic universals about women's condition, arguing that differences between Western society and other societies were not pronounced where women were concerned.

> "Coming-out" is a custom not peculiar to civilization. Our debutantes are apt to be older, to be sure, than those elsewhere. Instead of a year or two "abroad" or in a "finishing school," savage girls usually spend but a few weeks or months in a lonely hut or in a bed or in a hammock or cage in a corner of the house or on the roof. But once "out," a debutante's life is everywhere much the same. Everywhere at this time particular attention is paid to a girl's looks.[130]

Such anecdotes show Parsons establishing a kind of gender identification across culture, moving to a universal conception of womanhood based on positive shared characteristics.

In later work, she amplified instead the notion of women's shared oppression, arguing, "From the domination of her family [a woman] passes under the domination of her husband, and, perhaps, in addition, of his family."[131] Thus at the same moment Parsons established a form of gender identification that acknowledged the relative high status and autonomy of women in "primitive" cultures, her move to equalize sources of oppression among diverse groups of women posed a break with evolutionist thinking that proposed patriarchy as the form of civilized society. Parsons's intervention, building upon the insights of the Victorian feminists, was to suggest that it was patriarchal social organization that universally oppressed women, not the low placement of nonwhite cultures on an evolutionary grid.

Yet if Parsons drew upon and developed one tendency within Victorian feminism to resituate the meaning of patriarchy, she was also critical of many of its tenets. *Social Rule*, written in 1916, shows Parsons's thinking in transition, as she moved away from the category of "woman" itself as a basis of categorization.

> Even the movement we have called feminism has not succeeded by and large in giving women any control over men. It has only changed the distribution of women along the two stated lines of control by men, removing vast numbers of women from the class supported by men to the class working for them.
>
> The redistribution of women may be, of course, just an incident of feminism. It may be that this movement is primarily not concerned with the control of one sex by the other at all. The main objective of feminism, in fact, may be defeminization, the declassification of women as women, the recognition of women as human beings or personalities.[132]

Parsons advanced her argument not only by contrasting the "New Woman" to the "Old Fashioned Woman" of the nineteenth century but by radically redefining the New Woman:

The more thoroughly a woman is classified, the more easily is she controlled. The vernacular phrase, the "New Woman," has the psychological significance so curiously attaching to popular phrases. The New Woman means the woman not yet classified, perhaps not classifiable, the new woman not only to men, but to herself. She is . . . dissatisfied with expressing her own will to power merely through the ancient media, through children, servants, younger women and uxorious men. She wants to be not only a masterless woman, one no longer classified as daughter or wife, she wants a share in the mastery men arrogate.[133]

Paradoxically, Parsons's turn to fieldwork actually effaced the notion of sex inequality that Progressive Era feminism, and her own popular writing before 1915, helped to foreground. Writing for the *Scientific Monthly* in 1919, she asked, "Are the women of the community still thought of . . . even in scientific or pseudo-scientific circles, as a separable class? If so, there is nothing for us but to keep on with the categories of feminist and anti-feminist tiresome though they become."[134]

Like Fletcher, Parsons, too, was utimately wary of "disentangling work according to sex." Like the Victorian women, Parsons also sought to characterize the whole of a society, and understanding relations between the sexes was a means to this end. But while the work of both women reflected a notion of the cultural construction of gender, it was Parsons who developed the proposition that gender was marked by unequal relations of power. In her popular writing before 1915, she argued that recognition of this inequality meant recourse to "woman" as a universal category. In her professional writing after 1915, recognition of inequality between the sexes meant the de-categorization of women.

The understanding of cultural difference that was imbedded in evolutionist racism prevented Victorian feminists from fully reversing the evolutionary dictum about patriarchy; but in ways not yet fully understood, the impetus for cultural relativism, the quest to portray cultures as meaningful, coherent wholes, actually emerged from the need to understand sexual difference. For even as Parsons sought to move away from the notion of women as a sex class, paradoxically once again it was she, of all the anthropologists discussed in this essay, who actually wrote the most specifically on women and children in her quest to portray cultures as integrated wholes. It is this double movement that marks both the emergence of gender and the consolidation of cultural relativism within the discipline.

NOTES

I would like to thank Adam Green, Louise Lamphere, and Helene Silverberg for their comments on drafts of the essay, and Jennifer Burrell and especially Nicolas Prat for their help in locating materials. I thank also the library collections staff at the University of Texas (Austin) Center for American Studies and Harry Ransom Center for the Humanities for their assistance.

1. Henry Tibbles, *Buckskin Blankets* (New York: Doubleday, 1905), 236.
2. Elsie Clews Parsons's fondness for seeing the country from horseback on her eth-

nological tours was well known, and Fletcher referred to her allotment postings as the "wilderness." See Frederick Hoxie and Joan Mark, eds., *With the Nez Perces: Alice Fletcher in the Field, 1889–92. Letters of Jane E. Gay* (Lincoln: University of Nebraska Press, 1981), xxxiv. Desley Deacon, "The Republic of the Spirit: Field Work in Elsie Clews Parsons's Turn to Anthropology," *Frontiers: A Journal of Women's Studies* 12, no. 3 (1992): 13–38, and idem, *Elsie Clews Parsons: Inventing Modern Life* (Chicago: University of Chicago Press, 1997).

3. See Nancy Parezo, "Anthropology: The Welcoming Science," in *Hidden Scholars*, ed. Nancy Parezo (Albuquerque: University of New Mexico Press, 1993); Nancy Cott, *The Grounding of Modern Feminism* (New Haven: Yale University Press, 1987).

4. See the entries for these women in *Women Anthropologists*, ed. Ute Gacs et al. (Urbana: University of Illinois Press, 1989): Charlotte Frisbie, "Frances Densmore"; Vimala Jayanti, "Erminnie Platt Smith"; Nancy Parezo, "Matilda Cox Stevenson"; Andrea Temkin, "Alice Fletcher"; Christine Moon Van Ness, "Sara Yorke Stevenson."

5. The public success of this group of women also earned them less flattering attention. Nuttal's notoriety inspired D. H. Lawrence's characterization of Mrs. Norris in his novel *The Plumed Serpent*, while the reformist zeal of Fletcher and Cox Stevenson garnered them epithets for their uncompromising positions. Fletcher was seen as "dreadfully opinionated," and Cox Stevenson was variously described as "humorless," "aggressive," and "overbearing" (See Nancy O. Lurie, "Women in Early American Anthropology," in *Pioneers of American Anthropology*, ed. June Helm [Seattle: University of Washington Press, 1966]," 58–59). In a *Punch* satire, Yorke Stevenson was more tamely referred to as "Philadelphia's patriotic matron" (Martin Meyerson and D. P. Winegrad, "Sara Yorke Stevenson: The First Women at the University," in *Gladly Teach, Gladly Learn: Franklin and His Heirs at the University of Pennsylvania, 1740–1976* [University of Pennsylvania Press, 1978], 127), while Parsons's male colleagues addressed her as "dear propagandist."

6. Joan Mark, *A Stranger in Her Native Land: Alice Fletcher and the American Indians* (Lincoln: University of Nebraska Press, 1988), 32–33.

7. Ibid., 38.

8. See Cott, *The Grounding of Modern Feminism*.

9. See Edward B. Tylor, "How the Problems of American Anthropology Present Themselves to the English Mind," *Science* 4 (1884): 545–51. Still, Cox Stevenson was the only one to begin collecting ethnographic data by her husband's side, though Zelia Nuttal's entry into anthropology was probably also inspired by her marriage to French ethnologist Alphonse Louis Pinart. In 1906, Parsons also held that women could aid ethnology because a "woman student would have many opportunities for observing the life of women that male ethnographers lacked." Elsie Clews Parsons, *The Family: An Ethnographical and Historical Outline* (New York: G. Putnam and Sons, 1906), 198. Parsons was, however, the only one of this group who published specifically on women and children. But see Alice Fletcher, "Glimpses of Child-Life among the Omaha Tribe of Indians," *Journal of American Folklore* 1 (1888): 115–23.

10. See Lurie, "Women in Early American Anthropology," and Mark, *A Stranger in Her Native Land*.

11. Lurie, "Women in Early American Anthropology."

12. Fletcher and Yorke Stevenson were among the first members of the Archeological Institute of America, founded in 1879. In 1885, Platt Smith was the first woman honored as a fellow of the New York Academy of Sciences, and one of the first women members of the AAAS, serving as secretary of Section H (Anthropology). Yorke Steven-

son was a founding member of the American Exploratory Society of Philadelphia. In 1895, Fletcher was elected vice president of Section H of the AAAS; in 1905, she was elected president of the American Folklore Society.

13. While Fletcher, Densmore, and Cox Stevenson all relied upon the BAE for their livelihoods, and while on more than one occasion Densmore and Cox Stevenson demonstrated anxiety over their BAE funding, Fletcher received heavy financial support from a number of society women (including a life fellowship at Harvard gifted by Mary Copley Thaw), and both she and Cox Stevenson were well connected in Washington political circles. Parsons and Nuttal had the most contact with Franz Boas as he actively solicited their wealth and patronage for various projects. Alice Fletcher, along with Yorke Stevenson and Nuttal, also lobbied Phoebe Apperson Hearst for financial support of various anthropological ventures. Frederick Putnam, writing of his efforts to preserve an archaeological site in Ohio, said that they would "have come to naught if Miss Alice C. Fletcher meeting in Newport a few Boston ladies, had not taken the opportunity to appeal to them for assistance in the work. . . . Her earnest presentation of the subject had the desired effect. . . . Boston's noble and earnest women issued a private circular. . . . Subscriptions were solicited to purchase Serpent Mound. . . . and in June 1886 I was provided with nearly $6,000 with which to buy such land." See "The Serpent Mound of Ohio," *Century Magazine*, April 1890, 871–88; also Luric, "Women in Early American Anthropology," Parezo, "Welcoming Science," and Ross Parmenter, "Glimpses of a Friendship: Zelia Nuttal and Franz Boas," in *Pioneers of American Anthropology*, ed. June Helm (Seattle: University of Washington Press, 1966), 83–148.

14. Parsons earned a Ph.D. in sociology from Columbia in 1892, and Yorke Stevenson was awarded an honorary doctorate by the University of Pennsylvania in 1894. Platt Smith and Cox Stevenson both studied geology: the former graduated after two years of study from the Freiburg School of Mines, and the latter pursued advanced course work in law and chemistry. Both Fletcher and Densmore worked as schoolteachers before turning to anthropology; Densmore had completed advanced music study.

15. Yorke Stevenson was one of the founders of the University of Pennsylvania Museum and at one point sought to recruit Franz Boas to establish a Department of Anthropometry there. Parsons established the Southwest Society to fund anthropological research, while Nuttal helped found the International School of American Archaeology and Ethnology in Mexico City, and was instrumental in the establishment of the anthropology department at Berkeley, as well. Fletcher's role in establishing the School of American Archaeology (now the School of American Research in Santa Fe), over the objections of Frederick Putnam and Franz Boas, meant that she was also seen as a formidable rival.

16. Joan Mark has made this point forcefully. In addition to Platt Smith, Fletcher, and Nuttal, Putnam also encouraged the work of Cordelia Studley in physical anthropology (Mark, *A Stranger in Her Native Land*, 35).

17. Several of Boas's biographers suggest that it was Boas's experience of anti-Semitism in Europe that led him to encourage women's and African Americans' initiative in the field.

18. A cursory glance at their biographies reveals a number of overlapping friendships and organizational memberships. Fletcher served as a mentor for both Nuttal and Densmore (Mark, *A Stranger in Her Native Land*, 1088; Frances Densmore, *Pawnee Music* [Washington, D.C.: U.S. Government Printing Office, 1929]). Fletcher and Cox Stevenson worked together to make Mesa Verde a national park in 1887. Yorke Stevenson and

Nuttal were good friends who were both admitted to the American Philosophical Society in 1895.

19. Zelia Nuttal and Alice Fletcher were both mentored by Frederick Putnam; both Fletcher and Nuttal served as Putnam's assistant at the Peabody Museum before Boas held that position in 1893. It is likely that Putnam, a cousin of Platt Smith's, introduced her to the AAAS. Lewis Henry Morgan is said to have encouraged both Fletcher and Platt Smith, resulting in the latter's earning a staff appointment at the Bureau of American Ethnology (BAE) in 1880. Both Platt Smith and Cox Stevenson were trained by Powell, and although Cox Stevenson focused on the ethnographic particular and did not consider herself a theorist, her findings supported the evolutionary schemas of Powell and McGee. Yorke Stevenson also had close ties to Daniel Brinton, an evolutionary anthropometrist at Pennsylvania.

20. Joan Scott, *Gender and the Politics of History* (Chicago: University of Chicago Press, 1988).

21. See Elizabeth Fee, "The Sexual Politics of Victorian Social Anthropology," in *Clio's Consciousness Raised: New Perspectives on the History of Women*, ed. M. Hartman and L. Banner (New York: Harper and Row, 1974); idem, "Science and the Woman Problem: Historical Perspectives," in *Sex Differences: Social and Biological Perspectives*, ed. M. S. Teitelbaum (New York: Anchor Press, 1976), 175–223.

22. See Gail Bederman, *Manliness and Civilization: A Cultural History of Gender and Race in the United States, 1880–1917* (Chicago: University of Chicago Press, 1995).

23. I am to some extent conflating "gender" with the category of "woman." The emergence of woman as a universal category is of course problematic in feminist theory. For a discussion of its relationship to anthropology, see my "Histories of Feminist Ethnography," *Annual Review of Anthropology* 26 (1997).

24. See Judith Friedlander, "Elsie Clews Parsons," in Gacs, *Women Anthropologists*; Louise Lamphere, "Feminist Anthropology: The Legacy of Elsie Clews Parsons," *American Ethnologist* 16 (1989): 518–33.

25. See A. I. Howell, "The Beginnings of Anthropology in America," in *Selected Papers from the American Anthropologist, 1888–1920*, ed. Frederica de Laguna (Evanston, Ill.: Row, Peterson and Co., 1960); Curtis Hinsley, *Savages and Scientists: The Smithsonian Institution and the Development of American Anthropology, 1846–1910* (Washington, D.C.: Smithsonian Institution, 1981).

26. However, see Curtis Hinsley, "The World as Marketplace: Commodification of the Exotic at the World's Fair Columbian Exposition," in *Exhibiting Cultures: The Poetics and Politics of Museum Display*, ed. Ivan Karp and Steven Levine (Washington, D.C.: Smithsonian Institution Press, 1991).

27. See Henry King, "The Indian Country," *Century Magazine*, August 1885, 599–606; E. V. Smalley, "The New Northwest. First Paper: The Dakota Wheatlands, the Bad Lands, and the Yellowstone Country," *Century Magazine*, August 1882, 504–12; idem, "The New Northwest. Second Paper: Across the Rockies in Montana," *Century Magazine*, September 1882, 769–79; idem, "The New Northwest. Third Paper: From the Rockies to the Cascade Range," *Century Magazine*, October 1882, 863–72; idem, "Features of the New Northwest," *Century Magazine*, November 1882, 529–37; idem, "The New Orleans Exhibition," *Century Magazine*, May 1885, 3–14; "In and Out of the New Orleans Exhibition," *Century Magazine*, June 1885, 185–99.

28. See Frank Cushing, "My Adventures in Zuni," *Century Magazine*, 1882, 191–207; idem, "My Adventures in Zuni, II," *Century Magazine*, February 1883, 500–511; idem, "My Adventures in Zuni, III," *Century Magazine*, May 1883, 28–47; Putnam, "The Ser-

pent Mound of Ohio"; Alice Fletcher, "On Indian Education and Self Support," *Century Magazine*, 1883, 312–15; idem, "Personal Studies of Indian Life: Politics and Pipe-Dancing," *Century Magazine*, 1893, 441–55; idem, "Indian Songs: Personal Studies of Indian Life," *Century Magazine*, January 1894, 421–31; idem, "Hunting Customs of the Omahas: Personal Studies of Indian Life," *Century Magazine*, September 1895, 691–702; idem, "Tribal Life among the Omahas: Personal Studies of Indian Life," *Century Magazine*, January 1896, 450–61.

29. Cited in George Stocking, ed., *A Franz Boas Reader: The Shaping of American Anthropology, 1883–1911* (Chicago: University of Chicago Press, 1974), 44. Boas was less successful in having his own work appear in the *Century Magazine*. Reacting to an article by Robert Bennett Bean, "The Negro Brain," in a 1906 issue, Boas sought to have his reply to Bean's argument on racial inferiority published the following year. However, his article was rejected by the *Century*'s editor. See Marshall Hyatt, *Franz Boas, Social Activist* (New York: Greenwood Press, 1990), 91–94.

30. An abbreviated version of this account was first published as the introduction to Fletcher's 1893 monograph *A Study of Omaha Indian Music*, reissued in 1994 by the University of Nebraska Press.

31. Fletcher, "Indian Songs: Personal Studies of Indian Life," 422.

32. Her notion that "if one would hear Indian music and understand it, one must ignore as he does, his manner of singing" was also cited by her protégée Frances Densmore in ethnomusicology. See Frances Densmore, "What Intervals Do Indians Sing?" *American Anthropologist* 31 (1929): 274, and Charles Hoffman, "Frances Densmore and the Music of the American Indian," *Journal of American Folklore* 59 (1946): 45–50.

33. Fletcher, however, did take an evolutionist view of Native-American music (Helen Myers, introduction to Alice Fletcher, *A Study of Omaha Indian Music* [Lincoln: University of Nebraska Press, 1994]), while Densmore also emphasized the "primitive" tonal character of Native-American music, and an early essay attempted to account for the high tonal pitch of Native-American song by noting that this is a feature of "love songs" within the animal kingdom, thus proving that there was an "emotional origin to the musical expression of the [Indian] race." See Frances Densmore, "Scale Formation in Primitive Music," *American Anthropologist* 11, no. 1 (January–March 1909): 1–2, 5.

34. Sara Yorke Stevenson, *Maximillian in Mexico: A Woman's Reminiscences of the French Intervention* (New York: The Century Co., 1899).

35. Zelia Nuttal, "Ancient Mexican Superstitions," *Journal of American Folklore* 10 (1897): 265–81, quotation on 265.

36. Ibid., 266.

37. Fletcher, in her popular writing for the *Southern Workman*, did contest stereotypes of Native Americans, but without reflection on the origin and function of such stereotypes. See "The Indian and the Prisoner," *Southern Workman* 17 (1888): 45; "Flotsam and Jetsam from Aboriginal America," *Southern Workman* 28 (1898): 12–14; "Indian Speech," *Southern Workman* 28 (1899): 426–28. In "Indian Characteristics," *Southern Workman* 29 (1900): 202–5, she mused, ". . . at a lunch party, the conversation turned upon Indians, and such were the characteristics imputed to them that it was difficult to believe that at this late date they should still be so misunderstood. One of the ladies had spent several years on the frontier, and as she narrated her observations of the 'savages,' my mind reverted to some of my own experiences while staying in an Indian camp, where I had listened to similar comments among natives discussing my own race."

38. Matilda Cox Stevenson, "The Sia," *Bureau of American Ethnology, Eleventh Annual Report (1889–90)* (Washington, D.C.: Government Printing Office, 1894), 9.

39. Alice Fletcher, *Indian Story and Song from North America* (Boston: Small, Maynard and Company, 1907), 120.

40. Cox Stevenson, "The Sia," 15.

41. Mark, *A Stranger in Her Native Land*, 266.

42. See Alice Fletcher, "Indian Education and Civilization," *Bureau of Education Special Report* (Washington, D.C.: Government Printing Office, 1888), and Joan Mark, "Alice Fletcher," in her *Four Anthropologists: An American Science in Its Early Years* (New York: Science History Publications, 1980), xxxviii.

43. See Mark, "Alice Fletcher," 68.

44. Mark, *A Stranger in Her Native Land*, 265.

45. Alice Fletcher and Francis La Flesche, *The Omaha Tribe, Bureau of American Ethnology, Twenty-Seventh Annual Report (1905–6)* (Washington, D.C.: Government Printing Office, 1911), 29.

46. Hoxie and Mark, *With the Nez Perces*, 49.

47. Ibid.

48. Gay editorializes that this might be a "hard idea" for Indians to grasp, remarking caustically: "The prospect of standing beside the white man is not a very brilliant one. The unadulterated Indian looks down upon the species of white men he knows anything about. As to the law, all they know about the law is, that it is some contrivance to get ponies and cattle and land out of the red man's possession into that of the white man; it is a one-sided machine; it never brings back an Indian's stolen horse, or takes the border ruffian's fence or his cattle off the Indian's land" (ibid.).

49. Frances Densmore, *Chippewa Music*, Smithsonian Institution, BAE Bulletin 45 (Washington, D.C.: Government Printing Office, 1910), 88.

50. See Frances Densmore, "Traces of Foreign Influences in the Music of the American Indians," *American Anthropologist* 46 (1944): 106–12, 108.

51. Hoxie and Mark, *With the Nez Perces*, 10–11.

52. Quoted in Lurie, "Women in Early American Anthropology," 59.

53. Ibid., 34.

54. Matilda Cox Stevenson, "The Zuni Indians: Their Mythology, Esoteric Fraternities, and Ceremonies," *Bureau of American Ethnology, Twenty-Third Annual Report (1901–2)* (Albuquerque, N.M.: Rio Grande Press, 1904), 253.

55. Though the WCTU did not recognize alcohol on the reservations as an issue arising out of colonialism and political domination, it attempted in 1879 to contact chiefs of the Five Nations to persuade them of the importance of temperance, and pressure was put upon the U.S. government to see that liquor laws were enforced on the reservations. Crusaders like Fletcher also found it more effective to point to examples of Native-American self-regulatory temperance. Writing of the salutary effects of Christianization, she argued that missionary labor "has borne good fruit among the Omahas . . . due to the responsive influence of some of the leading Indian men who accepted Christianity as the standard of life and . . . industry and morality. It was largely the result of the energetic rule of head Chief La Flesche and his corps of soldiers or police, that 20 years ago intemperance was so severely punished that no man dared to risk the terrible flogging given the drunkard." See Alice Fletcher, *Historical Sketch of the Omaha Tribe of Indians in Nebraska* (Washington, D.C.: Judd and Detweiller Printers, 1885), 11; and Ruth Bordin, *Woman and Temperance* (Philadelphia: Temple University Press, 1981), 85.

56. Ann Ardis, *New Women, New Novels: Feminism and Early Modernism* (New Brunswick, N.J.: Rutgers University Press, 1990), 14.

57. Lurie, "Women in Early American Anthropology," 37.

58. Ardis, *New Women, New Novels*, 16.

59. Hoxie and Mark, *With the Nez Perces*, xxix.

60. Mark, *A Stranger in Her Native Land*, 258.

61. See Joan Jacobs Brumberg, "The Ethnological Mirror: American Evangelical Women and Their Heathen Sisters, 1870–1910," in *Women and the Structure of Society*, ed. Barbara Harris and Jo Ann MacNamara (Durham, N.C.: Duke University Press, 1984), and Billie Melman, *Women's Orients: English Women and the Middle East, 1718–1918* (Ann Arbor: University of Michigan Press, 1992).

62. Melman, *Women's Orients*, 167.

63. Rosalind Rosenberg, *Beyond Separate Spheres: Intellectual Roots of Modern Feminism* (New Haven: Yale University Press, 1982), 25; and Elisabeth Lasch-Quinn, *Black Neighbors: Race and the Limits of Reform in the American Settlement House Movement, 1890–1945* (Chapel Hill: University of North Carolina Press, 1993).

64. Mark, *A Stranger in Her Native Land*, 269.

65. Alice Fletcher (with Erminnie Platt Smith) was a member and later secretary of the pioneer women's organization Sorosis, a professional club for aspiring writers and journalists; she also helped found the Association for the Advancement of Women in 1873.

66. Mark, "Alice Fletcher," 67.

67. Hoxie and Mark, *With the Nez Perces*, 49.

68. Cox Stevenson, "The Zuni Indians," 380.

69. See Mark, *A Stranger in Her Native Land*, 106; and Parezo, "Welcoming Science."

70. Lurie, "Women in Early American Anthropology," 55.

71. Cox Stevenson, "The Zuni," 204.

72. Ibid., 406.

73. Mark, *A Stranger in Her Native Land*, 106–7.

74. Ibid.

75. See Frances Densmore, *The Plea of Our Brown Brother* and *Ke-wa-kun-ah* (Chilocco, Okla.: Indian Print Shop Press, 1900, 1906).

76. Densmore, *Plea*, 1.

77. Ibid., 2.

78. Smalley, "The New Orleans Exhibition," 13.

79. Fletcher, *Historical Sketch*, 12. In an article for the *Southern Workman*, however, Fletcher lamented somewhat contrarily, "The Indians are not represented at the Exposition among those who can exhibit proofs of their labor and education. They are present only in promise. Their story of struggle is set forth by the history of a single tribe, used as a type only to show how they are emerging from a past barren of results." See "The New Orleans Exposition," *Southern Workman* 14 (1885): 79.

80. See Smalley, "In and Out of the New Orleans Exhibition," 188–89.

81. Mark, *A Stranger in Her Native Land*, 109.

82. Cited in Meyerson and Winegrad, "Sara Yorke Stevenson," 126.

83. See Zelia Nuttal, "The Periodical Adjustments of the Ancient Mexican Calendar," *American Anthropologist*, n.s., 6 (1904): 486–500; Parmenter, "Glimpses of a Friendship," and Jeanne M. Weimann, *The Fair Women* (Chicago: Academy Chicago, 1981), 437.

84. See Mark, *A Stranger in Her Native Land*, 210. Fletcher was eventually appointed a member of Putnam's staff and served as a member of the Board of Judges for Ethnology, but it was Boas's Northwest Coast exhibit that dominated the Anthropology Build-

ing, while her collections of Nez Perce, Omaha, and Winnebago objects were among the smaller displays mounted by Putnam's many assistants. Although Fletcher read papers for the Congresses on Music, Ethnology, and Religion, the success she had hoped for with "Love Songs of the Omaha" eluded her. W. H. Holmes, in his 1893 *American Anthropologist* report on "The World's Fair Congress of Anthropology," characterized her paper as "interesting" and accompanied by "vocal illustrations most pleasingly rendered," but gave more attention to Fillmore's paper, "Primitive Scales and Rhythms," which had generated considerable discussion at the congress. Reprinted in de Laguna, *Selected Papers from the American Anthropologist*, 426.

85. See Weimann, *The Fair Women*, 393. Also see Frances K. Pohl, "Historical Reality or Utopian Ideal? The Woman's Building at the World's Columbian Exposition," *International Journal of Women's Studies* 5 (1982): 289–311.

86. See Bederman, *Manliness and Civilization*, 33.

87. Among the objects displayed were embroidery from the Nez Perce, Chippewa, Kiowa, and Haida; and Apache, Choctaw, Attacapa, Moki, Micmac, Eskimo, and Aleut baskets. One case consisted entirely of Navaho blankets, another of Eskimo skins and dolls; still others contained Kiowa and Sioux spoons, Eskimo and Haida dishes. Collections of Native-American handicrafts from the states and territories supplemented the Smithsonian display. Alaska contributed 204 exhibits, and Colorado 28. South Dakota sent an altar cloth of embroidered white deerskin from the Pine Ridge Agency, and New Mexico sent a collection of artifacts as well as a blanket commissioned by women in San Juan County of an "old weaver named Miranda." The weaver was paid $150 and given a picture of the Woman's Building showing the south window near which her blanket was to hang.

However, the high point of the Woman's Building exhibits turned out to be the lace collection of Queen Margherita of Italy, transported to the Woman's Building in a gold-harnessed horse-drawn carriage, accompanied by nineteen guards. The custodian of the Italian laces was the Countess di Brazza, the American wife of an Italian nobleman, who also arranged a musical drama called "The Seven Ages of Columbus," which was presented in the Assembly Room on Columbus Day, October 12, 1893. Harriet Monroe wrote the verse, Zelia Nuttal played a court lady, and "Colonel Cody lent twelve Indians" for the cast. See Weimann, *The Fair Woman*, 404, 406–7.

88. Paul A. Tenkotte, "Kaleidoscopes of the World: International Exhibitions and the Concept of Culture-Place, 1851–1915," *American Studies* 28 (1987): 5–29.

89. Quoted in Bordin, *Woman and Temperance*, 115.

90. Eventually six black women did address the congress. See Hazel Carby, *Reconstructing Womanhood* (New York: Oxford University Press, 1987).

91. See Bederman, *Manliness and Civilization*, 39–40.

92. Bordin, *Woman and Temperance*, 122.

93. Quoted in Robert Rydell, *All the World's a Fair: Visions of Empire at American International Expositions* (Chicago: University of Chicago Press, 1984), 63.

94. Buffalo Bill's "Wild West Show" also attracted four million visitors in a six-month period. See Tenkotte, "Kaleidoscopes of the World," 18.

95. Somewhat ironically, given Fletcher's failure to protest treatment of the Sioux at the exhibitions, she has been credited with understanding the Ghost Dance Movement as the Sioux response to the loss of buffalo on the plains, being crowded onto barren tracts of land, and coping with their children's being forced into English education. At her lecture on the "Indian Messiah" at a meeting of the American Folklore Society in December 1890, Franz Boas initially suggested that "crazes like these were probably

nervous diseases and should not be attributed to any great extent to politics." See Mark, *A Stranger in Her Native Land*, 209.

96. Rydell, *All the World's a Fair*, 51.

97. Fletcher, *Indian Story and Song*, preface.

98. The Indian Congress opened with a parade of 150 Indians, with those on horseback waving hunks of a recently slaughtered cow, while Buffalo Bill Cody headed another "ethnological parade" held in his honor. Fairgoers could wander through the Indian encampment at will, while mock battles between whites and Indians, or between groups of Indians themselves, were performed at scheduled times. Geronimo along with twenty-one other Apaches had been brought as prisoners of war from Fort Sill; he would sell his autograph for ten cents at this fair, as at the Buffalo and St. Louis fairs. Three Native Americans died while the exhibit was open, and one Indian woman attempted suicide. BAE ethnologist James Mooney protested faintly that the Indian Congress had degenerated into a "wild west show," but he himself staged performances of the Ghost Dance and footraces designed to show the stamina of the Indians. In a later article for the *American Anthropologist*, he detailed the ethnological characteristics of the Indians who participated in the exhibit, noting that the display had increased interest in anthropology. See Rydell, *All the World's a Fair*, 21, 51, 117.

99. See Alice Fletcher, "The Indian at the Trans-Mississippi Exposition," *Southern Workman* 27 (1898): 216–17.

100. Walter Williams, "Round the World at the World's Fair: Strange and Curious Sights at the Louisiana Purchase Exposition," *Century Magazine*, 1904, 794–803, 794.

101. By consulting with Boas and Ales Hrdlicka on setting up labs at the fair, McGee established an aura of scientific legitimacy, such that when the deaths of Filipinos being transported to the exposition were confirmed, Boas and Hrdlicka's discussion of obtaining the corpses for study raised little objection. McGee also continued the emphasis on Native-American progress from savagery to civilization, with a focus on "Indian school work." See Rydell, *All the World's a Fair*, 163.

102. Ibid., 20.

103. Williams, "Round the World," 801.

104. See Lurie, "Women in Early American Anthropology," 40; and Densmore, "Scale Formation."

105. Frances Densmore, "The Music of the Filipinos," *American Anthropologist* 8, no. 4 (1906): 611–32, quotation on 611.

106. Ibid., 632.

107. See William Schneider, "Race and Empire: The Rise of Popular Ethnography in the Late Nineteenth Century," *Journal of Popular Culture* 11 (1977): 78–109.

108. Fee, "Sexual Politics."

109. George Stocking, *Victorian Anthropology* (New York: The Free Press, 1987), 205.

110. Alice Fletcher, "The Indian Woman and Her Problems," *Southern Workman* 28 (1899): 172–76, quotation on 173.

111. Quoted in Stocking, *Victorian Anthropology*, 203.

112. Ibid., 205–6. Much has been written of Boas's contribution to the shattering of the evolutionary paradigm of the nineteenth century, but without attention to how he asserted the equivalence of women's mental capacity with men's to work against the theory of progressive racial types. Thus in his 1894 essay "Human Faculty as Determined by Race" he argued: "When men and women of the same stature are compared it is found that the brain of the woman is much lighter than that of the man. Neverthe-

less, the faculty of woman is undoubtedly just as high as that of man. This is, therefore, a case in which smaller brain weight is accompanied throughout by equal faculty. We conclude from this fact that it is not impossible that the smaller brains of males of other races should not do the same work that is done by the larger brain of the white race." See Stocking, *Franz Boas Reader*, 233.

113. Otis T. Mason, *Woman's Share in Primitive Culture* (New York: Appleton, 1894), 213.

114. Ibid., 205.

115. Fee, "Sexual Politics," 96–97. See also Thomas Trautmann, *Lewis Henry Morgan and the Invention of Kinship* (Berkeley and Los Angeles: University of California Press, 1987).

116. Stocking, *Victorian Anthropology*, 207.

117. Cited in Weimann, *The Fair Women*, 393.

118. Fletcher, "The Indian Woman," 175.

119. Helen Watterson, "The Woman Question Once More," *Century Magazine*, March 1895, 796. See also Elenora Kinnicutt, "The American Woman in Politics," *Century Magazine*, 1895, 302–4.

120. Erminnie Platt Smith, *Myths of the Iroquois, Bureau of American Ethnology, Second Annual Report* (Washington, D.C.: Government Printing Office, 1883).

121. Marta Weigle, *Spiders and Spinsters: Women and Mythology* (Albuquerque: University of New Mexico Press, 1982).

122. Cox Stevenson, "The Zuni," 293.

123. Elsie Clews Parsons, *Social Rule: A Study of the Will to Power* (New York: G. Putnam and Sons, 1916), 44.

124. Fletcher, "On Indian Education," 314.

125. Fletcher, "The Indian Woman," 172–76.

126. Fletcher, "The Indian and the Prisoner," 45.

127. My point here is not to dispute Parsons's feminism but to ask why it it does not occur to her to be one among the Zuni. The last sentence of the quotation that follows suggests Parsons's surprise that a Zuni woman would be subservient to men in ways similar "to [those of] the peoples of western civilization." "The first time was at Cochiti when late at night my tired and sleepy Indian hostess grumbled in the soft tone no Pueblo woman ever loses, grumbled because she had to sit up for the young husband who was spending the evening at the club. . . . 'I'll have to get him something to eat,' she said, 'no man here would ever cook for himself at home. They say if they did they would lose their sense of the trail.' Rationalization of habit or desire is not confined to the peoples of western civilization." The second time Parsons remembers she is a feminist is when she is asked to write an article on Zuni women, and she resists because she is working for the declassification of women. See Elsie Clews Parsons, "Waiyautitsa of Zuni, New Mexico," in *Pueblo Mothers and Children*, ed. Barbara Babcock (Santa Fe, N.M.: Ancient City Press, 1991).

128. See the following articles by Elsie Clews Parsons: "Zuni Conception and Pregnancy Beliefs," *Proceedings of the Nineteenth International Congress of Americanists*, 1915; "The Zuni La'mana," *American Anthropologist* 18 (1916): 521–28; "Nativity Myth at Laguna and Zuni," *Journal of American Folklore* 31 (1918): 256–63; "Mothers and Children at Laguna," *Man* 17–18 (1919): 34–38; "Mothers and Children at Zuni, New Mexico," *Man* 19 (1919): 168–73; "Waiyautitsa of Zuni, New Mexico," *Scientific Monthly* 9 (1919): 443–57. These essays have all been reprinted in Babcock, *Pueblo Mothers and Children*. See also Babcock's introduction, "Elsie Clews Parsons and the Pueblo Con-

struction of Gender," and Pauline Turner Strong's introduction to Elsie Clews Parsons, *Pueblo Indian Religion*, vol. 1 (Chicago: University of Chicago Press, 1995).

129. Elsie Clews Parsons, "Higher Education of Women and the Family," *American Journal of Sociology* 14, no. 6 (1909): 758–65.

130. Elsie Clews Parsons, *The Old Fashioned Woman: Primitive Fancies about the Sex* (New York: G. Putnam and Sons, 1913), 24.

131. Elsie Clews Parsons, *Social Rule: A Study of the Will to Power* (New York: G. Putnam and Sons, 1916), 44.

132. Ibid., 53–54.

133. Ibid., 55.

134. Parsons, "Waiyautitsa," 443.

PART TWO

Gender as Constitutive of Social Science

Hull-House Maps and Papers: Social Science as Women's Work in the 1890s

KATHRYN KISH SKLAR

THIS ESSAY views early women social scientists in the United States through the experience of Florence Kelley, a leading member of that group. Between 1892 and 1894 Kelley was closely involved in the production of *Hull-House Maps and Papers: A Presentation of Nationalities and Wages in a Congested District of Chicago, Together with Comments and Essays on Problems Growing Out of the Social Conditions* (1895).[1] She arranged its publication, authored two of its papers, and supervised the creation of its pathbreaking maps. The result was the single most important work by American women social scientists before 1900.

In November 1882 Kelley, then a recent Cornell graduate, published a pronouncement on the need for women to work as social scientists. Contained in an article, "Need Our Working Women Despair?" that analyzed the plight of wage-earning and professional women, Kelley's statement reflected her society's sex-segregated division of labor, but it also showed how women could turn that division to their advantage. "In the field of sociology there is brain work waiting for women which men cannot do," she wrote, emphasizing the compassionate character of recent social science.

> While the science of man was a science of wealth, rest and self-interest, there was slight inducement for women to touch it. The new social science has humane interest, and can never be complete without help from women.

Women were a necessary and integral part of the "brain work" of social science, she insisted.

> It is the science of human relations. These must be studied as they exist, with patient care; but exact tabulation of facts is the beginning only; afterward comes the work of interpretation. That can be complete only when accomplished by the whole human consciousness, i.e., by that two-fold nature, masculine and feminine, which expresses itself as a whole in human relations. Any attempt made by a part of the race to explain phenomena produced by complementary beings must be inadequate.[2]

Here Kelley expressed a complex truth about the relationship between American women and social science in the second half of the nineteenth century:

while social science expertise in many ways made the men and women who used it more equal, it also deepened the distinctions between them. That is, it accentuated the "masculine and feminine" aspects of human identity.

Ten years later as she was working on the components of *Hull-House Maps and Papers*, Kelley stood preeminent among a generation of college-trained women social scientists who worked not in universities but in women's reform organizations. The power and influence of this group of women outside academic life derived very significantly from their ability to maintain their own social science–oriented institutions, conduct their own social science studies, and advance their own social science goals. They only occasionally marched in the same processions as the (mostly male) social scientists of academia; generally they carried their own banners and kept step with their own music.

Historians have only recently begun to study American women social scientists who were not affiliated with universities—that is to say, women who used social science methods before 1900. The first to broach the topic was William Leach in his 1980 book, *True Love and Perfect Union: The Feminist Reform of Sex and Society*, which focused on the decades preceding 1880. In 1982 Margaret Rossiter's book, *Women Scientists in America: Struggles and Strategies to 1940*, and Rosalind Rosenberg's *Beyond Separate Spheres: Intellectual Roots of Modern Feminism* reminded us that women social scientists in the early decades of the twentieth century established small but important beachheads in the new social science disciplines then taking shape within universities. Mary Jo Deegan's *Jane Addams and the Men of the Chicago School, 1892–1918* (1988) reclaimed Jane Addams as a sociologist occupying a central place in that discipline around 1900, despite her lack of a university affiliation. Ellen Fitzpatrick's recent book, *Endless Crusade: Women Social Scientists and Progressive Reform*, focuses on Edith Abbott, Katharine Bement Davis, Frances Kellor, Sophonisba Breckinridge, and "how academic social science helped influence Progressive social reform."[3] These women inherited many of the same constraints that dominated the lives of their nonacademic predecessors. For them, social science served as the same two-edged sword. On the one hand it supplied them with language and analytic tools equal to those of their male peers. On the other hand it deepened their identification with female-specific topics and issues.

In this respect Kelley's experience, along with that of her colleagues—Jane Addams, Julia Lathrop, Grace Abbott, Lillian Wald, and others born before 1880 who affiliated with the social settlement movement—is paradigmatic for women reformers in the Progressive Era generally. The more capable they became in addressing social problems, the more closely they became affiliated with female-specific social problems. *Hull-House Maps and Papers*, published in 1895, exemplified this process. Five of its ten articles focused on what might be called female-specific issues: sweatshop labor, Cook County charities, child labor, labor organizations for working women, and the work of Hull House residents. Of the remaining five articles, one was titled "Receipts and Expenditures of Cloakmakers in Chicago, Compared with Those of That Trade in New York," and three described different ethnic groups in the settlement neighborhood. But the most significant of these exceptions were an article analyzing the volume's maps and, of course, the maps themselves, based on data collected by agents employed by the U.S. Department of Labor under the direction of Florence Kelley. Yet in a larger sense the entirety of *Hull-House Maps and Papers* was the product of female social science, since it was collectively produced by the residents of a female institution. Thus a full understanding of the volume requires us to consider the origins of gender-specific social science in the United States. Two dimensions of gender relations in early social science seem especially crucial to such an effort: its institutional setting and its moral values.

.   .   .

Historical writings on women and early social science have overlooked the institutional connections between "traditional" women's organizations and emerging social science in the 1860s. In that decade social science readily and enthusiastically incorporated women's institutions and women's issues. Women were not only present at the birth of American social science; they came with its territory. We know that Caroline Dall (1822–1912), author of *The College, the Market, and the Court* (1867), was a cofounder of the American Social Science Association, and that by 1874 six of the thirteen members of the ASSA board were women.[4] William Leach has described the multitude of women's social science associations that sprang into being in the 1870s and 1880s, and the general compatibility of social science and feminism in that era.[5] Yet the centrality of women in the American Social Science Association in the 1870s had earlier roots. It came from women's benevolent and charitable institutions, which since the 1830s had employed rational approaches to solving social distress. For example, in their efforts to improve education for free black girls in the 1840s members of the Philadelphia Female Anti-Slavery Society systematically visited all black schools in the city before determining to launch their own new school.[6] Initially, these modest efforts at rationalized benevolence carried no meaning beyond the moral or social goals they served; the technique itself was not empowered or valued. After 1870, social science techniques *were* empowered and valued, and so too were women's efforts to use them to solve social problems.

A good example of the way that women and women's interests were institutionally incorporated into American social science in its early years can be seen in the prominence of women in three of the five divisions of the American Social Science Association in the 1880s: "Education," "Public Health," and "Social Economy." (The other two were "Jurisprudence" and "Finance.") "Social Economy" was decisively female-dominated. Franklin Sanborn, head of the division in 1887, characterized "Social Economy" as "the feminine gender of Political Economy" because it was "very receptive of particulars" and dealt with "Social welfare."[7] Women responded to this friendliness in social science by forming their own organizations as well as by joining those led by men. As

William Leach has shown, in New York in the early 1870s women formed the New York City Sociological Club, the Women's Progressive Association, and the Ladies Social Science Association.[8]

Kelley's experience as a Cornell undergraduate exemplified the difficulty women had in eluding gendered features of social science. Raised in an elite Philadelphia family of mixed Quaker and Unitarian backgrounds, the daughter of William Durrah Kelley, who served fifteen consecutive terms in the U.S. House of Representatives between 1860 and 1890, she was reading governmental reports at the age of ten and began using the Library of Congress at the age of twelve. In 1878 in the fall of her junior year, Kelley cofounded the Cornell Social Science Club; her signature was the first to endorse the club's constitution, and she was elected secretary. "We students have formed a Social Science club which vows its intention of discussing 'all live questions social, moral, and political,'" she wrote her father.[9] According to the club's minutes, its purpose was "to give a broader culture to its members by making them familiar with the vital questions of the day." But the gendered approach to those questions can be seen in the fact that, as the club's only female member, she sponsored the only woman to speak before the club during her years at Cornell. (The guest lecturer was Mrs. Clara Neymann of New York City who spoke on "Rationalism in Germany," at the club's first meeting.)[10] Reflecting her orientation toward female-specific issues at Cornell, Kelley's honors thesis, "Some Aspects of the Legal History of the Child since Blackstone," forcefully analyzed recent social, legislative, and judicial changes that permitted the state to intervene in family life to protect the interests of children.[11]

These institutional sources of gendered social science deepened in the late 1880s and early 1890s, when women escaped the political repression experienced by male social scientists in those years. Located in universities, many leading male social scientists had nowhere else to go when they were attacked for political bias by powerful persons in those institutions. Henry Carter Adams at Cornell in 1886, Richard T. Ely at Wisconsin in 1893, and Edward W. Bemis at the University of Chicago in 1894 were among the many university social science faculty who were either fired or threatened with firing for advocating "radical" ideas. Richard Ely typified the accommodationist response to this threat when he recanted his radicalism during a trial staged by the University of Wisconsin Board of Regents in 1894. He declared himself "a conservative rather than a radical" and withdrew from the American Institute of Christian Sociology, which he had helped found in 1893.[12] "Objectivity" took precedence over advocacy as the most basic value of the new university disciplines.

Situated as they often were in their own institutions outside academic life, women were sheltered from this political repression. While this purging of opinion was taking place among university social scientists, the social settlement movement grew by leaps and bounds, attracting women and men who continued the older social science heritage that combined a "hands-on" approach to social welfare work with advocacy for social change. In 1891 there were six social settlements in the United States; in 1897, seventy-four; by 1910, over four hundred.[13] Most male settlement leaders were ministers. While most settlements (including Hull House) included residents of both sexes, almost all of these institutions were clearly identifiable as "male" or "female" by the gender of their chief resident. The settlement movement offered more to women than it did to men because women lacked the ministerial and professorial alternatives available to their male colleagues. Women's settlements and other women's organizations enabled a generation of college-trained women to forge lifelong commitments to social science–based reform organizations that were independent of the political climate in universities.[14] These same organizations also channeled women's energies deeper in gender-specific topics and issues.

Florence Kelley's own career exemplified this process in fascinating ways. Confined within gendered limits, she and her colleagues constructed an effective bridge to the "whole human consciousness" by focusing on working-class women and using them as a means of constructing a class analysis of contemporary society. In this way they used gender as a surrogate for class. Thus Florence Kelley, as the chief factory inspector of the state of Illinois at the time that *Hull-House Maps and Papers* was published, was appointed primarily because of her expertise in combating the spread of sweatshop labor in Chicago, a phenomenon associated with wage-earning women and children. She extended that expertise to embrace a critique of the working conditions of men, but her political-social-rhetorical base was female.[15]

Hull-House Maps and Papers exemplified this base. In it Kelley and her colleagues combined female-specific issues with social science methods to move themselves closer to the center of political power. The main power of social science in their hands was its ability to explain the causes of social ills. Kelley's essay on child labor, for example, summarized data about the industrial employment of children in the United States: "it is not where labor is scarce, but where competition for work is keenest, that the per cent of children is largest in the total number employed."[16] Her causal explanation led to policy suggestions. For example, she concluded, "there has been and can be no improvement in wages while tenement-house manufacture is tolerated." Thus like men, women used social science to gain leverage for particular policies in the public domain. Yet while women participated in social science discourse as equals with men, they worked within their own institutions and maintained their own legislative program.

Important as is this "institutional" perspective on the history of early women social scientists in the United States, however, it is not the whole story. It explains why women were active within American social science, but it cannot explain why Kelley and her cohort put social science methods to such effective use in shaping the transition from the "liberal" state of the early nineteenth century to the regulatory "positive" state of the early twentieth century. It explains their presence within social science but not their power in the polity.

One important source of their power, which has been underappreciated in our understanding of social science in general and of women social scientists in particular, was the moral emphasis within early social science in the United States. Entrenched American traditions of limited government meant that social science was not only an important arm of public policy but also a crucial means of overturning the fundamental premises of the liberal, laissez-faire state. In England, France, and Germany social science served as an important arm of public policy in the late nineteenth and early twentieth centuries, but in none of those nations was government qua government so suspect as it was in the United States. Therefore, in the United States more than elsewhere in the industrializing West, social science acquired something of the character of a moral crusade against social Darwinist laissez-faire public policies. The gendered aspects of early social science were constructed within this strongly moral context.

A good example of the moral roots of American social science in the 1860s was Franklin Sanborn, chief founder in 1865 of the American Social Science Association and the association's secretary from 1873 until 1897. In 1859 Sanborn had been a major financial supporter of John Brown's raid on Harpers Ferry in 1859.[17] Throughout his long career Sanborn linked antebellum moral values with a degree of state activism unknown in the antebellum era. In the pages of the *Journal of Social Science* he persistently urged "that civilization itself is an affair of . . . mutuality of help among individuals," and denounced "The chimera of non-interference by government," which "has been conjured up so many times to thwart wise statesmanship and a decent public policy."[18]

Sanborn's ally in this moral view of the activist state was Richard T. Ely, who founded the American Economic Association in 1885 for the express purpose of discrediting social Darwinist theories and laissez-faire public policies. At the AEA's founding Ely appealed to religious values.

> We wish to accomplish certain practical results in the social and financial world, and believing that our work lies in the direction of practical Christianity, we appeal to the church, the chief of the social forces in this country, to help us, to support us, and to make our work a complete success, which it can by no possibility be without her assistance.[19]

Ely did not have women in mind when he voiced this religious appeal, but his emphasis on "practical Christianity" inevitably encouraged women to join him. Early AEA members included about fifty-five women—slightly less than 10 percent of the whole, but a much larger proportion than could be found in analogous professional organizations in law or the ministry. (Interestingly enough, women protested against institutional sex segregation at AEA conventions in the 1880s, boycotting a separate reception arranged for female members when they were excluded from the association's main reception.)[20]

The transition from a liberal to an activist state in the United States was bumpier and fraught with more difficulties than was the case in England or Europe, and the moral commitment of women social scientists gave an essential boost to that transition. Their ability to construct moral arguments on behalf of less privileged social groups—immigrants, workers exposed to industrial hazards, women and men working more than ten hours a day, poor families generally, child laborers—was central to the creation of the "welfare state." Their task was not only to justify particular gender-specific social programs but to justify the validity of *any* social initiative by the state.[21]

This Kelley and her colleagues did with great persistence and skill, utilizing their politically autonomous institutions to emphasize the need for state initiatives with regard to women and children. As we will see, this moral stance was emphatically evident in *Hull-House Maps and Papers*. "Objectivity" did not constrain their language. Of course some of their moralism was misplaced, some exaggerated, some downright hurtful.[22] But we need to understand it as flowing from the intersection of their own institutions, the values inherent in American social science, and intractable traditions of limited government in the United States.

.   .   .

As Kelley's 1882 manifesto about women and social science demonstrated, the college-trained women of her generation were in a position to make larger contributions to social change than their mothers and grandmothers had been able to achieve through women's traditions of voluntary associations. Those traditions, which had taken shape in the economic, social, and intellectual contexts of the 1830s through the 1850s, were ineffective in the face of the scale of social problems introduced in the 1870s and 1880s.[23] Economically, rapid industrialization was generating struggles between capital and labor on an unprecedented national scale, accompanied by unprecedented bloodshed. Socially, millions of immigrants from eastern and southern Europe were beginning to reconstitute the American working class. Intellectually, the "humane" social science of the American Social Science Association, which since its founding in 1865 had been sustained by older values of radical individualism, now was challenged by evolutionary modes of thought that seemed to undermine human agency. Social Darwinism and its laissez-faire consequences for public policy mocked these older earnest notions of social intervention on behalf of the poor or needy. These economic, social, and intellectual changes demanded new, more systematic, approaches to social problems.[24]

In 1883 Lester Ward's *Dynamic Sociology* marked the beginning of a new era in which Sanborn's radical individualism was replaced within reform-oriented social science theory by a more organic view of social relations and the impact of "mind" on social progress. Evolutionary modes of thought, previously the enemy of state intervention, now were harnessed to it. Radical antebellum reformers had a love-hate relationship with government—loving its potential for ensuring individual rights, but hating its ability to sustain corrupt social hierarchies. This dualism dissolved in the 1880s, when organic views of society blurred the distinction between state and social order, naturalizing the relation between the two. For many social scientists in the 1890s the question became:

how could the power invested in social institutions like church and state best be brought to serve the interests of social progress?—especially in the American political context, where traditions of limited government inhibited state action.[25] Needing more skills to answer such questions than she could acquire through voluntary associations or during her undergraduate training at Cornell, Florence Kelley applied for graduate study to the University of Pennsylvania but was rejected on the grounds of her gender. Instead, she traveled in Europe after her family assigned her the task of accompanying her older brother while he recovered from alcoholism. There she encountered a Cornell acquaintance, M. Carey Thomas, who advised her to study at the University of Zurich, an institution that not only admitted women but—unlike Oxford or Cambridge— actually awarded them degrees.[26]

Joined in Zurich by her mother and younger brother in 1883–84, Kelley studied government and law. Duplicating the experience of Richard T. Ely, W.E.B. Du Bois, and other early social scientists who studied in Germany, she found in German evolutionary thought ideas that countered social Darwinism much more effectively than did British empiricism. Indeed, through her conversion to socialism she gained a wholly new perspective on social problems that would never have been possible had she studied at the University of Pennsylvania. Aware of "baffling human problems" at home and abroad, she wrote in a brief autobiography,

> here in Zurich among students from many lands, was the philosophy of Socialism, its assurance flooding the minds of youth and the wage-earners with hope that, within the inevitable development of modern industry, was the coming solution.[27]

Kelley's conversion to socialism was solidified by her marriage to a Jewish socialist medical student from Poland, Lazare Wishnewetzky. After her marriage she began translating the writings of Marx and Engels, her most important work being that of Engels's *Condition of the Working Class in England in 1844*, a study that placed early factory reports and other forms of British social science into evolutionary context. Alienated from her family and former friends, but thoroughly immersed in new "materialist" perspectives on social science and committed to her new life, she gave birth to three children in three years.[28]

Florence Kelley returned to New York with her family in 1886 and, with Lazare, joined the Socialist Labor Party. Her insistent advocacy of the writings of Marx and Engels, combined with her forceful manner at meetings not usually attended by women, earned her expulsion from the party in 1887. Thereupon, she returned to her earlier interest in promoting the welfare of children through state intervention. By 1889 she had become the nation's most serious and systematic critic of efforts by state bureaus of labor statistics to collect data on and recommend legislation against child labor. Apart from the U.S. Census, which before 1890 was dismantled after every decadal census and assumed no responsibility for the advancement of social science, state bureaus of labor statistics were the only governmental agencies gathering social data in the United

States. Yet these bureaus were often ineffective because they were caught in the political cross fire between state legislatures and organized labor. In June 1889, in Hartford, at the Seventh Annual Convention of Commissioners of State Bureaus of Labor, Florence Kelley presented a thorough critique of their moral timidity and methodological inadequacy. Meanwhile Lazare's medical practice faltered and he began physically abusing her. Sometime around Christmas 1891, she borrowed money from a neighboring governess and fled with the children to Chicago.[29]

There Kelley joined a group of talented women reformers at Hull House, founded four years earlier by Jane Addams and Ellen Gates Starr, as a social settlement in the Nineteenth Ward of Chicago, to build civic institutions and further social reform in the district. In this female institution her training as a social scientist finally took root in fertile ground. Kelley's children boarded with the family of reformer Henry Demarest Lloyd and his wife Jessie Bross Lloyd in suburban Winnetka. The settlement offered her a radically different but extremely satisfying alternative to married family life. She wrote her mother:

> We are all well, and the chicks are happy. I have fifty dollars a month and my board and shall have more soon as I can collect my wits enough to write. I have charge of the Bureau of Labor of Hull House here and am working in the lines which I have always loved. I do not know what more to tell you except this, that in the few weeks of my stay here I have won for the children and myself many and dear friends whose generous hospitality astonishes me.[30]

Her opportunities for social observation were magnificent. As she wrote to Engels, "I am learning more in a week of the actual conditions of proletarian life in America than any previous year."

> We have a colony of efficient and intelligent women living in a working men's quarter with the house used for all sorts of purposes by about a thousand persons a week. The last form of its activity is the formation of unions of which we have three, the cloakmakers, the shirt makers, and the book makers.[31]

Here as never before was the chance for women to connect "brain work" with social realities.

Kelley's first major employment as a Hull House resident came in May 1892, when she was appointed as a special agent of the Illinois Bureau of Labor Statistics to "investigate the sweating system in Chicago with its attendant child labor."[32] She had suggested herself for such work soon after her arrival, but the post took some time to develop. "Miss Addams is wirepulling with fair prospect of success for a position here in the bureau of labor statistics for me," she had written her mother in mid-March.[33] Popular furor over sweatshop labor—launched by a woman journalist's exposé, and sustained by an investigation by the Chicago Trades and Labor Assembly—created the need for such a report, and Kelley convinced the bureau that she was the person to research and write it.[34]

Soon after her appointment Kelley proudly informed Engels of her new status in a letter that enclosed the "schedule" used to record data at the household and shop level. "For a full schedule, I receive the munificent compensation of fifty cents," she wrote. "This is piece work for the government with no regular salary. It remains to be seen how many I can fill in a month." She was expected to supervise "1000 schedules to be filled in by 'sweaters' victims' in the clothing trades." Among these were "Poles, Bohemians, Neapolitans, Sicilians, and Russian Hebrews." "The work consists in shop visitation followed by house to house visitation and I find my polyglot acquisitions invaluable. The fact of living directly among the wage earners is also an immense help."[35] Crucial in getting her the special agent position in the first place, her location at Hull House was also critical in her successful completion of this important "brain work."

.   .   .

A year later Kelley began work on what were to become the maps of *Hull-House Maps and Papers* (*HHM&P*). Authored and compiled by residents of the settlement, and published in 1895 as part of the Library of Economics and Politics, under the general editorship of Richard T. Ely, professor of economics at the University of Wisconsin, the book's essays called attention to the innovative work of the burgeoning new settlement movement. Uneven in quality and reflecting the diverse talents of settlement residents, in many ways the articles convey more reliable information about the day-to-day life of the settlement than about the larger city. Some residents jokingly called the volume "the jumble book."[36] Nevertheless, the volume's maps were unique in contemporary American social science, and they deserve to be better known.

These maps were the American equivalent of Charles Booth's stunning "Descriptive Map of London Poverty," published in five parts in 1891 with volume 2 of *Life and Labour of the People in London*—a study that eventually reached seventeen volumes.[37] Until the publication of the multivolume *Pittsburgh Survey* in 1909, *HHM&P* represented the state of the art of social science analysis of working-class urban life in the United States.[38]

In many ways *HHM&P* imitated Booth's volumes. Both works contained maps that vividly depicted social conditions; both were collectively produced. Both were framed by moral approaches to social problems, and both expected their analysis to shape public policy. Both gave special attention to questions about labor, ethnicity, and geography. And, perhaps most significant, both were undertaken on a voluntary basis by nongovernmental agencies. These similarities reveal the multiplicity of shared Anglo-American traditions that informed the two works.

Yet differences between *HHM&P* and *Life and Labour of the People in London* point to revealing dissimilarities in the American and British contexts, which in turn lead us back to the female identity of the American authors. Most obvious were the different scales of the two works and the degree to which their authors were committed to social science as a handmaiden to social change.

Booth's was the lifetime project of an independently wealthy, gifted amateur whose main energies went into his business career. Though his palatial family residence, Gracedieu Manor, placed him in the wealthiest rank of English society, Booth had a lifelong fascination with the lives of the poor. He began his project by outlining his rigorous methods in papers presented to the Royal Statistical Society, which later became the base of his operations. He quickly attracted loyal assistants, seven of whom were employed on the essays for volume 1, published in 1889. Three of these were residents of Toynbee Hall, the original social settlement and the prototype for all others, including Hull House, even though Toynbee Hall excluded women. Booth's most talented assistant was his wife's younger cousin, Beatrice Potter (later Beatrice Webb), who like Florence Kelley was seeking work commensurate with her talents. Booth made her "aware that every conclusion derived from observation or experiment had to be qualified as well as verified by the relevant statistics."[39] Although Booth was the presiding genius behind the inquiry, its collective nature was especially visible in the production of the maps accompanying volume 2, published in 1891. For these he utilized the services of "School Board Visitors," who classified every block in London by estimating the average income of families on it. Some specific households were visited in parts of East London, but the scale of the project forced him to rely on more general estimates. These were then reviewed by agents of the Charity Organization Society. His goal was, above all, to compile accurate information.[40]

The Hull House volume, by contrast, was a much smaller production by women who saw social action rather than social surveys as their chief lifework. As Jane Addams wrote in the preface to *HHM&P*, the energies of Hull House residents "have been chiefly directed, not towards sociological investigation, but to constructive work."[41] Indeed it was Florence Kelley's employment as the paid agent of the U.S. Bureau of Labor that generated the volume's chief claim to fame—its extensive and detailed maps of Chicago's Nineteenth Ward.

Pathbreaking maps characterized both studies. This was no accident, for maps, with their incisive depiction of the interactions between population and geography, were especially appropriate tools for analyzing the problems of late-nineteenth-century cities. Maps evoked the physical dimensions of those problems and their spatial scale, exposing the realities of social problems more concretely and more convincingly than prose descriptions or statistical charts. Through their omniscient perspective on social problems, maps empowered the observer in ways that prose or statistics could not match. Through their exacting detail the maps of *HHM&P* also depicted, along with the concentration of certain ethnic groups in certain blocks, a striking range of moral relationships: between poverty and race; between the isolated brothel district and the rest of the ward; between the very poor who lived in crowded, airless rooms in the rear of tenements and those with more resources in the front; between the observer and the observed. If in many respects social science replaced religion as the interpreter of moral priorities, maps best exemplified this substitution. They conveyed more than information. They also communicated moral imperatives. If this was true of maps generally, it was doubly

true, given their magnificent scale, of the five Booth and two *HHM&P* maps
(they measured twenty-four by twenty-two inches and forty-five by fourteen
inches, respectively).

Revealingly, whereas Booth's maps resulted from a master plan for mapping poverty throughout London, *HHM&P*'s maps were a spin-off of Florence
Kelley's very practical need for an income capable of supporting her and her
children while she campaigned against sweatshop labor in Chicago. She described her routine to Henry Demarest Lloyd in November 1892, with only a
passing reference to the work for Carroll Wright and the U.S. Department of
Labor that would eventually produce the remarkable maps of *Hull-House Maps
and Papers*.

> I have swarmed off from Hull House into a flat nearby with my mother and my
> bairns. . . .
>
> I am teaching in the Polk Street Night School Monday to Friday evening inclusive.
> By day I am a "temporary agent" in the employ of the Department of Labor—Carroll
> D. Wright—and, on Dec. 4 (Sunday) I go to Geneva, [Illinois,] Dec. 11th to Madison
> to tout for Hull House under the auspices of Mr. Ely, and Dec. 17th and 18th to Oak
> Park to speak on Hull House and the Sweating System on Sat. and Sunday eves. Me
> Voila! There is only a limited amount of me at best; and, such as it is, it works twelve
> hours on weekdays for "grub and debts" and on Sundays it goes out of town to tell the
> outlying public how life looks in the nineteenth. By way of consoling the small fry for
> these absences I take one with me. Puss [Margaret, her daughter] is going to Geneva
> and Ko [Nicholas, her son] to Madison with me.[42]

Although Booth resided briefly in working-class London neighborhoods, and
although he utilized the aid of settlement residents, his work was not undertaken in the heat of the battle for social change. Kelley's was.

Did this lend any advantages to Kelley's work? The obvious disadvantage lay
with her inability to survey the entire city and document the extent of its poverty as Booth had done for London, showing that about 30 percent of the entire
London population lived in poverty. Kelley's work was also constrained by
limits imposed by her employer, the U.S. Department of Labor. Yet these limits
could be turned to her advantage. Her work as a "special agent" for Carroll
Wright in the winter of 1892–93 lay in selecting the portion of Chicago to be
studied for *The Slums of Baltimore, Chicago, New York, and Philadelphia*
(1894). She convinced Wright that his study should focus exclusively on the
Nineteenth Ward, where Hull House was located.[43] This decision enabled her
to study a small area in minute detail. The labor for that work arrived in the
spring and summer of 1893 in the form of four government "schedule men" and
their piles of printed questionnaires.[44]

Kelley seized that opportunity to produce the unprecedented maps of
HHM&P. The four agents worked full time between April 6th and July 15th,
visiting "each house, tenement, and room" in the Nineteenth Ward, and collecting data about tenements and their inhabitants, which they then gave to
Florence Kelley. Before she sent the information on to Wright, however, "one

of the Hull-House residents"—almost certainly Agnes Holbrook—copied "the nationality of each individual, his wages when employed, and the number of weeks he was idle during the year beginning April 1, 1892."[45] Hull House residents then transferred the nationality and wage information in graphic form onto maps of the ward.

This created vivid spatial depictions of the range and distribution of ethnicities and weekly incomes throughout the district. Colored keys attached to the maps explained the symbols, fifteen for the "Nationalities Map," six for the "Wages Map." First used in public health maps in the 1840s, after 1850 such color coding became increasingly feasible through the development of lithographic techniques. Yet not until the 1860s was it widely used—and then still primarily for the depiction of urban sanitary conditions.[46] Thus Kelley and Holbrook's application of this technique to measure poverty and its extension to nationalities and wages in the Hull House maps represented a distinct departure. (Though Kelley and Holbrook seem to have contemplated an "unemployment" map, and collected data for it, none was ever produced.)

While the government enumerators collected a vast array of data in response to the sixty-four questions posed on their schedules for each household, and Carroll Wright used those data to produce dozens of tables in the *Slums* volume, the "Nationalities Map" and the "Wages Map" utilized only two types of data, but by displaying spatial relationships these maps told more than all of Wright's charts combined. For they revealed systematic patterns that informed many of the empirical details collected by the agents. As Agnes Holbrook put it, "The partial representation here offered is in more graphic and minute form; and the view of each house and lot in the charts, suggesting just how members of various nationalities are grouped and disposed, and just what rates of wages are received in the different streets and sections, may have its real as well as its picturesque value."[47] These large maps are unique for their period, and, apart from Booth's, we have none to compare them with. But Booth's do not map ethnicity, and they do not contain information at the household level.

In her "Map Notes and Comments" Holbrook paid tribute to "Mr. Charles Booth's maps of London [which] have served as warm encouragement." Although the small area of the Hull House maps was dwarfed by "the vast area covered by Mr. Booth's incomparable studies," Holbrook thought "the two works have much in common." She thought that the "aim and spirit" were similar, but that the "greater minuteness" of the Chicago survey would entitle it to a rank of its own, both as a "photographic reproduction" and "as an illustration of a method of research."[48]

Holbrook told the reader a great deal about their methods, for the maps would, she hoped, "be of value, not only to the people of Chicago who desire correct and accurate information concerning the foreign and populous parts of the town, but to the constantly increasing body of sociological students more widely scattered." Conscious of this scholarly audience, she defended their methods. "The facts set forward are as trustworthy as personal inquiry and intelligent effort could make them," she said. Not only was each house, tenement, and room visited, "but in many cases the reports obtained from one person were corroborated by many others and statements from different workers at the same trades and occupations, as to wages and unemployed seasons, served as mutual confirmation."[49] Referring to Florence Kelley, Holbrook continued, "experience in similar investigation and long residence in the neighborhood enable the expert in charge to get at all particulars with more accuracy than could have attended the most conscientious efforts of a novice."

Holbrook discussed some of the methodological choices they had made. Where a building contained residents of more than one ethnicity, the mapmakers allocated space proportionate to the number of individuals in the "Nationalities Map," and to the number of families in the "Wages Map." Thus the basic unit for the "Nationalities Map" was the individual, while for the "Wages Map" it was the family. Yet, oddly enough, the mapmakers defined as a "family" every self-supporting individual—"every boarder, and each member of the family who pays board"—classifying him or her as a separate wage-earner and therefore a separate "family."[50] In spite of this atomistic categorization system, Holbrook recognized the collective process of the family wage economy:

> In this neighborhood generally a wife and children are sources of income as well as avenues of expenses; and the women wash, do "home finishing" on ready-made clothing, or pick and sell rags; the boys run errands and "shine;" the girls work in factories, get places as cash-girls, or sell papers on the streets; and the very babies sew buttons on knee-pants and shirt-waists, each bringing in a trifle to fill out the scanty income. The theory that "every man supports his own family" is as idle in a district like this as the fiction that "every one can get work if he wants it."[51]

Yet in spite of this important conceptual leap that recognized the family economy, she nevertheless excluded the wages of any board-paying family member from the family economy.

Whether based on individuals or on families, these calculations did not indicate population density. Density (as well as the presence of a boardinghouse) could be inferred where one house was represented as containing "negroes, Italians, Chinamen, Russians, Poles, Germans, Swiss, French-Canadians, Irish, and Americans," but one had to read Holbrook's notes to learn that "sixty men sleep every night in one basement room at No. 133 Ewing Street," or that the Negro and Italian districts were the most densely populated, or that "almost everybody" kept boarders in the most densely populated eastern portion of the ward.[52] However, the map did reveal that in tenements containing more than one nationality, Italians or Russian Jews usually occupied the rear, and that Jews and Italians rarely inhabited the same buildings.

The Nineteenth Ward included a red-light district, the substantial scale of which was abundantly clear on the "Wages Map," which contained a special color code—white—for brothels. The researchers classified as brothels only those places that defined themselves as such; "the many doubtful 'dressmakers'" were also classified according to their own statements.[53] Matching these residences with the "Nationalities Map" reveals that most of these prostitutes were American-born women. According to Holbrook, "few of the girls" were Chicago-born, most having migrated from central and eastern states. Some, however, were Irish, and some black. Holbrook noted that "in some houses the whites and blacks are mixed."[54]

The maps were not without problems. Native-born white Americans were represented on the "Nationalities Map" in white, indicating the presence of American-born children of American-born parents, as well as American-born children of foreign-born parents, who, culturally speaking, were actually part of their ethnic communities. Despite or perhaps because of her pride in the maps, Holbrook readily acknowledged some methodological limitations. "Carelessness and indifference on the part of those questioned" doubtless led to errors. Change and irregularity of employment probably generated inaccuracies. During the period of the investigation buildings and tenants changed in ways that could not be reflected in the schedules. Families moved constantly. Yet in spite of these limitations, she thought that the "charts paint faithfully the character of the region."[55]

In notes designed "to make the maps intelligible" rather than to furnish independent data, Holbrook described life within the "third of a square mile" they embraced. Her own values were clear, and she did not pretend to objectivity. She noted the presence of "a criminal district which ranks as one of the most openly and flagrantly vicious in the civilized world," and an area that was "the poorest, and probably the most crowded section of Chicago." The main thoroughfares were "semi-business streets," which contained "a rather cheap collection of tobacco-stands, saloons, old-iron establishments, and sordid looking fancy-shops, as well as several factories, and occasional small dwelling-houses tucked in like babies under the arms of industry."[56] Bent figures stitching at basement windows testified to the presence of sweatshops. Signs abounded in Bohemian, German, Russian, and Italian advertising furnished rooms for rent, wineshops, dressmakers, calciminers (for wall whitening), and cobblers, "while the omnipresent midwife is announced in polyglot on every hand." The schedules revealed the presence of eighty-one saloons in this tiny area, "besides a number of 'delicatessen,' 'restauranten,' and cigar-stands where some liquor is sold."[57]

Most of the ward's population lived in rear tenements accessible through alleys. There "the densest crowds of the most wretched and destitute congregate." There urban problems were most acute. "Little idea can be given of the filthy and rotten tenements, the dingy courts and tumble-down sheds, the foul stables and dilapidated outhouses, the broken sewer-pipes, the piles of garbage fairly alive with diseased odors, and of the numbers of children in every room, eating and sleeping in every window-sill, pouring in and out of every door, and seeming literally to pave every scrap of 'yard'. . . . surging in and out of passage-ways, and up and down outside staircases, like a veritable stream of life."[58] Tuberculosis was widespread, child mortality was high, and many babies looked "starved and wan."

While Holbrook paid homage to Charles Booth's example, she and other authors in *HHM&P* conveyed much more distinctly than did the Booth authors their hope of effecting social change. Holbrook insisted that "Hull-House offers these facts more with the hope of stimulating inquiry and action, and evolving new thoughts and methods, than with the idea of recommending its own manner of effort." The searchlight of inquiry "must be steady and persistent if it is to accomplish definite results," she continued, but "merely to state symptoms and go no farther would be idle; but to state symptoms in order to ascertain the nature of disease, and apply, it may be, its cure, is not only scientific, but in the highest sense humanitarian."[59] *Hull-House Maps and Papers* was more than a contribution to knowledge; it was a part of its authors' quest for social change.

.   .   .

Florence Kelley and other women in the social settlement movement occupied an especially fortunate niche in the expanding and partially overlapping worlds of social science and social reform in the 1890s. The splendid maps of *HHM&P* could not have been produced without the institutional resources of Hull House. It drew together the diverse talents of the maps' originators—Florence Kelley's knowledge of social science techniques employed by state bureaus of labor statistics; Agnes Holbrook's appreciation of the value of transcribing social data into graphic form; and the availability of other residents (in addition to Holbrook) to do that transcribing.

Within their privileged setting in the midst of the social environment they studied, Hull House residents continued earlier "humane" social science traditions that joined an appreciation for empirical details to a moral vision of social change. That link was evident in the essays of *Hull-House Maps and Papers*.

The first two of these were hard-hitting attacks on oppressive labor practices: "The Sweating-System," by Florence Kelley, and "Wage-Earning Children," by Kelley and Alzina P. Stevens. These articles marked Kelley's progress as both a social reformer and a social scientist, for they reflected her appointment by Governor John P. Altgeld as Illinois's first chief factory inspector. With a staff of twelve that included Alzina Stevens, an experienced labor organizer who had begun her working life at the age of thirteen in New England textile mills, Kelley was charged with the enforcement of a pathbreaking eight-hour-day law for women and children workers that she herself had drafted. Enacted in 1893, partly through middle-class support mobilized by Jane Addams, that law was the fruit of Kelley's early investigations for the Illinois Bureau of Labor Statistics and the U.S. Department of Labor. The merger of her perspectives as a social scientist and social reformer was visible in her persistent efforts to link social patterns with legislative actions. For example, she wrote that "The condition of the sweaters' victim is a conclusive refutation of the ubiquitous argument that poverty is the result of crime, vice, intemperance, sloth, and unthrift; for the Jewish sweaters' victims are probably more temperate, hard working, and avaricious than any equally large body of wage-earners in America." Yet, she continued, "the reward of work at their trade is grinding poverty, ending only in death or escape to some more hopeful occupation." These conditions led her to conclude that "there has been and can be no improvement in wages while tenement-house manufacture is tolerated."[60]

The same link between social data and social action characterized her essay on child labor. It summarized patterns of the industrial employment of children as revealed in U.S. census data nationally and in Illinois, concluding that "it is not where labor is scarce, but where competition for work is keenest, that the per cent of children is largest in the total number employed."[61] Drawing connections between child labor and oppressive working conditions for adults, the authors pointed out that long years of hard physical labor often disabled fathers by the age of forty, that periodic unemployment among adult men and the "loss of a limb which is regarded as a regular risk in the building-trades and among railroad hands" led to increases in child labor. Revealing the moral grounds of their argument, they insisted upon "the sacred right of children to school-life and healthful leisure," and viewed "the prohibition of child-labor [as] a humanitarian measure, to be adopted in the interest of the children themselves." This could be accomplished, they wrote, "by means of scholarships" in grammar schools. "Ample help to the poorest of the working children," they insisted, would "make our public schools not class institutions, but in deed and in truth the schools of the people, by the people, for the people."[62]

Not all *HHM&P* essays linked social science findings with public policy recommendations. One simply presented data on cloakmakers. One, by Ellen Gates Starr, cofounder of Hull House, urged settlements and schools to help urban dwellers express their need for art. Three were not part of the women's social science tradition; the articles on Chicago's Jewish, Bohemian, and Italian communities demonstrated the settlement's desire to include other perspectives than their own, and to let the ward's ethnic groups speak for themselves.

Two remaining articles, like the volume's first three, demonstrated the ability of women to use social understanding as a moral and political lever for social change. "The Cook County Charities," by Julia C. Lathrop, and Jane Addams's article, "The Settlement as a Factor in the Labor Movement," show that more was happening here than the "domestication of American politics."[63] Women were not only using new methods in their approach to arenas long familiar with their activism; their public culture was expanding to fill crucial gaps in the larger political culture.

This move on their part was due partly to the vitality of their participation in American traditions that linked social understanding with social action, but it was due also to the fact that American men were steering clear of these new fields, leaving them wide open for women to exploit. Neither social scientists, nor civil servants, nor organized labor, nor politicians were competing with Julia Lathrop's construction of a reform agenda for Cook County charities.[64] Florence Kelley's appointment as chief factory inspector for Illinois was made within a set of gendered power relations in which no man equaled her competence both as a social investigator and as a formulator of public policy. One reason for this was her remarkable combination of talents and experience, but others included the persistence of the American tradition of limited government, the lack of a civil service bureaucracy in the United States that might have trained men for such work, the dominance of most public sector jobs by political machines, and the tendency for organized labor to rely on nonpolitical methods to achieve its goals.[65] Middle-class men also formed settlements and generated important social data, but most talented male social scientists were shifting their institutional location from voluntary agencies like the Chautauqua Literary and Scientific Circle and the American Social Science Association to the newly emerging modern research universities.[66] An unusual, reform-minded governor like John P. Altgeld knew only a very small pool of qualified applicants for such an appointment. Not surprisingly, the best-qualified was a woman.

Jane Addams's essay, "The Settlement as a Factor in the Labor Movement," rounded out the volume's presentation of an alternative social vision based on "humane" social science. Focusing on sweatshops in the garment industry around Hull House as an example of modern labor problems, Addams explained why "in industrial affairs lack of organization tends to the helplessness of the isolated worker, and is a menace to the entire community." The settlement could play a useful role, she thought, in accentuating "the ultimate ethical aims of the [labor] movement," since among business interests as well as workers "there is a constant temptation towards a class warfare."[67]

Class warfare raged in its most ferocious modern manifestation in the United States between 1890 and 1920. In no other Western democracy were the interactions between capital and labor so unmediated. Elsewhere through civil service bureauracies, labor parties, or traditions of active government, men used the tools of social science to promote what they saw as the welfare of the whole society. But political traditions of limited government, the absence of civil service bureaucracies, and the lack of a labor party in the United States created few such opportunities for men, increasing the risk of class war on the one hand, and on the other opening opportunities for women reformers. Women like Jane Addams, Florence Kelley, and Julia Lathrop were able to make the most of those opportunities because they could draw on a social science tradition that informed their practical approach and validated their ethical solutions to social problems.

Hull-House Maps and Papers concluded with an appendix, "Outline Sketch Descriptive of Hull House." There Addams itemized the settlement's myriad daily, weekly, and monthly activities, which during an average week attracted two thousand visitors and one hundred teachers, lecturers, or aides. Addams again emphasized the importance of geographical location in this enterprise.

> This centre or "settlement," to be effective, must contain an element of permanency, so that the neighborhood may feel that the interest and fortunes of the residents are identical with their own. The settlement must have an enthusiasm for the possibilities of its locality, and an ability to bring into it and develop from it those lines of thought and action which make for the "higher life."[68]

Florence Kelley echoed that geographic sentiment when she wrote in 1898,

> You must suffer from the dirty streets, the universal ugliness, the lack of oxygen in the
> air you daily breathe, the endless struggle with soot and dust and insufficient water
> supply, the hanging from a strap of the overcrowded street car at the end of your day's
> work . . . if you are to speak as one having authority and not as the scribes in these
> matters of the common, daily life and experience.[69]

Thus, as practiced at Hull House, "social science" was rooted in geography and
the human relations that geography shaped.

Much of the settlement's work was too practical to be called "social science."
A nursery for the babies of working mothers, girls' and boys' clubs for constructive after-school activity, and Sunday concerts could not qualify as such. Revealingly, however, social science appeared in the settlement's activities as a
vehicle for adult discussions of social issues. A framework of social investigation
and social inquiry provided the context for sometimes raucous debates of class
relations. The Working People's Social Science Club was one such context;
others included the Arnold Toynbee Club and the Chicago Question Club. A
French visitor to the first of these called it "a club where social science gladly
uses the language of anarchy." The membership was cosmopolitan, she said,
"plenty of those Russian Jews." She was shocked at the "rage and rancor"
hurled by the working-class audience at the evening's speaker, a University of
Chicago professor, and surprised that "Miss Addams allow[ed] the guests to be
so ill treated." But she was impressed by the respect Addams elicited from the
rough-and-ready working men, who strictly observed the six-minute limit she
suggested for the length of their remarks.[70] Addams later acknowledged that "it
was doubtless owing largely to this club that Hull House contracted its early
reputation for radicalism."[71] Social science smoothed the edges of that radicalism. In a variety of ways, some profound, some superficial, it helped Hull
House bridge the gap between its own middle-class realities and those of its
working-class constituencies. It also demonstrated the competence of Hull
House residents on topics that embraced "masculine" portions of "the whole
human consciousness."

.   .   .

The multiple achievements of *HHM&P*, like those of the settlement itself,
could never have been accomplished without institutional autonomy. Addams
attracted sufficient financial backing from those who trusted her form of "practical Christianity" to permit her to ignore critics who thought she went too far.[72]
Salaried university professors had no such luxury. Yet necessary as it was to the
process by which its residents composed the maps and essays of *HHM&P*, the
settlement's autonomy did not put it in a position to publish the volume unas-
sisted. In this and other ways the power of Hull House residents derived from
their contact with male allies as well as from their own independent institution.
To exercise power of the sort represented in *HHM&P*, women reformers in the
Progressive Era needed to control their own institutions, but they also needed
to tap into the power invested in male-dominated institutions.

Richard Ely was a natural ally for the publication of *HHM&P*. He and Florence Kelley had been corresponding since 1890, and in 1892 she had stayed at the Ely home in Madison. Thereafter her letters usually ended on a personal note—"please give my kind regards to Mrs. Ely."[73] Moreover, Ely's publication series, the Library of Economics and Politics, published by Thomas Crowell of Boston, would bring the Hull House volume to the attention of interested readers. Other volumes that preceded *HHM&P* in the series included William Scott, *Repudiation of State Debts in the United States* (1893); Ely's own *Socialism and Social Reform* (1894); and *American Charities*, by Amos Warner (1894).[74]

The agreement apparently dated from May 1894, when Ely told Kelley that the volume would "be in the market" in September. In June she gave up plans to publish her two essays with a German periodical that paid "liberally and promptly," but by October the book was still delayed. That month Jane Addams entered into its editorial work, writing Ely that she agreed with his criticism of Miss Eaton's paper. "Mrs. Kelley and I have gone over it very carefully," and, she believed, "it is now clearer." She also expressed anxiety that the book's information would be outdated by the time of publication if further delays occurred.[75] "We have letters every week asking about it. Prof. Small told me the other day that he could not 'get on' any longer without it, and we feel that the matter will be so old and out of date if we wait much longer. Mrs. Kelly's office is already making great changes in the condition of the sweater shops in the neighborhood, the Jewish population is rapidly moving Northward, and all the conditions are of course, more or less, unlike what they were July 1st, 1893, when the data for the maps was finished."[76] She wondered if it would help to have Robert Woods, of Andover House, Boston, see Mr. Crowell.

Delays were the least of their problems in November, however, when Ely conveyed Crowell's suggestion that the maps be reduced in size. Kelley responded fiercely, revealing how much the maps meant to her:

> But the disappointment over the delay is trivial in comparison with the dismay which I felt when you suggested cutting the maps. This I positively decline to permit.
>
> The charts are mine to the extent that I not only furnished the data for them but hold the sole permission from the U.S. Department of Labor to publish them. I have never contemplated, and do not now contemplate, any form of publication except as two linen-backed maps or charts, folding in pockets in the cover of the book, similar to Mr. Booth's charts.
>
> If Crowell and Co. do not contemplate this, it will be well to stop work at once, as I can consent to no use of my charts in any other form.[77]

After Ely wrote Addams that he had lost patience with Kelley, Addams explained that Kelley's anger was sparked by "accumulated annoyances" from her work as factory inspector. She assured Ely that she realized it would have been impossible to get the book published without his aid, and that he would "have no further annoyance in regard to the book" from Hull House. A week later Addams wrote Ely yet another soothing letter after the page proofs had been returned to Crowell.[78] Kelley may have upset Ely, but she got her way—the maps were published with linen backs in pockets in the book's cover. A cheaper edition was available without linen backs, but there too the maps appeared in full.

Reviews of the book saluted its close look at one of the nation's most impoverished urban neighborhoods. A New York newspaper was typical. It emphasized the example set by the Hull House report "of how to go about dealing with the problem of congested areas, what to investigate, what to ascertain and how both to investigate and ascertain." Congratulating the residents for copying Booth, whose "monumental example" might well "discourage, if not appall imitation," the review identified the volume's most fundamental characteristic as "precision." "It is quantitative—it counts noses; in other words, it is scientific. Hence it gives a firm point of departure for study: discussion need not be all in the air; there is a base-line, or a bench-mark."[79] The most complete review appeared in *Atlantic Monthly*, which noted that the "industrial conditions of city life" had previously come to "'the reading public' mainly through the medium of fiction and the treatment of fact which pictures and the magazines render easily digestible." The maps of the Hull House volume presented information of new complexity, which the reviewer did not try to summarize, concluding that "the maps render possible an easy apprehension of the nature and condition of the community in which Hull-House is doing its work," but that "the details of what they reveal must be seen upon the maps themselves." This periodical recommended the volume as giving "a very adequate conception of the work done by the American Settlement which has probably had the widest opportunities and activities," and noted the growing familiarity of the middle class with settlement work: "Happily, the time is past when everybody need be told just what these enterprises are."[80]

Samuel Lindsay, reviewing *HHM&P* and two other works in Ely's series in the *Annals of the American Academy*, found the volume "interesting and valuable," and the maps, which "teachers of social science and settlement workers will do well to study," of "equal excellence" with those of Charles Booth.[81] Yet while the maps seemed to be valued by "the reading public," their expense meant that the book was not a profitable publication for Crowell, and it was not reprinted after the first thousand copies were sold.

Mary Jo Deegan has analyzed the neglect of *HHM&P* by university sociologists, as well as their imitation of its methods.[82] In many ways the book's neglect was in keeping with its birth. Dedicated more to social action than to the collection of data, its chief authors, Addams and Kelley, had many more urgent matters demanding their attention than the reception or subsequent treatment of their book. Kelley may have felt that her own obligation was completed when she succeeded in getting the maps printed to her specifications. In 1898 she moved to New York, where she became general secretary of the National Consumers' League, a position she held until her death in 1932. Under Kelley's directorship the NCL became the single most successful lobbying agency on behalf of legislative protections for working women and children—lobbying based on social data, carefully collected and analyzed.[83] In New York Kelley continued until 1926 to live collectively with other women at Lillian Wald's Henry Street Settlement.

More than a century after its publication, however, it is clear that *HHM&P* deserves more attention than it has received—from historians and sociologists alike. It demonstrated an important link between social science and governmental action—a link that ultimately aided the birth of what we now call the welfare state. Precocious for what it anticipated about the future of social inquiry, and valuable for what it revealed about the history of American social science, it set new standards for social investigations. Those standards arose from the most profound appreciation for the importance of geography as the basis for social analysis. They also sprang from the gendered features of contemporary social science.

NOTES

Originally published in *The Social Survey in Historical Perspective, 1880–1940*, ed. Martin Bulmer, Kathryn Kish Sklar, and Kevin Bales © Cambridge University Press, 1991. Reprinted with the permission of Cambridge University Press.

1. [Residents of Hull House,] *Hull-House Maps and Papers: A Presentation of Nationalities and Wages in a Congested District of Chicago, Together with Comments and Essays on Problems Growing Out of the Social Conditions* (Boston: Thomas Crowell & Co., 1895).

2. Florence Kelley, "Need Our Working Women Despair?" *International Review* 13 (November 1882): 517–27. The *International Review* was a New York periodical in which her father published frequently.

3. William Leach, *True Love and Perfect Union: The Feminist Reform of Sex and Society* (New York: Basic Books, 1980); Margaret W. Rossiter, *Women Scientists in America: Struggles and Strategies to 1940* (Baltimore: Johns Hopkins University Press, 1982); Rosalind Rosenberg, *Beyond Separate Spheres: Intellectual Roots of Modern Feminism* (New Haven: Yale University Press, 1982); Mary Jo Deegan, *Jane Addams and the Men of the Chicago School, 1892–1918* (New Brunswick, N.J.: Transactions Books, 1988); Ellen Fitzpatrick, *Endless Crusade: Women Social Scientists and Progressive Reform* (New York: Oxford University Press, 1990).

4. Leach, *True Love and Perfect Union*, 315; Caroline H. Dall, *The College, the Market and the Court, or, Woman's Relation to Education, Labor and Law* (Boston, 1867).

5. Leach, *True Love and Perfect Union*, 292–347.

6. Carolyn Williams, "The Philadelphia Female Anti-Slavery Society, 1833–1873" (Ph.D. diss., University of California, Los Angeles, 1991), chap. 5. See also Lori D. Ginzberg, *Women and the Work of Benevolence: Morality, Politics and Class in the Nineteenth Century United States* (New Haven: Yale University Press, 1990). Women's institutions enabled women to interact with men and men's institutions from positions of collective strength. Within their own institutions women also developed their own leadership, formulated their own goals, and controlled the distribution of their own resources.

7. *Journal of Social Science* 16 (December 1882): 98, quoted in Thomas Haskell, *The Emergence of Professional Social Science: The American Social Science Association*

and the Nineteenth-Century Crisis of Authority (Urbana: University of Illinois Press, 1977), 137.

Limited in its purview as it might be, the Social Economy Division of the American Social Science Association became the chief arm of the association's efforts to influence public policy. In 1881 Sanborn said that the association's "work of agitation and indoctrination" sprang out of "our department of social economy." *Journal of Social Science*, November 1881, 33.

8. Leach, *True Love and Perfect Union*, 317, 139.

9. Florence Kelley to William Durrah Kelley, Ithaca, December 2, 1878, Nicholas Kelley Papers, Box 66, "FK Papers, WDK Letters from His Daughter, 1865–1888."

10. Social Science Club Records, October 30, 1878, Cornell University Archives.

11. See Kathryn Kish Sklar, ed., *Florence Kelley, Notes of Sixty Years: The Autobiography of Florence Kelley* (Chicago: Charles Kerr, 1986), 1–57.

12. Mary O. Furner, *Advocacy and Objectivity: A Crisis in the Professionalization of American Social Science, 1865–1905* (Lexington: University of Kentucky Press, 1975), 150–58.

13. Allen F. Davis, *Spearheads for Reform: The Social Settlements and the Progressive Movement, 1890–1914* (New York: Oxford University Press, 1967), 12.

14. For the history of women on university faculties, see Barbara Miller Solomon, *In the Company of Educated Women: A History of Women and Higher Education in America* (New Haven: Yale University Press, 1985), 57, 133–39, 189, 210.

After 1900 women continued to make important contributions to the development of social surveys in the United States. For example, by creating the Russell Sage Foundation, Margaret Olivia Sage launched the single most important institutional support for American social surveys after 1900. In 1910 the Russell Sage Foundation published, as part of its sponsorship of the *Pittsburgh Survey*, Margaret Byington's *Homestead: The Households of a Mill Town*, which contained the most detailed maps of the six-volume survey and today is probably the survey's most frequently read volume. See John M. Glenn, Lillian Brandt, and F. Emerson Andrews, *Russell Sage Foundation, 1907–1946* (New York: Russell Sage Foundation, 1947), 3–12, and passim for Mrs. Sage's initiative in its founding and the foundation's research agenda before 1946.

The settlement movement's significance for American women reformers was highlighted by that movement's failure to serve the same population in England. There prominent women reformers did not form lifelong affiliations with the movement; instead many married male reformers and worked within male-dominated movements, such as Fabian socialism or the Labour or Liberal Parties. Although the American settlement movement was dominated by women, this was not the case in England. Many talented British women made important contributions to social reform and the history of social surveys through the settlement movement: Florence Bell, Violet Butler, Maude Davies, Eglantyne Jebb, and Maud Pember Reeves, to name a few. Women's settlements in England, beginning with the Women's University Settlement in Southwark (1887) and followed by St. Hilda's, Bethal Green, Lady Margaret Hall, Liverpool Victoria, Birmingham, Passmore Edwards, and others offered women important opportunities for social activism. Yet differences in the social, political, and economic structures in the two societies meant that settlements served different purposes, and one of those differences lay in the degree to which the societies' most politically powerful reformers affiliated with the movement.

I am grateful to Michael Rose for generously sharing his current research on women in the British settlement movement. For the lack of a sustained presence of prominent women reformers in the British social settlement movement, see Martha Vicinus, *Inde-*

pendent Women: Work and Community for Single Women, 1850–1920 (Chicago: University of Chicago Press, 1985). For an example of how the Labour Party provided the single best umbrella for Beatrice Webb, Margaret Llewelyn Davies, Margaret Bonfield, and other contemporary English equivalents of Florence Kelley, see their contributions to *Women and the Labour Party by Various Women Writers*, ed. Marion Phillips (New York: Heubsch, 1918). For the relationship between the British Civil Service and British social settlements, see Standish Meacham, *Toynbee Hall and Social Reform, 1880–1914: The Search for Community* (New Haven: Yale University Press, 1987).

15. Kathryn Kish Sklar, "Hull House as a Community of Women Reformers in the 1890's," *Signs: Journal of Women in Culture and Society* 10 (Summer 1985): 657–77.

16. Florence Kelley, "The Sweating-System," in *HHM&P*, 41 and 50.

17. Benjamin Blakely Hickok, "The Political and Literary Careers of F. B. Sanborn" (Ph.D. diss., Michigan State University, 1953), 135–245; and Haskell, *The Emergence of Professional Social Science*, 49, 129, 216; William R. Brock, *Investigation and Responsibility: Public Responsibility in the United States, 1865–1900* (Cambridge: Cambridge University Press, 1984), 1–57.

18. *Journal of Social Science*, November 1886, 7 and 10.

19. Quoted in James Dombrowski, *The Early Days of Christian Socialism in America* (New York: Columbia University Press, 1936), 51. See also John R. Everett, *Religion in Economics: A Study of John Bates Clark, Richard T. Ely, Simon N. Patten* (New York: King's Crown Press, 1946); and Dorothy Ross, "Socialism and American Liberalism: Academic Thought in the 1880's," *Perspectives in American History* 11 (1977–78): 5–80.

20. Richard T. Ely, *Ground under Our Feet: An Autobiography* (New York: Macmillan, 1938), 147; *Publications of the American Economic Association* 1, Constitution and List of Officers and Members of the American Economic Association, Supplement, American Economic Association, July 1889, 27. This volume listed a total of 604 members; 55 were women. Nine of those fifty-five female members were affiliated with Mount Holyoke College.

21. British social science embraced similar trends. Frances Power Cobbe, a social reformer who later became an advocate of women's rights, led the way within the British Social Science Association. In an 1861 publication she quoted an address by Lord Shaftesbury that commented on "the value and peculiar nature of the assistance" women gave to social science. "Men may do what must be done on a larger scale; but, the instant the work becomes individual, and personal, the instant it requires tact and feeling, from that instant it passes into the hands of women. It is essentially their province, in which may be exercised all their moral powers, and all their intellectual faculties. It will give their full share in the vast operations the world is yet to see." Frances Power Cobbe, "Social Science Congresses and Women's Part in Them," *Macmillan's Magazine*, December 1961, 94. I am grateful to Eileen Janes Yeo for this reference. For more on British women and social science, see her book *The Contest for Social Science: Relations and Representations of Gender and Class* (London: Rivers Oram Press, 1996).

See Fitzpatrick, *Endless Crusade*, for examples of important policy initiatives by women social scientists that were bolstered by moral imperatives. An enormous body of historical writings, embracing a wide range of historiographic issues, contributes to our understanding of why the transition from "liberal" to "positive" state was so difficult in the United States. However, very little has been written on how social science helped ease that transition. While social science provided an important discourse among civil servants, politicians, and social scientists elsewhere, such discourse was especially crucial in the United States where the "liberal" or laissez-faire state remained stronger longer. Social science was not a magic remedy that healed all socioeconomic or political problems in the United States—for women or men reformers. Yet for both it offered a crucial means of justifying state activism.

Good examples of this were the state bureaus of labor statistics created in the 1860s and 1870s by most state governments in industrializing regions. In his 1984 book, *Investigation and Responsibility*, William Brock quoted Carroll D. Wright, founder of American social statistics, on the sacred qualities of the bureaus' duties. "No matter for what reasons they were appointed, no matter how inexperienced in the work of investigation and of compilation and presentation of statistical material, no matter from what party they came and whether in sympathy with capital or labor, and even if holding fairly radical socialistic views; the men have, almost without exception, at once comprehended the sacredness of the duty assigned to them, and served the public faithfully and honestly, being content to collect and publish facts without regard to individual bias or individual political sentiments." Carroll D. Wright, "The Value and Influence of Labor Statistics," *Bulletin of the Bureau of Labor* 54 (1904): 1087, quoted in Brock, *Investigation and Responsibility*, 154.

Historians usually mention four major aspects of the American polity that diminished the extent to which class could serve as an effective vehicle for political action. All four of these factors created political gaps—that is, they generated political vacuums in the United States in places where, in England, France, and Germany, elites, labor activists, and politicians were interacting more effectively to generate new, positive actions by the state to address social problems. I have argued elsewhere that these gaps created special opportunities for women in the United States. See Kathryn Kish Sklar, "The Historical Foundations of Women's Power in the Creation of the American Welfare State, 1830–1930," in *Mothers of a New World: Maternalist Politics and the Origins of Welfare States*, ed. Seth Koven and Sonya Michel (New York: Routledge, 1993); and idem, *Florence Kelley and the Nation's Work: The Rise of Women's Political Culture, 1830–1900* (New Haven: Yale University Press, 1995).

A. The simultaneous development of political democracy and industrialization in the United States meant that before 1850 popular political values and elite-driven economic goals both endorsed "liberal" or laissez-faire policies. In no other nation did universal white male suffrage emerge simultaneously with industrial capitalism. Elsewhere—in England, France and Germany—industrialization occurred among a disfranchised populace whose political consciousness was shaped by the goal of acquiring state power in order to bend it to its own purposes. Not so in the United States, where in the antebellum era working-class men wanted to prevent elites from using the state for their own ends; elites benefited from the unregulated interaction of capital and labor.

B. In England, France, and Germany traditions of positive government combined with traditions of elite governance to produce formidable civil service bureaucracies, which led the way in formulating solutions for the problems created by industrialization and urbanization in the late nineteenth and early twentieth centuries. In the United States, civil service bureaucrats are not yet effectively severed from patronage politics. In the Progressive Era this severely limited their ability to advocate positive governmental action to solve social problems, and it preempted reformers' ability to use social science to justify positive government.

C. Massive immigration into the United States between 1880 and 1920 transformed the American working class into a predominantly foreign-born class. This meant that working-class politics turned on an ethnic rather than a class fulcrum; and it diminished middle-class sympathy for working-class social problems.

D. Organized labor, under the leadership of Samuel Gompers and the American Federation of Labor, quickly learned that American political structures, especially the ability of courts to overrule legislative enactments, rendered governmental institutions ineffective in labor's struggle to advance the interests of working people.

For the lack of "positive" or administrative capacities in American government, see Stephen Skowronek, *Building a New American State: The Expansion of National Administrative Capacities, 1877–1920* (Cambridge: Cambridge University Press, 1982). For the American lack of a civil service equivalent to England's, see Ari Hoogenboom, *Outlawing the Spoils: A History of the Civil Service Reform Movement, 1865–1883* (Urbana: University of Illinois Press, 1961). For the dominance of political machines, see Morton Keller, *Affairs of State: Public Life in Late-Nineteenth Century America* (Cambridge: Harvard University Press, 1977). For the absence of a labor party in the United States, see David Montgomery, *The Fall of the House of Labor* (Cambridge: Cambridge University Press, 1987).

22. Linda Gordon offers telling criticism of the tendency of white middle-class women reformers to view their working-class "clients" as "the other," especially in comparison with black women equivalents, in "Black and White Visions of Welfare: Women's Welfare Activism, 1890–1945," *Journal of American History* 78 (September 1991): 559–90.

23. See Ginzberg, *Women and the Work of Benevolence*; and Anne Firor Scott, *Natural Allies: Women's Associations in American History* (Urbana: University of Illinois Press, 1991).

24. Industrial strife and immigration are discussed in Herbert G. Gutman, *Work, Culture and Society in Industrializing America* (New York: Knopf, 1976). One of the best discussions of social Darwinism remains Richard Hofstadter, *Social Darwinism in American Thought*, rev. ed. (Boston: Beacon, 1955).

25. See Brock, *Investigation and Responsibility*, 1–57.

26. See Kelley, *Notes of Sixty Years*, 68.

27. Ely, *Ground under Our Feet*, 36; Jurgen Herbst, *The German Historical School in American Scholarship: A Study in the Transfer of Culture* (Ithaca: Cornell University Press, 1965), 1–22; and Kelley, *Notes of Sixty Years*, 71–72.

28. Kelley, *Notes of Sixty Years*, 61–74.

29. The best discussion of state bureaus of labor statistics is Brock, *Investigation and Responsibility*, 148–84. Kelley's critique was printed in the *Fifth Annual Report of the Bureau of Labor Statistics of the State of Connecticut* (Hartford: Case, Lockwood & Brainard, 1889), 43–45.

30. Florence Kelley to Caroline Kelley, February 24, 1892, Nicholas Kelley Papers, New York Public Library.

31. Florence Kelley to Friedrich Engels, Hull House, April 7, 1892, Archive, Institute of Marxism-Leninism, Moscow, 8489 a & b. Also quoted in Dorothy Rose Blumberg, *Florence Kelley: The Making of a Social Pioneer* (New York: Augustus M. Kelley, 1966), 127.

32. Florence Kelley to Caroline Kelley, Hull House, March 16, 1892, Nicholas Kelley Papers.

33. Ibid.

34. The stories by Nell Nelson appeared in the *Times* of Chicago, a pro-labor paper. Women garment workers called a meeting attended by representatives of twenty-six women's organizations in October 1888. Clipping, October 24, 1888, Thomas J. Morgan Collection, University of Illinois, Urbana. See Sklar, "Hull House as a Community of

Women Reformers"; and Meredith Tax, *The Rising of the Women: Feminist Solidarity and Class Conflict, 1880–1917* (New York: Monthly Review Press, 1980), 65–93.

35. Florence Kelley to Frederick Engels, Hull House, May 27, 1892. Reprinted in Blumberg, *Florence Kelley*, 128.

36. Allen F. Davis, *American Heroine: The Life and Legend of Jane Addams* (New York: Oxford University Press, 1973), 100.

37. T. S. Simey and M. B. Simey, *Charles Booth, Social Scientist* (New York: Oxford University Press, 1960), 115 and 128. Publication dates of the early volumes were: vol. 1, 1889; vol. 2 with "Map of Poverty," 1891; vols. 3 and 4, 1896.

38. The earliest thematic maps in the United States were also problem-solving instruments. Sanitary survey maps for New York City in the 1860s, showing household variables such as privy facilities, utilized the advances that lithography made possible. Thus the basic technological steps were in place twenty years before *HHM&P*. See Jon A. Peterson, "The Impact of Sanitary Reform upon American Urban Planning, 1840–1890," in *Introduction to Planning History in the United States*, ed. Donald A. Krueckeberg (New Brunswick, N.J.: Center for Urban Policy Research, Rutgers University, 1983), 13–39; and Arthur H. Robinson, *Early Thematic Mapping in the History of Cartography* (Chicago: University of Chicago Press, 1982), 24, 143, and 193.

The major studies containing thematic maps by social reformers between *HHM&P* and the *Pittsburgh Survey* were Robert Woods, ed., *The City Wilderness: A Settlement Study* (Boston: Patterson Smith, 1898); and idem, ed., *Americans in Process: A Settlement Study by Residents and Associates of the South End House* (Boston: Houghton, Mifflin and Co., 1903). The maps in the 1898 volume were extremely minimal and rudimentary compared to those of *HHM&P*, but improved color-coded maps appeared in the 1903 study. Based on Booth's method of block rather than household analysis, the maps depicted "Nationalities in the North End," "Nationalities in the West End," "Buildings in the North End," "Buildings in the West End," "Industrial Grades in the West End," and "Industrial Grades in the North End."

Neither these nor the maps in the six volumes of the *Pittsburgh Survey*, published between 1909 and 1911, approached the sophistication and detail of the maps in *HHM&P*. See, for example, Paul U. Kellogg, "Community and Workshop," in *Wage-Earning Pittsburgh*, ed. Paul U. Kellogg (New York: Russell Sage Foundation, 1914), 3–30. Depicting the whole city on one page, these maps gave a general portrait of "Congestion," "Growth," "Hospitals," and "Health." Six versions of the latter depicted "Comparative Mortality by Ward Groups, 1903–1907": "Tuberculosis," "Pneumonia," "Diarrhoeal Diseases," "Other Violence (than suicide)," "Typhoid Fever," and "All Causes." The most detailed maps in the *Pittsburgh Survey* can be found in Byington, *Homestead*. One, following p. 132, shows the "location of 22 courts studied; number of children under 14 in each; location of churches and saloons; absence of playgrounds."

All *Pittsburgh Survey* maps were drawn by Shelby Harrison, cocompiler of A. Eaton and S. M. Harrison, *A Bibliography of Social Surveys: Reports of Fact-Finding Studies Made as a Basis for Social Action: Arranged by Subjects and Localities: Reports to January 1st 1928* (New York: Russell Sage Foundation, 1930).

39. Simey and Simey, *Charles Booth*, 102.

40. Ibid., 113.

41. "Prefatory Note," *HHM&P*, vii and viii.

42. Florence Kelley to Henry Demarest Lloyd, 327 W. Harrison St., November 28, 1892, Henry Demarest Lloyd Papers, State Historical Society of Wisconsin.

43. Carroll D. Wright, Commissioner of Labor, *Seventh Annual Report: The Slums of*

Baltimore, Chicago, New York, and Philadelphia (Washington, D.C.: Government Printing Office, 1894).

44. Agnes Sinclair Holbrook, "Map Notes and Comments," *HHM&P*, 7.

45. Ibid. There Holbrook clarified the classification methods of each map:

In recording the nationality of each person, his age, and in the case of children under ten years of age the nationality of his parents and his attendance at school were taken into account. All under ten years of age who were not pupils in the public school, and who were not of American extraction, were classified with their parents as foreigners.

In estimating the average weekly wage for the year, first the number of unemployed weeks in each individual case was subtracted from the number of weeks in the year, the difference multiplied by the weekly wage when employed, and the result divided by fifty-two; then the amounts received by the various members of each family, thus determined, were added together, giving the average weekly income of the family throughout the year.

46. Robinson, *Early Thematic Mapping*, 24, 143, and 193.

47. Holbrook, "Map Notes," *HHM&P*, 9.

48. Ibid., 11.

49. Ibid., 11–12.

50. Ibid., 20.

51. Ibid.

52. Ibid., 8, 20.

53. Ibid., 23.

54. Ibid.

55. Ibid., 13.

56. Ibid., 3–4.

57. Ibid., 4.

58. Ibid., 5–6.

59. Ibid., 14.

60. Florence Kelley, "The Sweating-System," *HHM&P*, 41.

61. Ibid., 50.

62. Florence Kelley and Alzina Stevens, "Wage-Earning Children," *HHM&P*, 61, 72, 74–75.

63. In "The Domestication of Politics: Women and American Political Society, 1780–1920," *American Historical Review* 89 (June 1984): 620–48. Paula Baker's otherwise fine article uses a model of separate spheres to explain women's political culture rather than a model that emphasizes the interaction and change over time between women's political culture and the larger political culture.

64. Ellen Gates Starr, "Art and Labor," *HHM&P*, 178–79.

65. See n. 21 above.

66. This process is described in Dorothy Ross, "The Development of the Social Sciences," and Edward Shils, "The Order of Learning in the United States: The Ascendancy of the University," both in *The Organization of Knowledge in Modern America, 1860–1920*, ed. Alexandra Oleson and John Voss (Baltimore: Johns Hopkins University Press, 1979), 107–38 and 19–47. See also Martin Bulmer, *The Chicago School of Sociology: Institutionalization, Diversity, and the Rise of Sociological Research* (Chicago: University of Chicago Press, 1984), 1–44.

67. Jane Addams, "The Settlement as a Factor in the Labor Movement," *HHM&P*, 188–204.

68. Jane Addams, "Appendix, Outline Sketch Descriptive of Hull House," *HHM&P*.

69. Florence Kelley, "Hull House," *New England Magazine* 18 (July 1898): 550–66, quotation from 550.

70. Mme. Marie-Thérèse Blanc, *The Condition of Woman in the United States* (Boston: Roberts Bros., 1896), 74–82.

71. Jane Addams, *Twenty Years at Hull House* (New York: Macmillan, 1910), 183.

72. See Kathryn Kish Sklar "Who Funded Hull House?" in *Lady Bountiful Revisited: Women, Philanthropy and Power*, ed. Kathleen McCarthy (New Brunswick, N.J.: Rutgers University Press, 1990).

73. For example, Kelley used this phrase in letters to Ely dated October 3, 1892, and August 20, 1893. Richard T. Ely Papers, State Historical Society of Wisconsin, Madison.

74. Subsequent titles in the series included: E. W. Bemis, *Municipal Monopolies* (1899); John R. Commons, *Proportional Representation* (1902); Frank H. Dixon, *State Railroad Control* (1896); Frederic C. Howe, *Taxation and Taxes in the United States* (1896); Edward Ingle, *Southern Side Lights* (1896); Lauros G. McConachie, *Congressional Committees* (1898); Charles B. Spahr, *An Essay on the Present Distribution of Wealth in the United States* (1896); William P. Trent, *Southern Statesmen of the Old Regime* (1897); W. F. Willoughby, *Workingmen's Insurance* (1898); F. H. Wines, *Punishment and Reformation* (1923).

75. Jane Addams to Richard Ely, Chicago, October 31, 1894, Ely Papers.

76. Ibid.

77. Florence Kelley to Richard Ely, Office of Factory Inspector, Chicago, November 14, 1894, Ely Papers.

78. Jane Addams to Richard Ely, November 27, 1894, and December 4, 1894, Ely Papers.

79. Unidentified news clipping [*New York Times*, March 1896], Hull House Scrapbook, 1896, in *Jane Addams Papers*, ed. Mary Lynn McCree Bryan et al. (Sanford, N.C., 1985), microfilm, reel 73.

80. "Settlers in the City Wilderness," *Atlantic Monthly* 77 (January 1896): 118–23.

81. Samuel McCune Lindsay, review of *Hull-House Maps and Papers*, *Annals of the American Academy of Political and Social Science* 8 (September 1896): 171–81.

82. Deegan, *Jane Addams and the Men of the Chicago School*, esp. 63–66.

83. See Josephine Goldmark, *Impatient Crusader: The Life of Florence Kelley* (Urbana: University of Illinois Press, 1953).

"A Government of Men": Gender, the City, and the New Science of Politics

HELENE SILVERBERG

THE GENDER of American political life was fundamentally transformed in the years between 1880 and 1920.[1] Nowhere were these transformations more visible than in the turn-of-the-century city. Working through the General Federation of Women's Clubs, the National Women's Trade Union League, the National Consumers' League, and a multitude of purely local groups, middle-class women boldly entered political terrain once considered part of the male "sphere." They lobbied state legislatures and testified before legislative committees for woman suffrage, labor legislation, mothers' pensions, and other programs that set the cornerstone of the American welfare state. And in city after city, women's organizations and settlement houses became arenas of policy experimentation and advocacy as they vied with male reformers, party politicians, and academic experts for authority over the scope and purposes of government. Ratification of the Nineteenth Amendment in 1920 merely confirmed, rather than initiated, the thoroughgoing reconstruction of the American political community that had occurred during the previous forty years.[2]

The fluid boundaries of American politics severely complicated the professional aspirations of political scientists at the turn of the century. During the nineteenth century, they had operated at the margins of politics, ignored by politicians and voters alike. The rise of municipal reform activities in the 1880s, however, spurred political scientists to new ambitions; they hoped to use these activities to catapult their discipline to the center of American political life. But how to seize the realm of "the political" at a time when its meaning had been destablized by women's new civic activism was by no means clear. As political scientists recognized, their long-standing claim to expertise on "the State" would not easily be transformed into new authority over city politics.

The historiography of political science has paid little attention to the problem that women's political mobilization posed for political scientists as they sought to reorganize their discipline during these years. Instead, it has developed two rather different, though equally gender-neutral, portraits of the discipline. One portrait, largely the creation of political theorists and historians of political science, has focused primarily on its theories and ideas, and secondarily on developments within the American Political Science Association (APSA). Most of this work locates early-twentieth-century political science in a Whiggish narrative describing its transition from reform politics to social "science." Others have explored its intellectual links to American political culture and depicted a discipline deeply constrained during these crucial years by its attachment to American liberalism and the ideology of American exceptionalism. Still others have identified the beginnings of a distinct intellectual tradition that attempted to resolve the ostensible conflict between science and reform.[3]

Alternatively, in their exploration of early-twentieth-century municipal reform, historians of urban politics have somewhat indirectly provided a sketch of political scientists' political activities. This work has revealed political scientists' key role in the campaign to overhaul the structure and administrative practices of American city governments as they struggled to remedy the effects of immigration, industrialization, and urbanization. Most of this work views political scientists as members of this era's liberal coalition because of their prominent role in the state-building initiatives of this period. The mirror image of the disciplinary histories, these studies have shed light on political scientists' commitments outside their universities and professional organizations.[4]

Despite their substantial differences, however, both approaches represent the discipline in gender-neutral terms. Political scientists, as well as their perspectives and conceptual tools, appear in both accounts as genderless. The overwhelming predominance of men in the discipline during these formative years has passed without comment, as if this feature of political science's history had no important consequences for its character, organization, or analytical framework—then or today. Many of political science's most distinct features at this time—its concern with the institutional and administrative organization of government, and its representation of the political world as a wholly male sphere, for example—have been viewed as a "natural" and gender-neutral extension of its nineteenth-century interest in the "the State."

One possible explanation for this inattention to gender is the near absence of one of the great markers of gender—women—from the discipline at this time. Although most political science departments were opened to women graduate students in the 1890s, the discipline attracted so few that their presence generated little controversy.[5] More important, the few women who actually obtained a Ph.D., held an academic post, and achieved some measure of professional prominence, such as Deborah Ellen Ellis of Mount Holyoke and Louise Overacker of Wellesley College, do not seem to have differed very much politically or intellectually from their male peers, and in any case remained too far from the centers of disciplinary power to have caught the attention of recent scholars.[6] Nor has political science's intellectual domain included such obviously gendered topics as the family or sexuality, for example, through which its involvement with the turn-of-the-century debate about gender could be traced.

The more important explanation, however, lies in the narrow, partial framework within which the history of the discipline has been written. Specifically, scholars of the discipline have taken at face value the shape and character of the political world that political scientists evoked in their texts, taught in their classes, and debated at their professional meetings. That is, they have assumed that political scientists' depiction of the political world reflected an existing consensus about the scope and meaning of "politics." This assumption has been reflected in, and reinforced by, the research methods of scholars in this field, who have relied upon the published work of the discipline's "Great Men," the official proceedings and reports of the APSA, or the discipline's professional journals to inform their analysis. But this assumption is incorrect, and it takes for granted several aspects of the discipline's formation that need to be explained. To the extent that these historians have allowed turn-of-the-century political scientists to set the terms of their analysis, they have overlooked some of the most important questions concerning the discipline's development during these crucial years: Why was the mention of women in political science texts so rare as to be nonexistent during the peak years of their political mobilization? Why did political scientists come to represent political life as a strictly male affair at a time when women's political involvement was so broad and visible? How did political scientists come to set the boundaries of "the political" in ways that excluded women's participation?

Restoring gender to the history of political science is complicated by the dominant historiographical framework of Progressive Era women's history. Since William O'Neill's 1969 book *Everyone Was Brave: The Rise and Fall of Feminism in America*, research in women's history has employed the concept of "social feminism" to describe women's civic activities (other than the demand for the vote) during these years.[7] This term, which O'Neill juxtaposed with the "hard-core feminism" of proponents of woman suffrage and other women's political and civil rights, helped capture the feminist impulse in women's social welfare activities in ways that had not previously been recognized. This framework was eagerly embraced by a generation of feminist scholars who used it to dramatically expand the research agenda of women's history.

Recently, however, it has been criticized as particularly inadequate for an era in which women were self-consciously redrawing the political boundaries of urban public space. Its rigid demarcation of "the social" from "the political" obscured the extent to which the shape and character of "politics" was itself a matter of dispute between middle-class men and women. It also concealed the breadth and vitality of women's specifically *political* history prior to their enfranchisement by casting women's civic activism as "social" rather than political. The conceptual problem with this framework, as feminist scholars would subsequently note, was its implicit acceptance of a definition of politics based on the specific forms of men's political activity in this period: activity was political only if it occurred through the parties and/or in the electoral arena. Because voteless women most often operated through voluntary organizations, rather than parties, and directly lobbied legislators and administrators, rather than working through electoral channels, their political activity was deemed to be social.[8] A history of political science that accepted these terms would find little fault with the current historiography: since women's civic activism was not "political," there would be little reason to expect political scientists to "see" it.

Its absence from political scientists' representation of the political world would be explicable by reference to the ostensiblly "nonpolitical" character of women's activity rather than to the logic of political scientists' own conception of their disciplinary realm.

A more accurate history of political science during its formative years requires that we readjust our thinking about the relationship between political science and political life in two specific ways. First, we must expand our definition of politics to better accommodate the many forms of women's political activity that did not have a direct male counterpart. This broader definition is not only more historically accurate, it also better captures women's own understanding of the meaning and purposes of their activities.[9] Second, we must recognize that political scientists' view of their domain did not simply and straightforwardly mirror a societywide consensus about the scope and character of politics. Rather, it reflected parameters set by the new conceptual principles on which political scientists reorganized their discipline in the opening decades of the twentieth century.

In this essay, I explore the ways in which gender influenced the development of this conceptual framework. During these formative years, I suggest, political scientists reorganized their discipline around a set of principles drawn from the political agenda of male municipal reformers.[10] In the 1890s, political scientists entered the city's political life in search of new ground for their discipline. Following a path shaped at every turn by the structures of middle-class manhood, they encountered urban politics as it was perceived and practiced by male reformers. Working in this context, they mixed their discipline's traditional interest in institutions with male reformers' perspective on municipal reform to create new "scientific" principles of good government. As they refashioned these new principles into the basis for a new, more authoritative political science, they incorporated male reformers' perspective on politics into the very foundations of the discipline. Predictably, this new "science of politics" represented politics in ways that obscured women's political activism in the cities.

GENDER AND URBAN POLITICAL REFORM

The historiography of municipal reform at the turn of the century usually assumes that male and female reformers embraced different agendas: that male reformers were primarily concerned with the structure of municipal government while women focused on social welfare measures for women and children. Recently, historians have focused most often on women reformers and have explained their distinct program by pointing to gender-related factors: the influence either of a female culture, inherited from the early nineteenth century, or of the more immediate experience of women's daily lives in their home and family.[11] The few efforts to explore the agenda of male municipal reformers through a gender lens have similarly pointed to the content of their daily lives, especially their immersion in the world of business, to explain their support for proposals promoting the "fiscal efficiency and financial profitability" of both private business and city government.[12] But men's close contact with the business world, and their embrace of its values, cannot alone explain their specific political strategies and municipal proposals. Rather, their reform proposals and political strategies were also deeply informed by their relationship to the structure of American politics at this time.

The municipal reform battles of urban America took place against the background of the peculiar dynamic of the nineteenth-century American polity. Because the vote was extended to all (white) men prior to state bureaucratization in the United States, public administrative arrangements were colonized by the political parties and used to nourish their organizational and electoral needs through patronage. By the late nineteenth century, especially in American cities in the Northeast and Midwest, Democratic party machines had put down strong roots among the immigrant working class and thoroughly dominated urban political life. These arrangements encouraged very high levels of popular mobilization; outside the South, turnout regularly reached the 85–90 percent range among white men during presidential elections, and these high levels were sustained almost evenly across socioeconomic groups.[13] Moreover, the extension of the suffrage to men (and women's formal exclusion) firmly tied partisan and electoral politics to gender; rituals of male fraternalism were central during the "party period" of U.S. governance. Shared voting rights and party loyalties also linked men together across class lines—so much so that partisan political participation was part of the very definition of American manhood.[14] But "patronage democracy," as Ann Orloff has characterized these arrangements,[15] also produced serious opposition.

The initial campaign to end patronage practices in government was led by the mugwumps, upper- and upper-middle-class Protestant male reformers located in the Northeast, especially New York and Massachusetts. The mugwumps were deeply distrustful of American democracy; they believed that the parties' patronage practices had discouraged the "Best Men" from assuming political leadership.[16] In the 1870s, these men spearheaded the campaign for federal civil service reform and, after passage of the Pendleton Act in 1882, turned their attention to municipal affairs, creating local "good government" groups outside the party system from which to launch their attack on the urban machines. In most cities and states, however, civil service reform made only limited headway. Party leaders successfully mobilized opposition by marshaling the class and gender symbols of nineteenth-century politics. They regularly mocked civil service reformers as "man-milliners"—a catchall term for anything from unmanliness to homosexuality[17]—and characterized civil service reform as an attack on popular democracy.[18]

The mugwumps were joined in the 1890s by middle-class business and professional men, who added a concern for "honesty and efficiency" in city government to the mugwumps' quest for moral regeneration. They also helped place the booming municipal reform movement on a more permanent footing. By

1894, there were more than eighty local groups, of which sixty had been created since 1890. Over half of them were concentrated in the big cities of New York, Pennsylvania, and Massachusetts, and many of them explicitly barred women from membership.[19] The Municipal League of Philadephia, established in 1891, and the City Club of New York, established in 1892, were the recognized leaders of the reform movement. Each club boasted a membership of over a thousand men (both groups barred women members), and both were organized to actively participate in local electoral politics.[20]

These men perceived the problems of the city through the lens of their gender (and class) experiences. Mugwump reformers decried the corruption of the manly, republican "virtue" that had once flourished in the morally pure public sphere when "better men" had ruled. Middle-class professionals and businessmen were far more concerned with poor municipal services, underdeveloped commercial infrastructure, and high taxes. Both groups blamed the party machines—their patronage practices, profligate spending, ties to local corporations—for the city's deplorable condition. But their strategy for addressing these problems directly reflected middle-class men's distinct relationship to local political institutions. American men's primary route to political power lay through the political parties and electoral politics; yet both paths were blocked for middle-class men by the machines' firm hold on the working-class electorate. Unable to gain control of a local party, New York City male reformers, for example, often pursued their aims through spectacular fusion campaigns or independent reform tickets—but, usually, to no avail.[21]

By the mid-1890s, male reformers had settled on a handful of proposals they hoped would weaken the machine. Their chief goal remained civil service reform in order to deprive the machine of its patronage and install honest men in government. They also favored "home rule," which would give cities the authority to conduct their own affairs without interference from the state legislature. State legislatures had previously withdrawn this authority in response to the widespread corruption of city politics. Finally, male reformers favored the separation of municipal from national elections in the belief that this would eliminate from local politics the spoils provided in return for support for national party candidates and allow elites of different national party preferences to join forces in a "nonpartisan" local politics against their common enemy, the machine. Middle-class men hoped that these reforms would sufficiently restructure the local electoral arena to enable them to assume political power in the city.[22]

Reform challenges to the urban machines, however, were seldom fully successful. Mayors Tom Johnson and Newton Baker of Cleveland, Hazen Pingree of Detroit, Seth Low and John Purroy Mitchel of New York City, and John P. Altgeld and Edward F. Dunne of Chicago each managed to assemble the cross-class coalition needed for victory at the polls. Once in office, they tried to institute civil service rules, improve administrative and budgeting methods, change the procedures for authorizing city contracts, and, in some cases, also build better parks and schools. But reformers' victories were most often short-lived;

especially in the Northeast and the Midwest, reform mayors were rarely in office long enough to fully implement their agenda and consolidate reform control of city government.[23] At election time, party politicians routinely rallied working-class voters against reform administrations by framing reform as an assault on working-class interests. Reformers invariably confirmed these charges with their attacks on immigrants, the Catholic Church, and the "ignorant masses" more generally.[24]

The gender dimension of male reformers' program and strategy is particularly clear when set against the agenda and tactics of the middle-class women also active in turn-of-the-century municipal reform. These women clearly understood the problems of the city through the lens of their gender (and class) experience: they fashioned a broad and innovative social welfare agenda aimed especially at remedying the plight of poor women and children.[25] Their political strategy and modes of participation were also deeply shaped by their relationship to the American polity—which, of course, differed from the men's in critical ways. Formally excluded from electoral and party politics, American women pioneered both a new, gender-conscious discourse of authority that recast the meaning of "politics," and a new, nonelectoral style of political participation involving interest groups and the lobbying of city officials.[26]

These women did not simply fit themselves into a landscape of male public space, in which men decided the meaning of politics and the purposes of city government. Rather, they challenged male political authority by exploding the distinction between public and private that had long justified women's formal exclusion from politics. In their view, the city was simply an extension of the home and therefore a place particularly appropriate for women's activism. Speaking at the first National Conference for Good City Government in 1894, Mary E. Mumford asked why women "take an especial interest in municipal government." Her explanation evoked a broad conception of politics and city government and placed women fully within it. "Good city government is good house-keeping, and that is the sum of the matter," she replied. "If she follows her broom into the street she is confronted with a problem upon which she has been at work for centuries."[27] The language of municipal housekeeping greatly facilitated women's entry into politics by capitalizing on, rather than challenging, contemporary views of women's proper "sphere." It served also as a powerful source of political authority for women, since these ideas were also shared by men.[28]

Moreover, middle-class women's groups capitalized on the fluid boundaries between city government and private organizations (precisely those arrangements that male municipal reformers so strenuously opposed). Formally excluded from electoral politics, they constructed alternative paths of influence that bypassed the parties and the electoral arena and led directly to local city agencies. The close relationships between women's groups and municipal agencies took several forms. In Chicago, for example, lobbying by women's organizations resulted in the appointment of women matrons and probation officers to juvenile courts and jails, and women health inspectors to the health department. These appointments frequently opened regular, if informal, channels of communication between the women's groups and the department. In other cases, there was a more complex mixing of public power and private purpose, in which city departments granted public authority to women's organizations to facilitate their social welfare activities. The success of these ventures often led city governments to take them over, both financially and administratively, in a process that feminist and historian Mary Beard (wife of Charles Beard) aptly termed "municipalization."[29] The Henry Street Settlement's visiting nurses program was typical. Created by head resident Lillian Wald and funded by private donations, the program was administered from the Henry Street Settlement for many years. Initially, the New York City Health Department simply granted official status to the settlement's nurses to help them gain access to the homes of sick patients in the city's tenements. But the department soon took over the provision of these services, employing several Henry Street nurses to carry out the city's own expanded program.[30]

These institutional arrangements, which blurred the boundaries between public and private, government and society, accorded women a crucial role in administering city programs. They also sustained women's broader and more flexible conception of politics and government. In her 1915 book describing women's work in municipal reform, Mary Beard described women's view of their important role in city government. Through their activities, Beard observed, women

> have moved step by step into the municipal government itself, pushing in their activities through demonstrations of their value to the community and often going with their creations into municipal office; . . . in brief it may be claimed that women have broadened into the democratic and governmental point of view . . . at the same time that they have been perfecting the machinery by which democracy may lay its foundation of health, happiness, and power in governmental functions.[31]

Predictably, women reformers were more concerned with achieving their social welfare goals than with reforming election procedures or ending the "spoils system." They supported civil service measures, but the independence of their political influence from the electoral arena and political parties led them to a more benign opinion of the machine. Jane Addams, for example, viewed the boss as a "big manifestation of human friendliness" that would disappear naturally once the city itself provided the services the machine offered impoverished workers and their families.[32] Indeed, machine politicians, with their roots in poor working-class neighborhoods, were often more sympathetic to women's ideas for expanded city services than were the economy-minded reform administrations supported by middle-class men. Thus middle-class women directed their extraordinary energies toward social welfare policies, leaving their male counterparts to scheme endlessly to end the reign of "the boss."

POLITICAL SCIENCE GLIMPSES MUNICIPAL AFFAIRS

In the late nineteenth century, political science was a self-assured but cultur-ally marginal profession. The number of college and university instructors giving all or most of their time to what we now call political science was some-where between fifty and one hundred.[33] The discipline was dominated by Ger-man-trained men, such as Columbia's Francis Lieber and John W. Burgess, Johns Hopkins's W. W. Willoughby, and Yale's Theodore Dwight Woolsey, who worked within a tradition of Hegelian idealism that more closely resem-bled moral philosophy than it did what we now call political science. Their scholarship was devoted to elaborating a theory of "the State" that they under-stood to concern, in part, the great "art of statecraft."[34] The rapid expansion of American universities and the introduction of the elective system, which opened the curriculum to the new social sciences, dramatically increased em-ployment opportunities for political scientists and filled them with a new sense of possibility. In the 1880s, they set out to bolster their cultural authority by demonstrating political science's usefulness.

Political scientists tried first to capture for their discipline the task of training the male governing class so clearly needed in America. Burgess at Columbia and Herbert Baxter Adams at Johns Hopkins, like other mugwumps, had long been much concerned with the poor quality of the American civil service. Both educated in Germany, they were aware that European men trained for the civil service much the way they would for careers in law and medicine. Almost simultaneously, both men initiated plans to transplant the European system for training civil servants to American soil. Adams's proposal for a school at Johns Hopkins never got off the ground because of Johns Hopkins's financial straits.[35] In 1880, Burgess also proposed to the Columbia Board of Trustees the estab-lishment of a school of political science, arguing that "the Republic has now reached those mighty proportions demanding the finest training, as well as the finest talent, for the successful management of its affairs. . . . " Burgess believed the time was especially ripe for such a school because "the Government itself has recognized this fact, and in its civil service reforms, . . . has opened the way for an honorable career to the young men of the nation in the government service. . . . " Burgess modeled the school, the first autonomous graduate pro-gram in political science in the United States, on the Ecole Libre in Paris, where France's powerful civil servant class was trained.[36]

This vision of political science, however, could not take root in America. The Pendleton Act's impact on federal patronage practices was quite small and, together with the limited headway of civil service reform in the states and cities, failed to create the opportunities in government for men trained by polit-ical scientists in "the art of statecraft."[37] Columbia's School of Political Science had little to offer politically ambitious young men when the best route to public office remained the political party. As Frank J. Goodnow, professor of adminis-trative law in the School of Political Science, acknowledged in 1900, "For what should be its strictly professional work, that of helping to train men for the civil service, [the school] is better prepared than ever; but the development of this side of [the school's] political usefulness is still retarded by the fact that public service in the United States is not yet a career to which a man without independent financial resources can yet safely devote his life."[38] The small number of men seeking training for public service reflected this reality and soon forced Burgess and his colleagues to abandon their initial plans for the school. Undeterred by this false start, political scientists again set out to search for ways to establish their usefulness.

A handful of men, drawn primarily from the first generation of American-trained political scientists, now stepped forward to assume this task. Politically, they shared the mugwump skepticism of American democracy that had dominated the discipline since the early nineteenth century. Most were also mainstream Protestants and lacked the backgrounds in dissenting evangelical piety and social millenarianism that inspired the political radicalism and feminist sympathies of their counterparts in economics and sociology.[39] Many had entered political science after training in, and often practicing, law, a conservative profession with deep roots in nineteenth-century male political culture. They were also clearly uncomfortable with the changing relations between the sexes then under way. Opposition to higher education for women could be found among both conservative and progressive members of the discipline. Burgess vehemently opposed coeducation at Columbia in general, and at the School of Political Science in particular, which delayed the admission of women to courses in his field of public law until after his retirement in 1912. Woodrow Wilson, who taught for three unhappy years at Bryn Mawr, clashed often with the young feminist dean M. Carey Thomas, disliked his women students, and quickly left for the more "congenial masculine surroundings" of Wesleyan.[40]

These ambitious men understood that the study of "the State," no matter how broadly defined, could not sustain their large professional goals. They realized that political scientists would have to demonstrate their importance in matters far more central to "actual politics." But political science's conceptual resources for a new departure of this kind were limited. At Columbia, political science was deeply constrained by the formalism of its institutional and intellectual relationships to law. Both Francis Lieber, the first American appointed to a professorship of political science, and Burgess held positions at Columbia's law school, and three of the School of Political Science's five full-time faculty prior to 1890 held law degrees and pursued research specifically on the law.[41] Political science at Johns Hopkins University, which had evolved quite independent of Columbia, was rooted in the historical study of local institutions as they evolved out of the distant folk-assemblies of Anglo-Saxon England. The discipline's investigative practices borrowed heavily from these intellectual traditions, as well as from moral philosophy. They consisted largely of library research, philosophical speculation, detailed examination of historical documents, and especially the close analysis of constitutional law and legal cases.

The political science departments at the University of Chicago under Frederick N. Judson, the University of Pennsylvania under Edmund J. James, and Harvard University under Albert Bushnell Hart pursued some combination of these approaches.[42]

The growth and modernization of American law schools in the 1880s also put pressure on political scientists to strike out in new directions. During most of the nineteenth century, when the practice of law did not require a law degree and involved primarily the enforcement of private contracts and other private rights, American law schools had been heavily oriented toward vocational training. The rise of the administrative state, as well as the campaign for professionalization among lawyers, quickly transformed law schools into major postgraduate institutions concerned also with public law and legal scholarship.[43] As law professors ventured into constitutional terrain, they increasingly encroached upon territory that political scientists had once called their own. Some political scientists, most notably the University of Chicago's Ernst Freund, even abandoned departments of political science for the higher-prestige law schools.[44] Others reluctantly recognized that constitutional jurisprudence alone could no longer support their discipline, and they remained alert to new possibilities.

Fortuitously, legal and political developments in urban America were pointing toward a solution. The city's growing autonomy, implicitly registered in the mugwump campaign for the separation of local and national elections, was first legally recognized in Thomas Cooley's important *Constitutional Limitations* (1868), which designated city government as a separate arena of legal practice. Reflecting the court's prominence in nineteenth-century American government, Cooley's formulation had retained judicial responsibility for determining the city's "proper province." But in a precedential ruling in 1881, Judge J. F. Dillon decided that the authority to define municipal powers lay properly with the state legislatures rather than with the federal courts. One effect of "Dillon's rule," as it came to be called, was to transform the state legislatures into the key arena for conflicts over the scope and character of the city's "province." In doing so, Dillon's rule also opened new opportunities for experts in the specifically political (as opposed to legal) character of municipal affairs. Political scientists set out to make this territory their own.[45]

Frank J. Goodnow, Judge Dillon's former law clerk and a professor at Columbia's School of Political Science, was the first political scientist to recognize this opportunity for his discipline. Employing the old legal methodology of political science but reaching beyond the strictly constitutional, Goodnow's early work explored the activity of the new quasi-legal, administrative agencies (such as the Interstate Commerce Commission, for example) that Congress had recently established.[46] He borrowed the concept "administration" from his old teacher, the German scholar Rudolf von Gneist, to help bring into focus these extrainstitutional activities of government, and he proclaimed them a "new subject" for political science. By bringing this new concept into political science,

Goodnow laid the foundations for the new field of administrative law. Although law professors would later dominate this area, at this point Goodnow and his colleagues considered this very fertile ground for their discipline.[47]

In the meantime, New York City's reform campaign of 1894 turned Goodnow's attention toward city politics. Columbia's social scientists, including Goodnow, maintained close personal links to the City Club of New York, and they were drawn into the election campaign through these channels. Goodnow declined an invitation from his Columbia colleagues economist E.R.A. Seligman and fellow political scientist Abraham Charles Bernheim to join the all-male Committee of Seventy (the group of reformers organizing the anti-Tammany campaign that year) because he believed that social scientists should "stay out of politics."[48] But Goodnow surreptitiously reentered politics on other grounds, taking up the issue of home rule, one of the reform ticket's central concerns, in his next book. Seeking to explore the terrain implied in Dillon's rule, Goodnow extracted from the court cases the first set of principles for defining an independent realm for the city. Although Goodnow acknowledged that "the science of municipal government" was at "an early stage of development," he nonetheless proceeded to distinguish between those areas of municipal government that belonged to the state and those that were strictly local and belonged to the city alone.[49] The enthusiastic response to *Municipal Home Rule* encouraged Goodnow and his fellow political scientists to venture more boldly into municipal affairs.

Goodnow was not alone in his growing interest in the city's political life. Some political scientists, most notably Woodrow Wilson and Charles Merriam (who was active in Seth Low's mayoral campaign in 1897 while a graduate student at Columbia, was later elected a Chicago alderman, and ran unsuccessfully for mayor in 1911 and 1919) participated directly in electoral politics.[50] But others joined Goodnow in seeking to capture the rising interest in municipal affairs for their discipline. The University of Pennsylvania's Leo S. Rowe, for example, staked political scientists' claim to the important problem of municipal public utilities franchises. Albert Shaw, a Johns Hopkins Ph.D. who had studied with Adams, published two pioneering studies of European local government to wide acclaim in both scholarly and popular circles.[51]

Nevertheless, political scientists recognized that they were still struggling to define the concepts on which their new science of politics could be based. They desired more direct engagement with "actual politics" yet realized that their discipline's formalism continued to consign them to the margins of political life. "[H]ow much do statesmen turn to professors of political science for guidance?" A. Lawrence Lowell asked the members of the APSA during his presidential address. "Surely students of politics do not lead public thought as much as they ought to do [because] they do not study enough the actual working of government."[52] The problem, Leo Rowe complained, was that political scientists suffered from "[t]he tendency to reason from definitions rather than facts."[53] At the same time, however, their exciting new work on municipal affairs could not yet

be counted "scientific." Reviewing Albert Shaw's book on European municipal
government, Goodnow admitted in 1895 that "at the present moment, we are
probably more at sea, so far as the municipal problem is concerned, than at any
other time in our history."[54] Predictably, then, the handful of political scientists
puzzling over municipal affairs looked with great expectations to the new National Municipal League.

"ESSENTIAL PRINCIPLES": THE MUNICIPAL PROGRAM OF 1899

In January 1894, the Municipal League of Philadelphia and the City Club of
New York cosponsored the First National Conference on Good City Government to discuss "the best means" to further the campaign for municipal reform.[55] The many lawyers, journalists, businessmen, and government officials
who met in Philadelphia concluded that a national organization, composed of
local reform groups and facilitating the exchange of ideas and strategies, was
much needed. Established four months later, the National Municipal League
(NML) quickly emerged as the national leader of the municipal reform movement. It served as a speakers bureau, provided assistance to local clubs, tracked
political developments in cities large and small, and assembled the largest and
best collection of material on city government (from city charters to municipal
salary systems) in the nation.[56] But though NML secretary Clinton Rogers
Woodruff expansively proclaimed his group, and the municipal reform movement it led, "a movement for citizenship reform,"[57] the NML's conception of
citizenship, and politics more generally, was strictly tied to gender. When
Susan B. Anthony and Isabella Beecher Hooker appeared before the NML in
1901 to request a formal endorsement of woman suffrage, the group refused to
consider the matter, viewing suffrage as a "political" issue and contending that
an endorsement would violate the group's nonpartisan agenda.[58]

At the time the NML was organized, little agreement existed among reformers on the remedies for the city's many problems. The wide variation in cities'
relationships to state government, their internal organization, and the configuration of local actors continued to support a diversity of views. The mugwumps
in the group emphasized good character and manly virtue as the basis for disinterested public service, insisting that good city government was "dependent
not so much upon good laws and good charters as upon good men."[59] Others
supported the few isolated reforms, especially civil service and home rule, that
had dominated the male reform agenda for a decade.[60] There was agreement on
the need to elect reformers to public office and to consider, as one NML conference paper was entitled, "How to Arouse Public Sentiment in Favor of Good
City Government."[61] But beyond these proposals, reformers were deeply skeptical that *any* general principles could be applied to city politics, since reform
in each city seemed to depend upon wholly unique and idiosyncratic factors.
The format of the league's highly regarded annual conferences between 1894

and 1897 reflected this prevailing view: they consisted almost exclusively of detailed reports on individual cities that emphasized the local and particular dynamic of municipal reform.[62]

Political scientists, especially in New York City and Philadelphia, where they already had ties to reform clubs, were immediately drawn to the new organization.[63] They saw in the NML, and in the rising interest in municipal affairs that it represented, new opportunities to participate *as political scientists* in the national debate about the scope and purposes of government. But their efforts only revealed that the conceptual boundary between political "reform" and political "science" remained weak. They had little to offer beyond the usual nostrums of male reformers. Edmund J. James of the University of Pennsylvania told the NML's first annual conference that the problem of municipal corruption was "partly a moral and partly an educational one." Similarly, Jeremiah W. Jenks of Cornell urged the adoption of a proportional voting system "so that the power of the reformers will be increased, and so that the great middle class, which really controls, will be led to vote the right way instead of the wrong."[64]

In May 1897, the NML decided to pursue a new approach. Aware that the municipal reform movement lacked a common focus, the NML appointed a committee of "experts" and charged them with designing a program "which shall embody the essential principles that must underlie successful municipal government" and with "set[ting] forth a working plan . . . for putting such principles into practical operation." The committee, which the *Outlook* magazine considered "as well informed a body of specialists on municipal matters as could easily be secured," marked political scientists' entrance on the national stage. Horace Deming, a prominent New York City lawyer and municipal reformer, was chosen chairman. Serving also on the seven-member committee were Goodnow of Columbia, Rowe of the University of Pennsylvania, and Shaw, a Johns Hopkins Ph.D.; John A. Fairlie of the University of Michigan and Delos Wilcox, a prominent Michigan reformer and former student of Goodnow's at Columbia, also played important roles.[65]

The committee had, first, to fashion the conceptual tools with which to undertake a task that was, by all accounts, unprecedented. Their implicit starting point was Dillon's rule; they understood their charge to involve defining, and giving substance to, the city's independent sphere. Leading the way, the committee's political scientists turned to their disciplinary inheritance, freely embracing, discarding, or combining its different elements as they served the committee's purposes. Abandoning—temporarily—the conventions of their "science," they plunged into "actual politics." First, they borrowed the institutional focus of political science as it had taken shape at Johns Hopkins. Scrapping the historical context in which it had been located, the committee placed the institutional framework of city government at the center of their analysis. Second, the committee borrowed the focus on "administration" and the extrainstitutional activities of government from political science as it had developed at Columbia. They left behind the legal formalism in which it had been embedded, and used the concept to bring into view the separate realm of practices through which city government actually discharged its duties. Under this new rubric, the committee gathered several old reform measures, such as civil service reform, as well as such new ideas as "budgeting." Employing this analytical framework, the committee devised a uniform program to which, they believed, all cities could—and should—conform.

The committee's final proposal, presented to the NML in November 1899, definitively cast the city as an independent political entity and defined broadly the powers and responsibilities of its sphere. Indeed, the Municipal Program, as it was called, offered an especially bold interpretation of Dillon's rule by placing responsibility for the definition of city government's powers with the cities themselves, rather than with the state legislatures as Dillon had intended. At the center of the program were the issues of governmental structure and administrative practice. The committee wrote a new municipal corporations act and state constitutional amendments that defined the relationship between the state and the city and limited the state legislature's role in city affairs. It also detailed the proper structure and the broad powers of city government. The committee recommended the mayor–city council form as best able to maintain the separation of political and administrative responsibilities. Finally, the committee prescribed specific procedures for city government's vast administrative realm. It recommended a civil service system, created (by charter) a new office of city controller, established an executive budget system, imposed new record-keeping and reporting requirements, and closely regulated the city's methods for granting franchises to public utilities.[66]

Over the next decade, the Municipal Program would revolutionize municipal reform in several ways. The program's importance to specific reform efforts in individual cities was, in fact, limited. Few local groups sought to implement it wholesale; moreover, the mayor–city council form of government never achieved the popularity among reformers that the commission or city manager forms of government did.[67] The Municipal Program's central contribution lay elsewehere: in fundamentally recasting the conceptual underpinnings of municipal reform politics in two ways. First, the Municipal Program opened the way for the emergence of a truly national municipal reform movement. Prior to 1899, real political power lay with local leaders, since it was assumed that only they were in a position to evaluate the unique context of the local politics. The conceptual power of the Municipal Program's general principles, ostensibly more fundamental than the apparent ways in which each city was unique, persuaded local groups that the program's underlying principles were applicable to their circumstances. This recognition permitted political power to move upward to a new leadership able to pursue a genuinely national vision of local political reform.

Far more important, however, the Municipal Program lifted male reformers' interest in insulating the city's administrative realm from politics out of the class, ethnic, and gender conflict in which it had been embedded. According to the Municipal Program, the city's failures were not due primarily to the moral depravity of the working class, as the mugwumps claimed, or even to the corrupt patronage practices of the machine, as business and professional men insisted. Nor would simply arousing public opinion or electing reformers to public office solve the problem. The program's central insight—that the problems of the city concerned government structure and administrative procedures— enabled reformers to jettison the anti-immigrant, anti–working class sentiment that had led to their defeat, and to focus on the problem of government structure, and to build a broader political coalition on this basis.[68] It similarly lifted their concerns out of the masculine corridors of local city clubs, chambers of commerce, and bar associations, and disconnected them from the language of strict economy that had alienated women reformers. Institutional reform was now free to be tied to social welfare issues of concern to women.

The activity surrounding the Municipal Program also inspired a new impulse for organization among political scientists. Contact with municipal reformers in the NML galvanized their distinct sense of professional identity, and the program's enthusiastic reception[69] emboldened them to desire a group that would help them "take the scientific lead in all matters of political interest."[70] The Committee on the Municipal Program's extensive correspondence with political scientists around the country had also helped knit local contacts into a national network that laid the groundwork for a national professional organization. At a conference in December 1902, called to consider the formation of an organization to promote the study of comparative legislation, participants decided instead to form a "general association for the study of Political Science." When the APSA was officially established one year later, in December 1903, the men responsible for devising the Municipal Program speedily assumed the new positions of professional leadership. Frank Goodnow was elected the APSA's first president; Rowe, Shaw, and Fairlie were elected to the executive committee, and each of them would later also serve as president. Moreover, the APSA's early membership was largely drawn from good government organizations and others associated with municipal reform.[71]

The APSA's origins in the male municipal reform movement helped, in part, to fix political science's identity as a largely masculine profession. Women were not formally excluded from the organization, nor was membership restricted to academics or holders of the Ph.D., which would have implicitly barred most women from participation. Indeed, in contrast with that of later years, the APSA's early membership was predominantly nonacademic.[72] But the new organization attracted little interest among women reformers. Its social practices, drawn from the masculine world of good government clubs and chambers of commerce, signaled that this was male terrain. Leadership positions were clearly reserved for men; the holding of annual meetings by invitation of a university and the obligatory "smoker" for the "gentlemen" of the association at the conclusion of each annual meeting also signaled that the APSA was not a likely venue for the female sociability and gender autonomy women sought in their organizations.[73]

But political scientists' disciplinary project was still incomplete. The Municipal Program was, after all, a program of political "reform" and not of political "science." Although it, implicitly, represented an extraordinary act of disciplinary synthesis, it lacked the telling conventions of science: the language was too accessible, local, and specific, and the program was practical rather than theoretical. Its principles would have to be recast as a distinctly conceptual framework, one with scientific authority that could also bring political scientists nearer "actual politics." This was the key element of their disciplinary project, and it was to this crucial task that political scientists now turned.[74]

The Framework for a New Science of Politics

Having finished his work for the NML, Goodnow turned his attention back to political science. His experience with the Municipal Program seems to have sharpened his insights concerning the sources of his discipline's marginality. On the very first page of the book that would catapult him to professional prominence, published in 1900, he boldly asserted that political science's failure "to get back of the formal governmental organization and examine the real political life of the people" was due to "the fact that most writers who have left their impress on American political science have been lawyers, and are therefore not accustomed to look beyond the provisions of positive law." In Goodnow's view, however, it was the "extra-legal institutions" that more fundamentally impart "character to a political system than the mere legal form in which it may be framed." It was these institutions that Goodnow set out to claim for political science.[75]

He rejected the tripartite separation-of-powers scheme, which nineteenth-century political science had lifted from the U.S. Constitution and used to organize the discipline. Seeking to get behind "mere" legal forms, Goodnow brought the concept of "function" into political science for the first time to show that governments everywhere consisted of two functions: "expressing the will of the state" and "executing the will of the state." No mere inventions of political science, these functions, Goodnow declared, were rooted in human nature as well as in historical development. These functions were more fundamental than but not coextensive with the tripartite framework: on the one hand, a single institution might serve both functions; on the other, some functions were carried out by extraconstitutional institutions. To give these functions conceptual life, Goodnow conferred on them scientific terminology. He designated the domain of the expression of the will "politics" and the realm for the execution of the state will the realm of "administration." Goodnow then proceeded to constitute these as discrete realms of social scientific inquiry.[76]

Goodnow had to make his way through a tangle of language to fashion "politics" as a new scientific concept. His own use of the term, he cautioned, was "not the meaning which has been attributed to that word by most political writers," who used it to refer to the "spoils system."[77] Patronage democracy had transformed the entire realm of government into "politics" in this sense. But Goodnow sought to extract out of this morass a specific set of processess and procedures and to give them conceptual autonomy. Thinking in terms of functions permitted Goodnow to bring such matters as political parties (including "the boss") and such electoral mechanisms as the initiative, referendum, and recall (favorites of the reformers) into the realm of "science" for the first time.

Goodnow had less trouble distinguishing his scientific use of "administration." But he had more trouble evoking its sphere. Patronage democracy had so permeated American bureaucracy that the realm of administration also lacked conceptual autonomy. These supervisory tasks, largely new for government, were fundamentally different from politics, Goodnow insisted, because they were "quasi-judicial," "scientific," "statistical," or "quasi-commercial," and they were therefore properly the realm of the expert. Goodnow sought here to capture government as an organization, not merely as a framework of constitutional powers, and to bring into focus the "general work of government."[78]

Political scientists instantly placed the concepts of "administration" and "politics" at the center of their agenda. Clearly alert to its possibilities, they began to reorganize their discipline around it. The APSA's new structure of "departments" was the first signal of political scientists' resolve to explore the possibilities latent in these tools. Five of the seven departments reflected the discipline's nineteenth-century heritage in law and philosophy. But the two new areas political scientists had marked for exploration were "politics" defined as "questions of political dynamics" and "administration," defined as "the methods by which the business of government is carried on."[79] More important, political scientists used their new conceptual framework to investigate, debate, and classify the myriad problems of city government, and they moved outward from there. Federalism substantially expanded their new scientific realm as they explored central administration, state administration, and local administration, methods of administration, as well as the many city services that now came within their scientific ambit. Nothing, from streets to sewage, was beyond their reach.[80]

These new concepts enabled political scientists to enter the debate about the character and scope of government from new, scientific ground. American political parties had long defended the "spoils system" on democratic grounds. The concept of admininistration provided a rationale for limiting the parties' patronage practices that could not easily be construed as an attack on popular democracy; it proved powerful precisely because it promised to reconcile "popular government and efficient administration."[81] It also derived its conceptual power precisely from the murkiness of the activities it sought to capture. At the same time, the concept of "administration" underwrote political scientists' claim to scientific standing. Political scientists deployed the concept of "administration" to support their claim to a distinct realm, which they staunchly defended against the encroachment of lawyers, and it would later support the claim of "experts" to autonomy from politicians.

These new conceptual tools enabled political scientists to cast themselves as neutral arbiters of contemporary debates over the shape and purposes of city government. Having assumed, at least in their own mind, the mantle of "science," they now sought to push aside their competitors. They were especially dismissive of male reformers, those "henheaded theorists whose temperament contained few grains of practical common sense." They promoted their own objectivity by announcing its absence in others. A reformer, Harvard's William Bennett Munro intoned, though "loud in his professions of non-partisanship," is "in many cases a bigoted partisan of his own class or creed or theory."[82] They also sought to shoulder aside the business and professional men, whose outlook and demand for economy had dominated municipal reform. In their view, government's scope and purposes were more appropriately decided by those without vested interests. "The modern industrial city, with its wide social functions, must act in many things involving the heaviest expenditures," Woodrow Wilson told an audience at Johns Hopkins in 1896. "For my part, I do not believe that the persons who pay the largest taxes are the best judges of the needs of the city."[83] Finally, political scientists resorted to condescension to turn aside women reformers' claims to authority over municipal affairs. "So far as American political experience goes," Munro asserted, "it has been found that women rise to their public responsibilities no better, and perhaps no worse, than men do."[84]

To strengthen their hold on their precious new terrain, political scientists recognized their need for more regular access to the new "raw material" of their discipline, that is, to "actual politics." Their involvement in municipal reform had begun as incidental to their scholarly concerns, but its role in establishing their new political prominence led them to move it to the center of their disciplinary endeavors. This need was especially urgent in light of the limits of the discipline's traditional research venues. University libraries, where nineteenth-century political scientists had fashioned their "science of the state," were useless to the discipline's new urban explorers. The huge Bluntschli Library at Johns Hopkins, widely regarded as the best political science collection in the country, contained few books on contemporary politics. According to Cleveland reformer Frederic Howe, a Johns Hopkins Ph.D., "actual politics" seemed to interest only the muckruckers, "who were held in contempt, and . . . the yellow newspapers, which were not permitted in the university library."[85]

To this end, political scientists commenced an ambitious program of institutional innovation to expand and routinize their contact with the city's political life. Charles Beard took the lead when he established Columbia's "Politics Laboratory" (with its evocations of the quintessential setting for scientific inquiry) in 1911 to enable Columbia faculty and graduate students to examine "the actual working of political machinery in federal, state, and local government" without ever leaving their university.[86] Similarly, William Bennet Munro conceived of Harvard's Bureau of Municipal Research, established in 1912 as an adjunct to the Department of Government, as a "workshop" in which Harvard faculty and students could directly explore the problems of city administration.[87] Several land-grant universities, including Wisconsin, Kansas, Nebraska, Iowa, Illinois, and Texas, also established bureaus of municipal research. These "laboratories" enabled political scientists to capture and scrutinize political life—in the form of a steady stream of daily newspapers, weekly periodicals on contemporary public issues, and reference works on state government, franchises, and city charters—in "scientific" settings that could never be confused with mere reform. By 1916, forty-six universities and colleges maintained a "workshop or laboratory" in connection with their program in municipal government.[88]

Political scientists also sought to designate private bureaus of municipal research as relevant to political science's purposes. These bureaus offered unique and especially enticing posssibilities, for they offered political scientists direct access to the inner workings of government. But casting political scientists' relationship with them as "scientific" rather than "political" required some real sleight of hand. The APSA's Committee on Laboratory Methods in Political Science (later renamed the Committee on Practical Training), established in 1912 to explore how "laboratory work for graduate students in political science can be done," noted the problem. The committee observed that, in political science, unlike other science in which a laboratory within the university was sufficient, "training requires that the students shall leave the university to go to the place where the thing needs to be done." Yet such departures could be easily misconstrued. The committee devised a new rubric of "practical training" and "field work" to infuse these activities with scientific significance and enable political scientists to safely and scientifically enter government as part of their training.[89] The University of Michigan, for example, established a program in which political science graduate students wishing to obtain a degree in public service spent one year with the Detroit Bureau of Governmental Research.[90] Similarly, the University of Cincinnati's S. Gayle Lowrie, director of the Cincinnati Municipal Research Bureau, used the bureau as a "laboratory" for teaching and placed his students in city departments, where he supervised their work.[91] Years later, Charles Beard credited these bureaus with "transforming" political science from a "branch of law and political theory into [a] division of natural science and experimental thought."[92]

One effect of these new institutional settings and disciplinary practices was to focus the discipline's attention more narrowly on the realm of politics largely dominated by men. Extracting their new knowledge from their "laboratories" and "field work" in city agencies enabled political scientists to capture and examine the city's tumultuous political life. At the same time, however, their inspection of politics—and their conception of the shape of politics—was confined to the government documents and city charters that flowed through these settings. Women's larger political sphere lay outside these boundaries.

The effects of this new conceptual framework can be seen at work in William Bennett Munro's widely acclaimed *Principles and Methods of Municipal Administration* (1916). Here, his own gender experience subtly guided the ways in which he deployed his disciplinary framework. Munro sought to assure Americans that the principles of administration guaranteed that a more active government could also be an efficient one. But his vision of city government, constructed within a masculine frame, focused on services broadly concerned with economic activity and business prosperity. City government's role in providing water, for example, one of many areas in which machine control resulted in poor municipal services, was also a central issue for women reformers because of its impact on health conditions in the crowded tenements. Munro transformed this long-standing domain of corruption into an efficient and well-run city department by recasting it as a problem of public administration. Of the three uses for the city's clean water supply—public, industrial, and domestic—Munro viewed the public and industrial purposes as central and relegated domestic use to an insignificant place in the life of the city. He framed clean water as a technical issue, concerned with the purification of groundwater and the building of aqueducts, and boldly asserted that administrative procedures would assure the delivery of clean water in an efficient and economical manner. Moreover, at the center of these new administratives, he placed male experts— chemists, medical personnel, and engineers—whose gender, as well as technical training, promised neutral competence. Munro's examination of other areas of city government followed a similar pattern.[93]

The gendered contours of political science's new conceptual framework are especially clear when compared to the vision presented in Mary Beard's equally popular *Woman's Work in Municipalities*, published only one year earlier and covering much the same ground. Beard foregrounded the women holding administrative positions in city government, chronicling their battles and commending their achievements. Her conception of municipal government was spacious and flexible, and she celebrated the fluid connections between city government and women's organizations, which often underwrote crucial city services. She applauded the "little club in Vallejo, California [that] owned and managed a fire engine until the town authorities grew ashamed and decided that the city should have a fire department," and praised the Women's Municipal League of New York, which routinely reported violations of the tenement laws to the city's notoriously delinquent Housing Department, for its role as a de facto housing inspectorate. She also quoted with approval the comment of Martha Bensley Bruere (wife of Henry Bruere, director of the New York Bureau of Municipal Research) that "one prime function of public utilities should be to serve the home in order that science may supplant excessive drudgery there." In Beard's political world, and that of other middle-class women reformers, political science's analytical categories—which saw a rigid boundary between politics and administration and a government run only by men—were simply irrelevant. Thus Beard ignored them, fashioning an alternative language that better captured women's extraordinary place in the rich texture of municipal government and political life.[94]

By about 1915, signs of political scientists' disciplinary success were visible everywhere. Within the university, they had succeeded in persuading once-skeptical university presidents that municipal government was not simply an object of reform but also a legitimate area of social science inquiry. Around 1900, barely a handful of institutions offered one separate course or more on the subject, but by 1916 the number had reached ninety-five. "Nothing akin to it has taken place in any other country," Munro exulted. These courses could now also boast mounds of new knowledge, a regularized curriculum, and an opportunity for "field work." Only recently, the "usual equipment" of these courses had included "a haphazard collection of local histories, stray municipal reports, old charters, and reform pamphlets." The new field now possessed textbooks, the Census Bureau's *Statistics of Cities* and other reference material, new journals, much improved government publications, and workshops and laboratories.[95]

Perhaps more important, politicians now turned to political scientists for advice. Their achievement was most visibly confirmed in 1912 by political scientists' prominent place on President Taft's Commission on Economy and Efficiency. Charged with recommending reforms that would strengthen the president's hold over the executive branch, the commission included among its five members Frederick Cleveland, one of the directors of the New York Bureau of Municipal Research and creator of the "budgeting" idea; W. F. Willoughby, assistant director of the census; and, of course, Frank Goodnow. The commission authored several studies of governmental organization, personnel procedures, and financial practices (which included the first comprehensive chart of the existing organization of the federal government) and offered the president an unprecedented plan for institutionalizing executive control over the federal bureaucracy. Although the commission's proposals were rejected by Congress, which rightly saw them as a threat to its own control of the federal bureaucracy, the president's recognition of political science's expertise was its own reward. For the next twenty years, political scientists would remain the recognized experts in this field. When Franklin Roosevelt launched the next great moment of state building, he, also, turned to political scientists for guidance.[96]

CONCLUSION

During the first two decades of the twentieth century, political scientists recast the foundations of their discipline. In the late nineteenth century, they had operated at the margins of politics, ignored by politicians and voters alike. By World War I, they had successfully defined the administrative realm of government and claimed it as their own. In developing and deploying a new "science of government administration," political scientists gave conceptual life to a realm of politics previously embedded in partisan practices. Politicians now turned to political scientists because the new "science of administration" enabled public officials to build an autonomous state that appeared to reconcile popular democracy with "efficient government." The concept of administration thus proved to be the primary means by which political scientists effected the shift from the politically marginal discipline of the nineteenth century to one that instructed presidents in the early twentieth.

But while the new science of administration appeared to be gender-neutral, neither it nor the discipline constructed around it actually was. In particular, the circumstances in which political scientists redefined the discipline were marked by the gendered concerns of male reformers. Blocked by the machine from assuming political power through partisan and electoral channels, male municipal reformers were particularly concerned to create an autonomous realm of administration. In assembling their new science of politics in part out of male reformers' concerns, political scientists incorporated a gendered perspective on politics into the very foundations of their discipline. In offering male reformers a way of drawing a sharp line between government and society, political scientists' focus on administration excluded the vast scope of middle-class women's activism. This focus on adminstration had a powerfully formative consequence for the field of political science: it institutionalized a narrow conception of political activity and implicitly excluded a range of questions that have only recently been revived by scholars interested in women's history and gender studies. The discipline of political science has not yet fully recovered from these formative years.

NOTES

I would like to thank Amy Bridges, Ken Finegold, Jack Gunnell, and Elizabeth Lunbeck for helpful comments on earlier drafts of this essay.

1. "A Government of Men," the phrase that constitutes this essay's title, is the title of Albert Bushnell Hart's presidential address to the American Political Science Association, given December 28, 1912. See *American Political Science Review* 7, no. 1 (February 1913): 1–27.

2. The literature on the role of gender in the late nineteenth and twentieth centuries is now quite extensive. See, for example, Michael E. McGerr, "Political Style and Women's Power, 1830–1930," *Journal of American History* 70, no. 3 (December 1990): 864–75; Paula Baker, "The Domestication of Politics: Women and American Political Society, 1780–1920," *American Historical Review* 89, no. 3 (June 1984): 620–48; Seth Koven and Sonya Michel, eds., *Mothers of a New World: Maternalist Politics and the Origins of Welfare States* (New York: Routledge, 1993); Kathryn Kish Sklar, *Florence Kelley and the Nation's Work: The Rise of Women's Political Culture, 1830–1900* (New Haven: Yale University Press, 1995); Theda Skocpol, *Protecting Soldiers and Mothers: The Political Origins of Social Policy in the United States* (Cambridge: Harvard University Press, 1992).

3. The historiography of political science has generally focused on the "science" in political science rather than the delineation of the "political." The most important studies include Dorothy Ross, *The Origins of American Social Science* (New York: Cambridge University Press, 1991); Bernard Crick, *The American Science of Politics: Its Origins and Conditions* (Berkeley and Los Angeles: University of California Press, 1959); Dwight Waldo, "Political Science: Tradition, Discipline, Profession, Science, Enterprise," in *Political Science: Scope and Theory*, ed. Fred Greenstein and Nelson Polsby

(Reading, Mass.: Addison-Wesley Publishing Co., 1975), 1–130; Albert Somit and Joseph Tanenhaus, *The Development of American Political Science* (Boston: Allyn and Bacon, 1967); David Ricci, *The Tragedy of Political Science: Politics, Scholarship, and Democracy* (New Haven: Yale University Press, 1984); Raymond Seidelman, with the assistance of Edward Harpham, *Disenchanted Realists: Political Science and the American Crisis, 1884–1984* (Albany: State University of New York Press, 1985).

4. See, for example, Michael Frisch, "Urban Theorists, Urban Reform, and American Political Culture in the Progressive Period," *Political Science Quarterly* 97, no. 2 (Summer 1982): 295–315; Kenneth Fox, *Better City Government: Innovation in American Urban Politics, 1850–1937* (Philadelphia: Temple University Press, 1977); David C. Hammack, *Power and Society: Greater New York at the Turn of the Century* (New York: Russell Sage Foundation, 1982); Kenneth Finegold, *Experts and Politicians: Reform Challenges to Machine Politics in New York, Cleveland, and Chicago* (Princeton: Princeton University Press, 1995).

5. In 1910, only 8 of 120 dissertations then under way were being written by women. "List of Doctoral Dissertations in Political Science," *American Political Science Review* 4, no. 3 (August 1910): 420–25. Although the number had doubled (17 out of 145) sixteen years later, the numbers were still very small. "Doctoral Dissertations in Political Science," *American Political Science Review* 20, no. 3 (August 1926).

6. Mary Breese Fuller, "Department of History and Government in Smith College, 1875–1920," *Smith College Studies in History* 5, no. 5 (April 1920): 139–70; Ruth C. Lawson, "Ellen Deborah Ellis: A Pioneer among Women Political Scientists" (n.d.), Mount Holyoke College Archives (copy in author's possession).

7. William O'Neill, *Everyone Was Brave: The Rise and Fall of Feminism in America*, rev. ed. (Chicago: Quadrangle Books, 1971).

8. Nancy F. Cott, "What's in a Name? The Limits of 'Social Feminism': or, Expanding the Vocabulary of Women's History," *Journal of American History* 76, no. 3 (December 1989): 809–29; Baker, "The Domestication of Politics"; Mary Ryan, *Women in Public* (Baltimore: Johns Hopkins University Press, 1990).

9. For an excellent discussion of the importance of a broader definition of politics for the study of women's politics, see Louise Tilly and Patricia Gurin, "Women, Politics, and Change," in *Women, Politics, and Change*, ed. Louise Tilly and Patricia Gurin (New York: Russell Sage Foundation, 1990), chap. 1.

10. Of course, not all political scientists during these years studied municipal affairs. But this field's special importance to the discipline, both intellectually and professionally, is revealed in the professional and political prominence of men—such as Frank Goodnow, Leo S. Rowe, Albert Shaw, William Bennett Munro, and Charles Merriam—who worked in this field.

11. Maureen A. Flanagan, "Gender and Urban Political Reform: The City Club and the Women's City Club of Chicago in the Progressive Era," *American Historical Review* 95, no. 4 (October 1990): 1032–50; Baker, "The Domestication of Politics"; Koven and Michel, *Mothers of a New World*.

12. Flanagan, "Gender and Urban Political Reform," 1044. See also Arnaldo Testi, "The Gender of Reform Politics: Theodore Roosevelt and the Culture of Masculinity," *Journal of American History* 81, no. 4 (March 1995): 1509–33. Although the class basis of male reformers' challenges to the machine has long been recognized, the gender dimension of these battles has received very little attention.

13. Walter Dean Burnham, "The Changing Shape of the American Political Universe," *American Political Science Review* 59, no. 1 (March 1965): 7–28.

14. Baker, "The Domestication of Politics"; Michael E. McGerr, *The Decline of Popular Politics* (New York: Oxford University Press, 1986), chaps. 1–2. The term "party period," referring roughly to 1830–1900, comes from Richard McCormick, "The Party Period and Public Policy; An Exploratory Hypothesis," *Journal of American History* 66, no. 4 (September 1979): 279–98.

15. Ann Orloff, "The Political Origins of America's Belated Welfare State," in *The Politics of Social Policy in the United States*, ed. Margaret Weir, Ann Shola Orloff, and Theda Skocpol (Princeton: Princeton University Press, 1988), chap. 1.

16. Gerald McFarland, *Mugwumps, Morals, and Politics* (Amherst: University of Massachusetts Press, 1975); Mathew Josephson, *The Politicos* (New York: Harcourt, Brace, 1938).

17. On the "man-milliner" charge, see Fox, *Better City Government*, 46.

18. Martin Schiesl, *The Politics of Efficiency: Municipal Administration and Reform in America, 1800–1920* (Berkeley and Los Angeles: University of California Press, 1977), chap. 2; Ari Hoogenboom, *Outlawing the Spoils: A History of the Civil Service Reform Movement, 1865–1883* (Urbana: University of Illinois Press, 1961); Stephen Skowronek, *Building a New American State: The Expansion of National Administrative Capacities, 1877–1920* (Cambridge: Cambridge University Press, 1982), chaps. 3, 6.

19. Frank Mann Stewart, *A Half Century of Municipal Reform: The History of the National Municipal League* (Berkeley and Los Angeles: University of California Press, 1950), 12; William Howe Tolman, *Municipal Reform Movements in the United States* (New York: Fleming H. Revell Co., 1895), pt. 2.

20. Stewart, *A Half Century*, 13; Hammack, *Power and Society*, 140–41; Fox, *Better City Government*, 49–51.

21. Hammack, *Power and Society*, 145–57.

22. Stewart, *A Half Century*, 12–13; Fox, *Better City Government*, chap. 3; Schiesl, *The Politics of Efficiency*, chaps. 1–2, 4; Maureen Flanagan, *Charter Reform in Chicago* (Carbondale: Southern Illinois University Press, 1987), esp. chaps. 2–3; Jon Teaford, *Unheralded Triumph: City Government in America, 1870–1900* (Baltimore: Johns Hopkins University Press, 1984), chap. 5.

23. Reformers would, however, dominate local politics in the southwest after 1900. See Amy Bridges, "Winning the West to Municipal Reform," *Urban Affairs Quarterly* 27, no. 4 (June 1992): 494–518.

24. Amy Bridges, "Creating Cultures of Reform," *Studies in American Political Development* 8, no. 2 (Spring 1994): 4–7. See also sources cited above, n. 22.

25. See, for example, Kathryn Kish Sklar, "The Historical Foundations of Women's Power in the Creation of the American Welfare State, 1830–1930," in Koven and Michel, *Mothers of a New World*, chap. 2 and Skocpol, *Protecting Soldiers and Mothers*.

26. Elisabeth Clemens argues that women's new models of political participation transformed the repertoire of political activity in America during the Progressive Era and were "central to the invention of modern interest-group politics." Elisabeth Clemens, "Organizational Repertoires and Institutional Change: Women's Groups and the Transformation of U.S. Politics," *American Journal of Sociology* 98, no. 4 (January 1993): 755–98. See also Suzanne Lebsock, "Women and American Politics, 1880–1920," in Tilly and Gurin, *Women, Politics, and Change*, chap. 2.

27. Mary E. Mumford, "The Relation of Women to Municipal Reform," Proceedings of the National Conference for Good City Government (1894), 136–37.

28. On the political significance of the language of "municipal housekeeping," see Flanagan, "Gender and Urban Political Reform," 1048–50; Skocpol, *Protecting Soldiers and Mothers*.

29. Mary Beard, *Woman's Work in Municipalities* (New York: D. Appleton and Co., 1915), 55. "Municipalization" is clearly an important, yet unexplored, aspect of the emergence and expansion of the American welfare state.

30. Lillian Wald, *House on Henry Street* (New York: Henry Holt, 1915), 46–53. The Henry Street Settlement provides several examples of "municipalization." In 1900, for example, the settlement persuaded the New York City Board of Education to hire Elizabeth Farrell to teach special classes for children with disabilities, which led to the establishment of the Department of Special Education in 1908. Two years later it persuaded the board to hire the first school nurse, Lina Rogers, also a Henry Street resident.

31. Beard, *Woman's Work*, 45–46.

32. Jane Addams, "Political Reform," in Jane Addams, *Democracy and Social Ethics*, ed. Anne Firor Scott (Cambridge: Harvard University Press, 1964), chap. 7.

33. Anna Haddow, *Political Science in American Colleges and Universities, 1636–1900* (New York: Octagon Books, 1969), 258.

34. Ross, *Origins*, 280–81; Crick, *American Science of Politics*, 58–59, 95–101.

35. He also began plans for a "civil academy" in Washington, D.C., to train American civil servants, in which Johns Hopkins would play a major role. Raymond J. Cunningham, "'Scientia Pro Patria': Herbert Baxter Adams and Mugwump Academic Reform at Johns Hopkins, 1876–1901," *Prospects* 15 (June 1990): 117.

36. R. Gordon Hoxie, *A History of the Faculty of Political Science, Columbia University* (New York: Columbia University Press, 1955), 11–15, 29.

37. Skowronek, *Building a New American State*, 68–69.

38. Hoxie, *History of the Faculty*, 75.

39. Ross, *Origins*, 257–59, and Terence Ball, "An Ambivalent Alliance: Political Science and American Democracy," in *Political Science in History*, ed. James Farr, John S. Dryzek, and Stephen T. Leonard (New York: Cambridge University Press, 1995), 43–55.

40. Quoted in Henry Wilkinson Bragdon, *Woodrow Wilson: The Academic Years* (Cambridge: Harvard University Press, 1967), 163. The Columbia School of Political Science opened all strictly graduate courses in history and economics to women holding a B.A. in 1898, though men were admitted to the school without a first degree. Hoxie, *History of the Faculty*, 67.

41. Hoxie, *History of the Faculty*, 35.

42. Haddow, *Political Science*, chap. 11; Hoxie, *History of the Faculty*, chap. 2; John Martin Vincent, "Herbert Baxter Adams," in *American Masters of Social Science*, ed. Howard Odum (New York: Henry Holt, 1927); Carol F. Baird, "Albert Bushnell Hart: The Rise of the Professional Historian," in *The Social Sciences at Harvard*, ed. Paul Buck (Cambridge: Harvard University Press, 1965), 129–74.

43. William C. Chase, *The American Law School and the Rise of Administrative Government* (Madison: University of Wisconsin Press, 1982); Robert Stevens, *Law School: Legal Education in America from the 1850s to the 1980s* (Chapel Hill: University of North Carolina Press, 1983), chap. 2.

44. Haddow, *Political Science*, 215.

45. Fox, *Better City Government*, 25–33. Given the silence of the Constitution on local issues, cities were by definition invisible in constitutional legal theory, so there was no preexisting body of legal or political knowledge specific to municipal affairs at this time.

46. Frank J. Goodnow, *Comparative Administrative Law*, 2 vols. (New York: G. P. Putnam's Sons, 1893). This was the first English-language book on administrative law.

47. John A. Fairlie, "Public Administration and Administrative Law," in *Essays on the*

Law and Practice of Government Administration: Essays in Honor of Frank Johnson Goodnow, ed. Charles G. Haines and Marshall Dimock (Baltimore: Johns Hopkins University Press, 1935).

48. Lurton Blassingame, "Frank J. Goodnow and the American City" (Ph.D. diss., New York University, 1968), 12, 18; Hoxie, *History of the Faculty*, 211.

49. Frank J. Goodnow, *Municipal Home Rule: A Study in Administration* (New York: Macmillan and Co., 1895).

50. Barry D. Karl, *Charles E. Merriam and the Study of Politics* (Chicago: University of Chicago Press, 1974), 28–30; Bragdon, *Woodrow Wilson*, chaps. 10–11.

51. Albert Shaw, *Municipal Government in Great Britain* (New York: The Century Co., 1895) and *Municipal Government in Continental Europe* (New York: The Century Co., 1895).

52. A. Lawrence Lowell, "The Physiology of Politics," *American Political Science Review* 4, no. 1 (February 1910): 4.

53. Leo S. Rowe, "The Problems of Political Science," *Annals of the American Academy of Social and Political Science* 10 (July–November 1897): 171.

54. Frank J. Goodnow, "Review of Albert Shaw, *Municipal Government in Continental Europe*," *Political Science Quarterly* 11 (1896): 160.

55. Stewart, *A Half Century*, 15.

56. Ibid., esp. chap 8.

57. Ibid., 26.

58. Proceedings of the Rochester Conference for Good City Government and Seventh Annual Meeting of the National Municipal League (1901), 20–23, 47–48.

59. Proceedings of the Fourth National Conference for Good City Government and Second Annual Meeting of the National Municipal League (1896), iii.

60. Stewart, *A Half Century*, 28.

61. Ibid., 25.

62. Proceedings of the Second National Conference for Good City Government (1894); Proceedings of the Third National Conference for Good City Government and First Annual Meeting of the National Municipal League (1895); Proceedings of the Fourth National Conference for Good City Government and Second Annual Meeting of the National Municipal League (1896); Proceedings of the Fifth National Conference for Good City Government and Third Annual Meeting of the National Municipal League (1897).

63. Edward W. Bemis, an economist from the University of Chicago, presented a paper at the national conference in December 1894 but did not return, and economists played no further role in the organization.

64. Proceedings of the Second National Conference for Good Government and First Annual Conference of the National Municipal League (1894), 26, 131.

65. Stewart, *A Half Century*, 22–29.

66. "Report of the Committee on 'Municipal Program,'" Proceedings of the Columbus Conference for Good City Government and Fifth Annual Meeting of the National Municipal League (1899), 7–25; Stewart, *A Half Century*, 28–45.

67. Fox, *Better City Government*, 60; Stewart, *A Half Century*, 48–49.

68. Bridges, "Creating Cultures of Reform," 4–15, specifically notes the change in language (and object of reform) of municipal reformers (and object of reform) after 1900.

69. The Municipal Program was widely considered "the most clear and authoritative presentation yet made of the general character and working of American municipal organizations and of the changes that are desirable in them." E. Dana Durand, *Political Science Quarterly* 15 (1900): 330.

70. "The Organization of the American Political Science Association," *Proceedings of the American Political Science Association* 1 (1904): 11.

71. A brief history of the origins of the APSA can be found in ibid., 5–15. The network of scholars working on city government and public administration would be unusually well-represented on the APSA's Executive Council into the 1930s. Material on APSA officers can be found in the APSA *Proceedings* and the *American Political Science Review*.

72. Over 60 percent of the association's two hundred members were lawyers, businessmen, government officials, or participants in various good government movements. Somit and Tanenhaus, *The Development of American Political Science*, 55.

73. W. W. Willoughby, "Report of the Secretary for the Year 1904," *Proceedings of the American Political Science Association* 1 (1904): 29; on the meaning of club life for women, see Clemens, "Organizational Repertoires."

74. Michael Frisch perceptively notes the strong similarity between the league's Municipal Program and the new political science. But Frisch's formulation, that "when the League's Municipal Program was unveiled in 1899, it bore the clear stamp of the new political science," is only partially correct, because it suggests that there was a fully formed political science *prior* to the writing of the Municipal Program. Rather, I suggest, the Municipal Program and the new political science emerged *together* and were constitutive of each other. Frisch, "Urban Theorists, Urban Reform, and American Political Culture in the Progressive Period."

75. Frank Goodnow, *Politics and Administration* (New York: Russell and Russell, 1900), 1.

76. Ibid., chap. 1.

77. Ibid., 18–19.

78. Ibid., 76, 85–87.

79. Paul S. Reinsch, "The American Political Science Association," *Iowa Journal of History and Politics* vol. 2 (April 1904): 157–58.

80. See, for example, Leo S. Rowe, *Problems of City Government* (1908); John Fairlie, *The National Administration of the United States* (New York: The Macmillan Co., 1905).

81. Goodnow, *Politics and Administration*, 93–95.

82. William Bennett Munro, *Government of American Cities* (New York: The Macmillan Co., 1912), 382.

83. Quoted in Schiesl, *The Politics of Efficiency*, 95.

84. Munro, *Government of American Cities*, 123.

85. Frederic C. Howe, *The Confessions of a Reformer* (New York: Scribner's, 1925), 174–75.

86. "News and Notes," *American Political Science Review* 6, no. 1 (February 1912): 106; Ellen Nore, *Charles A. Beard: An Intellectual Biography* (Carbondale: Southern Illinois University Press, 1983), 35.

87. William Bennett Munro, "Instruction in Municipal Government in the Universities and Colleges of the United States," *National Municipal Review* (July 1913): 433.

88. Edward M. Sait, "Research and Reference Bureaus," *National Municipal Review* (January 1913): 48–56; William Bennett Munro, "Instruction in Municipal Government in the Universities and Colleges of the United States," *National Municipal Review* 5, no. 4 (October 1916): 568.

89. "Preliminary Report of the Committee on Practical Training for Public Service," *Proceedings of the American Political Science Association* (1912): 307–10.

90. "Detroit Bureau of Government Research," *National Municipal Review* (July 1916): 501.

91. W. J. Norton, "A University That Is Serving Its City," *National Municipal Review* (April 1916): 326–27.

92. Charles Beard, *Government Research: Past, Present, and Future* (New York: Municipal Administration Service, 1926), 4.

93. William Bennett Munro, *Principles and Methods of Municipal Administration* (New York: The Macmillan Co., 1916), 74.

94. Beard, *Woman's Work*, 86, 205, 291, 320.

95. Munro, "Instruction in Municipal Government in the Universities and Colleges of the United States," 565–69.

96. Peri Arnold, *Making the Managerial Presidency: Comprehensive Reorganization Planning, 1905–1980* (Princeton: Princeton University Press, 1986), 26–51, chap. 4. Merriam served on Roosevelt's Committee on Administrative Management (the "Brownlow Committee"), and the key position of executive director was filled by Joseph P. Harris, also a political scientist.

CHAPTER 7

The Establishment of an Applied Social Science: Home Economists, Science, and Reform at Cornell University, 1870–1930

NANCY K. BERLAGE

BETWEEN the 1870s and the 1920s, home economics emerged and matured as an academic discipline. In contrast to almost all other social sciences, this discipline was centrally defined by women, who, in shaping the field, responded to a constellation of forces both within the university and in the broader culture. First, they drew upon a widespread tradition of female reform that allowed women to claim authority in realms beyond the home. Second, they appealed to the growing cultural authority of science in formulating a professional identity inside the university. While these two traditions advocated different, and often seemingly incommensurate, ideals, home economists readily drew upon both in their academic pursuits. At the same time that they worked within prevailing gender conventions, they also redrew the boundaries that constrained women's activities. What emerged from this process was an applied social science that bridged the gap between public institutions and private homes.

In forging a new applied social science, home economists combined science with reform and advocacy for "women's issues," as well as with individual self-interest. Home economists amalgamated all of these elements, yet historians have not explored their integral interrelationship in examining the development of home economics. Their tendency to separate out single elements rather than acknowledge the interplay among them has provided an inadequate understanding of the whole. In focusing on particular concerns, we have lost sight of the women who became home economists and their actions, as well as their responses to broad developments over time.

The various histories that female home economists have written of their field, for example, affirm without question that the scientific nature of home economics emulates that of other academic sciences. They highlight events of the kind that scholars usually use to delineate the "professionalization" of a field. Depicting an upward slope of progress, these women describe how home economics developed from piecemeal attempts to train young girls in "housewifery" to a systematic, scientific profession. While celebrating its evolution into a scientific, professional, and academic field, they also cite, at least implicitly, the success of home economics as evidence of the gains in status that women have made over the last century. More recent works by scholars outside the field have focused primarily on home economics as a site for rhetorical arguments about the place of women in society. Thus home economics has become a context for analysis of questions about gender, authority and subordination, and power and control. Those works have concluded that the field's development served either as a rationale to expand the boundaries of "women's traditional functions into the arena of social housekeeping," or as an oppressive movement designed to keep women locked in the "traditional" arena of domesticity. Further, rural historians have focused on the application of home economics outside the university. Concerned with the impact of extension service home economists on rural life, they have been for the most part critical. Describing extension home economists as the handmaidens of government-supported business agriculture or as purveyors of "urban" values, they have argued that home economics reinforced domestic ideologies that were detrimental to rural women.[1]

Rather than any single factor, the complex interrelationship of gender with science, reform, and self-interest shaped the development of home economics as an applied social science. This interrelationship also points beyond the standard narratives of traditional social science, which focus on academic disciplines.[2] The multifariousness of home economics also cannot be captured by recent analyses that have challenged those orthodox accounts by "bringing the role of gender in." Robyn Muncy, Joyce Antler, and a few other female scholars have drawn attention to women's experiences and shown that female social scientists often encountered a different professional culture from that experienced by men. Working from the premise that the women they describe were professionals and social scientists (albeit of a type distinct from the academic model), they have expanded the traditional meanings of the terms *social science* and *professional*. But perhaps because the male-centered paradigm of professionalization has continued to serve as a point of departure, the conclusions of these works about social science practice emphasize a male/female dichotomy. These works have posited an alternative, female professional culture that developed and operated primarily (although not completely) outside the university and depended on homosocial networks. They have also stressed that females created a professional culture pivoting on advocacy of women's interests, reform, and politicization, rather than "objectivity" and technocratic neutrality. This tendency to root female social scientists and other female professionals in an enclosed "women's culture" has polarized women's and men's experiences.[3] Home economists, however, embraced many of the same ideals as did their male social science colleagues—the importance of an empirical, scientific tradition, national professional associations and journals, and ever higher standards of academic credentialism. While they remained committed to the reform of "women's work," home economists, in their search for authority, were bound to the broader professionalization process that men inaugurated in their world of practice and study.

The following analysis examines how home economists shaped their discipline as it emerged from its diffuse origins in the 1870s and moved through university academicization, to alliances with outside constituencies, and finally toward maturity in the 1920s as an academic specialty. Home economists straddled both a female reform tradition and the male-dominated academic social science tradition to form an applied social science. They merged science, reform, and gender issues with personal imperatives to construct a professional identity. Home economics initially emerged as an applied academic field designed primarily to enhance women's domestic skills. Around 1900, home economists aggressively redrew the field around nutrition and fortified its scientific character. Nutrition, grounded in chemistry, provided a scientific knowledge base yet was not inconsistent with notions about women's sphere. After 1914 home economists, going beyond the activities of other Progressive Era reformers, fused scientific and reform agendas by forging links to the federal government. These women expanded their support base by establishing a rural clientele outside the university. Finally, after gaining greater autonomy within the university and while Progressive reform networks contracted and reorganized, some home economists turned to child science and Rockefeller philanthropy in the 1920s as new bases for support. Emphasizing the social scientific orientation of child science, which was gaining importance, home economists were able to shore up their scientific base while maintaining a commitment to application and reform.

As both an "Ivy League" and an agriculturally based land-grant institution that received private and public funding, Cornell University provides an excellent focal point for tracing the development of home economics after 1900.[4] I have concentrated primarily on Cornell because the reach of home economics at private research universities was less extensive in this period than at land-grant institutions. Moreover, the New York State College of Home Economics, after a belated start, became one of the foremost institutions in home economics education and practice, often producing innovations in specialized fields.

ESTABLISHING HOME ECONOMICS APPLIED SCIENCE, 1870–1914

In the years between 1870 and 1914, home economics developed from a means to teach women domestic duties into an applied social science. When it initially materialized during the 1870s in coeducational land-grant universities, it was not yet defined as a scientific field, but as an applied one that might accommodate rising numbers of female students.[5] Land-grant institutions, created by federal legislation, emphasized agricultural and industrial arts training, and advocates affixed home economics to this utilitarian ideal. Partnered with agricultural colleges, home economics courses (under the label "domestic economy" or similar formulations) emerged first in midwestern institutions, but by 1900 about thirty colleges had developed domestic science and art departments.[6]

The development of academic home economics broke down some of the barriers facing female students and faculty and opened up space for them in coeducational academia. It provided many young women with new opportunities to break out of and at the same time fulfill many of the gender expectations they grew up with. Through 1870, a minority of women went to college, and those who did attended single-sex institutions; thereafter, the number of opportunities expanded.[7] Women who would previously have been excluded from faculty positions and professions in accordance with prevailing gender conventions now could find a legitimate niche in the university for "practical," domestic-oriented work.[8]

Proponents of the discipline used various rhetorical arguments about women to promote their differing ideals of what purpose applied home economics training would serve, and such justifications suited several motivations. Home economics could equally be depicted as empowering women, or as keeping them in their place. Discourses positing that women needed training in domestic skills (which historians credit Catherine Beecher with launching) dovetailed neatly with a general belief in the value of education for national progress and with a budding agricultural reform movement.[9] Against opposition to higher education for women, arguments that women needed education in "practical" domestic tasks to better perform their duties as wives and mothers mobilized support for domestic arts courses. When rooted in a powerful "separate spheres" logic, home economics did not seem to pose a radical challenge to the gender order. But at the same time, such rationalizations also refuted arguments (propagated in Edward Clarke's *Sex in Education*) that higher education was physically detrimental to women and thus compromised their maternal office as guardians of "the race."[10] As Adonijah S. Welch, president of Iowa State College, argued in his 1869 inaugural address, the "people's college" must "make labor as attractive not only to the boys who are seeking knowledge in their department but to the girls who can never become accomplished and thoroughly educated women without a knowledge of the art of housekeeping and the best methods of conducting every household occupation with system, intelligence and womanly grace."[11] Other advocates at Kansas State supported education for women to improve women's productive capabilities on the farm or in the dairy and poultry sheds, and in business.[12] Such training suited the rural town and agricultural backgrounds from which many students came, environments where women often partnered husbands and families in work, rather than conforming to urban-oriented middle-class domestic ideologies. As several historians of the period have argued, rural women's domestic power often pivoted on their economic and productive roles.

Home economics courses reflected and reproduced traditional notions about gender and work. Framed as useful training for women, early collegiate home economics and its body of knowledge did not explicitly challenge gender codes, although certainly early feminists discussed more radical domestic ideologies (often rooted in socialist or communitarian ideologies) in the latter part of the nineteenth century. Instead, since home economics courses were organized

around traditional notions of "women's work," gender codes served as an organizing principle, for the field lacked the sort of established "professional tradition" that characterized medicine, engineering, and the humanistic sciences
out of which traditional, academic social science emerged.[13] The field centered
on the home and family—far more tangible entities than abstract, theoretical
problems about the polity or economy that would come to define university
social science. For example, Mary Welch, who helped establish home economics at Iowa State University, organized the "Ladies Course" there around domestic matters. While Welch concentrated on food and cooking, the program
also included lectures and practical training in sewing, laundry work, the care
of children and the sick, home furnishings, hospitality and entertainment, and
dairying and poultry, as well as in slightly more theoretical areas such as hygiene, sanitation, and chemistry.[14] This course work was similar to that offered
at other land-grant institutions.

While home economics emerged as an applied field, home economists
sought to introduce an element of science to their students. For example, Kansas State home economist Mary Cripp taught courses in physiology and hygiene as well cooking and sewing, instruction that she considered "thoroughly
practical and of permanent use to the students when they go forth to meet life's
realities." Others also consciously sought to pass along some scientific knowledge to all homemakers. Nellie Kedzie Jones, a younger Kansas State home
economist, suggested in her M.A. thesis, "Science in Women's Life," that
women and their homes would undoubtedly benefit from science. And prominent University of Illinois home economist Isabel Bevier later summed up this
goal when she concluded that the idea of working on a scientific basis, in everyday domestic life, was a great contribution made by the land-grant institutions
to women's education.[15]

The early land-grant home economists' attempts to cultivate science in
"women's work" reflected values of scientism that were penetrating many other
arenas of study.[16] One of the ways home economists at Iowa and Kansas State
Universities introduced science was by setting up "experimental kitchens,"
where students received training in laboratory methods in addition to practical
experience. This experimental bent reflected the national trend toward emphasizing the empirical and scientific study of even the most mundane matters.
Although the department laboratory was sometimes little more than a glorified
kitchen, it was important for furthering claims that home economics indeed had
scientific aspects. Science, the home economists must have realized, was a
means of elevating the domestic arts field.[17]

Around 1900, home economists broke away from those amateurish attempts
at science, and, reinventing home economics, they turned it into an applied
science and, ultimately, an applied social science. They helped define human
nutrition,[18] rooted in chemistry, as a scientific field and, as a result, built a
strong disciplinary knowledge base.[19] Several "pioneering" home economists
tapped deeper into the cultural authority of science than previously and entered the field at a key moment when systematic study of nutrition was only just

beginning. Agricultural scientists had constructed the bases of the field with their chemical findings on animal nutrition. Dr. Wilbur Olin Atwater led the experimentation with human nutrition under the auspices of the U.S. Department of Agriculture's Office of Experiment Stations, beginning around 1894. Several women with academic degrees or training in chemistry, including Isabel Bevier, Martha Van Rensselaer, and Caroline Hunt (who later became leading university practitioners), developed a foundation in nutritional study by working in Atwater's laboratory at Harvard University. Others attended some of the new, traveling graduate schools offering courses in nutrition and gained a foothold in the field.[20] Unlike "regular" chemistry, food chemistry became an acceptable field for women as an extension of traditional "women's work." As a result of these developments, home economists established a great deal of authority in the field. Indeed, they initially helped define the contours of nutritional science and channeled that specialty toward improving home life.

Nutrition enhanced the scientific character of their work and allowed home economists to define it as an applied science. By staking out this crucial scientific territory, these women sought to meet the criteria for empirical or "pure" research, with its connotations of objectivity, so important in the developing basic and social sciences. Claiming jurisdiction over scientific knowledge of food as well as generating it, they transformed "cookery" and related experimentation in food preservation and conservation into nutritional science. These nutrition "pioneers" probably found it easier to scientize food preparation than other home economics activities (like sewing and laundry) because of its integral relationship to chemistry, an already well-established science.

By moving into nutrition, home economists made a statement that science was indeed a proper realm for women, although that realm was still bounded by gender codes. Over the next several decades academic home economists would further develop nutrition as a home economics specialty, and they would make significant contributions to the body of nutritional knowledge. They would advance understanding about the quality and preservation of food and nutrients, about dietary standards, and about vitamins and minerals. Many practitioners would rely on laboratory methodologies (inside and outside the physical laboratory setting) and use new research technology such as the respiration calorimeter. Other nutritional investigations would engage experimental, scientific methodologies more as an ideal than in actual practice; some of the recipe making moved in that direction.[21] Such claims to science buttressed their professional authority, helping confirm their expertise to women in the home as well as to male colleagues. Yet, while distancing themselves physically from the home by taking up residence in the university, home economists remained intellectually tied to the home.

The expansion of home economics in the university during the late nineteenth century coincided with an upsurge of women's reform activities. Many female activists were building a hearty tradition of political and social reform, addressing many different concerns, from temperance and suffrage to immigration and urbanization, throughout the nation in rural as well as urban areas. United in various moral crusades through voluntary associations, clubs, and other networks primarily based outside the university, women attempted to claim a broader public role by "domesticating" the political sphere.[22] It is not coincidental that home economics developed simultaneously: to be sure, it drew its momentum from this reformist mood.

Some of these reformers were also influenced by ideas about food and diet. They fused domestic science ideology and dietary concerns to urban reform projects. While they were not nutritionists according to the definition that would develop in academia, these women attempted to wield knowledge about diet as the basis for authority over other socioeconomic groups. In the 1870s, women like Maria Parloa and Fannie Farmer opened urban cooking schools, offering lectures and demonstrations designed for both working-class and middle-class homemakers.[23] Many consider these women to be the first generation of home economists, although they were not academicians. Other more famous reformers with academic training, like Jane Addams and Ellen Swallow Richards, set up community diners in social settlement houses or opened experimental soup kitchens where they dispensed information on diet, food preparation, and the relative costs of cooking. Many of these activities can easily be read as attempts at social control, a response to new waves of immigrants and to "the servant problem." These reformers attempted to abet the "Americanization" process by educating the "intemperate" working classes in proper diet and by creating a "better" class of female servants. Yet they also incorporated new social scientific knowledge that was being developed into their work. While these food-oriented reform attempts failed to take hold and establish significant nutritional authority within society, they were an important indicator of where home economics was going.[24]

Just as ideas about nutrition moved in and out of the university and between reform and science, so did female home economists in this early period before 1914. Women with academic training in chemistry and nutrition who became home economists took their expertise outside academia. This paralleled efforts by a few female reformers—Jane Addams prominent among them—to combine social science and reform and expand the laboratory beyond the confines of the classroom in order to enhance and utilize their knowledge.[25] By now home economists could draw on the specific body of social scientific knowledge that they were defining along with the training they had in nutrition, grounded in chemistry. The studies that Isabel Bevier authored for the U.S. Department of Agriculture early in her career demonstrate how newer nutritional science ideas combined with older environmental and hereditarian reform logics. Bevier and her male chemist colleagues combined chemical analyses of dietary composition with surveys of food costs and social conditions (such as ethnic, occupational, and home background).[26] Trained in chemistry, not home economics, Bevier would later become the first head of the home economics department at the University of Illinois and would then remain in academia. Ellen Swallow Richards,[27] a strong force in establishing "scientific" home economics, also provides an example of how home economists combined science with domesticity, reform, and occupational opportunities. Barred from practicing traditional chemistry, Richards directed laboratory work in sanitary science at MIT; she became a respected expert in nutrition, wrote governmental bulletins, acted as consultant for various settlement houses and other reform interests, and was involved in numerous attempts to promote popular nutritional knowledge. Her studies on and attempt to reform working-class diets at the New England Kitchen are classic examples of the combination of investigative research, scientific experimentation, and reform efforts to solve social problems—an approach that would remain prevalent in home economics academic practice.

As these developments indicate, the lines between professional, academic, and reformer, and between science, knowledge, and reform logics remained quite blurry through this period. Home economics, as a field of endeavor and as a field of knowledge, remained amorphous. Even as home economics was developing in academic centers, efforts outside of academia contributed to the growth of the field. Yet as academic expansion occurred, university home economics tended to separate out from non-university-based popular efforts.[28] Along with this differentiation, the decade of home economics conferences at Lake Placid, New York, attended by individuals (mostly women) from a variety of backgrounds who were interested in improving home economics, helped to further solidify consensus among practitioners that higher education seemed the best route for the expansion and upgrading of home economics.[29] Home economics training, credentialing, teaching, and a significant amount of research became firmly centered in the universities. While these changes helped mask the explicitly reformist components of their agendas, which could be perceived negatively, home economists continued to invest in reform, albeit newly reconfigured as science.

Around the turn of the century, a new group of female actors contributed significantly to the development of academic home economics. With a great deal of optimism that large-scale social change was imminent, a number of women had undertaken collegiate and graduate studies in a variety of physical and social science–oriented fields, at new research universities such as Columbia and Chicago. But their optimism faded as it became clear that women could not secure academic posts in either "traditional" or newer social scientific fields at coeducational schools. Some enterprising women used their training in positions at women's colleges, or in reform and political organizations. Others, like Marion Talbot[30] and Sophonisba Breckinridge[31] at the University of Chicago, and Agnes Fay Morgan[32] at Berkeley, self-consciously adjusted their academic aspirations for success in other fields and entered that of home economics, committing themselves to building strong home economics departments. Others who practiced home economics between 1890 and 1920 had originally studied chemistry and, in some cases, obtained a degree in it.[33] The early period was thus characterized by both denial of opportunity and new opportunity for women. By becoming home economists, women were able to gain access to

faculty positions based on merit in their own field of study. But that very opportunity was based on prevailing gender conventions that excluded women from
faculty positions in more established fields and assigned them to specialized
work having to do with the home.[34]

This early context helps us to understand that home economists' search for
occupational security, professional and academic status, and reform were important interrelated issues, with significant impact on how they shaped their
practice. Home economists were well aware of the gender bias and double
standards that the first generation of academically trained women encountered.
But as the development of home economics at Cornell University illustrates,
such discrimination did not mean that women were unaffected by or passive
receptors of the dominant trends in academia.

Home economics was institutionalized at Cornell University primarily as a
result of a growing national movement for rural reform that contemporaries as
well as historians referred to as the Country Life Movement. Liberty Hyde
Bailey, a prominent agricultural scientist cum reformer and dean of the College
of Agriculture, helped make Cornell a locus of reform.[35] Agrarian-minded reformers argued that in order to preserve the family farm—threatened by physical and moral degeneration, inefficiency, and out-migration—as a last bastion
of democracy, rural institutions needed improvement.[36] Bailey and other advocates increasingly stressed "the need" to bring scientific information to rural
women, for farm wives were partners to their husbands in ways unparalleled in
most other businesses. In 1900, Bailey brought a woman, Martha Van Rensselaer, on campus to organize a reading course, comparable to the one the college
already offered to farmers, geared specifically toward farmers' wives. This move
was innovative, as previous national efforts to disseminate information about
"scientific farming" through university and USDA bulletins, demonstrations,
and traveling institutes had been primarily oriented toward men. Van Rensselaer supervised the publication of college bulletins that offered advice on farm
homemaking, handled the correspondence sent in by farm women requesting
advice, and organized study clubs for homemakers. Following the huge success
of these efforts, the College of Agriculture officially incorporated home economics for academic credit into its regular curriculum and established a Department of Home Economics in 1908.[37]

The inauguration of home economics at Cornell opened up a range of occupational and social opportunities for Van Rensselaer and her colleagues that
they would not have found in other academic disciplines. Van Rensselaer became cohead of the new department despite her lack of a bachelor's degree
(later gained through part-time study). She also did not have specialized, academic home economics training, but the familiarity with rural women's problems that she had gained while working as a teacher, a leader in women's clubs,
and a school commissioner in rural New York—some of the few jobs open to
middle-class women at that time—as well as the reading courses' success
helped qualify her for the position. She shared the headship with Flora Rose,
a degreed home economist who had taught at Kansas State Agricultural College

and had pursued graduate studies in nutrition at Columbia University before coming to Cornell. Inseparable lifelong companions, Van Rensselaer and Rose retained, like many of their contemporaries, a heady belief in science, and they sought to share scientific knowledge with rural women. Their efforts contrasted with those of the agricultural reformers, scientists, and extension workers who primarily focused on the male agricultural sphere because of its supposed relation to the "public" interest and national economic efficiency. Through home economics, these remarkable and powerful women welded together their belief in science, their hopes for changing rural women's quality of life, and their professional aspirations.[38]

While their department continued to flourish, home economists found that it was not easy for women, no matter how well qualified, to gain acceptance in the university world.[39] The department received additional funds from New York State for a new building, and it established a four-year undergraduate curriculum, summer sessions, and a graduate program.[40] Yet colleagues denigrated their academic status. The university succumbed to male faculty opposition and assigned the coheads lectureships rather than the full professorships that Bailey had planned. Opponents claimed that Cornell would lose status if women became faculty. They also invoked a well-worn rhetorical strategy maintaining that because women were not family wage-earners, they should not compete with men. Finally, in 1911, the faculty grudgingly voted that "while not favoring in general the appointment of women to professorships," it would not object to their appointment in the home economics department.[41] Despite this achievement, the early period of academicization was clearly quite painful: Flora Rose and other home economists later humorously remembered that male colleagues at first ridiculed their academic status, called them "cooks," and even had them use their culinary and hostessing skills to convince visiting legislators to increase university funding. Others more bitterly recalled how "women were never persona grata around Cornell."[42]

Although among social science academics the general trend was toward narrow specialization and theoretics, Cornell home economists defined their discipline as a broad, practical, applied science. According to a university publication, it treated "some of the more important phases of human welfare" including "foods and diet or health and efficiency; the use of income in food and shelter; the principles of art applied to decoration and person; social and industrial forces that govern the home; and the child and the conditions that control its inheritance and environment." The variety of course offerings upheld this mandate; students had to fulfill demanding science requirements in the first years (in chemistry, physics, botany, bacteriology, and biology). Then, in the upperclass years, they took technical classes applying those subjects to home decoration and nutrition, as well as to social scientific courses such as "Women and the Family" or "Household Management." The department also encouraged students to take political science, English, and electives from other campus colleges.[43]

Although some students thought that traditional chemistry was not as helpful as the "food chemistry" courses later established specifically for home economics majors,[44] heavy curricular requirements in the physical sciences were important in reflecting home economists' commitment to maintaining their scientific base. Departmental cohead Flora Rose clearly articulated the rationale for science: "Chemistry, particularly, was believed to give the field of Home Economics a scientific foundation which placed it on a basis of equality with other college departments. It represented respectability," she later explained, setting her field apart from "the social sciences," which "were far from any settled state, and [even] in 1925 were still in great confusion."[45] Albert Mann, a successor to Liberty Bailey as dean of the agriculture college, also lauded home economists' scientific approach. Confirming the power of science, he concluded that even though home economics was still questioned by some because of its relationship to women, "the chemistry, utility and reactions of foods are quite as scientific problems and as important to mankind as the chemistry, utility, and reactions of drugs."[46]

EXPERTISE AND REFORM: THE IMPORTANCE OF THE STATE AND CONSTITUENTS, 1914–1920

In the second decade of the new century, home economists placed their academic practice and their strategy of combining scientific and reform agendas on a new institutional footing. Home economics at Cornell and other land-grant schools burgeoned as a result of a newly legislated association with the national government that conferred a stamp of approval upon the field. This federal funding, filtered through the university, supported both empirical research and application projects. Now highly structured, home economics "reform" programs coherently unified the production and application of expertise with an organized rural client-group.[47]

While by 1914 home economists had gained an institutional base in the College of Agriculture at Cornell and other land-grant universities, their new relationship to federal authority increased opportunities for home economics across several fronts. The field gained a significant role in the innovative science and reform nexus that the U.S. government established by linking land-grant universities, research stations, government agencies, and constituencies; no other sector of science could claim such patronage through this period.[48] The Smith-Lever Act of 1914 appropriated federal funds to set up a complex national system for extension service demonstration work in both agriculture and home economics. Through formal cooperative agreements, national, state, and county governments, agricultural colleges, and private groups contributed resources to make this decentralized system function. Together, they funded the activities of home economists and agricultural extension agents who demonstrated scientific advancements to farm men and women. In 1917, the Smith-

Hughes Act provided additional funding to train and pay the salaries of secondary school home economics teachers. Federal initiatives (and funding), then, solidified the university commitment to home economics.[49]

Perhaps most important for the success of home economics, federal legislation established an institutional mechanism, in the extension services, through which home economists linked the university and home economics knowledge directly to rural clients. To work with the extension agents, governmental and university administrators and farmers promoted the formation of county-based, voluntary organizations called farm bureaus and home bureaus, and some of the first were incorporated in New York State. Advocates encouraged individuals who were interested in farm and home improvements to join the bureaus—organizations that were extremely popular across the nation and were not limited to educational roles, but came to fulfill a variety of political, economic, and social functions. Thus home economists at Cornell and elsewhere helped set up a highly organized system and an active rural, female constituency through which to diffuse their knowledge. In effect, these cooperative efforts built a market for and a supply of home economics expertise; they also gave academically trained home economists an effective monopoly over demonstration work.[50]

Even with expansion, however, controversy over the structure of extension work in New York State threatened home economists' authority. The institutional organization of home economics became a highly gendered site of conflict as home economists struggled to retain the balance of power. Despite governmental support, traditional ideas about gender roles continued to undermine home economists' control over their practice. As long as home economists remained under the administrative umbrella of agriculture, their autonomy was limited. Home economists at Cornell, federal extension administrators, and leaders of the agricultural college battled over who would control the demonstration program. They maintained differing visions of the qualifications and expertise required to drive the organizational structure. A persistent gender bias ran through this conflict. Helen Canon, the first recipient of the Ph.D. in household economics at Cornell, underscored this bias when she described the "unnecessary and grueling controversy" as representative "of the lack of respect for the intellectual equality of experienced women and their suggestions."[51]

College administrators Maurice C. Burritt and Howard E. Babcock,[52] and Dr. C. B. Smith, the chief of the federal extension service, wanted to retain managerial control over home economics demonstration. They wanted it subsumed under and subordinate to the agricultural extension administration, opposing a separate home economics line of command. Arguing that this was the best route to administrative efficiency, they placated home economists by conceding that it might later be appropriate to have women direct the home economics extension work; but they would need administrative abilities and not academic training in home economics. This reasoning cut sharply at the power and authority that Martha Van Rensselaer and Flora Rose were trying to construct. They had planned a direct line of control and communication between the home economics department and local women, and between resident research and extension service work. Rose and Van Rensselaer wanted to ensure that the department and its female staff—not men—would direct the transmission of home economics to its rural clients. They challenged the male administrators on both professional and gendered grounds by claiming that only a knowledgeable, trained, female home economist could understand and therefore administer the work that rural women needed. Van Rensselaer willingly offered to leave control over any "business administration" (that seemed a particularly touchy matter) to the agricultural directors; but when it came to the dissemination of subject matter, she staunchly affirmed that a female head of home demonstration work must be appointed, one who was trained in home economics, a member of the academic staff, and under the control of the home economics department. She also challenged the subordination of female county agents to the agricultural agents, fearing that the men would not take the time to become acquainted with women and their needs—a problem she felt had already been developing. Those male agents, she suggested, probably would not recognize or respect the specialized nature of home economics knowledge.[53]

Overpowered, Van Rensselaer and Rose found it necessary to share administrative control over demonstration agents. A female state leader of home economics was not appointed as they had wished, and male agricultural administrators, who seemed to know little about the field, also retained final approval over agents and home economics departmental appointments. Within a few years, however, when they were more established, the home economics administrators acquired greater control over home economics demonstration work. The office of the state leader of home demonstration agents was transferred to the department in 1919, and the department also acquired control over setting professional qualifications for the practice of home economics at Cornell. Leaving no room for disparagement, they initiated qualifying standards for home economics agents as stringent as those required for extension agents. Cornell based professional standards on *both* academics and experience: agents needed lengthy academic training in home economics as well as practical housekeeping experience. Such rigorous qualifications countered the objections of detractors by reinforcing claims to the highly specialized and professional nature of home economics—even its demonstration work.[54]

Those struggles for control notwithstanding, the rise of the extension service network undergirded and fortified academic home economists' particular mode of applied science. Now, they could securely practice a style of scientized, institutionalized, secular "reform"—one that hinged on the combined production of scientific knowledge at the university and its direct application among mostly rural constituents. "Knowledge" formulated primarily in academic and laboratory-type settings and applied by home economists played a central role in their "reform" campaigns, such as the nutritional projects that I discuss below. Aimed at particular problems that home economics science provided solutions for, these efforts were systematically organized as application projects. Home economists styled their programs as a means for rural women to voluntarily apply scientific knowledge to everyday farm life, a vocabulary that helped disguise the reformist character of their agendas.

Home economists relied explicitly on expertise and science to justify their intrusion into rural family life.[55] They established and nurtured a direct link between the knowledge that they constructed in the university and the application projects they worked on with the rural female members of the county home bureaus. A tight relationship between home economists and the home bureau allowed them substantial control over home demonstration subject matter. Home economics knowledge defined the general scope of application work, even though county home bureau leaders planned their annual "program of work," choosing which projects they would implement from among those developed by the college and extension services.[56]

Martha Van Rensselaer, Flora Rose, and other organizers believed that an organizational style resembling the separatist strategy used by other women's groups to further particular reform agendas would best meet the needs of rural women. Although the New York Home Bureau benefited from affiliation with the male-dominated Farm Bureau, it retained a more autonomous and powerful structure than its counterparts in most other states. Performing managerial functions, these academicians took an active role in shaping the New York Home Bureau into an autonomous, highly sophisticated, statewide federation, and into a strong organizational base and ready-made market for their work. Indeed, home economists performed official duties, were assigned ex officio positions, and for a number of years acted as secretary of the federation.[57]

Working through these rural client groups, the universities, the government, and science, home economists helped implement an important mechanism for initiating change in rural areas—one that contrasted sharply with the efforts at political reform through orthodox channels that drove much of the Progressive movement. Through the Progressive Era and into the 1920s, other female reformers invoked social scientific knowledge but relied primarily on the power of political advocacy and lobbying to increase support for domestic issues and legislation such as the Sheppard-Towner Maternity Act and child-labor laws.[58]

The home economists' style differed also from the "objectivist" ideal of social science that predominantly male-dominated academic professions were constructing. Aspiring to a model of practice in which the structure of authority was informed by an ideal of objective knowledge, academic social scientists tended to distance themselves from the advocacy practiced by those they labeled "amateurs," and they tried to draw boundaries separating research, managerial functions, and reform. Through the 1920s, they vacillated between technocratic and activist ideals, but they still located the foci of their various practices in the "public" arena of the national economy and polity, which they interpreted as more significant than the merely domestic.[59] In contrast, home economists entered the intimate realm of the home and family both in person and with their subject matter.

Clearly, even with its domestic focus, home economics work had broader political implications. The farm and home bureau groups with which the home economists worked undertook political functions by promoting certain political policies and an ideology that idealized the family farm; they also fulfilled some of the social and cultural functions that parties traditionally had served. Moreover, the organization of these institutions allowed home economists and female members a political voice that they might not otherwise have had. Yet home economics demonstration agents cast themselves as neutral in the realm of explicit political action, especially party politics, even though they had opportunities to politicize their fieldwork with ruralists. They denied the political connotations of their work and instead affirmed an ethic of "objective" professional service.[60] Still, home economists relied heavily on public backing and served as advocates for home economics and demonstration work. They often resorted to pressuring for more appropriations by appealing in person to the predominantly male county boards of supervisors, as funding allocated through the college gave agriculture priority. Some of the women found this entry into male public space at once exciting, "daring," and frightening.[61]

In general, the home bureau served as a point of contact between a broader population of rural women, hungry for new scientific knowledge, and academic professionals who needed a client and support base. During this period, belief in the efficacy of modern science spread outside the university. An "eager public" tried to imitate the university in the organization of and search for knowledge.[62] Many rural women joined the home bureau to alleviate social isolation; they also joined because of their interest in managing their work scientifically, as well as to emulate their husbands, sons, and fathers, who were gaining power and knowledge through the farm bureau. This combination of the increased acceptance of science and the merging of private and public resources broadened the "knowledge community."[63] Along the way, home economists and the bureau helped women achieve leadership skills and self-confidence grounded in the knowledge they acquired from home demonstration programs.[64]

Home economists ensured that their nutritional work provided a public service in order to justify public support. They created marketplaces for advice on food preparation that became viable as literacy rates rose, publications became cheaper, and the demand for scientific information increased. Initially, they styled nutrition work as a "service" for women who "needed" more nutritious, economical food and better diets. Drawing upon their research, home economists published innumerable recipes in magazines, university extension circulars, and the *Journal of Home Economics*. The various extension circulars prepared by academic home economists at Cornell University and elsewhere also focused on preservation techniques, meal planning, and food substitutions. So that farm women could save "time, labor and fuel," they promoted new, simple types of food preservation equipment that had become available such as the fireless cooker and the economical pressure cooker.[65] The rationale of Taylorism—improved productivity and efficiency—that changed the male managerial world of work also influenced the home economists in their promotion of this new equipment, although the discourse was made to fit the gendered analysis of rural women's particular drudgery.[66]

Home economists expanded nutrition into a rural "social problem" by embarking on ambitious and far-reaching "Better Health" campaigns geared toward women and children. In doing so, they refuted those critics who denigrated the use of public funds for nutritional work and ridiculed it as support for "frosting cakes."[67] Fusing the knowledge gained in scientific research about food and nutrition to applied work, home economists expanded their jurisdiction into the broad realm of public health. In the case of nutritional science and health issues, medical professionals had not yet consolidated control in rural locales. Home economists seized the opportunity that this gap afforded by claiming specialized health expertise in nutrition and linking it to social welfare action in the countryside. Although professionally trained health experts, armed with the new germ theory of disease, were gradually gaining control of public health, there was still room for a variety of professional groups like home economists to gain a foothold, particularly in rural areas.[68] Moreover, as women, they could lay special claim to family nutrition as "women's work" and take advantage of prevailing gender codes.

The "Better Health" projects paralleled social and public health reform campaigns developed by the antituberculosis, eugenics, better homes, and housing movements as well as the national agricultural initiatives against animal diseases such as bovine tuberculosis. Interaction on a national level among the professionals involved in these movements, their reform organizations, and voluntary associations helped to solidify rhetoric and support for the solutions of certain "scientific" problems discussed in technical language.[69] Various reform logics melded together in the concern over physical, intellectual, and moral health, often making the diagnostics transferrable between environments. As in the city, a general fear of health dangers increased in the countryside, although certainly "problems" of immigration, urbanization, and "Americanization" were more immediate for urban critics and reformers. Problematics similar to those informing urban health issues underlay rural reform, along with an implicit anti-urban bias; home economists translated urban anxieties into concerns about the health "defects" of rural children, the unhealthy "drudgery" of farm women, and rural out-migration caused by unhealthy rural conditions. Fears about poverty, intellect, ill health, degeneracy, and citizenship could be used as a rationale for rural reform—but in this case home economists scientized their efforts through a focus on nutrition.[70]

Home economists often promoted "Better Health" campaigns through the schools, and this coincided with other Progressive educators' efforts to improve the one-room rural schools. The "Hot School Lunch" was a popular project throughout New York and other states into the 1920s. As a result, parents and teachers cooperated to contribute the necessary equipment to prepare hot food that their schools lacked. Home economists argued that their experiments showed that warm foods, proper nourishment, and milk would help children perform better in school.[71]

Milk campaigns, also popular projects, stemmed in part from suspicions that impure milk spread diseases such as tuberculosis, and the notion that home economists' advice could help arrest contagion. Research also indicated that milk was very nutritious relative to its cost, and home economists helped women devise ways to use more milk in recipes and to promote milk drinking at county fairs by serving "Holstein Highballs" and "Jersey Fizzes."[72] They urged children to drink more milk to ward off illness and discussed other nutritional improvements as a way to alleviate, even cure, common ailments such as constipation, gastric distress, weight problems, and colds. Children rated themselves on their habits according to health guidelines, competed in statewide health contests, and were subjected to medical inspections by doctors who weighed them and looked for "defects" such as bad teeth, weight problems, or eye disorders. Children would then agree to develop practices—which in conjunction with other sanitary and personal hygiene measures, such as not sharing germ-laden "dippers" for drinking water from buckets—were designed to produce a healthier future citizenry.[73]

Home economists collected statistics and reported on the efficacy of these health measures, using the medical inspections to correlate the direct relationship of increased milk consumption and the practice of hygienic measures with better health. While such simple statistical research reflected the social scientific belief in the "empirical truth" that data collection showed, it also served another purpose. Congressional mandates required all federally funded extension workers to provide annual reports on all activities.[74] The correlations among education, implementation, and health measurement served to validate home economics work for future funding and to substantiate the discipline's legitimacy.[75]

Influenced by the emerging rural sociology field and its focus on "the community," home economists encouraged home bureau participants to perform their "municipal housekeeping" duties and cooperate on local health projects with such other groups as the Red Cross, the new public health nurses, and the state department of health.[76] Farm women and home economists linked up with a broader health reform network, which women continued to dominate on the local level, thus broadening the reach of home economics. Health issues drew out the relationship between better homes and the broader community and provided a rationale for tightening communal bonds—while serving as a not always subtle means of exerting social control.

For home economists and rural women, the differences between the "practical" and the "scientific" sometimes blurred. Rural members served as a living laboratory; they became a source of knowledge that was incorporated into the developing body of home economics thought. After it became more autono-

mous and powerful, the Home Bureau Federation assailed the authority
of home economists by more forcefully asserting the sorts of knowledge members wanted from them. At Cornell, home economists battled New York State
Home Bureau members over what they deemed properly scientific: they argued that the demonstration of arts and crafts was not science, but shortly gave
in to members' demands to incorporate it into the extension program. As the
conflict revealed, home economists relied on the support of rural women and
could not afford to alienate them. It seemed, according to home economist
Orilla Butts, "that many things got into the Extension program because of public pressure."[77]

This difficulty was related to that of diffusing scientific knowledge without
imparting too much expertise. After all, if that expertise were too easily appropriated, there would be no need for home economists. This is one aspect of
what historian JoAnne Brown has described as the dilemma of the "delicate
balance" between popularization and monopoly of knowledge.[78] In applied
work, the problem was especially acute, and individual home economists differed as to the relative value of science and practical knowledge for rural
women. The definitions of science and research as well as the discipline's objectives remained ambiguous—a situation that would obtain through the late
1920s. That career patterns remained fluid only exacerbated this situation, as
home economists moved in and out of extension work, academic and industrial
positions, graduate study, and motherhood.[79]

The careers of some of the home economists at Cornell illustrate the range of
positions its proponents took as the discipline developed. Catherine Personius
made it clear that her own doctoral research on dairy products was scientific
and that she was not "making toasted cheese sandwiches." She later suggested
that some application work disregarded the scientific base and endangered the
reputation of home economics.[80] Helen Vandervort expressed more sensitivity
to the need for public support, even as she differentiated the realms of knowledge of the expert and the housewife. She pointed out that home economists
studied a variety of complex theoretical subjects, although the general public
assumed this was not the case. Furthermore, home economists needed to translate this knowledge into a vernacular that the individuals they worked with
could understand and utilize. Even though this contributed to home economics' reputation as "cooking" and "sewing," it helped communications. When a
home demonstration agent was out in the field, she couldn't "talk about physics
and chemistry. These [were] unrelated to the public understanding."[81]

The relationship of home economics to gender, women, and social health
involves multiple layers of rhetoric and meaning. Home economists recast and
expanded notions of women's duties and sought to empower women. On one
hand, they reiterated traditional female roles and seemed to reaffirm women's
capacity for nurture. Yet, on the other, they raised the stakes and placed an
extra burden on the mother and homemaker as the guardian of the "social,
spiritual, and intellectual needs of her family as well as their physical welfare."
The provision of proper health care to children, such rhetoric ran, was about

"the most important duty that women would have to perform," and the "first step towards obtaining a better, more intelligent, motherhood for American babies" was training in that duty. While it was important that men, who usually "had no idea what went on in the home," be participants in this domestic work, home economists assumed that it would be women who would benefit from their work and derive the greatest satisfaction from a happy, contented family.[82]

While the "Better Health" campaigns restated the importance of women's role as protector of the home and family, they also critiqued men's action. Meal planning could not only alleviate health problems but could produce "better homes" and "better babies," particularly if it was employed in conjunction with other hygienic, sanitation, and efficiency measures.[83] Relying on the oft-used metaphorical assertion that "children were the most important crop of all," home economists did not hesitate to criticize male-dominated agricultural establishments for focusing science so exclusively on business operations. The farmer, they said, had more scientific knowledge about raising calves and chickens than the farm wife had of the baby who was of such "prospective value to the prosperity and efficiency of the community."[84]

Both home economists and their home bureau clients capitalized on their fusion of domestic ideology and science to seize a broad public role. While rural social reform thus emphasized women's roles as mothers and caretakers, it also proclaimed the importance of these roles for the broader community. Women's activities in the home were linked to other activities in the outside world. At the same time, the interrelationship of gender, domesticity, and home economics justified home economists' move into public health and gave them a special claim on this territory. Expanding the importance of women's role in health maintenance throughout the community also helped raise the status of home economics' subject matter. Yet home economists' stance, as evidenced in their concern for other women's professional, political, and economic standing (as well as their own), was more ambiguous than the concept of "community housekeeping"—usually used to describe such activities—allows. Home economists were not consistent in reinforcing "traditional" gender roles or in challenging them. But in their concern for women's professional, political, and economic standing, home economists challenged traditional notions. They shifted away from domestic ideology and gender stereotypes in demonstration projects on citizenship and voting, in projects on marketing, and in the collection of data on women's economic contributions to family farms. Their correspondence course on human relations, "The Family and the Progressive Home," which incorporated interpretations resembling those found in the work of feminist social scientist Elsie Clews Parsons, reflected this duality.[85]

Home economists endeavored to empower women inside and outside the home. They were not "objective" in their health work and other projects, but self-consciously expressed explicit concerns for women's lot. Women should not only prepare healthier meals, they should prepare them in a healthier manner: wives needed to reduce drudgery by preparing meals in ways that would save labor, time, and money.[86] Home economists advocated the reduction of women's farm work through the acquisition of labor-saving devices, and through efficient planning and management of work. This would allow farm women more time for rest and recreation—a necessary part of the "new," healthy farm lifestyle that social scientists felt farm families needed but rarely practiced. Leisure time would offer rural women the same opportunities that other middle-class women enjoyed, giving them time to learn about civics and using the right of suffrage wisely. After all, the progressive farm woman had interests outside the home, according to Cornell home economists.[87]

SHORING UP THE BASE: ROCKEFELLER PHILANTHROPY, CHILD SCIENCE, AND PARENT EDUCATION, 1920–1930

By the mid-1920s, further structural changes and specialization led home economics toward more autonomy within the university system. Home economics was stretching toward full maturity. In 1925, five years after its introduction, state legislation established the New York State College of Home Economics as an institution independent of the College of Agriculture. Home economists and constituents in the State Federation of Home Bureaus (with their newfound organizational power) had lobbied in classic interest-group style to influence this and other beneficial legislative outcomes; the passage of the Nineteenth Amendment no doubt gave these women more leverage on the state and local levels. With separation from the College of Agriculture, home economists gained more control over their finances, administration, and, most important, their disciplinary subject matter. The college now had formal, specialized departments each organized around some individual aspect of domestic life.[88] Along with this autonomy, the College of Home Economics in the 1920s increasingly addressed "the problem of women's education" as one of preparing women to support themselves. Home economists at Cornell and at other schools explicitly combined older objectives of preparing capable homemakers with newer goals of providing training for expanding occupational opportunities to the new economic woman.[89] Without abandoning the mission of helping "the home" adjust to the complex problems of a changing world, each department now designed curricula to prepare women for specific vocations. The college faculty also geared their resident teaching toward training women for professional careers as home economists, social workers, and educators, as well as future homemakers. Drawing on social scientific data, the college reported that changed conditions were affecting women's role in the home: industrialization had deflated women's economic value, marriage was being delayed, and many families were either unable or unwilling to bear the economic burden of "idle" adult women. As a result, women—married and single—were going out to work. Academic home economists were prepared to train women for "economic independence" as well as for homemaking. This report, however, was careful not to advocate career over homemaking—although that is indeed what many academic home economists had chosen.[90] Home economists' mediation of practical with professional interests served to accommodate, but still challenge, gender constructions about the traditional role of women as mothers and homemakers.

Along with shaping institutional change, home economists at Cornell also expanded their knowledge base to more aggressively incorporate social science into the new area of specialization known as "Family Life." A broad new specialty, "Family Life" incorporated such social scientific issues as the "standard of living." In many ways, it was still a wide-open field that was not yet dominated by any particular group of specialists. While chemistry and nutrition remained important, the rate of expansion in these fields slowed. Instead, practitioners turned to the exciting new opportunities opening up as academic social science gained greater authority within the university, governmental agencies, and philanthropic organizations.[91]

In order to capitalize on the opportunities social science now seemed to be offering, Cornell's home economists actively expanded their support base by forging an alliance with Rockefeller philanthropy. Home economists continued to depend on government and rural constituencies for support, but the influence of that support was limited in the university, even with the establishment of a new Bureau of Home Economics in the USDA. In addition, after peaking in the second decade of the twentieth century, national Progressive reform campaigns shriveled: although reform did not disappear, it took on a quite different institutional form as functional organizations displaced parties and traditional political channels. The tradition of female reform also became more institutionalized and rigid and also lost some momentum with the passage of the national suffrage amendment in 1920. Rockefeller philanthropy stepped into the gap, lending support to home economists, and thereby enhancing the power of these women. The Laura Rockefeller Spelman Memorial philanthropic organization had embarked on a programmatic effort to "systematically up-build the social sciences":[92] it lent comprehensive support to academic institutions and toward professional training in social science as an alternative to direct contributions for legislative and social welfare reform. One result was that social science (still a blend of new academic theoretics and older logics) was expanding across several fronts and increasing in stature. It was now less risky professionally for home economists to move in that direction.

The alliance between home economists at Cornell and Rockefeller philanthropy resulted in a new kind of applied social science that merged academic, philanthropic, private, and public resources. Rockefeller philanthropy provided funds to establish in 1925 a brand-new Department of Family Life, grounded in psychology.[93] The grant also helped to initiate resident work and courses in child training and to develop a nursery school. Academics in the College of Home Economics now delved deeper into child training and parent education, which they made into subspecialties in the new department.[94] In exchange for support from Rockefeller philanthropy, these home economists worked out a research and "reform" program of application projects in child science and parent education, subjects the Memorial was particularly interested in. The Memorial had been founded in 1918 with a mandate to improve the lives of women and children; as part of its effort to promote the social sciences, the foundation helped establish child study at Cornell and other academic centers. It donated significant sums to promote the field across institutions and encourage interdisciplinary work between psychology and other social sciences.[95] Home economists tied child study to the social sciences— intellectually through psychology, and methodologically through both research and reform models.[96] The Rockefeller grant to the college at Cornell was unique in that it was given to a home economics institution and controlled by women. The grants to other academic centers underwrote programs with different institutional, intellectual, and gender characteristics.[97] The agendas of the philanthropists and Cornell's home economists thus merged conveniently.

Home economists, with the Memorial's contributions, developed some of the first applied social science projects that were grounded in psychology. This, I believe, was quite innovative, even though Rockefeller philanthropy was also beginning to support male-dominated academic social scientific fields. We now know a great deal from historians about Rockefeller contributions to the development of social scientific research and institutions; but the Memorial's support for applied social science has received little recognition in those accounts. Rockefeller philanthropy established links connecting academia, government, private business, and managerial interests, helping to create new technocratic roles for social scientists, through such agencies as the National Research Council, the Social Science Research Council, and the Brookings Institute. But, in the case of home economics, it also fostered an interdisciplinary mode of social scientific practice that would *include* the dissemination of new knowledge to the broader public.[98]

Child science and parent education, as well as the whole specialty of family life, opened up space in the academy that home economists attempted to fill in order to further shore up their scientific base. The intellectual models for child science, rooted primarily in the field of psychology, drew home economics closer to orthodox social science. Academic psychologists who opposed the linkage of child study to psychology argued that the former was not a properly scientific subject for male scientists. They thus helped open up that space for home economists; they also reduced its status by disdainfully associating it with amateur female reform and political advocacy—endeavors that, in their belief, violated the standards of academic social science.[99] The affiliation with Rockefeller philanthropy served to fortify the position of home economics in the struggle over turf. In this instance, however, they had to jockey for control with many other groups; social workers, psychologists, and psychiatrists were also establishing child guidance clinics, often funded by the Commonwealth Fund.[100]

Clearly, some home economists understood that child study and philanthropical support offered opportunities they "could not afford to overlook."[101] Like other colleagues, Martha Van Rensselaer and Flora Rose were eager to expand resident and extension work in child study and parent education "as the next step in the development of home economics work."[102] Van Rensselaer used her influence to persuade the Memorial that it should include Cornell in its child study program because of the college's emphasis on the family. In contrast to the other centers the Memorial funded, Cornell could present the home economics point of view, according to Ethel Bushnell Waring, a former faculty member of the family life department.[103] Cornell home economists had publicized child welfare for years through extension work, by sponsoring lectures given by innovative child experts such as Dr. Helen Wooley (one of the first social scientists to challenge prevailing theories of differences in mental traits between the sexes); and nutritionist Helen Monsch had helped run nursery schools and child nutrition programs. Moreover, home economists at Cornell usually had extensive experience in applied science, a stable institutional base, as well as direct networks to local agencies and female voluntary associations.[104]

The academic background of the new staff hired in the Department of Family Life and the courses they taught reflected the changes taking place in the home economics knowledge base. These women often held doctorates, had academic training at research institutions, and had worked in social service jobs. Their training and experience were often grounded in new epistemologies developing in psychology and encompassed experimental, educational, and mental measurement methodologies.[105] But department members forged their own mode of practice by mixing the contemporary rival schools in child study—behaviorism and developmentalism, personality and mental testing—together with the traditional focus of home economics on environment, material aspects of the home, and the techniques of child care.[106] In addition, they relied on the concept of the "normal" child, an intellectual innovation of the new child science. The Department of Family Life also incorporated both old and new social scientific approaches: Dr. Ethel Bushnell Waring's "The Principles of Child Guidance" combined instruction in particular empirical research and observation methods derived from psychology models with older environmental concerns about health and hygiene.[107] But home economics courses also continued to mingle notions about gender, "experience," and "practical training" with research and experimentation. "Practice houses" offered students experience in home management and infant care.[108]

Home economists designed the nursery school to function as a laboratory for all departments within the college, although this sparked some debate over whether it should be available only for observation and parent and teacher training, or for research objectives as well.[109] The view expressed by one of the deans of the College of Agriculture that its function was to teach prospective homemakers "how to care for children" may have been representative of their male colleagues' opinions.[110] As the work developed, however, faculty drew input from university departments outside their own college in order to integrate courses or research in a wide range of disciplines—psychology, biology, sociology, and, particularly, rural sociology and rural education—with home economics work suggesting some acceptance by other academicians.[111] This compilation of knowledge resulted in a broad specialty: through detailed observation of "normal" children's behavior, home economists worked out the principles of education, psychology, hygiene, nutrition, and environment necessary to train children. Based on scientific research and authority, their published research attempted to standardize both parent education and child behavior.[112]

College administrators viewed application of child guidance research through parent education as an important part of their agenda, and highly organized programs carried out through the extension services and the home bureau associations began in 1925. Child guidance work relied on many of the same pedagogical techniques already used by the extension services.[113] As with the nutritional work, home economists relied heavily on cooperation with the home bureau: they formed study programs in which parents could learn how to train children to behave "normally"—i.e., according to standardized guidelines—and then prepared reports on their success.[114] These application projects deployed knowledge culled from several home economics specialties, combining material elements (correct toys, furnishings, clothing, hygiene) with psychological aspects that, home economists argued, would make for better homes and better children.[115]

Staff member Dr. Marguerite Wilker, however, noted the difficulty of translating the psychological basis of the work into extension programs and criticized the parent education program because it "emphasized procedures and rules for parents too much."[116] Home economist Flora Thurston amplified the problem and depicted it as a general tension that existed in all efforts to blend practical experience and academic expertise. She illustrated her point by mentioning others' reservations about the authority of spinsters who taught courses on home economics and family life: "There was always a little friction between people who have had homes and children and those who have not."[117] To help alleviate this tension, the department initiated a program in which teachers visited homes to become familiar with the environments students came from and "the realities of living."[118] Certainly this was a gendered solution; it is improbable that male social scientists would opt for access to the intimate realm of child raising and home life.

While they stayed within certain boundaries, some home economists directly challenged gender conventions by suggesting new mappings of sexual difference. Home economists' work at Cornell disregarded notions of sexual difference in their specialized knowledge of child development. In their investigative studies on children, home economists in the Department of Family Life paid little, if any, attention to gender. Rather, they based their observation on the individual in a particular environment. In part, the psychology models (broadly defined) on which they were drawing help explain these characteristics of their thought. Through the end of the nineteenth century, claims of sexual differences based on physical and natural attributes had gained authority from biological models. Psychology, however, had moved away from the evolutionary paradigms favored by the natural sciences toward investigation of the normal child and psychological behaviorism.[119] Home economists and other individuals who disagreed with such claims could more easily challenge them by changing the terms of the discussion—by moving away from biological strictures to another terrain. For example, home economists' work at Cornell assumed that exogenous factors like nutrition and training mattered in child development; growth patterns, they opined, were not predetermined or innate, and did not automatically follow sequential models.[120] As such conceptualizations paralleled the findings of female social scientists, work that mounted feminist counters to biological assumptions about women's innate qualities, one suspects these conclusions were quite self-conscious.[121]

Ethel Bushnell Waring, the department's director of research, had gained some of her theoretical background from her studies with Lewis Terman, who had developed mental scales of development among children. Perhaps Terman encouraged Waring to develop her own ideas regarding sexual difference, as he was, according to historian Rosalind Rosenberg, among the younger generation of social scientists who were coming to grips with feminist challenges to theories about sex and intelligence.[122] In her summary of the first decade of research at Cornell, Waring explained that the main endeavor had been to study the total personality of the child as manifested in observable behavior. In this research, children were grouped by various categories, but not by sex. Given the pervasiveness of ideas about inherited sexual difference, it is quite telling that the principles of child guidance which home economists worked out did not assume innate behavioral differences between boys and girls. Despite their antideterminist stance, home economists, tellingly, did not use this research to mount an aggressive challenge to biological assumptions about behavior. Of course, to maintain their support, home economists could not flout still-pervasive gender conventions too radically. And perhaps they found it possible to construe their own unwillingness to enrage the male establishment as a manifestation of the very spirit of objectivity—and, hence, authority—upon which the academic social sciences pivoted.[123]

CONCLUSION

At the end of an interview in 1964 about her career in child development at Cornell, Dr. Ethel Bushnell Waring (then retired) cited an article that had appeared in the *Cornell News*, invoking it as a parable to illuminate changes in the Department of Family Life and in the College of Home Economics since her arrival there in the mid-1920s. The article recounted the research contributions of Alfred Baldwin, a cognitive theorist who had been chairman of that department since 1953. In Waring's view, it showed that his work was "really indistinguishable from that of the psychology group on the lower campus—as though he had reached the zenith. He was now fully accepted as one of them, what more could be desired? I thought, well now that has worked out to the finale. He and the department should be well-satisfied. But where is the home economics contribution! Where is the family focus and emphasis?"[124]

Waring's analysis illustrates how very real the conflict between gender and the academy remained in the mind of at least one of its representatives. The colloquy among gender, science, and professionalism continued, although in a modified form, in home economics and academic social science long after the close of the period that I have described. For Waring, this was a story of decline from a golden age when women worked together at Cornell and elsewhere to build a professional basis for home economics organized around the study of the family. The profession, as she saw it, had moved into a time of crisis when home economics was disengaged from its original purposes.

Despite Waring's lament, in many ways home economics was quite successful and provided women, including Waring, with opportunities that they would not otherwise have had. In the latter half of the nineteenth century, the new field gathered a great deal of momentum as it evolved toward definition as a "scientific," academic, and professional field. And in the second decade of the twentieth century, the pace of change quickened and home economics approached the stature to which it had aspired. Denied access to academic positions in other social scientific fields but determined to be accepted on an equal basis, women jockeyed for space in the university through home economics. Constrained by gender norms, they renegotiated the boundaries set by those norms. While the home remained the locus of their activities, home economists rearticulated constructions of gendered spheres of activity to accommodate their search for professional status. They constantly shaped and reshaped their knowledge base in order to better support their pursuit of professional and academic status and the social and economic opportunities that such status afforded. And in many ways, home economists were highly successful. Many universities and colleges instituted undergraduate and graduate programs and, as at Cornell, even established separate schools for the discipline. The new female professors produced rising numbers of women graduates who, in turn, found job opportunities as home economists in elementary and secondary schools, in business and industry.[125]

In part, home economists were successful because they tapped into the power of a women's reform community that made domestic issues central to societal improvement. The expansion of home economics corresponded to the increasing political resonance of women's and children's issues in the second and third decades of the twentieth century. By focusing on the home, reformers gave the so-called concerns of womanhood political currency. These issues were further legitimated by legislation, the establishment of the Children's and Women's Bureaus, and the appointment of women to political and governmental positions. Home economists had a special position in that community. They differentiated themselves from those who were not highly educated experts. The mechanism of professionalism and home economists' claims to research, authority, and knowledge allowed these professionals to cooperate with other women while setting them apart. In order to retain support, they remained integrally linked to the everyday world of "women's work" and the dominant, gendered ideology which bolstered that world. Paradoxically, those claims to distinction were built on a gendered base of knowledge that supposedly bound all women together.[126]

The fluidity of the social sciences in this period worked to home economists' advantage. The boundaries between social science fields, its various practitioners, and disciplinary knowledge remained malleable enough to allow home economists entry into the academic world. One might distinguish who was an academic and who was not, yet it was (and is) more difficult to mark where social science began and ended. Although academics were attempting to differentiate between social scientific fields and to distinguish their practice from that of nonacademics, those distinctions had not yet rigidified. Despite the movement toward a more "objectivist" social science, home economists—typified by those at Cornell—constructed a mode of practice in which they produced, consolidated, and applied a broad range of social knowledge to contemporary problems. This knowledge, often borrowed and adapted from other developing "scientific" disciplines, did not conform to the ideal of academic social science. Home economics was thus able to utilize the resources of a variety of reform communities.

Home economists capitalized on the resources that governmental support offered in return for managerial functions, seizing the opportunity to expand their practice. They were also able to garner support from the administrators of Rockefeller philanthropy whose multiple contributions were hastening a particular process of professionalization in many social scientific fields. The value that the political climate bestowed upon home economists' scientific concerns for "the home" also had currency among those reform communities. In turn, support from powerful groups outside the university helped legitimate the academicization of home economics.

This early configuration of the field was changing, however, by the 1940s. New developments marginalized home economics. The postwar merger of government and orthodox social science displaced home economics, which was pushed out of the spaces where its practitioners had previously located support, leaving little room for the discipline. As the boundaries of social science became more rigid, institutions excluded practices that did not fit with what had become an orthodox tradition. Social science now placed overwhelming emphasis on the linkage between professionalism and a knowledge base defined as abstract, objective, and theoretical—a link that had always been suspect in home economics.[127]

To be sure, the applied nature of home economics and the borrowing of disciplinary knowledge made it difficult for home economists to maintain claims to jurisdiction over particular areas of their practice. But it was not only the lack of an abstract, theoretical knowledge base that marginalized home economics' ties to social science. The seeds of decline had already been planted. The success of home economics in the earlier period had at its most basic level pivoted on the logic of gender difference, but that logic would begin to lose its competitive power, particularly during the 1960s as new feminist critiques of domesticity emerged. Ironically, the gendered concept of "women's work" that had helped gain home economics a place in the university would no longer protect that space. Home economists had built their field around constructions of gender difference—and a dramatic change in that construction ultimately devalued their work.[128]

NOTES

For their helpful comments on drafts of this essay, the author would like to thank Helene Silverberg, Louis Galambos, Dorothy Ross, Rebecca Plant, Carolyn Goldstein, and Dirk Bönker. Research funding, for which I am grateful, was contributed by the Fellowship in the History of Home Economics, College of Human Ecology of the State University of New York, and Mann Library, Cornell University; Rockefeller Archives Center; the Frederick Jackson Turner Society of the Department of History, Johns Hopkins University, and the Ford Foundation/Women's Studies Department, Johns Hopkins University. I have also appreciated the skillful efforts of the editors at Princeton University Press.

1. Carolyn Goldstein, "Mediating Consumption: Home Economics and American Consumers, 1900–1940" (Ph.D. diss., University of Delaware, 1994): this is a groundbreaking work that shows how gender operated more ambiguously in home economics than in the separate spheres ideology that many of the works draw on, at least implicitly. And for other interpretations and accounts, see Sarah Stage, ed., *Rethinking Women and Home Economics in the Twentieth Century* (Ithaca: Cornell University Press, 1997). For home economists' accounts, see Flora Rose, *Pioneers in Home Economics* (East Stroudsberg, Pa.: Practical Home Economics, 1948); Hazel T. Craig, *The History of Home Economics*, ed. Blanche M. Stover (New York: Practical Home Economics, 1945); Keturah E. Baldwin, *The AHEA Saga: A Glimpse of the Origin and Development of the American Home Economics Association and a Glimpse at the Grass Roots from Which It Grew* (Washington, D.C.: American Home Economics Association, 1949), and for a more recent, less celebratory account, Marjorie East, *Home Economics: Past, Present, and Future* (Boston: Allyn and Bacon, 1980). For accounts focusing on the role of gender, see Sarah Stage, "From Domestic Science to Social Housekeeping: The Career of Ellen H. Richards," in *Power and Responsibility: Case Studies in American Leadership*, ed. David M. Kennedy and Michael E. Parish (New York: Harcourt Brace Jovanovich, 1986), and Barbara Ehrenreich and Deirdre English, *For Her Own Good: 150 Years of Experts' Advice to Women* (New York: Doubleday, 1978). On agricultural extension, see Carolyn Sachs, *The Invisible Farmers: Women in Agricultural Production* (Totowa, N.J.: Rowman & Allanheld, 1983); Katherine Jellison, *Entitled to Power: Farm Women and Technology, 1913–1963* (Chapel Hill: University of North Carolina Press, 1993); Mary Neth, *Preserving the Family Farm* (Baltimore: Johns Hopkins University Press, 1994); Marilyn Irvin Holt, *Linoleum, Better Babies and the Modern Farm Woman, 1890–1930* (Albuquerque: University of New Mexico Press, 1995). Also see, from *Agricultural History* 60 (Spring 1986), the following articles: Joan Jenson, "Crossing Ethnic Barriers in the Southwest: Women's Agricultural Extension Education, 1914–40," 169–81; Cynthia Sturgis, "'How're You Gonna Keep 'Em Down on the Farm?': Rural Women and the Urban Model in Utah," 182–99; and, a less critical account, Dorothy Schweider, "Edu-

cation and Change in the Lives of Iowa Farm Women, 1900–1940," 200–215. And see Kathleen R. Babbitt, "Producers and Consumers: Women of the Countryside and Cooperative Extension Service Home Economists, New York State, 1870–1935" (Ph.D. diss., State University of New York at Binghamton, 1995).

2. Traditional narratives of social science have been grounded in models of professionalization; excellent overviews of developments in the historiography can be found in Gerald L. Geison's introduction to *Professions and Professional Ideologies in America*, ed. Gerald L. Geison (Chapel Hill: University of North Carolina Press, 1983); Andrew Abbott, *The System of Professions: An Essay on the Division of Expert Labor* (Chicago: University of Chicago Press, 1988), 1–31. For versions of the politico-economic model of professionalization in the social sciences, see Mary O. Furner, *Advocacy and Objectivity: A Crisis in the Professionalization of American Social Science, 1865–1905* (Lexington: University of Kentucky Press, 1975), and Thomas Haskell, *The Emergence of Professional Social Science: The American Social Science Association and the Nineteenth-Century Crisis of Authority* (Urbana: University of Illinois Press, 1977). Those models primarily focus on nineteenth-century developments, and I believe we need more work on the functions of social science in later periods: intellectual models closing this gap include Dorothy Ross, *The Origins of Modern American Social Science* (Cambridge: Cambridge University Press, 1991), and Mark C. Smith, *Social Science in the Crucible: The American Debate over Objectivity and Purpose, 1918–1941* (Chapel Hill: University of North Carolina Press, 1994). Also see Guy Alchon, *The Invisible Hand of Planning: Capitalism and Social Science and the State in the 1920s* (Princeton: Princeton University Press, 1985), and Michael J. Lacey and Mary O. Furner, *The State and Social Investigation in Britain and the United States* (Cambridge: Woodrow Wilson Center Press Series and Cambridge University Press, 1993). The traditional and revisionist narratives are also limited in that they leave out gender and are drawn from the experience of male-dominated social science.

3. Penina Migdal Glazer and Miriam Slater, *Unequal Colleagues: The Entrance of Women into the Professions, 1890–1940* (New Brunswick, N.J.: Rutgers University Press, 1987); Judith Trolander, *Professionalism and Social Change: From the Settlement House Movement to Neighborhood Centers, 1896 to the Present* (New York: Columbia University Press, 1987); Robyn Muncy, *Creating a Female Dominion in American Reform, 1890–1920* (Oxford: Oxford University Press, 1991); Joyce Antler, *The Educated Woman and Professionalization: The Struggle for a New Feminine Identity, 1890–1920* (New York: Garland, 1987). On the conflict between constructs of gender and professionalism, see Daniel J. Walkowitz, "The Making of a Feminine Professional Identity: Social Workers in the 1920s," *American Historical Review* 95, no. 4 (October 1990): 1051–75.

4. General histories of Cornell University and its state-funded partners are Morris Bishop, *A History of Cornell* (Ithaca: Cornell University Press, 1962); Gould P. Colman, *Education and Agriculture: A History of the New York State College of Agriculture at Cornell University* (Ithaca: Cornell University Press, 1963). The various oral histories of home economists, part of the New York State College of Home Economics Project, have been invaluable. Those specific oral histories, extensively quoted or referenced, are cited individually below.

5. To avoid confusion I describe the discipline as "home economics" throughout this essay. Not all of these land-grant schools were technically universities in the period, but I use this term broadly to encompass all land-grant higher education institutions.

6. Craig, *Home Economics*, 4–6.

7. The midwestern land-grant universities first offered home economics, and then it spread nationwide. "Prior to 1915 almost 100% of the women in coeducational land-grant colleges enrolled in home economics, for it was the only curriculum available to women," according to Linda Marie Fritschner, "The Rise and Fall of Home Economics" (Ph.D. diss., University of California, Davis, 1973), 119; see also 121–23, figs. 7–10, "Total Undergraduate Female Enrollment Compared to Total Home Economics Enrollment [by institution, 1890 through 1970]." Note that home economics enrollment increased sharply compared to total female enrollment starting about 1905. Of course, the land-grant colleges drew students from predominantly rural or farm backgrounds.

8. For alternative discourses providing more radical alternatives to the structure of domestic economy and gender codes, see Dolores Hayden, *The Grand Domestic Revolution: A History of Feminist Designs for American Homes, Neighborhoods, and Cities* (Cambridge: MIT Press, 1981), esp. chap. 2. Also see Karen Elizabeth Altman, "Modernity, Gender, and Consumption: Public Discourses on Woman and the Home" (Ph.D. diss., University of Iowa, 1987), 68–78.

9. For one interpretation linking the rise of home economics to social control and to historical shifts in the labor force, see Fritschner, "Rise and Fall of Home Economics": chap. 2. On education and national progress, see Lawrence A. Cremin, *The Transformation of the School: Progressivism in American Education, 1876–1957* (New York: Vintage, 1964), 8. On Catherine Beecher, see Hayden, *Grand Domestic Revolution*, 55–57.

10. On the emergence of home economics in land-grant universities, see Ercel Sherman Eppright and Elizabeth Storm Ferguson, *A Century of Home Economics at Iowa State University: A Proud Past, a Lively Present, a Future Promise* (Ames: Iowa State University Home Economics Alumni Association, 1971), 19–35; Wayne D. Rasmussen, *Taking the University to the People: Seventy-Five Years of Cooperative Extension* (Ames: Iowa State University Press, 1989), 19; Virginia Railsback Gunn, "Educating Strong Womanly Women: Kansas Shapes the Western Home Economics Movement, 1860–1914" (Ph.D. diss., University of Kansas, 1992), 82; Bessie W. Spratt, "Development of the Home Economics Curriculums at Iowa State College from 1923 to 1953" (M.S. thesis, Iowa State College, 1953), 5–9; Rose, *Pioneers*, 1–9; Craig, *Home Economics*, 3–9. On the rhetorical usages of separate spheres ideologies, see Linda Kerber, "Separate Spheres, Female Worlds, Woman's Place: The Rhetoric of Women's History," *Journal of American History* 75 (June 1988): 9–39. On sex and education, see Rosalind Rosenberg, *Beyond Separate Spheres: Intellectual Roots of Modern Feminism* (New Haven: Yale University Press, 1982), 2–11.

11. "Foundations Laid Early for . . . Iowa's Home Economics Extension Work," Agricultural Extension Service, Iowa State College, MA-107, June 1953, in Box 25, Notebook "Iowa Farm Bureau Women," Ruth Buxton Sayre Papers, Iowa State Historical Society, Iowa City, Iowa, citing inaugural address of March 19, 1869.

12. Gunn, "Educating Strong Womanly Women," 61–66.

13. Agricultural scientists also lacked an academic, professional tradition; see Margaret W. Rossiter, "The Organization of Agricultural Sciences," in *The Organization of Knowledge in Modern America, 1860–1920*, ed. John Voss and Alexandra Oleson (Baltimore: Johns Hopkins University Press, 1979), 211; however, male agricultural scientists' gender probably made it easier for them to appropriate a tradition. Dorothy Ross describes the humanistic traditions of social science in "The Development of the Social Sciences," in Voss and Oleson, *Organization of Knowledge*.

14. Mary Welch was also the wife of Adonijah S. Welch, the president of Iowa State University (then College). On Iowa courses, see Spratt, "Development of the Home

Economics Curriculums," 1–11; Goldstein, "Mediating Consumption," 41–43. For representative descriptions at other land-grant universities, see Gunn, "Educating Strong Womanly Women," 104 and chap. 5; Lorene Keeler-Battles, *A History of the Oklahoma State University College of Home Economics* (Stillwater: Oklahoma State University, 1991), chap. 1; Craig, *Home Economics*, 3–9.

15. Gunn, quoting Mary E. Cripp (a fifty-five-year-old widow, mother, and milliner when she was hired by the university), "Educating Strong Womanly Women," 78; on Jones's thesis, see 107. For a biographical account, see Jeanne Hunnicutt Delgado, ed., *Wisconsin Stories: Advice to Farm Women*, reprinted from the *Wisconsin Magazine of History* 57 (Autumn 1973): 3–27 (Madison: State Historical Society of Wisconsin, 1973). Juliet Lita Bane describes Bevier's opinion in *The Story of Isabel Bevier* (Peoria, Ill.: C. A. Bennett Co., 1955), 40–44. For an example of political conflict over the new emphasis on science in home economics, see Gertrude E. Kaiser, "A History of the Illinois Home Economics Program of the Cooperative Extension Service" (Ph.D. diss., University of Chicago, 1969), 60–65; Kaiser cites Isabel Bevier, *Home Economics in Education* (Philadelphia: J. B. Lippincott, 1924), 134–41, and Bane, *Isabel Bevier*, 16–26.

16. On shifting historical variants of "scientism," see Ross, "Development of the Social Sciences." Also see Ronald G. Walters, ed., *Scientific Authority and Twentieth Century America* (Baltimore: Johns Hopkins University Press, 1997).

17. On the characteristic usages of "pioneering," "experimental," and "laboratory," see "Foundations Laid," Sayre Papers. On "laboratory" functions ca. 1908, see Anna Hunn, Oral History, #47/2/O.H. 73, Division of Rare and Manuscript Collections, Cornell University Library, Ithaca, New York (hereafter CU), 19; Goldstein, "Mediating Consumption," 41–43; Gunn, "Educating Strong Womanly Women," 79–81, 156; Keeler-Battles, *Oklahoma Home Economics*, 24–25. Historians have not explored in depth the role of the laboratory in home economics; thanks to Karen Stupski for sharing her innovative work that helps close this gap: "The Role of the Laboratory in the Home Economics Movement, 1909–1913" (paper presented to the Graduate Women's Studies Workshop, February 22, 1996, Johns Hopkins University, Baltimore).

18. I combine the various subjects of food preservation and conservation, diet, food chemistry, and recipe devising under the broad term *nutrition*: what differentiates this from "cookery" is that home economists incorporated an element of research and science into all of these topics.

19. For background on nutritional science and home economics, see Margaret Rossiter, *Women Scientists in America: Struggles and Strategies to 1940* (Baltimore: Johns Hopkins University Press, 1982), 199–203. On nutrition in general, see *The Science and Culture of Nutrition, 1840–1940* (Amsterdam: Rodopi, 1995).

20. Paul Vernon Betters, *The Bureau of Home Economics: Its History, Activities and Organization* (Washington, D.C.: Brookings Institution, 1930), 14–29. On Atwater and home economists, see Harvey Levenstein, *Revolution at the Table: The Transformation of the American Diet* (Oxford: Oxford University Press, 1988), 75–77, and Goldstein, "Mediating Consumption," 52.

21. Descriptions of nutritional science discoveries are in Ann Hertzler, "Food and Nutrition: Integrative Themes and Content," in *Definitive Themes in Home Economics and Their Impact on Families, 1909–1984* (Washington, D.C.: American Home Economics Association, 1984).

22. Paula Baker, "The Domestication of Politics: Women and American Political Society, 1780–1920," *American Historical Review* 89 (June 1984): 620–47. For more on the reform tradition and its domesticity, see Muncy, *Female Dominion*.

23. According to Craig, *Home Economics*, 5, Fannie Merrit Farmer was student, teacher, and principal at the Boston Cooking School, and published a best-selling cookbook in 1896. Parloa, a former teacher with reformist inclinations, gave public lectures and demonstrations at the Boston Cooking School and elsewhere.

24. For a home economist's linkage of "drunkenness" to the working classes, see Rose, *Pioneers*, 4; on courses for a range of socioeconomic classes, see Craig, *Home Economics*, 6–8. Levenstein, *Revolution at the Table*, describes the "kitchen movement" in chap. 4 and the servant problem in chap. 5; see also Laura Shapiro, *Perfection Salad: Women and Cooking at the Turn of the Century* (New York: Farrar, Straus, Giroux, 1986). For an interesting social control analysis, see Fritschner, "Rise and Fall of Home Economics," and her "Women's Work and Women's Education: The Case of Home Economics, 1870–1920," *Sociology of Work and Occupations* 4 (May 1977): 209–34.

25. On Addams and social science, see the contribution by Dorothy Ross in this volume.

26. H. S. Grindley and J. L. Sammis, E. F. Ladd, and Isabel Bevier and Elizabeth C. Sprague, "Nutrition Investigations at the University of Illinois, North Dakota Agricultural College, and Lake Erie College, Ohio, 1896–1900," United States Department of Agriculture, Office of Experiment Stations, *Bulletin*, no. 91 (Washington, D.C.: Government Printing Office, 1900). In the same series, Isabel Bevier, "Nutrition Investigations in Pittsburgh, PA., 1894–1896," *Bulletin*, no. 52 (1898); and H. B. Frissell and Isabel Bevier, "Dietary Studies of Negroes in Eastern Virginia," *Bulletin*, no. 71 (1899).

27. Richards was the first woman to study at and receive a bachelor of science degree from the Massachusetts Institute of Technology, in 1873. She received an M.A. in chemistry from Vassar, continued graduate studies in chemistry at MIT, and received a faculty appointment there in the sanitation laboratory, which she retained until her death in 1912. Richards helped organize the Lake Placid Conferences in Home Economics, and became the first president of the American Home Economics Association in 1908. In addition to her academic and scientific accomplishments, Richards was active in promoting popular education in sanitation and nutrition, as well as in other home economics subjects. John L. Rury, "Ellen Swallow Richards," in *Women Educators in the United States, 1820–1993*, ed. Maxine Schwartz Seller (Westport, Conn.: Greenwood Press, 1994), 412–19. On Richards's career, see Robert Clarke, *Ellen Swallow: The Woman Who Founded Ecology* (Chicago: Follett Publishing Co., 1973), chap. 13; Hamilton Cravens, "Establishing the Science of Nutrition at the USDA: Ellen Swallow Richards and Her Allies," *Agricultural History* 64 (Spring 1990): 122–33; Rose, *Pioneers*; Bane, *Isabel Bevier*; American Home Economics Association, *Home Economists: Portraits and Brief Biographies of the Men and Women Prominent in the Home Economics Movement in the United States* (Baltimore: American Home Economics Association, 1929); Ehrenreich and English, *For Her Own Good*, 150–57.

28. For mention of home economics' separation from popular institutions, see Rossiter, *Women Scientists*, esp. 70.

29. On these conferences, see Marjorie Brown, *Philosophical Studies of Home Economics in the United States: Our Practical Intellectual Heritage* (East Lansing: College of Human Ecology; Michigan State University Press, 1985), 248–57, 322–23, 287–94; Emma Seifrit Weigley, "It Might Have Been Euthenics: The Lake Placid Conferences and the Home Economics Movement," *American Quarterly* 26 (March 1974): 79–96; and, for some of the topics discussed, see *First Lake Placid Conference Proceedings, September 19–25, 1899* (Washington, D.C.: American Home Economics Association, 1899).

30. Marion Talbot, from an upper-middle-class family of New England reformers, was dean of women at the University of Chicago, 1899–1925. She had received B.A. and M.A. degrees from Boston University and a specialized degree in sanitation science under the guidance of Ellen Swallow Richards from the Massachusetts Institute of Technology. Fully aware of the obstacles to women's education, she turned to home economics and established the Department of Household Administration at the University of Chicago. C. H. Edson and B. D. Saunders, "Marion Talbot," in Seller, *Women Educators in the United States*, 480–89.

31. Daughter of a prominent Kentucky family, Breckinridge graduated from Wellesley College, was a teacher, and completed the Kentucky bar exam but was denied access to the profession. In 1901 she received a Ph.D. in political science and economics (the first woman to do so) from the University of Chicago, and then gained her J.D. degree. Unable to obtain a faculty position in those fields, she joined the faculty of that university in the Department of Household Science and became part of the Chicago female reform circle. John L. Rury, "Sophonisba Breckinridge," in Seller, *Women Educators in the United States*, 63–69.

32. Morgan had a Ph.D. in chemistry from the University of Chicago and reorganized home economics at Berkeley around a rigorous science and research agenda; Maresi Nerad, "Gender in Higher Education: The History of the Home Economics Department at the University of California at Berkeley" (Ph.D. diss., University of California, Berkeley, 1989).

33. Rossiter, *Women Scientists*, for background on nutritional science and home economics, 199–203; Bane, *Isabel Bevier*, 40–44, 59. On home economists' relationship to chemistry, see Rossiter, *Women Scientists*, 65–67, and 36, the suggestive table 2.1, "Institutions Awarding Doctorates to Women before 1900," which shows that women received more degrees in chemistry than in any other basic science. The number of women with chemistry degrees is based on my own compilation culled from primary sources, research collections, secondary books and articles, and newspapers.

34. On women's academic and career shifts, see Ellen Fitzpatrick, *Endless Crusade: Women Social Scientists and Progressive Reform* (Oxford: Oxford University Press, 1990), chap. 4, 81–87; Stage, "Domestic Science," 214–17.

35. Bailey (1858–1954) was instrumental in the overall scholarly growth of Cornell and served as chairman of Theodore Roosevelt's Country Life Commission. A botanist who had grown up on the Michigan frontier, he viewed the farming class as a balancing force in American politics and morality. According to Donald K. Pickens, he combined environmental and hereditarian philosophies, and he augmented them with eugenic conclusions about the need for a "fit" rural population. *Eugenics and the Progressives* (Nashville, Tenn.: Vanderbilt University Press, 1968), 197–201.

36. David Danbom, *The Resisted Revolution: Urban America and the Industrialization of Agriculture, 1900–1930* (Ames: Iowa State University Press, 1979), 25–35.

37. On the early history of home economics at Cornell from contemporaries' viewpoints, see Flora Rose, Esther Stocks, and Michael Whittier, *A Growing College: Home Economics at Cornell* (Ithaca: Cornell University Press, 1969), 13–28, 78; Colman, *Education and Agriculture*, 188; Ruby Green Smith, *The People's Colleges: A History of the New York State Extension Service in Cornell University and the State, 1876–1948* (Ithaca: Cornell University Press, 1949), 75–76. On the reading course, esp., see Sarah Elbert, "Women and Farming: Changing Structure, Changing Roles," in *Women and Farming: Changing Roles, Changing Structures*, ed. Wava G. Haney and Jane B. Knowles (Boulder, Colo.: Westview Press, 1988), 254–61.

38. For an anecdotal biography, see Caroline Percival, *Martha Van Rensselaer* (Ithaca: Alumni Association of the College of Home Economics at Cornell University, 1957). Although Van Rensselaer's lack of a degree at first hurt her candidacy, she later gained the credential through part-time study, and the university appointed her cohead of the new department. She also performed professorial and administrative functions; headed the Home Conservation Section of the U.S. Food Administration during World War I; participated in national presidential conferences, among others; and was a member of the Political Science Association. On the less well known Flora Rose, see Smith, *People's Colleges*, 78. Several of the oral histories in the Cornell collection provide home economists' impressions of the two leaders. Flora Thurston, Oral History, #47/2/O.H. 149, Division of Rare and Manuscript Collections, Cornell University Library, Ithaca, New York, 76–79; Helen Vandervort, Oral History, #47/2/O.H. 75, Division of Rare and Manuscript Collections, Cornell University Library, Ithaca, New York, 26, 37–38, 91–92. Rose and Van Rensselaer's close relationship perhaps represents a transitional stage in the types of bonds home economists relied upon. It resembled the nineteenth-century ties described in Carol Smith-Rosenberg, "The Female World of Love and Ritual: Relations among Women in Nineteenth Century America," *Signs: Journal of Women in Culture and Society* 1 (Autumn 1975): 1–29. Yet it differed from the style of personal relationships that developed by the 1920s; this matter needs further research. For insight on the possible functions of Rose and Van Rensselaer's friendship, see Muncy, *Female Dominion*, chap. 1, which describes the importance of these bonds for women's professional culture.

39. Rose is more critical of male academic domination in her *Pioneers*, 2–3, 14, than in the later Rose et al., *Growing College*, 12. Despite their value, accounts that describe the inclusion of home economics curricula as an example of the "promise of democracy" and as a vestige of the "equal rights" movement have overlooked gender discrimination in academia; e.g., see Colman, *Education and Agriculture*, 188, citing contemporary prominent educator Alfred True.

40. In 1910, New York State appropriated $150,000 for a home economics building. The "staff" became larger and more specialized, but had not yet produced any systematic research, according to one contemporary, because of lack of time, space, financial support, and training. For institutional expansion, see Rose et al., *Growing College*, 51–52 ff.

41. Smith, *People's Colleges*, 82–88; Rose et al., *Growing College*, 34–37; and Elbert, "Women and Farming," 260, all cite the University Faculty Records for October 1, 1911. After this approval, Liberty Hyde Bailey warned Rose and Rensselaer to wait a while before attending meetings of the university faculty.

42. The similarity of these narratives is striking; for these tongue-in-cheek accounts, see home economists Ruby Green Smith (Smith, *People's Colleges*, 84–85) and Flora Rose (Rose et al., *Growing College*, 40); Bane, *Isabel Bevier*, 37; Gunn, "Educating Strong Womanly Women," 100. Mabel Rollins, Oral History, #47/2/O.H. 242, Division of Rare and Manuscript Collections, Cornell University Library, Ithaca, New York, 40–42, CU. On gender discrimination against women in general, see Charlotte W. Conable, *Women at Cornell: The Myth of Equal Education* (Ithaca: Cornell University Press, 1977).

43. Quotation from "Four-Year College Course; Extension Teaching," misc. publication (Home Economics Department, New York State College of Agriculture, Cornell University, ca. 1912), in Box 25, Folder 21, New York State College of Home Economics Records, #23/2/749, Division of Rare and Manuscript Collections, Cornell University

Library, Ithaca, New York. In 1914, the four-year course in home economics included chemistry, physics, biology, botany, physiology, and bacteriology according to the listings of departmental offerings in the annual *Cornell University Register*; see the years 1915–1930.

44. The department in 1926 hired Edith Nasson, a young Ph.D. in chemistry from Vassar, to create a chemistry course that would better accommodate the goals of home economists than the liberal arts course did. This change coincided with independence from the College of Agriculture and the department's conscious move into social science fields. Mabel Rollins, CU Oral History, 41; Helen Hoefer, Oral History, #47/2/O.H. 104, Division of Rare and Manuscript Collections, Cornell University Library, Ithaca, New York, 42–43; Helen Vandervort, CU Oral History, 83; Cornell University, *Report of the New York State College of Home Economics* (1926), 19.

45. Rose et al., *Growing College*, 73–74. For a reiteration of the instability of social science in the early years of academic home economics, also see Rose, *Pioneers*, 9.

46. Albert R. Mann, "Report of the Dean and Director," *Thirty-Fourth Annual Report of the New York State College of Agriculture at Cornell University and the Agricultural Experiment Stations Established under the Direction of Cornell University* (1921), 40–54. Certainly, the establishment of government agencies such as the Pure Food and Drug Administration in 1906 and the World War I Food Administration indicated that others had also begun to accept the importance of "food science" to the national citizenry.

47. Several agricultural historians have established that the federal government contributed to the development of home economics (see n. 2 above): however, the interrelationships among gender, the academy, government, and social science have not been thoroughly explored. A groundbreaking work on home economics addressing professionalism in the USDA Bureau of Home Economics is Goldstein, "Mediating Consumption."

48. On the precedent-setting relationship between the state and the agricultural sector, see Rossiter, "Organization of Agricultural Sciences"; Brian Balogh, "Reorganizing the Organizational Synthesis: Federal-Professional Relations in Modern America," *Studies in American Political Development* 5 (Spring 1991): 119–72, esp. 150–52; David E. Hamilton, "Building the Associative State: The Department of Agriculture and American State Building," *Agricultural History* 64 (Spring 1990): 214, and Mary Jean Bowman, "The Land-Grant Colleges and Universities in Human-Resource Development," *Journal of Economic History* 22 (1962): 523–46. On governmental promotion of rural social science in the 1920s, see Harry C. McDean, "Professionalism in the Rural Social Sciences, 1896–1919," *Agricultural History* 58 (July 1984): 365–72, and idem, "Professionalism, Policy and Farm Economists in the Early Bureau of Agricultural Economics," ibid. 57 (January 1983): 64–82; and on females in the USDA, see Gladys L. Baker, "Women in the U.S. Department of Agriculture," ibid. 50 (1976): 190–201.

49. On the extension services, see Rasmussen, *Taking the University to the People*, esp. 50, 76–80, 86–87.

50. The standard analytical works on the American Farm Bureau Federation include Grant McConnell, *Private Power and American Democracy* (Chicago: University of Chicago Press, 1961); John Mark Hansen, *Gaining Access: Congress and the Farm Lobby, 1919–1981* (Chicago: University of Chicago Press, 1991); Theodore Lowi, *The End of Liberalism*, 2d ed. (New York: W. W. Norton & Co., 1979). I am grateful to Louis P. Galambos for encouraging me to develop my ideas about the "associationalist" governing style that government, professionals, and private groups participated in. For his groundbreaking analysis of organizational developments, see "The Emerging Organiza-

tional Synthesis in Modern American History," *Business History Review* 44 (Autumn 1970): 278–90 and "Technology, Political Economy and Professionalization: Central Themes in the Organizational Synthesis," *Business History Review* 57 (Winter 1983): 47–93. For a theoretical framework, see Ellis W. Hawley, *The Great War and the Search for a Modern Order: A History of the American People and Their Institutions, 1917–33* (New York: St. Martin's Press, 1979), and idem, "Herbert Hoover, the Commerce Secretariat, and the Vision of an Associative State," *Journal of American History* 61 (June 1974): 116–40. On this style of relations among government, universities, and farm and home bureaus, see Nancy K. Berlage, "The Early Farm Bureau: Organization and Community, 1914–1928" (paper presented to The American Seminar, Johns Hopkins University, Baltimore, Maryland, April 24, 1991).

51. Helen Canon, "Problems in the Organization of Extension Work in Home Economics, 1916–1923" (ca. 1940), Box 25, Folder 21, #23/2/749, CU.

52. In New York, Burritt was state leader of county agricultural agents, 1914–1916 and director of extension, 1916–1919, and Babcock was state leader of agricultural agents, 1916–1919.

53. Memorandum for Miss Van Rensselaer and Miss Rose from B. T. Galloway, July 3, 1915; M. C. Burritt to Mr. [*sic*] Forristal, March 4, 1916; Burritt to A. G. Knapp, April 6, 1916; C. B. Smith to B. T. Galloway, May 12, 1916; Martha Van Rensselaer to C. B. Smith, May 30, 1916; Van Rensselaer to A. R. Mann, November 20, 1916, and December 27, 1916; "Memorandum of Understanding Concerning Relations that shall obtain in the Central Organization of the Home Demonstration Work of the Farm Bureaus, agreed upon in Conference in the Dean's Office on November 13, 1916, Professors Van Rensselaer, Rose, and Burritt"; Helen Canon, "Reflections," all in Box 25, Folder 21, #23/2/749, CU; "President's Report 1918–1919," 38, Box 13, Folder 14, #23/2/749, CU; see also Rose et al., *Growing College*, 57–58. Mabel Rollins also notes the conflict between male administrators and home economists; CU Oral History, 74–75, 93–94.

54. On qualifications, see M. C. Burritt to W. L. Markham, March 3, 1916, Box 25, Folder 21, #23/2/749, CU. Van Rensselaer emphasized that extension service positions required a college degree with specialization in home economics; Martha Van Rensselaer to Lucy Swift, November 19, 1921, Box 25, Folder 24, #23/2/749, CU.

55. Rural social scientists and agricultural economists in the 1920s also entered into family life, yet they differed somewhat in the manner in which they focused and constructed space on the farm; they made it "public" by endowing it with implications for the national economy.

56. There are no comprehensive published works on the home bureau other than information included in farm bureau "company" histories or extension services histories including D. B. Groves and Kenneth Thatcher, *The First Fifty: History of Farm Bureau in Iowa* (Lake Mills, Iowa: Graphic Publishing Co., 1968), 51–52; Deacy Leanard, *The Vermont Farm Bureau Story, 1915–1985* (Montpelier: Vermont Farm Bureau, 1985), 20; Melvin Woell, *Farm Bureau Architects through Four Decades* (Dubuque, Iowa: Kendall/ Hunt, 1990), 244–45; Smith, *People's Colleges*, 145–57. For a more complete analysis and listing of citations on the home and farm bureau, see Nancy K. Berlage, "The Farm and Home Bureau: Organization, Family and Professionals, 1914–1928" (Ph.D. diss., Johns Hopkins University, 1997).

57. Ruby Green Smith to C. E. Ladd, November 5, 1928, Box 13, Folder 20, #23/2/749, CU.

58. The timing of home economics' hookup with the government and the rise of interest groups like the bureaus paralleled the decline of traditional party politics, indi-

cating change in the political economy. See Mark Lawrence Kornbluh, "From Participatory to Administrative Politics: A Social History of American Political Behavior, 1880–1980" (Ph.D. diss., Johns Hopkins University, 1987); Muncy, *Female Dominion*. Guy Alchon provides a useful analysis of how the exceptional van Kleeck established links between social science and social feminism, but this useful interpretation seems to rely on the older dichotomy dividing male social science from female reform: "Mary van Kleeck and Social Economic Planning," *Journal of Policy History* 3 (1991): 1–23.

59. Whether that separation ever occurred other than in the minds of those who wished it is a question that is open to further consideration. Lacey and Furner, *Social Investigation*; Smith, *Crucible*; Alchon, *Invisible Hand*.

60. Orilla Butts, Oral History, #47/2/O.H. 72, Division of Rare and Manuscript Collections, Cornell University Library, Ithaca, New York, 41, 42, 46; Frances C. Ladd, Oral History, #47/2/O.H. 87, Division of Rare and Manuscript Collections, Cornell University Library, Ithaca, New York, 34; Helen Hoefer, CU Oral History, 63–66, describes "political pressure" not as "party politics" but as the way "things were done locally."

61. Smith, *People's Colleges*, 149–57; *Annual Report of Extension Work in Home Economics in New York State* (1921), 9; Ruth Day, Oral History, #47/2/O.H. 98, Division of Rare and Manuscript Collections, Cornell University Library, Ithaca, New York, 22–30; Helen Vandervort, CU Oral History, 53; Orilla Butts, CU Oral History, 37; Lucille Cuningham, Oral History, #13/6/2082, Transcript #3856 and #3857, Division of Rare and Manuscript Collections, Cornell University Library, Ithaca, New York, 13–14, 75–76; Helen Hoefer, Oral History, 63–68, recounted how rural women made it clear to supervisors that if they wanted to be reelected, they would need to vote for appropriations.

62. Neil Harris, "The Lamp of Learning: Popular Lights and Shadows," in Voss and Oleson, *Organization of Knowledge*, 430.

63. This phraseology is from ibid.

64. For a rare positive analysis of the useful functions of home economics extension, see Schweider, "Education and Change"; on the experiences of rural women, see the collection of Unpublished Histories of County Farm Bureau Women, MS 18, Iowa State Historical Society, Iowa City, Iowa; Marie C. Wells, *Thirty Years of Progress with the Genessee County [NY] Home Bureau, 1917–1955* (n.p., n.d.), 11–14, in author's possession; Edna B. Scott Sewell, "This Is My Life," autobiographical unpublished manuscript of farm and home bureau member, Box 24, Sayre Papers; and Julie MacDonald, *Ruth Buxton Sayre: First Lady of the Farm* (Ames: Iowa State University Press, 1980), chap. 5.

65. Typewritten Report, November 5, 1918, 5, Box 1, Folder "New York State Federation of Home Bureaus Papers, 1917," #23/17/853, Division of Rare and Manuscript Collections, Cornell University Library, Ithaca, New York.

66. Frederick W. Taylor developed an array of new scientific management techniques to cut costs and enhance productivity, and his efficiency ideals impacted on several fronts across society during the Progressive Era. Martha Banta, *Taylored Lives: Narrative Productions in the Age of Taylor, Veblen and Ford* (Chicago: University of Chicago Press, 1993), 233–40; examples of gendered application of Taylorism in home economics practice can be found in Emily M. Bishop and Martha Van Rensselaer, "Saving Strength," no. 25; Mary Urie Watson, "Rules for Cleaning," no. 23; Helen Canon, "The Fireless Cooker and Its Uses," no. 95; all in *Cornell Reading Course for the Farm Home*. The Country Life Movement also provided a sociocultural analysis of the "drudg-

ery" of women's farm work; for an interpretation of the social construction of the problem of rural "drudgery," see Jellison, *Technology*, chap. 2, and Emily Hoag, "The Advantages of Farm Life: A Study by Correspondence and Interviews with Eight Thousand Women," Records of the Division of Farm Population and Rural Life and Its Predecessors, "Manuscript File," 1917–1935, Entry 149 Es-Fa, Box 2, RG 83, Records of the Bureau of Agricultural Economics, 1923. With this food expertise, home economists staffed the Food Administration Service during World War I to diffuse information about dealing with expected food shortages (which also boosted the reputation of home economics). "Circulars," 1916–1934, RS 8/3/804, University of Illinois Archives, Urbana, Illinois. Sometimes this food production advice exhibited a commercialism stemming from home economics' relationship with the College of Agriculture by promoting products produced in the state.

67. Ruth Day, CU Oral History, 39.

68. On the notion of professional jurisdictions, see Abbott, *System of Professions*. My interpretation of the broad reach of ideas about "health dangers" has been greatly influenced by Dr. JoAnne Brown, to whom I am very grateful for her generosity in sharing her work and thoughts: JoAnne Brown, *Matters of Life and Death* (working title, forthcoming), and her "Crime, Commerce and Contagionism: The Political Languages of Public Health and the Popularization of Germ Theory in the United States, 1870–1950," in Walters, *Scientific Authority*, 53–81. Scholars are only beginning to illuminate the cultural symbolism and material impact of fears about disease and how they reached a broad public outside of medical institutions. See JoAnne Brown, "The Social Construction of Invisible Danger: Two Historical Examples," in *Nothing to Fear*, ed. Andrew Kirby (Tucson: University of Arizona Press, 1990); Naomi Rogers, *Dirt and Disease: Polio before FDR* (New Brunswick, N.J.: Rutgers University Press, 1992), 18–19; and Alan M. Kraut, *Silent Travelers: Germs, Genes and the "Immigrant Menace"* (New York: Basic Books, 1994). Public health concerns were diffusing through the country in this period: e.g., several states initiated pure milk laws; the Cooperative Extension Service produced educational films—such as *Out of the Shadows*, Federal Extension Service, 1920, in Motion Pictures Record Group 33.148, United States Department of Agriculture, National Archives, College Park, Maryland—illustrating how men and women who joined the farm and home bureaus and worked with demonstration agents might defeat tuberculosis; and agricultural campaigns against bovine tuberculosis and hog cholera diffused public health concerns. See Berlage, "Farm and Home Bureau."

69. Academic home economists had contact with activists and specialists within that broad spectrum concerned with so-called women's issues, as well as children's issues, particularly through national conferences; for example, see *White House Conference on Child Health and Protection called by President Hoover, 1930* (New York: The Century Co., 1930).

70. On the timing of eugenics and nativism, see John Higham, *Strangers in the Land*, 3d ed. (New Brunswick, N.J.: Rutgers University Press, 1994), 149–53. Historians have, for the most part, written about urban and rural reform and home economics as if they were separate phenomena; the exception is David Danbom, who does not focus on women. On social science and agriculture, see Danbom, *Resisted Revolution*, 31–32; Emilia E. Martinez-Brawley, ed., *Pioneer Efforts in Rural Social Welfare* (University Park: Pennsylvania State University Press, 1980). Contrary to expectations, social scientific surveys like those done on the Jukes and the Kallikaks, and others, indicated that those in the countryside had the potential to be as defective as city slum-dwellers. Home economists cited studies showing the "health defects" of rural children compared to city

children; they attributed health problems in the countryside to home conditions as well as the lack of rural medical institutions. On "defects," see Helen Knowlton, "Suggestions for the Health of Children," *Cornell Reading Course for the Farm Home*, no. 103 (January 1, 1916); Mary Pack cites figures on "defects" from the New York City Bureau of Child Hygiene in "The School Lunch," *Extension Circular*, no. 41 (Urbana: University of Illinois, College of Agriculture, February 1921); "Half of These Children Needed Help," *Extension Service News*, February 1930, 10.

71. "Home Bureaus Influence Rural Community Life," *Extension Service News*, March 1921, 18; Florence Harrison and Olive B. Percival, "The Rural School Lunch," *Extension Circular*, no. 4 (Urbana: University of Illinois, College of Agriculture, December 1916); Nancy H. McNeal, "A Hot Dish for the School Lunch," Sample Set of Directions for Project Leaders, Box 37, Folder 2 "Extension Work," #23/2/749, CU; Neale S. Knowles shows how extension workers trained for nutrition projects, "Home Economics Annual Report, Iowa State University, 1920"; Dorothy Schweider, *Seventy-Five Years of Service: Cooperative Extension in Iowa* (Ames: Iowa State University Press, 1993), 51–52.

72. Helen Vandervort, CU Oral History, 3–4.

73. Nancy H. McNeal and Mathilda Bertrams, "Suggestive Course of Lessons on Milk"; Nancy H. McNeal, "Milk"; Flora Rose, "A Milk Catechism"—all in Sample Set of Directions for Project Leaders, Box 37, Folder 2 "Extension Work," #23/2/749, CU. The *Annual Report of Extension Work in Home Economics in New York State* (1921–1928) also provides information on these projects. Cornell home economist Mabel Rollins thought that the ability to provide useful, scientific knowledge was compromised by the commercial and political orientation of the agricultural college (New York was a major dairy-producing state). She was troubled by the impression given out that milk was "more like a patent medicine than like a food. There was a distinct implication . . . that it would prevent your having colds and a lot of things that I thought were questionable." Although she took this matter up with the dean of the College of Agriculture, she was warned not to get mixed up in certain aspects of milk. Mabel Rollins, CU Oral History, 63–64.

74. This was often taken to the extreme, as even a brief perusal of extension service reports shows; they can be found at university archives, local farm bureau and extension service offices, and on microfilm at the National Archives. Although extension reports were later standardized, there appears to have been no single report form for agents to complete in the various states through the 1920s.

75. Mabel Rollins, CU Oral History, s55; Albert R. Mann "Report of Dean and Director," *Thirty-Sixth Annual Report of the New York State College of Agriculture* (1923), 83–85; "Home Bureaus Influence Rural Community Life," *Extension Service News*, March 1921, 18; "Home: A Unit of Health," ibid., November 1921, 96; "New York Backs Better Homes Campaign," ibid., September 1922, 65; "Statistics—Nutrition's Measuring Stick," ibid., August 1922, 62; Ruth Day, CU Oral History, 76. On the relationship of medical inspections to broader public health fears, see Kraut, *Silent Travelers*.

76. "Home Bureau, Red Cross, and City Health Workers Unite for Health Betterment," *Extension Service News*, June 1920, 63. "Minutes of Meeting, New York State Federation of Home Bureaus" (1922), 24, and Report of Eastern District (1922), 15, Box 1, #23/17/853, CU. For an overview of "community" theory, see Lowry Nelson, *Rural Sociology: Its Origins and Growth in the United States* (Minneapolis: University of Minnesota Press, 1969).

77. On the arts and crafts conflict, see Kathleen R. Babbitt, "The Productive Farm

Woman and the Extension Home Economist in New York State, 1920–1940," *Agricultural History* 67, no. 2 (Spring 1993): 83–101. The quotation is from Orilla Butts, CU Oral History, 86–88, 93.

78. On the several functions of popularization and monopoly, see JoAnne Brown, *The Definition of a Profession: The Authority of Metaphor in the History of Intelligence Testing, 1890–1930* (Princeton: Princeton University Press, 1992), 54, 22.

79. Rossiter, *Women Scientists*, 201–3, links this to different types of home economists—administrators, researchers, and extension specialists. The differences that became evident in the Cornell oral histories stem from the constant flux in subject matter and differences in academic training between successive generations; this probably also had to do with personal goals and an individual's views on home economics as a career.

80. In the description of her career, home economist Catherine Personius revealed how she geared her study and work toward that professional model. Born in 1904 to a lawyer father and a homemaker mother not involved "in any special women's movements," Personius went to college expecting to become a dietician rather than a teacher, the only career choices she felt were open to women. She majored in chemistry and in home economics, which consisted of only a few courses in food preparation and clothing; she took some liberal arts courses, but nothing in child development or family relations. Elmira College in New York then hired her to teach cooking and supervise the "home management house" where students practiced homemaking. She attended Columbia summer school where she first heard of the pioneer work of Martha Van Rensselaer and Flora Rose at Cornell, and later taught at Cornell where she began to study again and teach part-time. Although the 1930s, when Personius was continuing her doctoral studies, are beyond the purview of this essay, her recollection of this work is valuable. She did her doctoral work not in home economics but in related basic sciences—dairy science, bacteriology, and physical chemistry—as study for the Ph.D. was not available in food science (although one could by that time get a Ph.D. in nutrition and home economics). She noted that "no one in the chemistry department would have been interested in directing a thesis problem which involved food," and that her course of study was primarily dominated by men who were headed for the food industry or teaching and research in food technology rather than in home economics. Personius drew a distinction between amateurish "food science" and the more professional nutrition science—a distinction that seemed to demarcate science and "pioneering" research from practical application and problem solving. Catherine Personius, Oral History, #47/2/O.H. 130, Division of Rare and Manuscript Collections, Cornell University Library, Ithaca, New York, 49, 51, 77–89.

81. Helen Vandervort, CU Oral History, 12. Specialists also prepared extension bulletins in nontechnical language for popular use, Neale S. Knowles, "Home Economics Annual Report, Iowa State University 1918–1919," Box 4, Folder "Home Economics," Records of Cooperative Extension Service in Agriculture and Home Economics, 16-3-01, Special Collections, Parks Library, Iowa State University, Ames, Iowa; Flora Thurston, CU Oral History, 54–55. Thurston read the *Journal of the American Medical Association* and textbooks regularly, but people criticized her for "popularizing" or simplifying the scientific material she used. Ruth Day, CU Oral History, 28–29, also thought that technical bulletins were too complicated, and noticed the widening gaps between factions within home economics, 118. See also C. B. Smith, "Is Extension a Profession?" *Extension Service News*, March 1931, 39 cited by Babbitt, "Productive Farm Women," 98. Orilla Butts noted the conflict between research and utility, CU Oral

History, 90–91. As the fields differentiated and specialized with the growth of the extension services, however, this basic tension between home economics researchers and extension workers would increase. Extension workers were likely to find research agendas less pertinent.

82. "Home Bureaus Stand on What They've Done," *Extension Service News*, October 1920, 108; Knowles, "Annual Report 1918–1919"; Grace Armstrong and Nathalie Vasold, "Manual for Meal Planning, and Preparation Clubs," *Circular*, no. 312 (Urbana: University of Illinois Agricultural Experiment Station, January 1927), 1–2.

83. A variety of home economics specialties were arranged around the concept of better homes, e.g., household decoration, and they included various aesthetic and economic conceptualizations. "New York Backs Better Homes Campaigns," *Extension Service News*, September 1922, 65. For economic and aesthetic facets of the better homes movement, see Janet Anne Hutchison, "American Housing, Gender, and the Better Homes Movement, 1922–1935" (Ph.D. diss., University of Delaware, 1990), and idem, "Better Homes and Gullah," *Agricultural History* 67 (Spring 1993): 102–18. For extension work on better homes at Cornell, see "Bedroom Arrangement," in State Federation of Home Bureaus Report, November 1930, Box 1, #23/17/853, CU.

84. Flora Rose, "The Care and Feeding of Children," *Cornell Reading Course for the Farm Home*, no. 1; Minutes, Annual Meeting of the New York State Federation of Home Bureaus (November 6, 1929), 2.

85. For a differing interpretation, see Sara Evans, *Born for Liberty: A History of Women in America* (New York: Free Press, 1989). On marketing, see Nancy K. Masterman and Helen B. Crouch, "The Roadside Market: An Opportunity for Rural Women," *Cornell Bulletin for Homemakers*, no. 193 (Ithaca: New York State College of Home Economics, June 1930); R. W. Quackenbush to Martha Van Rensselaer, March 9, 1929, Box 13, Folder 24, #23/17/853, CU; "Correspondence Course—Progressive Home" [unprocessed collection], Gladys Reid Holton, #4385, Division of Rare and Manuscript Collections, Cornell University Library, Ithaca, New York. On the value of household labor, see, e.g., Individual Records for Survey of Household Management, Finances, Nutrition, Clothing, in #23/18/1648, Division of Rare and Manuscript Collections, Cornell University Library, Ithaca, New York, and Helen Canon, "A Study of the Family Finances of 195 Farm Families in Tompkins Co., New York, 1917–1928" (Ph.D. diss., Cornell University, 1930). On Parsons, see Rosenberg, *Beyond Separate Spheres*, 156–57.

86. Armstrong and Vasold, "Manual for Meal Planning, and Preparation Clubs," 1–2.

87. Bane, *Isabel Bevier*, 143–44.

88. Rose et al., *Growing College*, 63–84. The college now included the Department of Food and Nutrition, the Department of Economics of the Household and Household Management, the Department of Family Life, the Department of Textiles and Clothing, the Department of Household Art, the Department of Institution Management, and the Department of Hotel Administration.

89. *Report of the College of Home Economics* (1928), 17. On the "new economic woman," see Dorothy M. Brown, *Setting a Course: American Women in the 1920s* (Boston: Twayne Publisher, 1987); Marie Dye, *History of the Department of Home Economics, University of Chicago* (Chicago: Home Economics Alumni Association, 1972), 351; "Roundtable on Household Economics, 1908," Box 2, Folder 39, #23/2/749, CU; Minutes of Meeting of Organization Committee of New York State Federation of Home Bureau Associations, Box 1, Folder "NYSFHB Organizational Meetings, 1919," #23/17/853, CU.

90. *Report of the College of Home Economics* (1928), 17. On the general expansion of women's participation in the labor market, the Women's Bureau's concern for conditions of women in industry, and protective labor legislation, see Brown, *Setting a Course*, chap. 4. It is important to note that in this period, many female reformers supported protective legislation for women workers and defended women's right to work for wages, even as they advocated seemingly contradictory ideals about family wages for men. For the varied uses of this rhetoric, particularly as the debate pertains to "homework," see Eileen Boris, *Home To Work: Motherhood and the Politics of Industrial Homework in the United States* (New York and Cambridge: Cambridge University Press, 1994), 57–60; esp. chap. 3.

91. Cornell home economist Catherine Personius notes this transition away from chemistry toward academic social science, CU Oral History, 124. The USDA in the 1920s built up rural social science; on "standard of living," see Records of the Division of Farm Population and Rural Life and its Predecessors, "Manuscript File," 1917–1935, Entry 149, RG 83, Records of the Bureau of Agricultural Economics, National Archives, College Park, Maryland. On the relationship between social scientists and government, see Alchon, *Invisible Hand*.

92. Alchon, *Invisible Hand*, 117. The director of the Memorial, Beardsley Ruml (a psychometrician with a doctorate from the University of Chicago), had chosen Dr. Lawrence K. Frank to help direct these efforts and to develop the child study program. Frank, who had close ties to leading social scientists, had gained a reputation in New York's reform circles for his ideas about family education. Both men believed that the social sciences had an important role to play in solving societal problems, but they criticized the contemporary state of social science for lacking the attributes of "basic science"—empirical research capabilities and adequate professional training.

93. Although planners consciously grounded the department in psychology, Rose claimed that this mapping became a source of conflict as several theories vied for dominance and made it difficult for staff to agree on methodological approaches. Rose et al., *Growing College*, 77–78. Ethel Bushnell Waring affirmed that there were various psychological theories taught on campus but did not recall any problems this caused in the department. Ethel Bushnell Waring, Oral History, #13/06/2480, Division of Rare and Manuscript Collections, Cornell University Library, Ithaca, New York, 181–84.

94. The grant was totally under control of the College of Home Economics, a new experience. The college was to receive $13,000 per annum for the four years beginning in 1924–1925, plus an initial grant of $10,000 for extension work and equipment. Rose et al., *Growing College*, 69–78, esp. 77. Funding was raised to $37,000 for the years 1926–1929. Beardsley Ruml to Cornelius Betten, March 3, 1926, Box 31, Folder 332, series 3.5, Laura Spelman Rockefeller Memorial (hereafter LSRM), Rockefeller Archive Center, North Tarrytown, New York (hereafter RAC).

95. In addition to Cornell, the Laura Spelman Rockefeller Memorial funded centers at Yale, Columbia Teacher's College, Berkeley, the University of Minnesota, and the State College of Iowa, and contributed a small grant to the Merrill-Palmer School in Detroit.

96. The emphasis on voluntary management in home economics programs is mine, influenced by Alchon, *Invisible Hand*. For an analysis describing the "professionalization" of child science, see Hamilton Cravens, *Before Head Start: The Iowa Station and America's Children* (Ames: Iowa State University Press, 1993); and on boundaries in social science, see Donald Fisher, *Fundamental Development of the Social Sciences* (Ann Arbor: University of Michigan Press, 1993), 42. On the importance of child-rearing as it

related to social order in the mental hygiene–child guidance movement, see John H. Ehrenreich, *The Altruistic Imagination: A History of Social Work and Social Policy in the United States* (Ithaca: Cornell University Press, 1985), 67–68; on Progressives and protective legislation, see Hamilton Cravens, "Child-Saving in the Age of Professionalism, 1915–1930," in *American Childhood: A Research Guide and Historical Handbook*, ed. Joseph M. Hawes and N. Ray Hiner (Westport, Conn.: Greenwood Press, 1985), 415–88; Ehrenreich and English, *For Her Own Good*, chaps. 6 and 7. In contrast, Muncy, *Female Dominion*, describes the parallel female dominion of child-saving and legislative actions, e.g., the Sheppard-Towner Maternity and Infancy Act, mothers' pensions, and minimum wage debates.

97. Flora Rose to Dr. Katharine Blunt, January 23, 1926, Box 2, Folder 4, #23/2/749, CU. Male directors were appointed at the child study centers, and women performed research functions or led the extension programs in parent education. The appointment of Helen Wooley to the directorship of the Columbia Institute was an exception, Cravens, *Before Head Start*, 35, 66–67, 97, 106–9, chap. 2; Theresa R. Richardson, *The Century of the Child: The Mental Hygiene Movement and Social Policy in the United States and Canada* (Albany: State University of New York Press, 1989), 137–43.

98. Fisher, *Fundamental Development*; Alchon, *Invisible Hand*, 117–23. Interpretations of the development of Rockefeller philanthropy place varying degrees of emphasis on the motivational force of social control and its influence on the production of knowledge. Social control helps explain how these philanthropists and home economists found a common meeting ground, but a primary focus on that obscures other reasons for the disciplinary shift. I would also suggest that administrators envisioned a relationship between gender and applied functions, making home economics a logical place to center the work in child study and parent education. This helps explain why the Memorial's directors linked home economics closely to child study when that field was steering, at least in many universities, toward psychology. No doubt, pervasive gender constructions about the role of woman as mother/homemaker also were a factor. We need further exploration of this issue. For varying perspectives on social control, philanthropy, and professionals, see Fisher, *Fundamental Development*, 12–13, and Barry D. Karl and Stanley N. Katz, "Foundations and Ruling Class Elites," *Daedalus* 116 (Winter 1987): 1–40; for a glimpse of participants' motivations, see Memorandum of Interview of Lawrence K. Frank with Flora Rose and Martha Van Rensselaer, November 30, 1924, Box 31, Folder 333, LSRM, RAC. Cravens mentions Lawrence Frank's applied science agenda in "Child-Saving," 440. For a discussion of other Rockefeller attempts to promote applied social science and agricultural and home economics techniques, see Nancy K. Berlage, "Rockefeller Philanthropy and Rural Professionals, 1900–1930" (research report prepared for the Rockefeller Archive, Tarrytown, New York, March 1994).

99. Cravens, "Child-Saving," 433, 437, 443.

100. On other child guidance clinics, see Dr. Margo Horn, "The Moral Message of Child Guidance, 1925–1945," *Journal of Social History* 18 (Fall 1984): 25–36. Cornell also ran consultation and guidance clinics for parents of nursery school children, as well as for the Ithaca Social Services. "Child Guidance Report 1927–1928," Box 31, Folder 333, series 3.5, LSRM, RAC; Ethel Waring, CU Oral History, 39; Lawrence K. Frank to Martha Van Rensselaer, March 29, 1926, Box 2, Folder 2, #23/2/749, CU; *Report of the College of Home Economics* (1928), 23–25.

101. Katherine Blunt (University of Chicago), Anna Richardson (Iowa State University), and Agnes Fay Morgan (University of California–Berkeley) all attended the conference on the general relationship of home economics departments to child welfare, and

"all felt that Home Economics had missed the boat and felt revision of home economics was coming." From Memorandum by Lawrence K. Frank, April 15, 1925, Box 32, Folder 342, LSRM, RAC.

102. Memorandum of Interview of Lawrence K. Frank with Flora Rose and Martha Van Rensselaer re Child Health Survey, October 30, 1924, Box 31, Folder 332, LSRM, RAC.

103. Ethel Bushnell Waring, CU Oral History, 42, 267. Waring suggests that Martha Van Rensselaer and Rose played an aggressive role, based on their prestige, connections, and authoritative knowledge of the family, in soliciting the Memorial's grants; secondary sources and Cravens, in *Before Head Start*, 60–71, assess their role as less significant.

104. On Wooley, see Rosenberg, *Beyond Separate Spheres*, 83. For Cornell home economists' work, see "Teachers and Children Learn Together," August 1924, 41; "Children Learn Conduct from Watching Parents," October 1924, 74; "Home Bureaus and Community Picnics," September 1919, 82; "Child Training Features for Home Makers," February 1924, 99—all in *Extension Service News*. On the link to women's groups in Iowa, see May Pardee Youtz to Lawrence K. Frank, May 15, 1924, Box 40, Folder 417; May Pardee Youtz to R. Haefner, n.d.; "Child Study and Parent Education in Iowa— Study Clubs," n.d.; both in Box 40, Folder 419; "Extracts from Report of the Work in Child Development and Parent Education of the Iowa Welfare Child Research Station," Box 40, Folder 421—all in series 3.5, LSRM, RAC. Ethel Waring, CU Oral History, 42. Frank was also organizing an innovative, but highly decentralized, child study and parent education program in Iowa that involved home economists from Iowa State College as well as other specialists, institutions, and volunteers throughout the state. Memorandum by Lawrence K. Frank, April 15, 1925; "Progress Report of the Iowa State College of Agriculture and Mechanic Arts," November 19, 1929; Frank to Bird T. Baldwin, June 11, 1925, all in Box 32, Folder 341; Memorandum of Interview with Flora Rose, Martha Van Rensselaer, and Lawrence K. Frank, October 30, 1924, Box 35, Folder 332—all in series 3.5, LSRM, RAC; Cravens, *Before Head Start*, 52–55.

105. Dr. Nellie Perkins was formerly a university lecturer in social psychiatry and director of a juvenile psychopathic clinic; Helen D. Bull, M.D., had studied at Cornell and the Merrill-Palmer School; and Dr. Marguerite Wilker used her training, numerous degrees in educational measurement and psychology, to coordinate the extension work in child guidance. Dr. Ethel Bushnell Waring was an accomplished researcher and supervised departmental research. In addition to her study in education at the University of Illinois, Waring had worked with Lewis Terman and Percy Davidson at Stanford; educational theorist William H. Kilpatrick had directed her dissertation in experimental psychology at Columbia, which formed the basis of her book published in 1927, *The Relation between Early Language Habits and Early Habits of Conduct Control*. Marie Fowler had previously been supervisor of education in Kalamazoo, Michigan. According to Waring, Fowler was active in the International Association of Childhood Education and the National Association for Nursery School Education, maintained contacts "inside and outside her profession," and had worked at Teacher's College under Dr. William Kilpatrick, John Dewey, and Patty Smith Hill; as a supervisor at Kalamazoo she supported her teachers to do "anything new or different or better." Waring, CU Oral History, 126, 184–87.

106. This suggestion of the combination of psychological, biological, and environmental models is mine, influenced by Ehrenreich's depiction of intellectual influences on social work and the mental hygiene movement, *Altruistic*, 66–69. Ehrenreich and English, *For Her Own Good*, 201–7; "Child Guidance Report 1927–1928"; and *Report*

of the College of Home Economics (1929), 25. On the paradigm of intelligence testing and its relationship to child development, see Brown, *Definition of a Profession*, 59, 91–92, 102, 136–37.

107. "Child Guidance Report 1927–1928."

108. Several universities had these practice houses: Catherine Personius, CU Oral History, 9; Eppright and Ferguson, *Home Economics at Iowa State University*, 204–5. "Practice" infants, usually orphans—"awful specimens"—who needed care were brought into the practice house where the young students were to get them into "better shape," according to Mabel Rollins. But that policy changed, she remembered, because the Department of Welfare thought that it was bad for babies to have "multiple mothers." Rollins (revealing her belief in empirical truth) disliked that change, because she did not think there was "any evidence that multiple mothers were bad for babies." Rollins, CU Oral History, 18–21, 32. Catherine Personius also thought the practice house gave students who were training for the home economics profession the opportunity to get "some experience" and not be "so idealistic." Personius, CU Oral History, 35–38. Also see *Report of the College of Home Economics* (1930), 46.

109. Ethel Bushnell Waring, CU Oral History, 128; "Child Guidance Report 1927–1928"; *Report of the College of Home Economics* (1918), 23. For example, the Foods and Nutrition Department, headed by Helen Monsch who specialized in infant nutrition, studied the relationship between certain foods and growth, and the Textiles Department studied children's clothing needs.

110. Ethel Bushnell Waring notes this conflict (CU Oral History, 233–40), and, in turn, she emphasized the research function of the nursery in a report that she probably prepared, "Child Guidance Report 1927–1928"; in contrast, an earlier overview of the LSRM program in child study emphasized the training functions of the nursery for teachers and social workers, "Child Study—Parent Training Budget," July 29, 1924, Box 31, series 3.5, LSRM, RAC; Cornelius Betten to Flora Rose, February 23, 1926, Box 2, Folder 4, #23/2/749, CU.

111. "Child Guidance Report 1927–1928"; *Report of the College of Home Economics* (1930), 40; Ethel Waring, CU Oral History, 126–29, 140, 183, 170–71. The department lost an "opportunity," however, to bring outside departments further into the work through a universitywide plan for study of the family funded by the Laura Spelman Rockefeller Memorial, apparently because of administrative problems. Ethel Bushnell Waring, CU Oral History, 138–39.

112. Home economists selected children between the ages of 2.5 and 4.5 years who had "all the behavioral problems familiar to any home," such as sleeping and eating difficulties, temper tantrums, etc., from "representative" homes of the community. *Report of the College of Home Economics* (1928), 23. Publications included Ethel B. Waring and Marguerite Wilker, *The Behavior of Young Children* (New York: Charles Scribner's Sons, 1929), and Ethel B. Waring and Marguerite Wilker Johnson, *Helping Children Learn* (Ithaca: Cornell University Press, 1941).

113. Descriptions of extension work in child guidance and parent education can be found in *Annual Report of Extension Work in Home Economics in New York State* (1927–1930). See also "Family Life Annual Report" (1926–1932), Box 16, and Margaret Wylie, "Child Guidance for the Lay Leader," Box 12, all in Holton Papers, CU. *Report of the College of Home Economics* (1930), 90–91; "Extension Report Child Training—New York, 1926," Box 26, Folder 270, series 3.5., LSRM, RAC.

114. As in all federally funded extension work, public support placed pressure on home economists to demonstrate the efficacy of their work. Home economics and the

extension services tried to denote this with statistics on all the work done, on numbers participating, and on those reporting behavioral changes in children. "Summary of the Year's Work: Extension Program in Child Guidance," September 30, 1926, Box 31, Folder 333, series 3.5, LSRM, RAC.

115. On work with local organizations, see *Annual Report of Extension Work in Home Economics in New York State* (1928), 15–16; "Extension Report Child Training, 1926"; "Summary of the Year's Work: Extension Program in Child Guidance." For discussion of farm family child guidance ranging broadly from child behavior, time schedules, and family rituals to household conveniences, see "Meeting of Morning of April 10, 1929," Box 2, Folder 15, #23/2/749, CU. Also see Marguerite Wilker, "Child Guidance—Extension Program, 1928–1929," in "Annual Report, Department of Family Life Child Guidance, 1928–1929, New York State College of Home Economics at Cornell University," Box 2, Folder 7, #23/2/749, CU. Material and psychological conditions related to ideas about the "standard of living" that home economists and rural social scientists in other departments and universities and at the USDA were trying to measure. Home economists also encouraged members to participate in exhibits at fairs and community plays—events that organizational specialists in the field of "rural life" (i.e., rural sociology) claimed were educational and recreational—for leisure time was something that, in their expert view, farm families and farm children lacked. "Crowds Testify Success of Home Bureau Exhibits [on child guidance]," *Extension Service News*, September 1926, 25. Ostensibly, the individual who participated not only could become a better parent but could utilize these skills for the benefit of the community.

116. Dr. Wilker concluded that those standardizations were "inconsistent with Dewey's philosophy and Progressive education." Memorandum, Marguerite Wilker to Martha Van Rensselaer and Flora Rose, February 11, 1930, Box 2, Folder 13, #23/2/749, CU.

117. Helen Vandervort, CU Oral History, 106–8; Flora Thurston, CU Oral History, 101.

118. Catherine Personius, CU Oral History, 35–38.

119. Cravens, "Child-Saving," 480; Cravens, *Before Head Start*, 45; Fisher, *Fundamental Development*, 42.

120. This occurred at a time when, according to historian Hamilton Cravens, other developmentalists were "beginning to act as if nutrition was not a component of the science of child development." Cravens, *Before Head Start*, 112–13. I would suggest that this trend was gendered in that academic child scientists tried to define their turf in a particular way and exclude those who practiced nutritional science by claiming nutrition did not really matter to child science; but this topic needs further research. On the synthetic fusion of gender and disciplinary practice and knowledge, see Elizabeth Lunbeck, *The Psychiatric Persuasion: Knowledge, Gender, and Power in Modern America* (Princeton: Princeton University Press, 1994).

121. Rosenberg, *Beyond Separate Spheres*. Colleagues at the Iowa Child Welfare Research Station also undermined orthodox maturation and deterministic theories by maintaining that child guidance procedures made a difference to mental and physical growth.

122. Rosenberg, *Beyond Separate Spheres*.

123. Ethel Bushnell Waring, "Ten Year Report of Studies in Child Development and Parent Education," *Bulletin*, no. 638 (Ithaca: Cornell University Agricultural Experiment Station, 1935).

124. Ethel Bushnell Waring, CU Oral History, 270.

125. On employment of home economists, see Goldstein, "Mediating Consumption," 204–5.

126. Muncy, *Female Dominion*; Boris, *Home to Work*. On the rhetorical variations and functions of the issue of "the home," see chap. 3.

127. On the postwar attack on female home economists, see Margaret Rossiter, *Women Scientists in America: Before Affirmative Action, 1940–1972* (Baltimore: Johns Hopkins University Press, 1995), chap. 8; Balogh, "Reorganizing the Organizational Synthesis."

128. On jurisdictional competition, Abbott, *System of Professions*. Goldstein, "Mediating Consumption," 7–9, describes feminist-informed historiographical reactions to home economics; on reactions to domesticity in the 1960s, see William H. Chafe, *The American Woman: Her Changing Social, Economic, and Political Roles, 1920–1970* (London: Oxford University Press, 1972), chap. 10; Ehrenreich and English, *For Her Own Good*, chap. 8. The history of home economics after 1940 needs yet to be filled out. Although women continued to obtain degrees in home economics through the 1970s, it has been increasingly difficult for home economics to maintain support; for statistics, see table 14, "Number and Percent of Home Economics Degrees Granted by Level for Women and Men for 1968–1977," in East, *Past, Present, and Future*, 152.

PART THREE

Social Science as Cultural Critique

Gendered Social Knowledge: Domestic Discourse, Jane Addams, and the Possibilities of Social Science

DOROTHY ROSS

OVER the past twenty years the history and sociology of the social sciences has demonstrated the historical contingency of disciplinary boundaries and definitions. However, it was not until historians of women addressed the subject that gender was taken seriously as a dimension in the social construction of social knowledge. In a pioneering study of sociology in 1972, Anthony Oberschall identified sociology with "sociological theorizing and social research in the contemporary sense" and, defining its origin as the moment of its institutionalization, traced its origin to the University of Chicago in the 1920s. In that perspective, Jane Addams and the Hull House women were cast as "reformers" who carried out "social research," but not as "sociologists." Culture, audience, financial and institutional support all appeared as factors that enabled and shaped sociology, but not gender.[1] After Oberschall, historians influenced by the New Left critique of the social sciences widened and deepened the story he had begun to sketch. Class became a major category of analysis, and the scientific identity that Oberschall regarded as sociology's essence was itself shown to be a misleading social construction. These historians historicized the mainstream social science Oberschall had defined, showing that "sociology" was not always identified with its contemporary markers. However, they largely ignored gender. My own book, for example, preoccupied with a critique of mainstream social science, only noted the masculine language and the exclusion of women that characterized it.[2]

The explosion of women's history and the move to gender have nonetheless made their way to the history of the social sciences. Mary Jo Deegan began as early as 1978 to chronicle the first generation of women in sociology and to argue that Jane Addams and the Hull House women were important sociologists. Her work does a great deal to suggest that women reformers and academic social scientists can be seen as actors in the same history.[3] We are now in a position to ask in a more nuanced way what sociology *was* in these formative decades and how gender was implicated in defining it, both as a dominant cultural representation and as the complex gender positions occupied by actual people.

The lessons of social constructionism are particularly apt in the case of the versatile women of Hull House and the amorphous discipline of sociology. Jane Addams, Florence Kelley, Edith Abbott, and their colleagues opened a variety of paths through sociological territory. While these varieties of social study had much in common, they also had distinctive characters. Kelley brought the statistical techniques of social investigation to Hull House, as well as Marxist theory, and developed them into a powerful tool of social reform. Abbott, more thoroughly trained in academic social science, carried social investigation into an academically grounded profession of social work and policy science. Addams, while supporting their work, theorized and practiced a distinctive kind of interpretive sociology: For Addams, sociological knowledge was interpretive, socially situated, relational, warranted by personal experience, and gendered.

In this paper I will look closely at the formation of Jane Addams's interpretive sociology.[4] Founder of the Chicago settlement in 1889, Addams spent her college years and the early part of her career deeply engaged with domestic discourse. By 1902 when she wrote *Democracy and Social Ethics*, she had used her domestic heritage, reading in romantic literature, settlement work, and study of pragmatism to construct a gendered conception of social knowledge different from that of her university contemporaries. Her struggles with that formulation and her use of it in social study will tell us something about how sociology might have been differently defined.

.   .   .

By domestic discourse I mean the connected discussion of the home as a privileged moral space, of women's nature, and of child-rearing and education, that took shape in the late eighteenth century in England and America and continued in the United States at least until World War I. By treating domesticity as a discourse,[5] I want to call attention to the range of cultural themes it brought together and the variety of uses to which its language could be put. While a didactic literature addressed to women and an ideology of "true womanhood" or "separate spheres" emerged within it, the discourse produced male-oriented discussions of paternity as well, and its prescriptions for child-rearing drew from and reached into the literature of educational reform. Women writers used its language to justify active public benevolence as well as passive familial duty.[6] Domestic discourse in nineteenth-century America often expressed the concerns of secularizing Protestants about the breakdown of traditional gender roles and morality in a fast-changing commercial society.[7] The native middle-class was a primary locus of these concerns and, in part, formed around the domestic pattern as a means of class differentiation and social reproduction. The intertwining of class and gender identities produced a highly gendered language of domesticity that both formed and reflected the new patterns of middle-class life.[8]

Although the language of domesticity is well-known to historians and critics, they have not examined carefully its ability to serve as a medium of social knowledge, that is, as a language that conveyed and promoted certain ways of understanding society. The discourse of domesticity offered a variety of resources for the cultivation of social knowledge. There was first, of course, the attribution to women of finer sensibilities, giving them intuitive insight into spiritual matters and sympathetic understanding of human and moral relations. A second was the domestic writers' model of child-rearing, urging that human nature was redeemable and could be shaped by environmental influences. In the dyadic relationship between parent and child, the parent or teacher was told to exert authority, not by fiat or force, but by example and by enlisting the child's own reason, interests, and feelings in good conduct.[9]

Environmentalist logic led domestic writers to emphasize learning from experience. Against mere intellectual or "book" knowledge, they urged concrete experience of the conditions of life. Experience of the world could be coded as masculine, but in women's domestic literature it appeared largely as feminine, the realm of the concrete and of interpersonal experience, like the didactic mother-child relations that taught duty and self-control. In its romantic form, such experience brought emotions into play and produced an understanding grounded in feeling. After the Civil War, domestic discourse absorbed in addition the worship of high culture and the desire for leisured sociability of the more secular, Gilded Age middle-class.[10]

The discourse of domesticity thus provided a variety of means to social knowledge: women's superior moral intuitions; an appreciation of the educative value of experience, particularly interpersonal experience, with its acute psychological focus on human relations; the parent-child model of learning based in sympathy, which middle-class women were fast extending to those outside middle-class domestic norms, like slaves and the poor; and the cultural authority of the middle-class home. In the new circumstances of the Gilded Age and Progressive Era, it was a heritage that could be engaged and transformed in a variety of ways, yielding both strengths and limitations for the understanding of society and social relations.

Jane Addams absorbed domestic discourse in a morally earnest and culturally elevated upper-middle-class home, where her stepmother was wholly committed to domestic values.[11] Born in 1860, she grew up reading in the domestic genre[12] and in 1877 enrolled in nearby Rockford Female Seminary, soon to become Rockford College. Rockford was modeled on Mount Holyoke and taught piety and domesticity as well as a basic college curriculum of classical languages, literature, and science.[13]

Addams's college essays show her to be thoroughly steeped in romantic writers: Goethe, Wordsworth, Coleridge, Scott, Emerson, and Carlyle constantly reappear. I use *romantic* here broadly, to denote the tendency to valorize feeling, subjectivity, individuality, and intuition. Framed in opposition to scientists' mechanistic understanding of the world, the romantics' intuition gave access to the world's aesthetic and spiritual meanings; it proceeded by sympathetic insight and synthetic grasp, rather than by distanced analysis. Despite their differences, these writers shared some or all of these themes. Romanticism reinforced domesticity's praise of intuition, feeling, and experience, but it also challenged the feminine limits that domesticity had placed on these terms.

Addams gives her highest praise to romantic intuition, the power of the "poet" or "prophetic priest" that "organizes the divine beauty in every object and can discern the loveliness of things."[14] The male romantic poets linked this power to Imagination, previously considered a female capacity, turning it into the high, intuitive form of Reason, the capacity to discern the fundamental order—at once rational, moral, and aesthetic—of the world. In the process, they demoted female imagination to mere "fancy."[15] It is romantic intuition in this softer, feminine vein that first attracts Addams. Such power, she says, comes from Mother Nature: "even as she feeds and nourishes her children with corn and wine, so likewise she contains that which would make them wise and learned, fill even the meanest with delicate fancies and tender thoughts."[16] Addams would soon abandon feminine fancy for the masculine aspiration to intuitive Truth, but nature as the feminine source of both bread and wisdom was a thread that ran throughout her college essays, joining romantic wisdom to domestic nurturance.

Beyond intuition, there was also the romantic penchant for experience. Reviewing Walter Scott, Addams lamented that study could "bury ourselves that much the deeper under a mass of books and other men's thoughts." Or "We lack real experiance [sic] and work to a disadvantage."[17] Likewise, with references to Carlyle, personal force and character were always at the center of her attention. Writing an essay on Cicero and Caesar, she discussed not political principle or historical consequence, but rather their characters as men of action or principle.[18]

For romantic writers, personal force was not only the focus of subjective experience but also the path of self-realization. One of Addams's most insistent notes was the romantic injunction to achieve her "own individuality," her "own life purpose."[19] One tradition of women's education, going back through Mary Lyon at Mount Holyoke to Catharine Beecher, urged young women to use their education in action, and like many women in her generation, Addams also could have found encouragement for independence in domestic heroines such as Louisa May Alcott's Jo.[20] But romantic writers like Emerson and Carlyle offered her a more direct invitation to heroism. "Unless each man follow independently his own star no one man can be a hero."[21] Including herself in the generic masculine, "man," Addams accepted the challenge. The desire for unique individuality could threaten all social conventions, and it soon encouraged her to stretch, if not break, the conventional bounds of domesticity. Yet she always contained individualism by stressing the harmony that romantics posited among all individualities, so that achieving one's own "life-purpose" also brought one "into sympathy with nature, and harmony with mankind." Romanticism could also lead to organic conceptions of society that meshed well with Addams's domestic ideal of a society bound by familial ties of charity and duty.[22]

At the end of her junior year at Rockford, Addams located her life purpose, vague though it still was, within the first-generation collegians' enlarged domestic ideal. Woman's aspiration, she asserted, has "passed from accomplishments and the arts of pleasing, to the development of her intellectual force, and her capabilities for direct labor." But, she continued, "we still retain the old ideal of womanhood—the Saxon lady whose mission it was to give bread unto her household. [Believing] that the only true and honorable life is one filled with good works and honest toil, we have planned to idealize our labor, and thus happily fulfil Woman's Noblest Mission." Addams goes back to the "Saxon lady," presumably to find a strong and noble role model untainted by contemporary social standards, as she goes forward to "idealized" labor in the society at large.[23]

During Addams's senior year, her romantic/domestic ideal was enlarged once again, and this time by a very different source, modern science. Her studies of science in college and with her stepbrother, who was an aspiring scientist, took on new force.[24] In one essay, she assigned to the scientist the godlike creativity that she had hitherto reserved for the romantic poet.[25] Addams praised science in romantic terms, but she also read Huxley and admired Darwin. She absorbed what David Hollinger has called the ethic of science, the claim of science to a high morality of diligence and integrity: what most impressed her was the scientist's commitment to painstaking observation of nature.[26] Her studies gave her a new perspective on her old ideal and, above all, a more confident romantic ambition.

Addams's valedictory essay is remarkable for its intellectual boldness. Using the myth of Cassandra, whose prophecy of the Greek victory over Troy was scorned by her Trojan countrymen, Addams now claimed for intuition, this "feminine trait of mind," all the power that its male heralds had put into it. Calling it "the old beautiful force which Plato taught," she insisted that "an intuition is a force in the universe, and a part of nature; that an intuitive perception committed to a woman's charge is not a prejudice or a fancy, but one of the holy means given to mankind in their search for truth." No longer just "fancy," it was a "mighty intuitive perception of Truth."

While Addams recognized this force, however, she lamented that the world did not. Women had used their intuitive power in occasional prophecy, in sentimentalism, in frustrated discontent, or under the aegis of love, particularly in the relation between mother and child, she said. But women had never gained "what the ancients called *auethoritas*, [the] right of speakers to make themselves heard." That authority was held by men, she said, because the masculine ideal of knowledge had been made effective by science. "While men with hard research into science, with sturdy and unremitting toil, have shown the power and magnificence of knowledge," women had "shirked to perform for intuition the same hard labor."

How could feminine intuition be made effective in the world? Women should study at least one physical science, she suggested, to make their intuition more "accurate" and self-critical. Addams's answer, to bring science into the orbit of romantic epistemology, was one that other romantics had taken. She was familiar with Goethe's romantic science, which sought the order of living forms rather than mechanical laws. Training in science could issue, she implies, in a kind of romantic science.[27] Or it could be put to the use of woman's socialized domestic ideal. In the sphere of "morals and justice . . . she must take the active busy world as a text for the genuineness of her intuition." Here science, particularly the naturalist's science of careful observation that she admired, could augment the romantics' familiar intellectual skills: insight, "the quick recognition of the true and genuine wherever it appears"; "broadened sympathies toward the individual man and woman"; and synthetic grasp, for "only an intuitive mind has a grasp comprehensive enough to embrace the opposing facts and forces."[28]

There are a number of things remarkable about this essay beyond its intellectual ambition. It suggests how seriously Addams took the problem of gendered knowledge set her by domesticity and how the romantic tradition both reinforced the problem and enlarged the intellectual resources available to her for its solution. Addams took with her into her early career this composite domestic/romantic epistemology, its feminine powers fortified by masculine ambitions. Likewise, sympathy, insight, and synthesis would remain the central terms in her understanding of her task, supplemented by an appreciation of science as their adjunct. Her domestic/romantic project propelled her out of the domestic sphere into the "active busy world," and it continued to define her approach to the modern complexities she found there.

.   .   .

When Addams graduated in 1881 and returned home, the reconciliation between domesticity and romantic ambition she had effected on the level of theory collapsed in practice. Her stepmother reasserted middle-class family claims and conventional social values, while Addams herself was uncertain how to realize her moral ideals.[29] She briefly attended and then abandoned medical school, embarking on a life of family duties, self-culture, and European travel, where the inspiration of art could satisfy both her romantic visions and domestic cultural values. But none of this satisfied her desire for moral social action, which grew sharper at the sight of European poverty and in response to her reading of Ruskin, the democratically inclined English positivists, and the social novels of Walter Besant. After visiting the first settlement house, Toynbee Hall in London, she decided to start a settlement in Chicago with her college friend Ellen Gates Starr.[30]

From the outset, Addams had to explain to many audiences what it was she was trying to do in this novel effort:[31] her doubting family, her new neighbors, potential contributors and supporters, a curious public, and, most demanding of all, herself. She was anxious to dissociate herself from charity or philanthropy, activities already tainted in the public mind and her own with condescension and with the strident self-righteousness of what she called "professional doing good."[32] For similar reasons, she rejected the title of "reformer."[33] Her initial goal, like that of her Toynbee Hall model, was to replace class barriers with Christian fellowship and bring to the poor the cultural benefits of middle- and upper-class life.[34]

While the men of Toynbee Hall, largely Oxford students and graduates, were engaged in a male class project, modeling their building and their style of fellowship on an Oxford college,[35] Addams was engaged in a female class project centered on the upper-middle-class home. The problem, she said in 1893, in her first major statement as unofficial spokesperson for the settlement movement, is that the people "who have the social tact and training, the large houses, and the traditions and custom of hospitality, live in other parts of the city."[36] Hull House was meant to be an upper-middle-class home, she furnished it as one, and it functioned in the ghetto as it did in the suburbs. The process of living there was crucial to the enterprise of sociability and socialization.[37] She hoped for an ideal future in which "this moving and living will at length be universal,"[38] a strikingly home-centered image of the triumph of middle-class family values in the society at large. Yet it was not domesticity's nuclear family that Addams produced at Hull House, but its "female world of love and ritual."[39] Under the shelter of domestic forms, Addams constructed a family largely of women, one that incorporated the sociability of her earlier female college world.

Addams soon folded her domestic class values into the larger goal of "social democracy." America may be a political democracy, she said, but socially it is sharply divided between rich and poor, Negroes, immigrants, and natives. The comfortable and educated have no way to put their fellow feeling into action. At the same time, the poor and immigrants are isolated from the benefits of social intercourse: "the blessings which we associate with a life of refinement and cultivation."[40] That Addams framed her discussion of unequal social relations as a problem of democracy was undoubtedly a product of the "civic" functions Hull House had taken on, "if indeed a settlement of women can be said to perform civic duties."[41] The social and educational activities she initiated soon led to tentative political forays concerning the neighborhood's public schools and cleanliness. Then, influenced by Mary Kenney, a working-class union organizer, Addams opened Hull House to union activities among local women workers. The arrival of Florence Kelley in December 1891, with her strong political consciousness and legislative goals, completed the process. Addams began to see that what Hull House workers were doing was taking on "the duties of good citizenship"[42] and arousing "the sense of responsibility of good citizenship" in their neighbors.[43]

Social democracy on the domestic model placed Addams in a tutorial relation to her immigrant neighbors and brought into play domesticity's parental model of moral training. Her own long struggle to attain independence, as well as her knowledge of domestic discourse, made the parental relationship crucial for her. Her struggles undoubtedly fueled her desire to both act the part of the parent and recognize the egalitarian claims of the child. The settlement, she says "aims, in a measure, to lead whatever of social life its neighborhood may afford, to focus and give form to that life, to bring to bear upon it the results of cultivation and training."[44] Leading here is a form of "training," and it operates by drawing out the child/immigrant's own social impulses. Addams struggled to reconcile the hierarchical authority and the mutuality of interests the process assumes and requires.

Her democratic instincts were aided by the revision of the domestic model of child training. By the 1890s, educational reformers like G. Stanley Hall and John Dewey were shifting the balance of power between adult authority and the inner powers of the child, giving more leeway to the child's desires and making less arbitrary the imposition of adult values.[45] Addams accepted the new view in her discussions of education and extended it to "similar relationships." She criticized charity workers who "ruthlessly force our conventions and standards upon [the poor man], with a sternness which we would consider stupid indeed did an educator use it in forcing his mature intellectual convictions upon an undeveloped mind."[46]

The most powerful statement she ever made of this dilemma, and indeed the most powerful testament to her domestic imagination, was an essay she wrote during the Pullman strike in 1894 that likened the class impasse between Pullman and his workers to the familial impasse between Shakespeare's King Lear and his daughters.[47] Her critical dissection of Pullman's philanthropy leads her to reflect on her own. The philanthropist must "discover what people really want" and then provide the channels in which their "moral force" can flow. Underpinned by the "multitude," progress will be "slower perpendicularly, but incomparably greater because lateral."

> To touch to vibrating response the noble fibre in each man, to pull these many fibres, fragile, impalpable and constantly breaking, as they are, into one impulse, to develop that mere impulse through its feeble and tentative stages into action, is no easy task, but lateral progress is impossible without it.[48]

This painful image of delicate fibers being pulled out of the human body, as it were, into leading-strings, reveals the transgression involved in the domestic effort to internalize authority. Addams assumes that what people "really want" conforms to her own conception of nobility, and she is determined to reach in and draw it out. Yet her assumption that nobility is there in each person, as it is in herself, and the delicacy and care she exerts suggest an attitude of respect. As she got to know her neighbors, her own views changed accordingly. Her attitude toward labor organization, for example, became less judgmental and more respectful of labor's intentions and desires. Her initial ideal of cultivation as the appreciation of high art shifted to the more democratic ground of immigrant crafts and the Arts and Crafts movement.[49] The intrusive and hierarchical family model was never abandoned, but it was mitigated by her democratic convictions.

What role, then, is played by social knowledge in Addams's project? She insisted on subordinating intellectual pursuits to social action. Recalling her postcollege years of frustrated purpose, she deprecated the impracticality of college education, the separation of theory from life, the failure "to translate our philosophy into the deed."[50] Likewise, thought not grounded in social feeling was inadequate.[51] As a result, despite her identification with college-educated women and despite the fact that colleges and universities quickly affiliated with urban settlements, Addams did not want to take on a collegiate identity. In 1894, when her talk at a state charity society was mistitled "Hull House as a Type of College Settlements," she rejected the designation.[52]

At the same time, however, she was starting to identify with what she called the "sociological movement." From the outset, Ellen Starr wrote, they hoped to "learn to know the people and understand them and their ways of life." That purpose took on new direction with the arrival of Florence Kelley, already a practitioner of "sociology," understood as the problem-oriented investigation of social conditions.[53] Residents began keeping a "ward book," Addams reported, in which they "noted matters of sociological interest found in the ward," like instances of sweated labor, child labor, and unsanitary tenements.[54] Under Kelley's direction, they also collected statistics for Carroll Wright at the Bureau of Labor Statistics and, inspired by the work of Charles Booth, put together a pioneering collection of urban studies and maps, *Hull-House Maps and Papers*, published in 1895 in Richard T. Ely's Library of Economics and Politics.[55]

Addams came into contact with Ely through Kelley, and when Albion Small founded the sociology department at the new University of Chicago in 1892, another academic connection to sociology was opened. In 1894, Addams noted that Ely and Small were sending students to them. Just as Hull House residents needed university study of languages so as to be able to speak to their neighbors, she said, they also needed to study "Social Science."[56]

In June of 1895, addressing Rockford College alumnae, Addams made her clearest statement of alliance with a larger enterprise called sociology. Apparently referring to the new work at Hull House that Kelley led and to the growth of college settlements, but now in a way that suggested identification with them, she claimed that "In the study of society which we call sociology," the settlement method of living among the people and "staying with them a long time" was the new method "coming into vogue. . . . They study their characters as a group, they try to help them in every way they can, they study them to learn their needs and their manner of thought." It is not encouraging work, she said, "because we are untrained as yet, and we go into the work without the keen observation and skill which are the product of training."[57]

Sociology in this formulation was based in both settlement house practice and university training. Perhaps the most striking thing about it was the female audience to whom Addams chose to make it. Addams thought of settlement work as specially suited to the moral concerns and capacities of educated women, and both in numbers and leadership women were the major force in the settlement movement.[58] But it was also a friendly audience to which to make her claim; she could not have made it to Chicago's sociology department, where she was not invited to speak. Addams had a variety of early contacts with Small, contributed a study of household labor to the first volume of his new *American Journal of Sociology*, and contributed periodically to the journal thereafter.[59] But Small was intent on making sociology a legitimate academic subject. While he needed contributions from practitioners to fill his journal, he would have been conscious that she was a woman, had no graduate degree, and was a social-political activist. For her part, Addams also had doubts about the Chicago sociologists. She was aware of the reluctance of Small and his colleagues to address controversial public issues directly, and she undoubtedly recognized the combination of academicism and fear for their positions that made them cautious. Her hope to get training from them in observational skills would have been soon disappointed by the abstract character of their university work.[60]

In the fall of 1895, in any case, an event intervened that turned Addams's interest away from making academic connections. At the death of the settlement's original benefactor, it appeared for a time that his will required the Hull House property to be transferred to the University of Chicago.[61] Addams was distraught and asked President William Rainey Harper to preserve its independence:

> Its individuality is the result of the work of a group of people, who have had all the perplexities and uncertainties of pioneers . . . living in the 19th Ward, not only as students, but as citizens, and their methods of work must differ from that of an institution established elsewhere, and following well defined lines. An absorption would be most unfair to them . . . who believe that the usefulness of the effort is measured by its own interior power of interpretation and adjustment.[62]

Hull House remained independent, but the event heightened Addams's desire to define settlement work as unique, rather than to show how it was part of a joint, practically oriented and university-based "sociological movement."

She was fortified in this effort by reading the pragmatic philosophy of John Dewey and William James. Dewey had arrived at Chicago in 1894 and was immediately impressed with Hull House and Addams. The kinds of socialized education that went on there and Addams's concept of social action quickly influenced his work. The Hull House social practice that tied social theory to specific practical situations and its mediating reform philosophy clarified and fortified his own similar ideas. Addams in turn began quoting Dewey's educational ideas in 1897 and began absorbing his pragmatic philosophy.[63] As she later recalled, it was not "announced" on his arrival but "slowly leaked out."[64] By 1899, pragmatism gave her the language to frame a theoretical justification of the settlement that realized her collegiate ambition for gendered knowledge.

Addams began by quoting Dewey and James to the effect that "the interest in [knowledge] has at last transferred itself from accumulation and verification to its application to life."[65] Thus having "the support of two philosophers," she attempted to locate the settlement in a "sterner and more enduring" project than even the attainment of social democracy—implicitly, the role of knowledge in the evolution of humanity. "Just as groups of men [n.b.], for hundreds of years, have organized themselves into colleges, for the purpose of handing on and disseminating knowledge already accumulated, and as other groups have been organized into seminars and universities, for the purpose of research and the extension of the bounds of knowledge, so at last," she said, "certain people [n.b.] have consciously formed themselves into groups . . . for the purpose of the application of knowledge to life."[66] Addams's shift here from "men" to "people" seems deliberate, a recognition both of the fact that some men as well as women performed settlement work and the fact that it was a feminine and human pursuit, distinctly not a masculine one.

Both Addams's gendered romanticism and her gendered desire for independence led her to separate the settlement's practical ideal from the university's: "The settlement stands for application as opposed to research; for emotion as opposed to abstraction, for universal interest as opposed to specialization."[67] Settlement people, she said, should "see to it that the university does not swallow the settlement, and turn it into one more laboratory; another place in which to analyze and depict, to observe and record." Having established this opposition, she was forced to regard it as something of an anomaly that "a settlement finds itself curiously more companionable with the state and national bureaus in their efforts in collecting information and analyzing the situation, than it does with university efforts," probably because such efforts were "in the line of applicability."[68]

Romanticism also colored how Addams understood the process of "application to life." It was a synthetic process of bringing all one's knowledge to bear, rather than an analytical one. Its closest analogue was art, for "the deed often reveals when the idea does not, just as art makes us understand and feel what might be incomprehensible and inexpressible in the form of an argument." Actual experience gives us the same kind of illumination as Zangwill's novel, *Children of the Ghetto*, and "personal acquaintance" adds to it "a consciousness of participation and responsibility."[69]

"Application to life" also involved the pragmatic function of knowledge: "to test its validity and to discover the conditions under which this knowledge may be employed." Here the primary standard is democracy. The settlement "finds itself challenging and testing by standards of moral democracy those things which it before regarded as good . . . and it sometimes finds that the so-called good things will not endure this test of being universalized."[70] Addams's chief example is the "experience and emotion" accrued by Hull House artists and teachers in the course of working with the traditional, elitest conception of high art. What they learned led them to support the Chicago Arts and Crafts Society, with its new conception of art as integral to everyday work and everyday objects.[71]

Addams clearly realized not only that experience might modify knowledge, but also that settlement experience might act as a leaven on the college and university ideals of "accumulating and transmitting" knowledge, perhaps even on the "thirst for data and analysis of the situation which so often distinguishes the 'sociologist.'"[72] Addams's quotation marks around "sociologist" here might well indicate a desire not to cede the term entirely to the university men. But Addams's romanticism and separatism kept her at this point from appreciating the fuller connection called for by the pragmatists' experimental conception of knowledge. Pragmatism suggested that Addams integrate "application" and the university ideal of "research and the extension of the bounds of knowledge," not separate them.

The knowledge that Addams wanted settlement workers to apply was "whatever knowledge they, as a group, may possess."[73] That meant the accrued body of intellectual and moral wisdom of her educated class: "the solace of literature . . . the stern mandates of science . . . the metaphysic . . . the moral code," which dictated "the transforming of the economic relation into an ethical relation."[74] Her formulation suggested a view of knowledge as ideal truths, progressively realized as they are "universalized" in history, that was closer to her romantic heritage than to the pragmatists' provisional, open-ended view of knowledge in which research and application fed into one another. She had good reasons for her romanticism and separatism, but they prevented her at this point from seeing how central the application of knowledge to life was to the construction of knowledge itself.

.   .   .

Having affixed the settlement movement to the large purpose of the application of knowledge to life, Addams shifted her attention to the concrete purposes served by settlement house knowledge and to a less ambitious vocabulary more compatible with pragmatism. The upshot of her 1899 theoretical statement was to reaffirm the functions the settlement house had already been performing: "interpretation and synthesis."[75] We have already seen that *synthesis* meant bringing a wide range of knowledge to bear in action. *Interpretation* was the principal term Addams used to designate her own and the settlement's intellectual task.

Interpretation, the act of explaining or elucidating meaning, is necessary when the meaning of something is not clear on its face. It flowed easily from Addams's domestic conception of interpersonal knowledge and her romantic preference for insight and synthesis over analysis on the model of science.[76] As we have already seen, when Addams wrote Harper in 1895, she was protecting the settlement's "own interior power of interpretation."[77] Addams's usage was also congruent with the pragmatists' understanding of language as a sign, rather than a mirror, of reality and hence in need of elucidation, and James and Dewey frequently used the term.[78]

If interpretation bridged the distance between language and meaning, it also traversed the social distances between Addams, her immigrant neighbors, and the respectable public she addressed. One of the first things Addams learned about her neighbors was that they were foreigners—Italians ("Neapolitans, Sicilians, and Calabrians, with an occasional Lombard or Venetian"), Germans, Polish and Russian Jews, Bohemians, Canadian-French, and Irish.[79] It was the inability of many of these foreigners to speak English that first led Addams to see the settlement as engaged, quite literally, in "interpreting" for them in their contacts with native Americans and each other.[80] At about the same time, she began to speak more broadly of the settlement function as "interpretation." As she later recalled, "The early settlements practically staked their future upon an identification with the alien and considered his interpretation their main business."[81]

Addams meant by the term a twofold process of gaining knowledge of her immigrant neighbors and then explaining them to the respectable public. Interpretation thus had to leap social distances in two directions. She had first to come to an understanding of her foreign neighbors, and she recognized this as a difficult task. It required belief in "the solidarity of the human race . . . which will not waver when the race happens to be represented by a drunken woman or an idiot boy." Settlement workers must also "be emptied of all conceit of opinion and all self-assertion." Only if devoid of fixed prejudices and convictions would they be free to understand their neighbors'. And "they must be content to live quietly side by side with their neighbors until they grow into a sense of relationship and mutual interests."[82] To steady sympathy, deep tolerance, and mutual social connections she most often added another, more reflective and distanced requirement: "long and continuous observation," her scientific ally of empathetic identification.[83]

Addams was not fully aware of the ambiguities of identification and distance, nor of the inherently problematic character of interpretation:

> Living eight years as I have, and seeing them early in the morning and all day long and late at night, and not being able to get away simply because one is caught with his sympathies, with his imagination, with his desires, with his interests, he does get a point of view which, I think, comes only to us on any subject when we give it continuous attention.[84]

The settlement worker's sympathetic, imaginative, personal involvement brought her so close that it threatens here to trap her inside the immigrants' world. But her immersion is not complete, as the move to impersonal pronouns ("*one* is caught with *his* sympathies . . .") and the fear of entrapment suggest. She turns in the end to a concerted and distanced "continuous attention," but it is not clear how it connects with her imaginative experience. Nor does Addams doubt that the interpretive process allows her actually to grasp her neighbor's "standpoint,"[85] to see things "from the point of view of the immigrant people themselves."[86] "The Social Gulf is always an affair of the imagination," she said in 1902, implying that an effort of imagination could leap across it.[87]

Addams's assurance that she could reach the immigrant standpoint undoubtedly owed something to the assurance of her own feminine intuitive power and class position. That she alternately speaks of her constituents as friends and neighbors, and as "the alien," suggests her ease in moving back and forth from the settlement milieu to her own class standpoint. She never pretends to speak "for" her neighbors; the distance that requires "interpretation" remains in view.

It was her own class position that allowed her to interpret her neighbors to the respectable public. Addams quickly realized that in order to fulfill her civic purpose and achieve legislative regulation and reform of the terrible conditions around her, she needed to "arouse and interpret the public opinion of their neighborhood" to the community at large.[88] She used her newspaper interviews, talks, journal and magazine articles, and books, in the city and then nationally, to explain her immigrant neighbors to audiences that were ignorant of and often hostile to them. Indeed, very soon, she found some of her neighborhood friends and acquaintances—like strikers and anarchists—under attack from respectable opinion, and herself along with them. The public mind, she complained, "falls into the old mediaeval confusion—he who feeds or shelters a heretic is upon *prima facie* evidence a heretic himself."[89] To defend herself, as well as to persuade her own class audience, she needed to maintain the separate stance of interpreter that distinguished her from the poor, the foreign, the heretical.

Addams's complex interpretive role generated what she had long sought for the female speaker, *auethoritas*. Drawing on her domestic/romantic belief in the educative value of experience, she based her authority to speak on the settlement experience. It was this experience of living together, with its shared sympathies and long observation, that gave settlement workers their unique understanding. The "settlement interpretation," based in "years of first hand information" and "opportunity for free intercourse," in turn gave settlements "exceptional opportunities for suggesting the best method for meeting the situation."[90] Firsthand experience authorized Addams's knowledge of the immigrant population, and of its problems and their solutions.[91]

Although Addams had used this concept of experience and occasionally the term itself since her earliest writings,[92] it was her reading of James and Dewey at the turn of the century that allowed her to see that experience had a philosophical status. In *Democracy and Social Ethics* she asserted it more forcefully as her warrant for authoritative knowledge. Apparently following James's description of the unimpeded flow of experience when it is in adjustment with the environment, Addams said that "experience gives the easy and trustworthy impulse toward right action." Hence "genuine experience [cannot] lead us astray any more than scientific data can."[93] It followed from that and from her own and Dewey's view of democracy that "Contact with social experience . . . is the surest corrective of opinions concerning the social order."[94]

Addams did not fully embrace James's and Dewey's pragmatic philosophies. It is doubtful that she followed them into an intersubjective theory of truth. Although Addams, like James and Dewey, sought *interpretive* knowledge, knowledge of human subjects and their meanings, the pragmatist philosophers modeled knowledge on the scientific experiment, while Addams continued to model it on literary production. Likening experiential knowledge to that of the naturalistic novelists Zola and Zangwill, she admitted that such knowledge always bore the stamp of personal interpretation—"no other men accepted the facts of human nature exactly as they did." But they approached their subjects with the scientist's "spirit of reverent truth seeking" as well as with an attitude of "sympathetic friendship and respect." Science thus remained an adjunct to aesthetic reflection. From the romantic standpoint, art modeled a fuller knowledge of the human subjects of social knowledge than did science, and it promised to rouse its audience more powerfully into moral action.[95]

It may nonetheless have been a result of this pragmatic assurance that Addams began to speak more easily about the *knowledge* function of the settlement. "May we not say that [the settlements'] first aim is to get into such social and natural relations with their neighbors that they can reveal to themselves and to the rest of the citizens the kind of life that exists in industrial neighborhoods?" Indeed, this revelation should be mutual: "We take very little pains to find out what [these foreigners] think of us, and the picture they draw is by no means flattering. A Settlement should be able to reveal the two sets of people to each other."[96]

Addams also for the first time closed the gap she had earlier left open between university research and settlement knowledge. The settlement method should also be the standard for "scholarship." Scholars must be asked, "What are your facts; upon what are your teachings founded? Are you sure you know about the people of whom you are writing and talking?" Scholarship, Addams said, "has to go into acquaintance with all kinds of conditions of men, if it would in any wise help us to understand and interpret them, if it would add to our working knowledge. . . . We are forced into fraternal relations not necessarily from conviction but from the nature of the case."[97] Authoritative social knowledge, "working knowledge," was necessarily interpersonal knowledge, and it required the settlement's domestic/romantic/pragmatic method.

.   .   .

Addams's assurance in 1902 regarding the settlement's interpretive method must also have been a recognition of what she herself had just accomplished in *Democracy and Social Ethics*. What kind of social knowledge did she produce in that book? It was, first, social knowledge undisguisedly rooted in the middle class and shaped by her gendered class outlook. The university sociology her male colleagues were formulating was equally middle-class in social position, but it spoke in an objective, universalistic voice that claimed the authority of nature or history. Addams positioned herself as a middle-class interpreter. In the introduction to the book, using the first person plural—"we," "us," "our"—she located herself within her middle-class audience.

She also located herself and her class at the point of evolutionary change between an older individualistic, personal and family morality and a newer social ethics. Addams's version of historical evolution was one among many influenced by Herbert Spencer's model of evolution from an individualistic to a more socialized society. Hers was a social democratic version that reformulated the middle-class cultural hierarchy. Art, duty to others, and democracy remain as the highest values but are given new, socialized forms. Standing with the some of "us" who had begun to adopt the new morality, the advanced guard of the middle class, as it were, she could urge the rest of "us" along. Indeed, she argued that the working class, with its sharing in times of need, its union organization and democratic politics, was further along than the "educated and self-conscious members of the community."[98]

Addams's sociology was an interpretive form of social knowledge. Unlike the academic sociology that treated social facts as objective things and sought the laws that governed them, Addams explained social relations among human subjects by reference to their meanings and the contexts that shaped those meanings. The book is a collection of six essays, "studies of various types and groups," that focus on the social psychology of her subjects, although that is too formal a term to capture the range of her interest. In each case she examines the values and norms of her subjects, showing how their beliefs and behavior emerge from their previous experience, the pressures of their social situation, and their own desires, a compound of instinctive human nature and contemporary urban culture.

Addams's sociology is relational in a double sense. Her knowledge was shown to emerge from the interpersonal experience and sympathetic relation between the sociological interpreter and her subjects. In addition, Addams showed her subjects to be equally engaged in a web of cognitive and social interpersonal relations. Throughout her book, Addams constructs social relations as intersecting points of view. Each essay plays off one representative social actor against another: the charity worker and the poor recipient of charity; the middle-class parent and the middle-class daughter; the domestic worker and the middle-class housewife who employs her; the industrial employer and the factory worker; the worker who needs education and the middle-class public that provides it; the political boss and his immigrant constituents. In each case we are shown not only the different points of view of the subjects but how each subject, often mistakenly, views the other. Addams has indeed employed her cross-class settlement experience to reveal "the two sets of people to each other."

Addams's complex view of social relations can be attributed to the complex social stance she took as an interpreter, but it also gained force from her domestic imagination. Most of the essays revolved around the parent/child dyad or a middle-class/working-class substitute, as had her familial analysis of the Pullman strike. Typically Addams took up a stance outside the "family," where she could alternately take both positions. On rare occasions when she allowed her own, interpreter's voice to merge with the parental figure, her tone became didactic and her insights, less original.[99]

Her desire to seek the point of view of both parties to often conflictual social relations entailed conscientious effort. She cultivated the ability to see the same logic at work in seemingly disparate class phenomena. She was at first appalled to discover, for example, that the richest Italian in the neighborhood, worth several hundred thousand dollars, still kept his wife picking rags and his children peddling on the streets.[100] Yet a few years later she used the example to her collegiate alumnae to illustrate their own failure to grasp their new opportunities. "The educated woman has much the same experience to pass through.

Her mind has been narrowed by the restrictions of the past and suddenly it is given the opportunity of broadening."[101] Perhaps the most noteworthy instance is one we have already examined, her ability to see in Pullman-Lear's self-righteousness "a constant and settled danger in philanthropy," including her own.[102] Addams put her experience through a conscientious and imaginative process of self-reflection.

That process did not eliminate, of course, her middle-class domestic bias. The educated daughter is allowed individuality and independence, but only if the claims of family and, more important, society, are recognized as well. Trade unions are defended, but what Addams finds most appealing is an educational program that would allow workers to understand the social context of their work. She only glancingly mentions the underlying economic system that sets the conditions of work.[103]

Still, Addams's ability to move imaginatively to both sides of her dyad allowed her to construct each of their points of view empathetically, yet realistically: the housewife's desires for her own family, based on a commendable but narrow ethic, conflict with her household worker's own human and domestic needs. The charity worker's middle-class attitudes, justifiable in their place, violate her immigrant clients' expectations of charity, so that she appears to them only as selfish, foolish, or mysterious. Perhaps Addams's most noteworthy essay, and one that suggests the reach of her social vision, was on the corrupt urban political machine that Hull House had been fighting for a decade. One of the first people to recognize the positive functions of the political boss, Addams described perfectly the web of traditional values, personal relations, and social functions that linked the boss and his immigrant constituents. At the same time, she played off this corrupt but democratic immigrant politics against the politics of the "better element,"[104] ineffectual administrative reformers on the one hand and businessmen allies of the boss on the other. It was undoubtedly this ability to take multiple vantage points in a complex social field and to see each of them from "within" that led William James to say that Addams "simply *inhabits reality*, and everything she says necessarily expresses its nature."[105]

By 1902 Addams had formulated a viable approach to social knowledge. She sought to explain the different "types and groups" of modern urban society to each other. She proposed to use this interpretive knowledge to enlighten and empower her lower-class neighbors and her middle- and upper-class friends in a joint public effort to democratize values (that is, the values forged in the experience of settlement house women), through education, social action, and legislation. She had a warrant for her knowledge and her social proposals in the experiential methods of settlement house work. If her aims and methods were inherently problematic, so too were the universalist aims and objectivist methods of the university sociologists.

The shape she implicitly proposed for sociology was that of a practice-oriented, rather than knowledge-oriented, profession, a kind of social-political medicine, in which the practitioners cast themselves not as scientific experts but as expert participants, whose knowledge emerged from their practice and who were active primarily in the aid of individuals and democratization of society, and secondarily in the generation of social knowledge useful to that purpose. Within her time and place, and again within class limits, she envisaged a feminist profession that would empower educated women and their social democratic values.

Addams's approach to social knowledge was, on one level, gendered feminine. Forged in the female communities of her women's college and Hull House, her sociology was rooted in discourses of domesticity and romanticism that echoed the dominant conventions of femininity in the nineteenth century. The paths of benevolent action rather than speculative knowledge, and of interpretation rather than science, were gendered tracks her culture prepared for her and that she deliberately chose. Yet the nineteenth-century gender system was in the process of change. And while the dominant gender representations of a culture are usually clear, their application to specific cultural products is unstable and their appropriation by different persons, highly individual.

Although Addams lived securely in the women's reform network based at Hull House, her settlement, university, civic, and reform activities also occurred in an increasingly heterosocial world. She continued to speak of women's special interest in domestic matters and special sensitivity to moral issues, but she also recognized that some differences between women and men would be worn away by their joint action in the social world.[106] Her use of and acknowledged ties with pragmatism brought her interpretive, practically oriented approach partially into a new orbit. Cast as a mediating doctrine between science and religion, theory and practice, pragmatism escaped easy gender typing.[107] Thus although the cognitive map she had drawn in her college essays remained, her language took on the neutral cast of her heterosocial milieu; none of her later writings explicitly assigned sociology to a "feminine trait of mind." Moreover, as we have seen, Addams enlarged the feminine sphere with masculine ambitions. If her imagination was deeply gendered, it moved in two directions and aspired to the generically human as well as the feminine. Her approach to social knowledge also bore this androgynous, human stamp.

.   .   .

Addams and her university contemporaries plotted the sociological field very differently. For Addams, the sociological movement was based in democratic social practice and the kind of interpretive, working knowledge practice yielded. For university sociologists, it was based in theoretical reflection and "objective" observation on the model of science and then tested or applied in practical settings. The institutional seat marked the cognitive center of power. Both sociologies aimed at practical use and required the middle-class expert or interpreter to effect, but the emphasis was different. As Addams implied, one model expected reform to come from "corporate effort inspired by social ideas and guided by the study of economic laws"; the other looked to citizens "who constantly see the harsh conditions of labor and who are incited to activity by their sympathies as well as their convictions."[108] For some, pragmatism served to mediate these differences, but it did not alter the polar forces that separated university from settlement work.

Conventional gender codes strengthened these polarities. Determined to raise the status of their field and make it a viable university subject, fearful of political controversy, and embarked on a nationalist project grounded in nature, the university men wanted the authority of a male and objective voice. In that context, Addams's work could be accepted only as an exception to the rule. Note the praise by the Columbia economist, E.R.A. Seligman, of *Democracy and Social Ethics*: "No other book by a woman shows such vitality, such masculinity of mental grasp and surefootedness."[109] Seligman's inclusion of Addams within the precincts of "real" social science in fact reveals the grounds on which women were pushed to the margins of the social science disciplines.[110] Given the university orientation and their own deeply held ideals of service and mutuality, Addams and her colleagues had powerful reasons to protect their interpretive viewpoint and reformist practice.

Addams nonetheless was attracted at moments in her career to a closer alliance with university sociology—as in her initial enthusiasm of 1895 and probably again at the time of her successful series of university extension lectures in 1899[111] and the publication of her 1902 book—but the attraction was not powerful enough to overcome diverging interests. The first was prematurely cut off by the sudden threat of completely losing her independence to the university. The second was only belatedly and partially reciprocated. In 1905 she was invited to deliver the Convocation address at the University of Chicago, a more formal acknowledgment of her intellectual stature than the university had hitherto conceded, but the following year, the university's conservative trustees cancelled a faculty vote to award her an honorary degree.[112] It was not until 1913 that the sociology department at the University of Chicago asked her to take a half-time position in the department, which she apparently declined.[113] By that time she had become a national political figure through her work for Theodore Roosevelt's Progressive Party and was past the point at which university work could engage her.

Addams herself was partly responsible for this missed connection. *Democracy and Social Ethics* was an exemplar of her interpretive approach and was very well received by sociologists and the public,[114] but it was neither a full statement of her views nor a fully articulated discussion of the paradigm it implied. Her statements about the character and role of social knowledge appeared as nuggets in talks and articles focused on other aspects of settlement house work and geared to a variety of audiences. Her major theoretical statement in 1899, although addressed to sociologists, was intent on establishing an identity for the settlement separate from the university and conveyed a bifurcated view of social knowledge. Nor did she use her Convocation address of 1905 to make a synthetic statement of her position. She surely stated her position. Urging scholars to study the recent immigration to the United States, she lamented that they had "furnished us with no method by which to discover

men, to spiritualize, to understand, to hold intercourse with aliens and to receive of what they bring."[115] The talk, however, was not one of her best, going
off in several directions, none of which were coherently developed. It missed
an opportunity to bring home her sociological vision. A woman of great energy
and ambition, Addams was also spread thin. She had an interest in theory, but
she had many other interests, as well, and was not in a setting that encouraged
theoretical reflection. She might also have felt some insecurity about telling the
university sociologists how to do their work.

The divergence in models of social knowledge marked the limits of Addams's
intellectual influence on the development of university sociology. There seems
little doubt that Addams and Hull House powerfully influenced Chicago sociology's focus on urban exploration, and Addams, along with Dewey and George
Herbert Mead, moved at least one line of Chicago development in an interpretive direction.[116] It is also likely that Addams's early conception of sociology as a study of "types and groups" and her frequent use of "the situation" in
a sociological context had some effect on William I. Thomas's and Robert Park's
later work.[117] However, direct evidence of intellectual impact is hard to find.
The pragmatist philosophers Dewey and Mead are the exceptions that prove
the rule. Closer to Addams in their understanding of social knowledge, they
also operated from a more secure professional position than did the sociologists
and from a more adventurous personal base.[118] One sociologist who left a record in his work of appreciation for Addams's interpretive sociology was, appropriately, Charles Horton Cooley, although it was Addams's democratic social
idealism that seemed most to attract him. One of the few articulate dissenters
from the scientific direction of the field, Cooley too had read deeply in romantic
literature as a young man. An introspective and reclusive man, his only sociological research was literally domestic, the observation of his children's psycho-
social development.[119]

As the example of Cooley suggests, it was the desire for scientific objectivity
and its masculine coloration that probably led the university sociologists
to discount Addams's model of social knowledge. William I. Thomas presents
a particularly striking example. His research protocol of 1912, designed to
send his students out into the city to study immigrants and Negroes, can be
taken as the founding document of the Chicago university's distinctive sociology.[120] In many ways Thomas's protocol overlapped with Addams's work. He
addressed practical workers as well as students. Originally an anthropologist,
he had an anthropologist's appreciation of subjectivity and sought interpretive
data. Like Addams, he drew on James and Dewey for his social psychology. Yet
the differences are equally striking. Thomas takes the stance not of the native
middle-class interpreter but of the visiting anthropologist. While Addams is
careful not to sensationalize her ethnic subjects' difference in favor of common
humanity, Thomas accentuates their strangeness. His attitude toward his subjects is distant and objective, intellectual rather than sympathetic, and framed
wherever possible by theoretical categories. Despite the many ways in which
Thomas's project might have acknowledged and included Addams, she is not

mentioned. Nor is her work even among the sources from which he draws illustrative examples.[121] Thomas might well have been influenced by Addams's work, but he was too intent on developing sociology in a different, more objectivist, direction to notice.[122]

There is still a great deal more to be said about Addams's later work, the Hull House women, and their relations with other sociological paths before we can properly assess this new sociological territory. But it seems clear that by 1902, Addams had developed an interpretive conception of sociology, the scope and originality of which was not fully appreciated at the time and has since been lost to view. Had the academy been more open to her work, sociology might have become a site for the production of a different kind of social knowledge and might perhaps have come closer to including a source both the university and the settlement admitted only in mediated form, the immigrants and workers themselves.

NOTES

I would like to thank Jean H. Baker, Lorraine Daston, Toby Ditz, Paula Fass, Louis Galambos, Linda Kerber, Elizabeth Lunbeck, Mary Poovey, Barbara Sicherman, Gabrielle Spiegel, Joan Williams, Theresa Wobbe, and the members of the Women's Studies Workshop at Johns Hopkins University for their extremely helpful comments. I am also grateful to the Gender Reading Group at the Center for Advanced Study in the Behavioral Sciences, 1992–1993, particularly Joanne Long DeMaria, Deborah Tannen, Susan Watkins, and Richard Yarborough, for helping me sort through the perplexities of gender analysis. A shorter version of this paper appears in German in *Klassikerinnen des soziologischen Denkens*, ed. Claudia Honegger and Theresa Wobbe (Berlin: C. H. Beck, 1997).

1. Anthony Oberschall, "The Institutionalization of American Sociology," in *The Establishment of Empirical Sociology*, ed. Oberschall (New York: Harper and Row, 1972), 187–251, quotation on 219.

2. Dorothy Ross, *The Origins of American Social Science* (Cambridge: Cambridge University Press, 1991), 59, 394–95. See also Mary Furner, *Advocacy and Objectivity: A Crisis in the Professionalization of American Social Science, 1865–1920* (Lexington: University Press of Kentucky, 1975).

3. Mary Jo Deegan, "Women in Sociology: 1890–1930," *Journal of the History of Sociology* 1 (Fall 1978): 11–34; idem, *Jane Addams and the Men of the Chicago School, 1892–1918* (New Brunswick, N.J.: Transaction, 1988). Special mention should also be made of Deegan's invaluable *Women in Sociology: A Bio-Bibliographical Sourcebook* (New York: Greenwood, 1991). Jennifer Platt takes up Deegan's lead, suggesting that the history of the Chicago school of sociology be rewritten to include the community of social workers and reformers, in which community university sociologists played a "minor and dependent" role: Jennifer Platt, "The Chicago School and Firsthand Data," *History of the Human Sciences* 7, no. 1 (1994): 72. Other important examples of women's and gender history that deal with sociology are Rosalind Rosenberg, *Beyond Separate Spheres: Intellectual Roots of Modern Feminism* (Ithaca: Cornell University Press, 1982); Barbara Laslett, "Unfeeling Knowledge: Emotion and Objectivity in the History of Soci-

ology," *Sociological Forum* 5, no. 3 (1990): 413–33; Ellen Fitzpatrick, *Endless Crusade: Women Social Scientists and Progressive Reform* (New York: Oxford University Press, 1990), and Robert C. Bannister, *Jesse Bernard: The Making of a Feminist* (New Brunswick, N.J.: Rutgers University Press, 1991).

4. I will thus not discuss in this essay Addams's support of the other kinds of social science going on at Hull House. To understand *Hull-House Maps and Papers*, for example, it is necessary first to look closely at Kelley.

5. My definition of discourse follows the usage of J.G.A. Pocock, "Introduction: The State of the Art," in *Virtue, Commerce, and History: Essays on Political Thought and History, Chiefly in the Eighteenth Century* (Cambridge: Cambridge University Press, 1985), 1–34; and David Hollinger, "Historians and the Discourse of Intellectuals," in *New Directions in American Intellectual History*, ed. John Higham and Paul Conkin (Baltimore: Johns Hopkins University Press, 1979), 42–63.

6. Historians of domesticity have not always considered these overlapping discussions together. Kathryn Kish Sklar, *Catharine Beecher: A Study in American Domesticity* (New Haven: Yale University Press, 1973); Nancy F. Cott, *The Bonds of Womanhood: "Woman's Sphere" in New England, 1780–1835* (New Haven: Yale University Press, 1977); and Mary P. Ryan, *Cradle of the Middle Class: The Family in Oneida County, New York, 1790–1865* (Cambridge: Cambridge University Press, 1981), recognize that strategies of child-rearing and moral training are integral to the nineteenth-century definition of domestic space. Richard H. Brodhead, *Cultures of Letters: Scenes of Reading and Writing in Nineteenth-Century America* (Chicago: University of Chicago Press, 1993), appropriately I think, draws in the rhetoric of school reform that, from much the same sources, urged a similar program of character-training through sympathetic identification with the maternal/paternal authority figure. Jay Fliegelman, *Prodigals and Pilgrims: The American Revolution against Patriarchal Authority, 1750–1800* (Cambridge: Cambridge University Press, 1982), is important for the eighteenth-century origins and paternalist uses of the discourse. On separate spheres as an ideology that legitimates market behavior, see Amy Dru Stanley, "Home Life and the Morality of the Market," in *The Market Revolution in America*, ed. Melvyn Stokes and Stephen Conway (Charlottesville: University Press of Virginia, 1996), 74–96.

7. Cott, *Bonds of Womanhood*, chap. 2; Linda Kerber, "Separate Spheres, Female Worlds, Woman's Place: The Rhetoric of Women's History," *Journal of American History* 75 (June 1988): 9–39; James Turner, *Without God, without Creed: The Origins of Unbelief in America* (Baltimore: Johns Hopkins University Press, 1985), 82–95, 126–32.

8. Ryan, *Cradle of the Middle Class*, esp. chaps. 4, 5. For an interesting critique, in the British context, of the link between domestic discorse and middle-class formation, see Dror Wahrman, "'Middle-Class' Domesticity Goes Public: Gender, Class, and Politics from Queen Caroline to Queen Victoria," *Journal of British Studies* 32 (October 1993): 396–432. Wahrman's analysis does not seem to me to disprove the existence of a discourse of domesticity, but only to show that the language of domesticity could be put to different uses in a variety of contexts.

9. Bernard Wishy, *The Child and the Republic: The Dawn of Modern American Child Nurture* (Philadelphia: University of Pennsylvania Press, 1968); Fliegelman, *Prodigals and Pilgrims*; Brodhead, *Cultures of Letters*, chap. 1.

10. Fliegelman, *Prodigals and Pilgrims*, chap. 1; Wishy, *Child and the Republic*, 29–32. On high cultural values in domestic discourse, see Brodhead, *Cultures of Letters*, chap. 3.

11. The standard biography of Addams is Allen F. Davis, *American Heroine* (New York: Oxford University Press, 1973). For an excellent recent treatment of Addams and Hull House, see Robyn Muncy, *Creating a Female Dominion in American Reform, 1890–1935* (New York: Oxford University Press, 1991), chap. 1. The perceptive essay on Addams in Christopher Lasch, *The New Radicalism in America, 1889–1963: The Intellectual as a Social Type* (New York: Knopf, 1965), chap. 1, is still useful, as is John C. Farrell, *Beloved Lady: A History of Jane Addams' Ideas on Reform and Peace* (Baltimore: Johns Hopkins University Press, 1967). A great deal of material on Addams, including bibliography, can be found in Deegan, *Jane Addams and the Men of the Chicago School*, and idem, *Women in Sociology*, 37–44. Jill Conway, "Women Reformers and American Culture, 1870–1930," *Journal of Social History* 5 (Winter 1971): 164–82, is the classic critique of the failure of Addams's generation to abandon domestic discourse; the implications of this failure for national social welfare policy are drawn by Linda Gordon, *Pitied But Not Entitled: Single Mothers and the History of Welfare, 1890–1935* (New York: The Free Press, 1994).

12. For example, *Little Women*. See Barbara Sicherman, "Reading *Little Women*: The Many Lives of a Text," in *American History as Women's History*, ed. Linda Kerber, Alice Kessler-Harris, and Kathryn Kish Sklar (Chapel Hill: University of North Carolina Press, 1996), 1; Addams also studied about domestic authors in an American literature course at Rockford (13–14).

13. Davis, *American Heroine*, 10–12.

14. Jane Addams (hereafter, in archival references, JA), "One Office of Nature," *Rockford Seminary Magazine* 7 (June 1879): 154–56 (University of Illinois Chicago Circle, JA Memorial Collection, hereafter UICC, JAMC), Reel 46, Jane Addams Papers (hereafter, JAP), ed. Mary Lynn McCree Bryan (University Microfilms International).

15. On the high masculine argument of the romantics, see M. H. Abrams, *Natural Supernaturalism: Tradition and Revolution in Romantic Literature* (New York: Norton, 1971). On the demotion of feminine imagination, see Lorraine Daston, "The Naturalized Female Intellect," *Science in Context* 5, no. 2 (1992): 209–35, and Marlon Ross, *The Contours of Masculine Desire: Romanticism and the Rise of Women's Poetry* (New York: Oxford University Press, 1989).

16. JA, "One Office of Nature." See also JA, "Resolved—The Civilization of the 19th Cent[ury] Tends to Fetter Intellectual Life and Expression. Aff.," February 18, 1880 (UICC, JAMC), Reel 46, JAP; JA, [Bellerophon], [1880–81] (UICC, JAMC), Reel 46, JAP.

17. JA, "The Gipsies of Romance. Meg Merrilies Their Queen" (UICC, JAMC), Reel 46, JAP.

18. JA, "Cicero and Caesar," November 10, 1879 (UICC, JAMC), Reel 46, JAP.

19. JA, "The Gipsies of Romance."

20. Sklar, *Catharine Beecher*, 76, 289n. For an excellent discussion of the way later readers of *Little Women* used it to support female independence, see Sicherman, "Reading *Little Women*."

21. JA, "Follow Thou Thy Star," *Rockford Seminary Magazine* 7 (July 1879): 183–85 (Rockford College Archives), Reel 46, JAP.

22. Ibid. Indeed, she clung to that ideal harmony, in which truth, beauty, and goodness merged, even as she braved an unconventional career. During her early years at Hull House, she believed that "if Hull House activities were ever misunderstood, it would be either because there was not time to fully explain or because our motives had

become mixed, for I was convinced that disinterested action was like truth or beauty in its lucidity and power of appeal." Jane Addams, *Twenty Years at Hull-House* (1910; New York: Penguin, 1961), 115.

23. Jane Addams, "Bread Givers [1880]," in *Jane Addams: A Centennial Reader*, ed. Emily Cooper Johnson (New York: Macmillan, 1960), 103–4.

24. Davis, *American Heroine*, 17.

25. "These men while compiling from nature do not work for learning but for the idea alone, they come close to the comprehensive Idea of the Creator himself and thus it is given them to produce something at last which is up to the limit of their power and to which they have nothing more to add. An Idea gaining from age to age must finally break forth in an event for it is productive." JA, "Compilers," 1881 (UICC, JAMC), Reel 46, JAP. To her friend Ellen Starr she declared, "I would rather get my inspiration from a dodicahedral crystal than even a genius because it would take a stronger mind to see a principle embodied by cohesion than embodied by vital personal force." JA to Ellen Gates Starr, February 13, 1881 (Ellen Gates Starr Papers, Sophia Smith Collection, Smith College), Reel 1, JAP.

26. Davis, *American Heroine*, 12; Addams, *Twenty Years*, 57–58; David Hollinger, "Inquiry and Uplift: Late Nineteenth Century American Academics and the Moral Efficacy of Scientific Practice," in *The Authority of Experts: Studies in History and Theory*, ed. Thomas L. Haskell (Bloomington: Indiana University Press, 1984), 141–56.

27. "There are discoveries to be made which cannot come by induction, only through perception, such as the mental laws which govern suggestion, or the place that rhythm holds in nature's movements." JA, "Cassandra" [June 22, 1881], in "Essays of Class of 1881, Rockford Seminary" (UICC, JAMC), Reel 27, JAP. For an excellent analysis of Goethe's science as "feminine" but not "feminist," see Lisbet Koerner, "Goethe's Botany: Lessons of a Feminine Science," *Isis* 84 (1993): 470–95.

28. JA, "Cassandra."

29. She wrote plaintively that "We are taught subtle theories of heredity, that our very nerve centres and muscular fibers have inherited tendencies, predispositions for benevolence, [that we] are bound not only to the right action, but also to disseminate the impulse—to increase the tendency. This view of ourselves is rather overwhelming." JA, "Our Debts: and How Shall We Pay Them" [1880s] (UICC, JAMC), Reel 46, JAP.

30. Davis, *American Heroine*, 34–51, untangles Addams's own account of her decision to found a settlement in *Twenty Years*, chap. 4. However, Lasch, *New Radicalism*, remains the better psychological account, although I read Addams's interest before the visit to Toynbee Hall as more a general benevolent intention than a decision to found a settlement house.

31. Another settlement house opened in New York City a week before Hull House, founded by a number of Smith College graduates, including Vida Scudder, also influenced by Toynbee Hall, Ruskin, and Besant. Davis, *American Heroine*, 51.

32. JA to Alice Haldeman, June 14, 1888, and January 5, 1890 (UICC, JAMC), Reel 2, JAP. Note Jane Addams, "The Subjective Necessity for Social Settlements and the Objective Value of a Social Settlement [1893]," in *Philanthropy and Social Progress: Seven Essays by Miss Jane Addams, and Others* (New York: Books for Libraries Press, 1969), 1–56: "I am always sorry to have Hull House regarded as philanthropy, although it doubtless has strong philanthropic tendencies . . ." (55).

33. JA, "Hull House as a Type of College Settlements," Wisconsin State Conference of Charities and Corrections *Proceedings* (1894), 112, Reel 46, JAP.

34. As she wrote at the end of her first year, we want "to fortify people, who need

fortitude above all others, with the best that we can procure for them. It is curious to see the helpful and warm friendships that are formed between people so diverse in circumstances and yet really alike in feelings; it is the opportunity given to both classes to form these ties that we care most for." JA to George Haldeman, December 21, 1890 (Swarthmore College Peace Collection), Reel 2, JAP.

35. Standish Meacham, *Toynbee Hall and Social Reform, 1880–1914: The Search for Community* (New Haven: Yale University Press, 1987).

36. Addams, "Subjective Necessity," 4.

37. It is interesting that Robert A. Woods, later a leader of the settlement movement, was sensitive to the feminine gendering of settlement house work and tried to escape the domestic identity ("Establishment of new centres of social activity . . . might possibly not demand residence in the neighborhood"). Robert A. Woods, "The University Settlement Idea [1893]," in *Philanthropy and Social Progress: Seven Essays by Miss Jane Addams, and Others* (New York: Books for Libraries Press, 1969), 57–97, 64, 82.

38. Addams, "Subjective Necessity," 26.

39. See Carroll Smith-Rosenberg, "The Female World of Love and Ritual: Relations between Women in Nineteenth-Century America," in *Disorderly Conduct: Visions of Gender in Victorian America* (New York: Knopf, 1985), 53–76.

40. Addams, "Subjective Necessity," 2–10.

41. JA, "Hull House, Chicago: An Effort toward Social Democracy," *Forum* 14 (October 1892): 226–41, esp. 229, Reel 46, JAP. This essay was reprinted as "The Objective Value of a Social Settlement," pt. 2, of Addams, "Subjective Necessity."

42. Addams often called on the republican theme of citizenship, and in *Twenty Years*, chap. 2, she emphasized her ties with Lincoln and her father's Republican Party. She less often mentioned the special availability of social mobility in the United States. (See, e.g., Jane Addams, "Trades Unions and Public Duty," *American Journal of Sociology*, 4 [January 1899]: 461: "A workingman in America . . . may become a carpenter only as a stepping-stone toward becoming a contractor and capitalist.") But her thought was not deeply rooted in the discourse of American exceptionalism, as was the case with most male social scientists. Her recognition that in taking on a civic identity she was invading male space suggests why. cf. Ross, *Origins*.

43. JA, "Hull House, Chicago," 241; idem, "Subjective Necessity," 23; JA to Katharine Coman, December 7, 1891 (Denison House Papers, Schlesinger Library, Radcliffe College), Reel 2, JAP. On Kenney and Kelley, see Kathryn Kish Sklar, "Hull House in the 1890s: A Community of Women Reformers," *Signs: Journal of Women in Culture and Society* 10, no. 4 (1985): 658–59.

44. Addams, "Subjective Necessity," 21.

45. Wishy, *Child and the Republic*, pt. 2; Dorothy Ross, *G. Stanley Hall: The Psychologist as Prophet* (Chicago: University of Chicago Press, 1972), 115–24.

46. Jane Addams, *Democracy and Social Ethics* (New York: Macmillan, 1902), 65–66. Much later, Addams said that Dewey's "insistence upon an atmosphere of freedom and confidence between the teacher and pupil, of a common interest in the life they led together, profoundly affected all similar relationships, certainly those between the social worker and his client." Jane Addams, ""A Toast to John Dewey [1929]," in *The Social Thought of Jane Addams*, ed. Christopher Lasch (Indianapolis: Bobbs-Merrill, 1965), 175–83, 178.

47. Jane Addams, "A Modern Lear," *Survey* 29 (November 2, 1912): 131–37. Pullman's well-known "paternalism" allowed the family analogy, although the more likely association for this political-economic context would connect paternalism with feudal-

ism, as Richard T. Ely did in "Pullman: A Social Study," *Harpers* 70 (February 1885): 452–66.

48. Addams, "Lear," 137.

49. Compare Jane Addams, "The Settlement as a Factor in the Labor Movement," in *Hull-House Maps and Papers* (New York: Crowell, 1895), with idem, "Trade Unions and Public Duty," *American Journal of Sociology* 4 (January 1899): 448–62. On her shifting conception of how to cultivate aesthetic values, see Jane Addams, "A Function of the Social Settlement," *Annals of the American Academy of Political and Social Science* 13 (May 1899): 330–34; "The settlement soon discovers how impossible it is to put a fringe of art on the end of a day" spent in industrial labor (332).

50. Addams, "Subjective Necessity," 6.

51. "Intellectual life requires for its expansion and manifestation the influence and assimilation of the interests and affections of others." The settlement movement, she proudly asserted, was "based not only upon conviction, but genuine emotion." Ibid., 9, 2.

52. See n. 45, supra.

53. Ellen Starr to Mary Blaisdell, February 23, 1889, quoted in Davis, *American Heroine*, 57; Sklar, "Hull House in the 1890s." On Kelley's early use of the term "sociology," see Florence Kelley, "Need Our Working Women Despair?" *International Review* 13 (November 1882): 517–27.

54. JA, "Hull House as a Type of College Settlements," 103.

55. *Hull-House Maps and Papers* (New York: Thomas Y. Crowell, 1895); Kathryn Kish Sklar, "Hull-House Papers: Social Science as Women's Work in the 1890s," in *The Social Survey in Historical Perspective 1880–1940*, ed. Martin Bulmer, Kevin Bales, and Kathryn Kish Sklar (Cambridge: Cambridge University Press, 1991), 111–47.

56. Davis, *American Heroine*, 98; JA, "Hull House as a Type of College Settlements," 113.

57. JA, "Claim on the College Woman," *Rockford Collegian* 23 (June 1895): 60 (UICC, JAMC), Reel 46, JAP.

58. John P. Rousmaniere, "Cultural Hybrid in the Slums: The College Woman and the Settlement House, 1889–1894," *American Quarterly* 22 (Spring 1970): 45–66, 46; Davis, *American Heroine*, 93.

59. Despite overstatement, Deegan, *Jane Addams and the Men of the Chicago School*, chap. 4, is useful on Addams's contacts with Small.

60. On Small and Chicago sociology in the 1890s, see Ross, *Origins*, chap. 4. Despite the practical, reform character of his work, Charles F. Henderson's suggestions for observation were as abstract and inappropriate for Addams's work as Small's theory. See his *Catechism for Social Observation: An Analysis of Social Phenomena* (Boston: D. C. Heath, 1894). Note also JA to Richard T. Ely, February 19, 1895 (Richard T. Ely Papers, State Historical Society of Wisconsin; hereafter, SHSW) Reel 2, JAP: "Dr. John Graham Brooks from Cambridge has been in Chicago for six weeks. He has been most valuable and inspiring to our plans here. Such a man makes us very discontented with the Chicago University men." A few years later, Florence Kelley, after a visit in Chicago, wrote Addams—in a manner suggesting shared views—that she was going off to a meeting of the American Social Science Association. "Perhaps I may get half an idea there. I did not get a decimal fraction of one in the University." Kelley to JA, August 28, 1899, enclosure in JA to Mary Rozet Smith, September 4, 1899 (JAP, Series 1, Swarthmore College Peace Collection), Reel 3, JAP.

61. Deegan, *Jane Addams and the Men of the Chicago School*, 38.

62. JA to William R. Harper, December 19, 1895 (President's Papers 1899–1925, University of Chicago), Reel 2, JAP.

63. C. Wright Mills, *Sociology and Pragmatism: The Higher Learning in America*, ed. Irving Louis Horowitz (New York: Oxford University Press, 1969), chap. 16 and 432 ff.; Andrew Feffer, *The Chicago Pragmatists and American Progressivism* (Ithaca: Cornell University Press, 1993), 113–15; Deegan, *Jane Addams and the Men of the Chicago School*, 249–53; JA, "Foreign-born Children in the Primary Grades," National Education Association *Journal of Proceedings and Addresses* 36 (1897): 104–12, esp. 104, Reel 46, JAP.

64. Addams, "Toast to John Dewey," 178.

65. In this and another quotation Addams uses, she seems to have made a loose transcription of passages from "The Significance of the Problem of Knowledge" (1897), probably the first major statement Dewey made of the larger implications of pragmatism for philosophy. See *John Dewey: The Early Works, 1882–1898* (hereafter, *EW*), ed. Jo Ann Boydston (Carbondale: Southern Illinois University Press, 1972), 5:4–24, esp. 20–21. Her quotations from William James were from an address to the Philosophical Union of the University of California, though the idea appeared repeatedly in James's writings: "Beliefs, in short, are really rules of action, and the whole function of thinking is but one step in the production of habits of action"; and "the ultimate test for us of what a truth means is indeed the conduct it dictates or inspires."

66. Addams, "A Function of the Social Settlement," 323–55, esp. 334–35.

67. Ibid., 336.

68. Ibid., 347, 348.

69. Ibid., 335–38. Although Addams's formulation rests on her own romanticism, she might have been encouraged to take this line of thought by Dewey's view of education as "the most perfect and intimate union of science and art conceivable in human experience." As to art, he continued, "I believe that the art of thus giving shape to human powers and adapting them to social service, is the supreme art; one calling into its service the best of artists; that no insight, sympathy, tact, executive power is too great for such service." John Dewey, "My Pedagogic Creed" (1897), *EW*, 5:84–95, esp. 94.

70. Addams, "A Function of the Social Settlement," 335, 340.

71. Ibid., 343–44.

72. Ibid., 350.

73. Ibid., 335.

74. Ibid., 340.

75. Ibid., 355.

76. In fields where human subjects and the elucidation of their meanings were central, *interpretation* was a common term of art. During the nineteenth century, it was often used in such fields as literature, biblical criticism, the law, and philosophy. Before Addams put it to special use in the settlement, "interpretation" was part of her everyday vocabulary as well as her discussion of literature and the Bible. For example, JA, [Essay on Biblical Prophets], [1880–81] (UICC, JAMC), Reel 46, JAP.

77. Note also Addams's description of a young woman for whom she was trying to secure fellowship money, so that this prospective colleague could work at Hull House on the problems of sexually delinquent girls: "She is a girl of rather unusual advantages, who has travelled and seen enough of different sorts of people to make her judgment lenient and at the same time penetrating, and who has an unfailing spring of sympathy. Perhaps her distinguishing trait is her ability of interpretation." JA to Anita McCormick Blaine, December 11, 1895 (Anita McCormick Blaine Papers, SHSW), Reel 2, JAP.

78. James T. Kloppenberg, *Uncertain Victory: Social Democracy and Progressivism in European Thought, 1870–1920* (New York: Oxford University Press, 1986), 100–107, and idem, "Democracy and Disenchantment: From Weber and Dewey to Habermas and Rorty," in *Modernist Impulses in the Human Sciences, 1870–1930*, ed. Dorothy Ross (Baltimore: Johns Hopkins University Press, 1994), 72–75.

79. JA, "Hull House, Chicago," 227, 230.

80. Ibid., 230, 236. At an early organizing meeting among cloakmakers at Hull House, she was confronted with a mixed group of "Russian-Jewish tailors, many of whom could command not even broken English … ill-dressed and grimy, suspicious … ," and American-Irish girls, "well-dressed, and comparatively at ease." Addams recognized that the two groups "were separated by strong racial differences, by language, by nationality, by religion, by mode of life, by every possible social distinction." Indeed she felt "There was much less difference of any sort between the residents and working-girls than between the men and girls of the same trade." As a result, "The interpreter stood between the two sides of the room, somewhat helpless." Addams, "The Settlement as a Factor in the Labor Movement," 183–204, esp. 189–90.

81. Jane Addams, "'Americanization,'" *Papers and Proceedings of the American Sociological Society* 14 (1920): 206–15, esp. 211. It is likely that Addams's frequent use of the term accounts for its spread among settlement house workers, although Florence Kelley was already using it in the context of sociology before coming to Hull House. Cf. Mary E. McDowell, "The Activities of the University of Chicago Settlement," *University [of Chicago] Record* 12 (1908): 111, 112, 113; Kelley, "Need Our Working Women Despair?" 521.

82. Addams, "Subjective Necessity," 23.

83. JA, "Social Settlements," National Conference of Charities and Corrections *Proceedings* (1897): 344, Reel 46, JAP.

84. Ibid., 344–45.

85. JA, "Hull House, Chicago," 236.

86. JA, "Social Settlements," 344–45.

87. JA, "Address of Miss Addams [on Settlement Work]," University Settlement Society of New York, *Annual Report for 1902*, 55, Reel 46, JAP.

88. Addams, "Subjective Necessity," 22–23.

89. Jane Addams, "The Chicago Settlements and Social Unrest," *Survey* 20 (May 2, 1908): 155–66, 155.

90. Ibid., 155.

91. Although there was a real distinction between the kind of experience Addams urged on sociologists and the kind practiced in universities at this time, her firsthand knowledge included, but was not limited to, direct personal observation. Note Florence Kelley's review of Addams's *A New Conscience and an Ancient Evil* (New York: Macmillan, 1912) in the *American Journal of Sociology* 18 (September 1912): 271: "The book grows out of the author's first-hand contact with neighbors whose daughters are, by their poverty, peculiarly exposed to the ravages of this ancient evil. Miss Addams' personal acquaintance of more than twenty years with a congested neighborhood is supplemented by active work in the Juvenile Protective Association." Addams's emphasis on personal experience was thus not entirely equivalent to firsthand data "in the sense implied by modern writers" that Jennifer Platt finds missing in the Chicago university sociologists. See Platt, "The Chicago School and Firsthand Data," 74.

92. JA, "Hull House, Chicago," 236. Note also: "The best teacher of life is life itself."

It was thus appropriate that many residents would come to the settlement with the "attitude of students" and regard it as a "classroom." Addams, "Subjective Necessity," 24.

93. Addams appears to be relying here on James's "The Sentiment of Rationality," in *The Will to Believe* (1897; reprint, New York: Dover, 1956), 63–110, esp. 105–6.

94. Addams, *Democracy and Social Ethics*, 5, 7.

95. JA, "The New Social Spirit," National Council of Jewish Women *Proceedings* (1902), 16–22, esp. 17–18, Reel 46, JAP. For an analysis that links Addams more closely to pragmatism, seeing her both as a source of Dewey's philosophy and as a practitioner of his method, see Charlene Haddock Siegfried, *Pragmatism and Feminism: Reweaving the Social Fabric* (Chicago: University of Chicago Press, 1996), and an unpublished paper, idem, "The Pragmatist Unity of Theory and Practice: Jane Addams and John Dewey."

96. JA, "Address of Miss Addams," 51–52, 54.

97. JA, "The New Social Spirit," 17–18.

98. Addams, *Democracy and Social Ethics*, 1–12.

99. One example is Addams's first discussion of the labor movement, "The Settlement as a Factor in the Labor Movement," esp. 195–204; another, chap. 6 on educational methods, in *Democracy and Social Ethics*.

100. JA, "Hull House, Chicago," 228.

101. JA, "Claim on the College Woman," 60.

102. Addams, "Lear," 136.

103. On the limits of Addams's view of racial equality, see Elisabeth Lasch-Quinn, *Black Neighbors: Race and Limits of Reform in the American Settlement House Movement, 1890–1945* (Chapel Hill: University of North Carolina Press, 1993), chap. 1; and of ethnic pluralism, see Rivka Shpak Lissak, *Pluralism and Progressives: Hull House and the New Immigrants, 1890–1919* (Chicago: University of Chicago Press, 1989).

104. Addams, *Democracy and Social Ethics*, 222.

105. William James, "Review of Jane Addams, *The Spirit of Youth and the City Streets*," *American Journal of Sociology* 15 (January 1910): 553.

106. Jane Addams, "Woman's Conscience and Social Amelioration," in *The Social Application of Religion*, ed. Charles Stelzle, Jane Addams, et al. (Cincinnati: Jennings & Graham, 1908); Jane Addams, "If Men Were Seeking the Franchise [1913]," in *Jane Addams, A Centennial Reader*, ed. Emily Cooper Johnson (New York: Macmillan, 1960), 111–12.

107. When William James, for example, placed pragmatism between "tough-minded" science and "tender-minded" religion, he referred to it as "she." James, *Pragmatism* (1907; reprint, Indianapolis: Hackett, 1981), 35.

108. Addams, *Democracy and Social Ethics*, 166.

109. Quoted in Davis, *American Heroine*, 128.

110. Deegan, *Jane Addams and the Men of the Chicago School*, argues that during the Progressive Era the Chicago sociologists welcomed Addams and other practical sociologists into a joint sociological community; only during the 1920s did professionalism and scientism redefine sociology to exclude them. I believe that the tensions with science and professionalism were present from the 1890s forward and that the evidence suggests a more limited and ambivalent relationship. Rosalind Rosenberg also shows that the welcome of women as social science graduate students at Chicago during the Progressive Era was always partial and never extended to full membership in the professors'

university community. Any rewriting of the history of sociology or the Chicago School of sociology will have to take account of the mixed perceptions and purposes of the subjects of those histories. Rosenberg, *Beyond Separate Spheres*; Ross, *Origins*.

111. JA, "Democracy and Social Ethics. A Syllabus of a Course of Twelve Lectures" [1899] (Anita McCormick Blaine Papers, SHSW), Reel 30, JAP.

112. Deegan, *Jane Addams and the Men of the Chicago School*, 175–77.

113. Ibid., 81–82.

114. Davis, *American Heroine*, 128; Deegan, *Jane Addams and the Men of the Chicago School*, 10–12.

115. Jane Addams, "Recent Immigration: A Field Neglected by the Scholar," *University [of Chicago] Record* 9 (January 1905): 275, 279.

116. Sociology at the University of Chicago was more heterogeneous and the interpretive approaches of some Chicago sociologists were less salient than the Chicago-inspired histories of sociology suggest. See Martin Bulmer, *The Chicago School of Sociology: Institutionalization, Diversity, and the Rise of Sociological Research* (Chicago: University of Chicago Press, 1984), and Robert C. Bannister, *Sociology and Scientism: The American Quest for Objectivity, 1880–1940* (Chapel Hill: University of North Carolina Press, 1987).

117. On Addams's use of the term "situation," see, for example, *Democracy and Social Ethics*, 3, 12, 18, 26, and 38.

118. In Deegan, *Jane Addams and the Men of the Chicago School*, most of the conclusions regarding mutual intellectual influence between Addams and the university men are assumed from their social, civic, and settlement contacts.

119. On Cooley, see Ross, *Origins*, 240–47; on his romantic reading and domestic child-study, Edward C. Jandy, *Charles Horton Cooley: His Life and His Social Theory* (New York: Dryden Press, 1942), 41–46, 98–105. Cooley cites and discusses Addams's work in *Social Organization: A Study of the Larger Mind* (New York: Scribner's, 1909), 25, 137, 190–91, 244, 350, 385. On his interpretive understanding of social science, see idem, "The Roots of Social Knowledge," *American Journal of Sociology* 32 (July 1926): 59–79.

120. William I. Thomas, "Race Psychology: Standpoint and Questionnaire, with Particular Reference to the Immigrant and the Negro," *American Journal of Sociology* 17 (May 1912): 725–75.

121. On immigrants and Negroes in the United States, Thomas takes his examples from the work of Jacob Riis and W.E.B. Du Bois.

122. On Thomas, see Ross, *Origins*, 347–57.

CHAPTER 9

Bringing Social Science Back Home: Theory and Practice in the Life and Work of Elsie Clews Parsons

DESLEY DEACON

ON November 17, 1906, just as the New York season was about to open, the front page of the *New York Times* informed its readers that Mrs. Elsie Clews Parsons, a doctor of philosophy and a former lecturer in sociology at Barnard College, had published a textbook for elementary students in sociology. Such an event did not usually warrant front-page treatment from the country's leading newspaper. But this textbook attracted public attention for two reasons: Elsie Clews Parsons was the daughter of a prominent New York banker and the wife of Herbert Parsons, who had recently been elected to the United States Congress; and this congressman's wife was suggesting what the *Times* headline put politely as "a Radical Change"—the idea of trial marriage.[1]

Newspaper accounts of Elsie Clews Parsons's textbook fueled an avalanche of condemnation from the clergy. The Reverend Dr. Morgan Dix, rector of the fashionable Trinity Church, had not read the book, but he told the *New York Times* that "The doctrines which . . . Mrs. Parsons advocates, are simply outrageous," and that his sermon the following Sunday would be aimed at counteracting "the influence which the spreading of such disgraceful theories have made on society." "The idea of men and women living like animals," he went on, "separating at will, and contracting new alliances, leaving the children to be nobody's children, and to be cared for by the State, is barbarous. The proposal to abolish the clause in the divorce law prohibiting the remarriage of divorced couples is almost as reprehensible. . . . The proposal to reduce the number of children in a family and keep down the progeny of married couples is also most offensive, and is a menace to morality and the stability of society." In his sermon Dr. Dix warned a congregation composed largely of women of the dangers of extreme radicals, "seditious communists," and "the murderous Anarchist," and their "schemes of social revolution." "The home should be a sanctuary," he emphasized; "a school of righteousness; a fortress of safety from outside foes."[2]

Elsie Clews Parsons's seditious textbook was aimed precisely at the conception of the home articulated by the Reverend Dr. Dix. In her opinion the home, as it was presently constituted, was the problem, not the solution. The home should be a school for life, preparing children for a changing world; instead, parents adhered unthinkingly to outmoded ideals that left young men and women dangerously unfitted for modern life. In attacking the home, Parsons was challenging head-on the domestic paradigm that stood at the center of nineteenth-century women's intellectual thought and political activity. According to this paradigm, women's self-sacrificial role in the family gave them a moral superiority, a gift for understanding and intuition, and a collective political program that compensated for and counteracted the amoral (and masculine) rationality of the market. The domestic paradigm had been pushed to its limits by one of its principal proponents, Jane Addams, during Parsons's years as an undergraduate and graduate student at Barnard and Columbia during the 1890s. As the founder of Hull House in 1889 and chief theorist of the burgeoning new settlement house movement, Addams had a paradoxical relationship with the middle-class family. On the one hand, everything she did was an implicit critique of the way the Victorian family absorbed and confined women's personality and actions: she wrote movingly of the "family claim" that kept young women from work outside the home; at Hull House she substituted a new "family of choice" for the "natural" family; and she carried "family values" outside the home into the new profession of social work and the new political organization, the pressure group. But she did all of this without explicitly critiquing the conception of the family that she was, in reality, rejecting.[3]

Addams and Parsons were part of the major turn-of-the-century intellectual and political project concerned with bridging increasing social divisions between classes, ethnic groups, and generations. Both shared a vision of greater social and economic democracy fostered through increased understanding between groups. Addams's *Democracy and Social Ethics* (1902) depicts with great insight the gap in experience and cultural understanding between the well-meaning young middle-class woman and the working-class and ethnic neighbors she wants to help. She brilliantly conveys the perplexities and blindnesses of her middle-class counterpart; but for Addams it is the immigrant and the worker who need explanation, and her main concern is to interpret working-class and ethnic group behavior to her middle-class audience. For Parsons, however, it was the middle class that needed explanation. As a young married professional woman and mother working in a mixed-sex environment, Parsons admired Addams's work; but she felt strongly that it needed to be pushed much further. Rather than interpreting the "other," Parsons turned her gaze onto her own kind. Focusing her critique on the middle-class home, the institution women had made their own under the domestic paradigm, Parsons looked unflinchingly at the those central aspects of family life that the domestic paradigm avoided—sexuality and the conventions that governed relations between the sexes.[4]

.   .   .

Elsie Worthington Clews was one of the first students trained by Franklin Giddings after his appointment as professor of sociology at Columbia University and Barnard College in 1894. In 1896–97 she wrote her masters thesis under

Giddings's supervision. Barred by her sex from registering for doctoral work in the Faculty of Political Science, where sociology was located, she gained her Ph.D. in 1899 in the Faculty of Philosophy, with a major in education and a dissertation supervised by Nicholas Murray Butler; but her minors in sociology, philosophy, and statistics and her choice of Giddings as an adviser on her dissertation indicated her continued interest in sociology. Giddings then appointed her to the Columbia faculty for three years as Hartley House Fellow, responsible for supervision of the fieldwork of his Barnard students, and from 1902 to 1905 she was lecturer in sociology at Barnard, where she taught what had been Giddings's course on the family.[5]

Giddings was an original, widely read, and energetic teacher who liked to shock his students "by drawing them up either to the edge of atheism or immorality or what not, and pressing them hard." He found his match in Elsie Clews, who had been pursuing an iconoclastic career since early childhood. Born in New York in 1874, she was the daughter of wealthy banker Henry Clews and his socialite wife, Lucy Madison Worthington Clews. Despite the material privilege in which she grew up, she was, like Gertrude Stein, "there to kill what was not dead, the 19th century which was so sure of evolution and prayers."[6]

Elsie Clews was one of that generation of Americans who were irrevocably cut off from the past by the trauma of the Civil War, the massive transformation of the nation through the processes of industrialization, urbanization, and immigration, and the Darwinian intellectual revolution. Her family history increased what Nietzsche called "the strength to forget the past" that was common to this generation. Her father was a self-made man who came to New York from England as a young man and made a fortune during the Civil War. He was a man without a past, never looking back to his British origins, yet free of any American heritage. As an Episcopalian, he had none of the introspection, guilt, and sense of social obligation of the native-born evangelicals and their descendants. Although he enjoyed the exercise of power, he did not share the obsessive concern with his children's souls that characterized a Lyman Beecher, or the strict sense of social obligation that marked the fathers of Progressives such as Jane Addams. Her mother came from a distinguished southern family; but they were ruined by the Civil War, and a major corruption scandal during the Grant administration involving her uncle, Minister of War General Belknap, cut her off decisively from her southern roots. She continued to exemplify, however, the aristocratic southern tradition of femininity. Like her husband, Lucy Worthington Clews escaped the evangelical indoctrination into good works and seems to have accepted without guilt her reputation as Newport's best- (and most expensively) dressed woman. The closest she came to the self-sacrifice and efficiency of the evangelical ideal was in her devotion to her "social duties." In a tartly worded description written in 1916, Elsie Clews Parsons targeted both the evangelical tradition and the "gynocratic caste" of American "Society" to which her mother belonged:

To be attractive to women a society life must impart a sense of achievement. Staying in society as well as getting into it must be arduous and calling for enterprise and skill. The American society life answers these requirements. That art of conspicuous wasting it relies upon is itself exigent. Other "social duties" are laborious, often exhausting. They require a kind of self-devotion which verges on asceticism. They appeal to the energetic and self-denying spirit of the American woman. Take the ceremonial, for example, of leaving cards. Afternoon calling gives a woman, I believe, a quasi-mystical sense of acquiring merit. I remember driving one lovely spring afternoon in Washington with a lady who was leaving cards. She paid little or no attention to the charms of forsythia or maple-tree blossoms, but each of the twenty-five calls she made appeared to give her the kind of satisfaction a Catholic or a Buddhist takes in telling the beads of his rosary.

As the weak sister of the gynocracy of reform, Society life had little resistance to change. According to Parsons's 1916 analysis of her mother's milieu, imitation and economic elasticity assailed it from without, while increasing outlets for feminine energy and ambition eroded it from within. "Without boundaries, without leaders, without matrimonial baits, without means of accrediting or advertising itself through crisis ceremonials or through newspaper notoriety what hope of a future is there," she asked, "for the gynocratic caste?"[7]

Alhough the obligations of Society were much stronger in the years when Elsie Clews was growing up, the "Rule of the Elders," as she later put it, was not as powerful where the evangelical impulse was absent. Elsie Clews could imitate her ambitious, goal-directed father and repudiate her "feminine," indolent mother to a degree that was not available to women such as Catharine Beecher and Jane Addams. It was relatively easy, therefore, for her to insist on going to college, especially since the opening of Barnard College in 1889 allowed her to live at home and participate in the form, if not the spirit, of her set's social obligations.[8]

The nature of Barnard College and the New York City constituency it served strengthened the rebellion against convention already permitted by Elsie Clews's background. Established as a sister school to Columbia University, Barnard was different from other women's colleges. Vassar, Wellesley, Smith, Mount Holyoke, and Bryn Mawr all catered to boarders, providing a total environment based on the idea of a separate women's culture. In contrast, Barnard students were scattered in private homes and accommodation. Unlike the Harvard Annex—later Radcliffe—which it resembled most closely, Barnard was able to insist on exactly comparable standards for its students, who were granted the Columbia degree, and after 1895 could exert considerable influence on those standards by its ability to appoint and share with Columbia its own talented faculty. Indeed, Barnard had something of the quality of a coeducational university. Barnard seniors and graduate students shared classes with Columbia men, and, despite social proprieties that inhibited informal interaction, men and women learned something of "the fiber of each other's mind."[9]

Barnard College also attracted a wider spectrum of students than the other colleges, ranging from women of moderate means who could not afford a residential school to the wealthy socialite who was unwilling to miss the New York season (or whose mother was unwilling to forgo her daughter's company). In addition, a significant number of its students were Jewish—at first the daughters of German Jewish intellectuals, and later poorer Eastern European immigrants.[10]

The New York intellectual milieu provided a diversity and tolerance that fostered Barnard's difference from other elite women's colleges. Its influx of Jewish intellectuals after 1848, its continuing absorption of recent British immigrants, and its constant exposure to international trends cut across the American evangelical tradition and the settled attitudes of more stable, long-established, and homogeneous communities such as Boston. This more cosmopolitan milieu fostered the development of the more radical, egalitarian branches of the nineteenth-century woman's movement. The acceptance by New York society of its most outrageous forms is caricatured by Henry James in *The Bostonians*, where Mrs. Burrage is content to encourage her son's marriage to Verena, the feminist orator who is considered beyond the pale by Boston matrons. In contrast to popular woman-focused organizations based on the evangelical religious tradition, such as the Woman's Christian Temperance Union, New York preserved much of the earlier tradition of the Seneca Falls Convention, with its emphasis on natural rights, equality, and the tyranny of custom and law in creating and maintaining a separate and oppressive women's sphere. Elizabeth Cady Stanton lived in New York from 1862 until her death in 1902, and New York was the headquarters of the National Woman Suffrage Association she and Susan B. Anthony established in 1869. The name of their short-lived journal, *The Revolution*, and its motto, "Men, their rights and nothing more; women, their rights and nothing less," epitomize the uncompromising stand toward women's rights that characterized this New York tradition.[11]

.   .   .

Elsie Clews had strong personal reasons to be receptive to the message of sociology in the fall of 1894. Earlier that year her love for Sam Dexter, a young lawyer who seemed in every way suited to her, was cut brutally short by his sudden death. After a dreary summer in which she followed her mother dutifully around Europe and the Parisian couturiers, Elsie found that the sociology she encountered in Giddings's class opened up a new world of experience, adventure, and wider social participation. Basing his sociology on the idea of "consciousness of kind," Giddings envisaged an ideal society in which rigorous discussion and debate and an ethical awareness of the wider society led to the highest, rational form of like-mindedness. Attracted by the notions of activity, effort, and change that imbued Giddings's work, Elsie plunged into the study of sociology, and at the same time into the world of philanthropy and social settlements that was closely associated with it. She was particularly impressed by the opportunities that settlements provided for women such as herself to develop their abilities in a socially useful way. In 1895 she began her ten-year association with the settlement movement; and over the next few years she gained a reputation as "the busiest young woman in New York," taken up with "multifarious tasks among the submerged."[12]

Although Elsie found Giddings's theoretical perspective attractive, she found his practice unsatisfactory as a guide to her own life and work. She became impatient with his cautious approach to social change, his emphasis on social consensus at any cost, and his essentially condescending "legislator's" attitude to underprivileged groups. Her later contempt for the Americanization movement and America's colonial pretensions demonstrated her strong condemnation of the social control his sociology stood for. More important to her were the work of the social psychologist Gabriel Tarde and the example of her friend and coworker Mary Kingsbury Simkhovitch, both of whom had a respect for individual difference and autonomy and an eagerness for radical social change that Giddings ultimately lacked.[13]

Elsie discovered Tarde's work in Giddings's introductory class in 1894, and she spent the summer before she entered graduate school in 1896 in the Bibliothèque Nationale translating his *Laws of Imitation* and *Social Logic*. The founder of social psychology, Gabriel Tarde (1843–1904) was a writer of great charm and brilliance who was widely regarded during the 1890s as France's leading sociologist. In his much-publicized debate with Durkheim, Tarde stood for an anti-institutional, anticollective perspective allied politically to anarchism and the less doctrinaire forms of socialism, while Durkheim represented reason, order, authority, and established institutions.[14]

It was exactly the anarchic and imaginative aspect of Tarde's work that made it so attractive to Elsie Clews and other social innovators of the period. Tarde appealed to what he called the "wild and undisciplined spirit[s]" who are "the inventors of the future." Pointing out that what has been historically achieved is only a fraction of what might have been or could be, he challenged the determinism of late-nineteenth-century sociology by asserting the range of possibilities open to societies. Within a general framework that incorporated innovation, conflict, and change as central elements, his emphasis on invention, imitation, and opposition set up a complex model of social life that allowed for chance and initiative in a way more mechanistic models did not.[15]

Tarde's emphasis on the freedom and creativity of the individual fitted well with Parsons's ideas on social change. For Tarde, change was more like a series of explosions than a gentle, consistent transformation. He emphasized "the accidental, the irrational . . . the accident of genius" rather than what he called "the rationale." "In his eyes, everything stemmed from the individual, and everything came back to him," wrote the French sociologist Bouglé. Where Durkheim emphasized coercion and social control, Tarde emphasized choice and freedom; where Durkheim saw science as productive of laws that could be used for what he called "the positive regulation of conduct," Tarde saw it as capable only of showing what is possible and impossible; where Durkheim emphasized reason, Tarde focused instead on "sensation, instinct, passion, all the base and obscure parts of ourselves."[16]

Although his name is always linked with the idea of imitation, Tarde was much more interested in the phenomena of nonimitation, invention, and what he called the "logical duel," in which rival innovations were brought into harmony. "When a people deliberately undertakes not to reproduce the examples of its forefathers in the matter of rights, usages, and ideas, we have a veritable disassociation of fathers and sons, a rupture of the umbilical cord between the old and the new society," he wrote. "Voluntary and persistent non-imitation in this sense has a purgative role which is quite analagous to that filled by what I have called the logical duel. Just as the latter tends to purge the social mass of mixed ideas and volitions, to eliminate inequalities and discords, and to facilitate in this way the synthetic action of the logical union; so . . . non-imitation of anterior models, when the moment has come for civilising revolution, cuts a path for fashion-imitation." For Tarde, the goal of progress was "the birth, the development, and the universal spread . . . of a unique society" in which "the growing resemblance of individuals between whom all customary barriers of reciprocal imitation have been broken down . . . makes them feel with a growing and, eventually, irresistible power the injustice of privilege." "When, instead of patterning one's self after one person or a few, we borrow from a hundred, a thousand, or ten thousand persons," he argued, the result is both "the purest and most potent individualism" and a "consummate sociability."[17]

In Tarde, Elsie Clews found an ally in her project of "killing the 19th century." He provided her with a vision of a new and better world where individuality would not be blotted out by tradition and where respect for individual difference would be the basis of social harmony. He also showed her the means of achieving that goal through the promotion of what he called "conversation." For Tarde, mass communications, extended patterns of loyalty, and the development of overlapping group memberships enabled people to shift ideological perspectives and form coalitions with greater flexibility. These processes in turn facilitated the development of rationality, tolerance, and peace. Through more democratic and spontaneous personal relationships, in other words, the effects of broader structural changes could be modified.[18]

. . .

Tarde's notions of imitation, invention, and conversation gave Elsie Clews a theoretical perspective and a program of action. But it was her fellow graduate student Mary Kingsbury who demonstrated the practical working out of this program. Mary Kingsbury entered the Columbia graduate program with Elsie in 1896 but soon left to become head worker at College Settlement. In 1898 she moved to Friendly Aid House, a settlement supported by the Unitarian Church. When she married Vladimir Simkhovitch in 1899, they lived on the upper floor of the settlement. In 1902 she founded Greenwich House in

Greenwich Village. There she lived with her husband and two small children, working with the immigrant communities of the area and forming a center for what has been called the "ethical bohemia."[19]

Mary Kingsbury Simkhovitch saw as the main role of settlements the empowerment of the community and its members through encouragement of community cohesion and local leadership. "If social improvements are to be undertaken by one class on behalf of another, no permanent changes are likely to be effected," she pointed out. Basic to this work was Tarde's idea of face-to-face conversation. "Before any help can be given the situation must be felt, realized and understood at first hand," Simkhovitch wrote. "Only that which is lived can be understood and translated to others." She insisted, therefore, on living in the community as a family like any other. She supported neighborhood theater, helped establish a settlement music school, and campaigned for local schools to be used as neighborhood centers. In her major reform effort to improve public housing, she emphasized restoration of old buildings and the reconstruction of small-scale traditional neighborhoods as well as supporting pioneering efforts in large-scale public housing. Her ideal was always the organic community combining business, housing, recreation, and educational and cultural institutions.[20]

Elsie Clews and Mary Kingsbury became firm friends and partners in these enterprises, with Mary often taking the part of doer and Elsie the facilitator. But they were also partners in another, more personal venture, again inspired by Tarde's injunction to reformers that they be inventors of the future. When Mary Kingsbury married Vladimir Simkhovitch in 1899 and Elsie Clews married Herbert Parsons in 1900, they were consciously embarking on an experimental life. Just as young women of M. Carey Thomas's day, "haunted by the clanging chains of that gloomy specter, Dr. Edward Clarke's *Sex in Education*," did not know whether women's health could stand the strain of education, those of Elsie Clews's day did not know if they could successfully combine work, marriage, and childbearing. Prejudice against the experiment was strong. Most career women of Thomas's—and Jane Addams's—generation eschewed marriage in favor of households of women or a loving relationship with another woman. New York City did offer, however, some prominent role models such as journalist Jane Croly and physician Mary Putnam Jacobi. Emily James, the brilliant young dean of Barnard College, remained in her position after her marriage to George Herbert Putnam in 1899, and Elsie's Barnard friend Alice Duer Miller had also married in 1899 and was continuing the career that would eventually make her a leading Hollywood writer. But just as Elsie and Herbert announced their engagement in April 1900, the pregnant Emily Putnam was losing her struggle to keep her position. The older generation of women Elsie worked with were skeptical of the experiment. A former professor wrote, typically, "I am not going to congratulate you at all. You and Alice Duer were the two girls I had made up my mind would make great names for yourselves, and show women what they can do, and now you just come down to the level of us ordinary mortals." Annie Nathan Meyer, who had insisted on Emily Putnam's resignation, was quite definite that "in time it seems wisest to change one's activities—you will find there are many to fill one's life." Elsie's students were, however, "very glad and surprised" to hear that she intended to continue her work with their class. Her settlement coworker James Reynolds wrote supportively. And to her College Settlement colleague Susan Walker, who was contemplating marriage herself, she was a welcome role model. "I am mightily glad you don't think matrimony incompatible with other things," Susan wrote. "I have similar views & so far have only Mary Simkhovitch to fall back upon for proof. May I long be able to quote you among the noble minority."[21]

Although Elsie had loved Herbert Parsons for several years, she had adamantly refused to marry him, believing, as Jane Addams had before her, that marriage would not be compatible with her self-development and her ability to contribute to the wider society. Tarde's vision of an invented world and Mary Simkhovitch's example gave her the strength to experiment. Elsie was pregnant within six weeks of the marriage, so she soon had the opportunity to put her theories to the test. Her daughter Lissa was born in August 1901 and her son John in August 1903, both pregnancies nicely timed so that she was only six months pregnant at the end of the academic year and had finished breast-feeding by the time the teaching year started again. Always the careful scientist, Elsie recorded the details of Lissa's birth in a special diary—but she added a feminist flourish: "The twentieth century is high time that women should shout and shout I did," she wrote in Lissa's persona. Mary Simkhovitch, herself pregnant with her first child, exclaimed excitedly, "What a modern young lady she will be."[22]

In January 1902, Mary's son Stephen was born. His arrival severely tested the young women's experiment. The board of Friendly Aid House objected to her bringing up a baby in the settlement and forced her to resign with much acrimony. Over the next year, with child care and financial help from Elsie, she established Greenwich House, even though she was again pregnant. The example of these two busy young mothers earned the admiration of their fellow workers. After Elsie's son was born in 1903, Katharine Coman wrote from the College Settlements Association, "You and Mrs Simkhovitch should be written up in vindication of the essential womanhood of the intellectual woman." But the final blow for Mary fell when Stephen contracted tuberculosis in 1905. By 1908 the Simkhovitches had bought a farm in New Jersey, where their two children were brought up with the help of a governess and the parents visited them for long weekends.[23]

. . .

Elsie's testing trials as a wife and mother were soon to come; but Mary's experiences, her own family's hostility to her flouting of convention, and her students' fieldwork convinced her that the area of social life most impervious to adaptation and innovation was that of the family and sexual mores. The course on family organization she taught beginning in 1902 introduced her to the burgeoning comparative ethnographic and psychological literature on the family and sexuality. She eagerly recognized its new message of cultural relativity as a reinforcement of her own rebellion against any fixed and timeless morality. Casting a clear eye over the women of her own family and class, she became increasingly critical of the three institutions she had been intimately involved with—the family, the women's college, and the settlement house. All, in her opinion, should be concerned with developing individual autonomy and responsibility to enable people to adapt readily to rapidly changing conditions. Yet the family remained enmeshed in outmoded conventions that left young women unready to cope with the actual conditions of modern life; the women's college had not developed an appropriate curriculum to prepare its privileged students for lives of self-development and social usefulness; and the settlement house, which was specifically designed to foster personal and local initiative, tended instead to replace local institutions and legislate for community members, breaking up in the process local and family life. And all of these institutions ignored the problem that was central to women's lack of autonomy and individuality—sex relations.[24]

Herbert Parsons's election to Congress in November 1904 coincided with this crisis in Elsie's thinking. Their move to Washington in 1905 enabled her to break her links with applied sociology and the settlement movement and to launch into a new, more detached, career as ethnographer and social critic. Tarde considered mass communications and face-to-face talk the most important ways of encouraging and spreading innovation. Parsons now envisaged a much more outspoken role for herself in which she used journals of social comment and the conversation of Washington society as forums for the propagation of new ideas.

The most urgent area of change for Parsons was the "tabooed" area of sexuality. Although she never lost sight of class inequality and the importance of women's access to work, both for personal development and for economic independence, she took sex relations and the situation of middle-class women as her particular sphere of expertise and interest. With the establishment of the Socialist Party in 1900, its support among young privileged men and women, and the organization of the Women's Trade Union League in 1903, women could talk about work and economic exploitation; but the topics of sex and sexual oppression, especially among women who appeared to be materially well-off, remained unacceptable.[25]

From about 1904, Parsons began to note down the social conventions of her own set. Turning herself into a native informant, she began an ethnography of everyday middle-class culture that formed the basis of her social critique (and of the dry wit that gave all her work its distinctive piquancy). She used this material for the first time in 1905 and 1906 in a series of articles that castigated the affluent home and the women's college for their failure to prepare women for a socially productive life. In particular she focused on their failure to challenge the sex taboos prevalent in economic life and to educate girls for what she called "democratic" sexual relations and childbearing. The Board of Education's attempt to outlaw married women teachers was "mere Rip Van Winkleism," she argued in an article titled "Penalizing Marriage and Child-Bearing" in the *Independent* in 1906. Instead of continuing to insist that women's place was in the home, the community should be facing up to what was actually happening and studying the conditions under which women could best work. In pursuit of this program three major concerns had to be addressed: the best education to help girls become socially productive under conditions most conducive to their health; the work women could best do to allow them two months' intermission at childbirth; and the changes in popular sentiment necessary to make childbearing socially more compatible with an economically and socially productive life. As a student of Tarde, Parsons was most interested in the question of popular opinion. What we need, she argued, is a lifting of the taboo on sex. Without frank discussion and acceptance of the moral and physical aspects of sex, girls develop a hostility toward marriage and sexuality, rejecting them as personally confining and physically unesthetic. The enforced retirement of the pregnant woman from social life, the taboo on the nursing mother, and the general lack of contraceptive knowledge were all serious handicaps to the useful activity of childbearing women.[26]

Taking up three aspects of sexuality that were being widely discussed, Parsons condemned this discussion as insincere, fallacious, and unenlightening. Why characterize prostitution as a "necessary evil" without discussing frankly the reasons it was "necessary" or the consequences if it was "evil"? she asked. Why condemn divorce without discussing the social and economic causes of marital incompatibility in a period of major social change? Why express horror of "race-suicide" without acknowledging that girls' ignorance of sex and maternity, the widespread resort to prostitution, and the overcultivation of the leisure-class wife were factors that had to be discussed? "In primitive communities taboo is a far-reaching and most effectual instrument and preservative of group tradition," she pointed out. "In modern civilization there are not a few survivals of taboo in out of the way mental corners, but the taboo of direct reference is perhaps the sturdiest. . . . In no other class of subjects . . . is taboo on clear thinking so onerous . . . and failure to 'think thru' so practically disastrous, as in our sex morality." "There is an ethical, as well as intellectual, obligation in seeing things as they were and are before concluding what they ought to be."[27]

One of the main enemies of open discussion, in Parsons's opinion, was religion, which "fosters the state of mind which is intolerant of innovation and respectful of whatever is traditional or authoritative." She fired the first volley in a lifelong battle against religious superstition in an article for the *American Journal of Sociology* in 1906 that examined the ways religion sanctioned the gift of women for sexual service to the gods. As she comments mordantly, "The occasion sometimes requires the immolation of the gift." Tracing the Christian idealization of celibacy to the custom of dedicating women to the service of the gods, she observed that this was one of the many cases in which religion conserves outgrown social practices. Christianity's condemnation of sexual desire is "a grave obstacle to the development of woman's personality," she argued in her controversial textbook *The Family* in 1906. Because women have been stigmatized as the means of satisfying unworthy desire, they have become objects of seclusion and repression. Developing her idea of a modern, ethical family, she argued that such a family must be capable of adapting the child to a changing environment and encouraging its capacity for individual variation. The only sort of family that could do this was, in her opinion, one that encouraged women's full development. Monogamy and equality of conjugal rights and duties are desirable, she pointed out, not because they are morally right, but because they allow the development of many-sided, free personalities fit to educate children. Given the importance of monogamy and reciprocal rights and duties, she went on, sexual choice is an important matter that should be made only by the relatively mature. But if late marriage was desirable, the question of premarital sex had to be faced honestly. The age-old solution of prostitution is as incompatible with modern democracy as slavery, Parsons argued. Given late marriage and the passing of prostitution, there remained only two alternatives, the absolute chastity of both sexes until marriage, or toleration of freedom of sexual intercourse on the part of the unmarried of both sexes before the birth of children. In the new family ethics Parsons proposed, sexual intercourse would be disapproved of only if indulged in at the expense of one's own health or emotional or intellectual activities, or those of others. As monogamous relations are most conducive to emotional and intellectual development and health, it would be sensible, she concluded, to encourage early trial marriage. Couples should enter into such a relationship with a view to permanency, but with the possibility of breaking it without public condemnation if it proves unsuccessful and if there are no children. The development of such a new morality depends, Parsons pointed out, on "the outcome of present experiments in economic independence for women," on "revelations of physiological science . . . through the discovery of certain and innocuous methods of preventing conception," and on "a more enlightened and purposive approach to parenthood." With the need for sexual restraint largely gone, the possibility of quite different relations between the sexes should emerge, she concluded.[28]

In speaking out on sexuality and the right to free speech, Parsons was treading on dangerous ground. These topics were the province of anarchists and freethinkers. As recently as 1900, sex reformer Ida Craddock had committed suicide rather than face another prison sentence for the publication of her pamphlet *Wedding Night*, and Moses Harman, editor of the anarchist *Lucifer, the Light-Bearer*, had been jailed in 1905 for his pamphlet *The Right to Be Born Well*. In 1905 Anthony Comstock, the man who had systematically guarded the purity of the nation since 1873, had attempted to prevent the staging of Shaw's *Mrs. Warren's Profession* in New York and had arrested *Physical Culture* editor Bernarr Macfadden for promoting a "Mammoth Physical Exhibition" with "obscene" photographs of young men and women.[29]

By 1906, however, the tide was turning on "comstockery," as George Bernard Shaw called it. Comstock was not successful in any of these prosecutions. At the same time, Emma Goldman, notorious for her connection with Alexander Berkman's assassination attempt on business magnate Henry Clay Frick, had recently begun to lecture publicly on sexuality, and her journal *Mother*

Earth became a forum for discussion of sexual emancipation from its first edition in March 1906. As the Reverend Dr. Dix underlined in his condemnation of *The Family* from the pulpit of Trinity Church, issues of free speech, political freedom, and sexual freedom were inextricably linked in the early years of the twentieth century. McKinley's assassination in 1901 brought in its wake a concerted drive by the United States postal authorities to ban radical newspapers and magazines from the mails. It also gave rise to federal laws banning the entry of anarchists to the United States. These laws, the first to exclude immigrants on political grounds, aroused middle-class liberal support for the anarchist cause in defense of civil liberties. By the end of 1903, Goldman was being invited to lecture at such liberal forums as the Manhattan Liberal Club, the Brooklyn Philosophical Society, and the Sunrise Club, and she became friends with Theodore Schroeder and other liberals involved in the Free Speech Leagues.[30]

Given the heated nature of the discussions of free speech and sexuality at the time, and their association with the most radical elements in the society, it is not surprising that Parsons found it difficult to publish her articles, even in censored form, and that *The Family*—intended as a textbook for college students—was greeted in many quarters with horror. By writing about sexuality, Parsons was deliberately linking the issues of family reform and women's emancipation with the incendiary cause of free speech. In the preface to a projected new book "Little Essays in Lifting Taboo," she emphasized the importance of language. "It does sometimes seem that the introduction in these days of a new descriptive term opens up a new vista of thought," she wrote. She found the Polynesian word "tapu" particularly useful for naming, and therefore recognizing and lifting, the modern taboos that surrounded sex and women's work. Social transitions in these areas were rapid; yet they were not being dealt with in a rationally self-directing, purposive way, she wrote. Women must think clearly about these changes if they were to control the conditions of their lives. "How much longer can misinterpretations of social facts lurk in the medieval corners of our minds?" she asked. "Sociology, the youngest of the sciences, is also the last to have its truths become commonplaces." Defending herself against the accusation that no "decent" woman would discuss sexual topics publicly, she argued that no one else could carry out the task of improving attitudes to sexuality. "Men merely because they are men, live or are reputed to live too firmly encased in glass houses to lead in the stone-throwing." The unmarried, the divorced, the unhappily married, and the childless woman is also handicapped in such a discussion. Privileged women have the duty to take up this task, she argued, especially if, like herself, they are familiar with other moral systems, in their own society or in other more remote cultures.[31]

. . .

Despite favorable reviews of her work from the liberal legal and scientific community, Parsons retreated for some years from her public refashioning of the family to deal with her own personal problems. Continually pregnant from July

1905 to September 1907, despite the fact that she considered herself sophisticated about birth control and had access to the "best" advice, she lost two children at birth, the first in March 1906 and the second in February 1907. A further pregnancy immediately after the loss of the second child ended in abortion or miscarriage, and another possible pregnancy early in 1908 proved to be a false alarm. This series of reproductive disasters left her seriously depleted in health and spirits; and in 1909, during another pregnancy whose outcome she awaited anxiously, she began a long battle with jealousy over Herbert's friendship with the conventionally feminine wife of a Washington colleague.[32]

Parsons strenuously resisted her decline in physical, mental, and moral strength, and increasingly turned to arduous and exciting trips as a means of shaking herself out of her depression and lack of energy. At first she tried to interest Herbert in the sort of travel she enjoyed, but he had little inclination for such adventures and the few trips they took together were unsuccessful. Beginning in 1908 she began taking demanding trips with a variety of men and women friends. In 1910, after a year in which Herbert's friendship with Lucy Wilson deepened and Parsons's second healthy son was born, she found the perfect travel and conversational partner in George Young, a secretary at the British Embassy, whose friendship strengthened her mentally and physically. In the summer of 1910, in a determined effort to reassert control over her life, she made the trip to the Southwest that was to be a turning point in her life. With a new sense of purpose and control, she determined to prepare herself for a life as an anthropological fieldworker. Already extraordinarily well-read in anthropology, she began reading voraciously about the Southwest. Over the next year, she established contact with the National Museum and the American Museum of Natural History, at the same time as she rode, played tennis, canoed, walked, and camped with George Young, despite the pregnancy that ended with the birth of her youngest son in September 1911.[33]

This new sense of purpose helped Parsons to bring her simmering jealousy out into the open and precipitate a crisis in her relationship with Herbert. In a fictionalized account, Parsons speaks of this period as marking the end of her love. This fits well with her "life-plan" over the next few years. She retained a strong affection for Herbert; but she deliberately diffused her emotional life among her work, her children, and her friends, some of whom became lovers. Her anthropological fieldwork became particularly important to this process of emotional diffusion and family reorganization.[34]

.   .   .

Parsons's re-creation of herself as an anthropological fieldworker was not just a retreat from painful personal problems. Anthropology provided her with the integration of theory and practice she had been searching for. The application of sociology in settlement house work had not satisfied this search. Her apprehension about the directions in which sociologists such as Giddings and Edward Ross were taking Tarde's work in justifying immigration restriction and colonialism distanced her further from sociology; and her anguish over sociological arguments for the suppression of minority opinion "in society's interest" during World War I cut her off completely from her old discipline. Anthropology, on the other hand, gave her ideological and structural reinforcement for her challenges to orthodoxy and habit. Her foray into the Southwest in 1910 brought her into contact with a group of young anthropologists based in the American Museum of Natural History and Columbia University. Over the next few years these young men, Robert Lowie, Alexander Goldenweiser, and Pliny Goddard, became her close friends and colleagues, welcoming her as a kindred spirit into the discipline they were reconstructing—or perhaps "*de*constructing" might be a more appropriate term.[35]

The weapon that Parsons's new friends and colleagues used in their deconstructive project was positivism—not the system-building positivism of Comte or Spencer, but the critical positivism of Ernst Mach. An Austrian physicist, mathematician, and historian of science, Mach was the author of *Science of Mechanics* (1883), *Analysis of the Sensations* (1886), *Popular Scientific Lectures* (1895), and *Knowledge and Error* (1905), which had an enormous impact on turn-of-the-century scientific and artistic worlds. Mach used history and studies of perception to question the bases of knowledge-claims and to critique accepted scientific concepts. His "positivistic chastity," as Robert Lowie called it, rejected all metaphysical speculation and abstract theorizing, and based all knowledge-claims in experience. In other words, Mach demonstrated what postmodernists call an "incredulity towards metanarratives." For Mach all knowledge was a provisional processing of sense-data for the purposes of survival. All we can know is given through our sensations, to which the mind gives shape according to need. Ideas of space, time, body, and ego are all personal cuts into the chaos of sensations according to current need, to be discarded in the face of new experiences and new needs. For Mach, theories were "like withered leaves, which drop off after having enabled the organism of science to breathe for a time." The metanarratives implicit in words, concepts, classifications, and theories were, therefore, temporarily useful fictions to be discarded before they became impediments to adaptation to new conditions.[36]

Mach's insistence on rigorously questioning current systems of thought was highly attractive to the modernist avant-garde, to revolutionary political groups, to innovative intellectuals, and to the women and men who were beginning to call themselves feminists. In the sciences and the arts alike, his emphasis on the provisional character of all knowledge initiated a wholesale critique of language and conceptual, classificatory, and theoretical systems. Robert Lowie and Alexander Goldenweiser discovered Mach's work as graduate students at Columbia between 1904 and 1909. Like others of their generation, they were seeking to form a new worldview from the intellectual ferment of a period of rapid change. Along with Paul Radin and Morris Cohen, they formed a reading group in which they read the new positivists—Mach, Pearson, Poincaré, and Ostwald. Unlike most of Parsons's settlement house and sociology colleagues, Lowie, Goldenweiser, Cohen, and Radin were all Jewish immigrants. This group of young intellectuals were drawn to the mixture of scientific rigor and critique in Mach's work. As immigrants with backgrounds in the European professional middle class, they could be characterized as secure outsiders, a status that allowed them to be critical of established intellectual thought and able to tolerate the uncertainties implicit in Mach's approach to knowledge. When Elsie Clews Parsons met Lowie and Goldenweiser between 1910 and 1912, they were embarked, under Mach's inspiration, on a wholesale critique of the central concepts and theoretical systems of nineteenth-century ethnology. "Like the generation of thinkers that preceded ours, we are living in an age of revolt," Lowie announced in a lecture series at the American Museum of Natural History in 1914, "but the object of our revolt is different from theirs. Our predecessors fought tradition as arrayed against reason. We have the task of exorcising the ghosts of tradition raised in the name of reason herself. There is not only a folklore of popular belief, but also a folklore of philosophical and scientific system-mongers. Our present duty is to separate scientific fact from its envelope of scientific folklore."[37]

Parsons, a secure outsider herself—secure by virtue of her wealth and social position, an outsider by virtue of her gender and radicalism—found these young men and their deconstructive project highly sympathetic. Through them she found a supportive group of colleagues and friends who eventually included Pliny Goddard at the American Museum of Natural History, Franz Boas at Columbia University, and Alfred Kroeber at the University of California at Berkeley. She also found in Mach's ideas a crystallization of her own attempts to fashion a more complex and flexible approach to life and work. Over the next seven years she used Mach's ideas as the basis of her critique of the family and the situation of women, and as the charter for the new way of life she created for herself. Between 1912 and 1917, at the same time as she established herself as a professional anthropologist, Parsons set out her critique in a series of popular books, articles, and unpublished manuscripts. Drawing on a variety of ethnographic material, assembled with a cool irony from contemporary American society and so-called primitive societies alike, she mocked the past, celebrated change, and looked forward to what she called "An Unconventional Society"— a future society that social science would help bring about by undermining the influence of "the Elders."[38]

The target of Parsons's critique is the nineteenth-century family and the "old-fashioned woman" who sustains it. But her vision of possible new relationships among women, men, and children is embedded in a general conception of social freedom in which people are no longer identified by their age, sex, class, marital status, or nationality. Just as Mach freed modern physics from outmoded and unnecessary concepts and categories, Parsons's project was nothing less than to free people from the imprisonment of social categories and institutions. Human beings have a passion for classification, she argued in *Social Freedom* in 1915, and a fear of anomalies—in other words, a fear of those people who are unclassified or unclassifiable. For her, the social categories were obsessive and imperial, spreading over the irrelevant; and they arrested innovative thought. The urge to classify, the fear of social change, and social control are closely interrelated, Parsons argued in *Social Rule* in 1916. "The social categories are an unparalleled means of gratifying the will to power. The classified individual may be held in subjection in ways the unclassified escapes."[39]

Given the power of classification, the main objective of the new feminism for Parsons was "the declassification of women as women, the recognition of women as human beings or personalities." "The more thoroughly a woman is classified the more easily is she controlled," she argued in 1916. "The *new woman*," therefore, "means the woman not yet classified, perhaps not classifiable." This unclassified, unclassifiable woman is new not only to men but to herself, Parsons goes on. For women were, in her opinion, more conventional than men. Parsons had a deadly eye for the conventionalities of daily life that women maintained to uphold the distinctions between the sexes and to conserve their positions of power within the family; and she delighted in turning Lévy-Bruhl's concept of "primitive thinking" on its head by demonstrating the "magical" and "sentimental" elements lurking in the beliefs and behavior of even the more "progressive" women of her social class.[40]

Mach had said that physics was only experience, arranged in economical order. Basic to Parsons's feminist critique of the family, therefore, was the notion of experience as the source of knowledge, adaptability, and power. The female traveler and the female stranger epitomize for Parsons the modern, independent woman. As she pointed out in 1914, women's development as creators of knowledge has been cramped as effectively as the feet of Chinese women crippled by the practice of binding:

> In no culture have women shown desire to do anything which requires running the risks of being alone. Women hermits are extremely scarce, there are few women explorers, there are no women vagabonds. . . . Rarely indeed do women go off by themselves—into the corner of a ballroom, into the wilderness, to the play, to the sacred high places of the earth, or to the Islands of the Blessed.

"Penelope stays at home," Parsons lamented. With women confined physically and psychically at home, men and women are like strangers from different countries; and their separation is further emphasized by all sorts of taboos. Feminism for Parsons is, therefore, an "adventure" involving the crossing of gender boundaries and the challenging of classifications. In the ideal "Unconventional Society" that she sets up at the end of *Fear and Conventionality* (1914), Parsons places the principle of unrestricted travel in the center of her vision. "The viability of the world will be taken advantage of," she predicts. "The habit of living in lairs will die out and. . . . We shall live at large, going where it is best for us to be, unperturbed by novel experience and not safeguarded against it."[41]

The most important outcome of the lifting of the social categories for women and men was the possibility of substituting "personality" for some more rigidly defined "ego." For Mach, the ego was only makeshift, designed for provisional orientation and for definite practical ends. This view of the ego as a theoretical construction, like the category "woman," opened the way for Parsons's view of the "personality." A personality did not have any preconceived characteristics or consistency. Instead, he or she reacted spontaneously to the environment. In conditions of social freedom men and women would have a wider scope in their different expressions of self, and these different expressions would be more frankly expressed in their relationships. "The day will come," she wrote in her "Journal of a Feminist, 1913–1914," "when the individual . . . [will not] have to pretend to be possessed of a given quota of femaleness or maleness":

> This morning perhaps I feel like a male; let me act like one. This afternoon I may feel like a female; let me act like one. At midday or at midnight I may feel sexless; let me therefore act sexlessly. . . . It is such a confounded bore to have to act one part endlessly. Men do not resent being treated always as men because, in the first place, of the prestige of being a man and because, in the second place, they are not treated always as men. And yet men too may rebel some time against the attribute of maleness. . . . The taboo on a man acting like a woman has ever been stronger than the taboo on a woman acting like a man. Men who question it are ridiculed as effeminate or damned as perverts. But I know men who are neither "effeminate" nor perverts who feel the woman nature in them and are more or less tried by having to suppress it.

Some day, she concludes, there may be a "masculinism" movement to allow men to act "like women."[42]

Parsons saw sexual relationships as particularly bound by conventions, and she looked forward to greater frankness, sincerity, and privacy between the sexes under conditions of social freedom. "Between a relationship all sex as in the ante-feminist past and the entirely sexless relationship of the Professional Feminist . . . I don't see much to choose from," she wrote in an article titled "Privacy in Love Affairs" in 1915. "Why keep sex so tagged and docketed? So shunted off from human relations? Sex is a part of every personality, and into any personal relations between a man and a woman it naturally enters—more or less. Whether more or less is to be decided for itself in each case, otherwise a relationship is not private at all, it's impersonal, a status relationship, a relationship of the old order."[43]

The greatest opportunity for the expression of personality, according to Parsons, was between friends, simply because friendship was "so regardless of conventions, so heedless of status." Friendship cuts through the barriers of sex, age, and family relationships and demands a personal relationship; it finds stimulation in difference, and does not expect unbroken companionship; it is more imaginative, more alert, spontaneous, and joyful than more convention-ridden relationships. Marriage and family relationships, on the other hand, tend to obliterate all expression of personality. In a chapter of her 1913 book *The Old-Fashioned Woman*, mordantly titled "One," Parsons documents ideas of conjugal identity across cultures. And in an article in the *New Republic* in 1916 she asked the question: "Must We Have Her?" arguing that "A husband or a wife is a personal taste" that should not be forced on others. She makes a plea, therefore, for separate invitations as a contribution to "a new, less institutional, more personal form of intercourse."[44]

.   .   .

For Parsons, social science could play an important part in bringing about an "Unconventional Society" by clarifying concepts and questioning classifications. In this new society, "differences in others will no longer be recognized as troublesome. . . . Nor will presumptions of superiority or inferiority attach to differences per se. Exclusiveness will cease to be a source of prestige. Blind efforts to produce types . . . will be condemned. Intolerance will be a crime. . . . Variation will be welcome. . . . complete freedom of personal contacts will be sought. The play of personality upon personality will become the recognized raison d'être of society instead of the greatest of its apprehensions."[45]

Elsie Clews Parsons's life was, from 1910 on, a deliberate attempt to create a life outside of conventions and institutions, to reconstruct her own life as a new woman who was, as she put it, unclassified, unclassifiable. She deliberately cultivated an adventurous life, physically, intellectually, and emotionally, a wide range of experience, and a variety of situations that forced her to interact in personal rather than conventional ways. Anthropological fieldwork provided her with the ideal vehicle for the sort of multifaceted self she wanted to create. After 1911, when her sixth and last child was born, she spent at least part of each year in the field, beginning with the pueblos of the American Southwest during the teens and twenties, which culminated in the monumental work *Pueblo Indian Religion* (1939); moving on to Mexico in the 1930s (*Mitla*, 1936); and, just before her death in 1941, to Ecuador (*Peguche*, 1945). Interspersed with these field trips were folklore-collecting expeditions close to home along the Atlantic coast while her children were young, and later sweeping through the West Indies, Egypt and the Sudan, and Spain and Mallorca. These trips were almost always both physically and mentally challenging—and deliberately so. And they always combined work and play. She was often accompanied on her fieldtrips by a lover or a colleague, and sometimes by one of her children. Her fieldwork and her wealth allowed Parsons to divide her life among several homes—winter in New York City, summer in Newport or Lenox or Maine, or somewhere in the field. And she cultivated a wide variety of relationships—as wife, mother, lover, colleague, and friend—allowing none of them to dominate or interfere with the integrity of the others.[46]

.   .   .

Randolph Bourne characterized his friend Elsie Clews Parsons in 1917 as "A Modern Mind"—"a fortunate anomaly" in an American intellectual world "still too much divided between hopelessly unporous science and popular sentimentality." What Bourne admired was Parsons's refusal to accept unquestioningly established ideas, conventions, and institutions and her equal insistence that the purpose of social science was to solve the everyday problems of personal interactions, relationships, love, friendship, of being a parent or a citizen. Parsons never separated her work from her life. In Tarde and Mach she found theoretical perspectives that were guides to a personal program of action. With their emphasis on inventiveness, breaking with the past, and personal transformation as a means of social transformation, Tarde and Mach helped Parsons to carry through more thoroughly the focus on the self that Jane Addams had begun. Unlike Addams, she was able to address specifically the problem that they both faced—how to create a new family for new times. In doing this, she had to demolish the concepts of self, gender, and home on which the nineteenth-century woman's movement was based.[47]

NOTES

1. "Suggests Trial Marriages. Mrs. Clews Parsons in 'The Family' Recommends a Radical Change," *New York Times*, November 17, 1906, 1. See also "Marriage on Trial. Elsie Clews Parsons Advocates Startling Reforms in New Book," in "For and About Women," *New York Daily Tribune*, November 17, 1906, 5; and "New York Society," *New York Daily Tribune*, November 18, 1906, 8; Elsie Clews Parsons (hereafter, ECP), *The Family: An Ethnographical and Historical Outline, with Descriptive Notes, planned as a Textbook for the use of College Lecturers and Directors of Home-Reading Clubs* (New York and London: G. P. Putnam's Sons, 1906).

2. "Dr. Dix on Trial Marriages. Rector of Trinity Says Mrs. Parsons's Views Are Barbarous," *New York Times*, November 18, 1906. See also "Criticised by Clergy. Dr. Morgan Dix Describes Mrs. Parsons's Book as 'Outrageous,'" and "Perilous Transportation" (a report on Herbert Parsons's campaign for better public transport), *New York Daily Tribune*, November 18, 1906, 4, 8. "Dr. Dix Speaks Out to Save the Home. Rector of Trinity Protests Against Loose Marital Relations. First Duty to the Child. The Home Is Its Predestination, He Says—When That Goes, Social Order Goes Also," *New York Times*, November 19, 1906, 5. But see on same page: "Wants Wider Divorce Laws. The Rev. M. C. Peters Says They Should Embrace Drunkenness." See also "Dr. Dix on the Home. Attacks Its Enemies. Says Future of State Depends on Sanctity of Marriage," and "Dr. Carsons on Divorce. Says Remedy Is To Be Found in Better Home Life," *New York Daily Tribune*, November 19, 1906, 12; "Calls Trial Marriage Barbarous. Bishop Coleman Says Any One Favoring It Should be Considered an Outlaw," *New York Daily Tribune*, November 20, 1906, 11.

3. For the "family claim," see Jane Addams, "The Subjective Necessity for Social Settlements," in *Philanthropy and Social Progress: Seven Essays*, ed. Jane Addams et al., with an introduction by Henry Carter Adams (1893; Montclair, N.J.: Patterson Smith, 1970), 1–26; and idem, "Filial Relations," in *Democracy and Social Ethics*, ed. Anne Firor Scott (1902; Cambridge: Harvard University Press, Belknap Press, 1964), 71–101. For Addams's life and work, see Scott, introduction to *Democracy and Social Ethics*. For domestic paradigm, see Dorothy Ross, "Gendered Social Knowledge: Domestic Discourse, Jane Addams, and the Possibilities of Social Science," in this volume. For Hull House and some of the dilemmas posed by the domestic paradigm for one of its mem-

bers, see Kathryn Kish Sklar, "Hull House in the 1890s: A Community of Women Reformers," *Signs: Journal of Women in Culture and Society* 10 (Summer 1985): 658–77; and idem, *Florence Kelley and the Nation's Work: The Rise of Women's Political Culture, 1830–1900* (New Haven: Yale University Press, 1995).

4. *Democracy and Social Ethics* comprises seven articles that appeared previously in *Atlantic Monthly, American Journal of Sociology, International Journal of Ethics,* and *Commons.* Chap. 1, based on "The Subtle Problems of Charity," *Atlantic Monthly,* February 1899, 163–89, laid out her general line of thought. The other chapters covered charitable effort, filial relations, household adjustment, industrial amelioration, educational methods, and political reform.

See ECP to Herbert Parsons (hereafter, HP), June 2, 1903, American Philosophical Society (hereafter, APS) for her reading of *Democracy and Social Ethics.* The APS holds two Parsons collections: (1) Ms. Coll. no. 29 contains the bulk of her personal correspondence, some professional correspondence, manuscripts, financial papers, and photographs; (2) 572/P25 contains professional correspondence, notebooks, and manuscripts. A third collection of personal and professional papers is in the Parsons Family Papers at the Rye Historical Society (hereafter, RHS). For a description of the APS 572/P25 collection, see Gladys Reichard, "The Elsie Clews Parsons Collection," *APS Proceedings* 94 (1950): 308–9.

5. Elsie Worthington Clews, "On Certain Phases of Poor-Relief in the City of New York" (A.M. thesis, Columbia University, 1897); *Educational Legislation and Administration of the Colonial Governments,* Columbia University Contributions to Philosophy, Psychology, and Education 6 (1899; New York: Arno, 1971). For Giddings's classes, see D.G.C. [Goddard Chase] to EC [June 1895], RIIS; EC, Schedule [November 1894?]; Second Term Report, June 7, 1895, APS; and R. W. Wallace, "The Institutionalization of a New Discipline: The Case of Sociology at Columbia University, 1891–1931" (Ph.D. diss., Columbia University, 1989), 127–28; also 139–45 for coeducation question.

6. Charles E. Merriam, "Merriam's Early Experiences as a Graduate Student of Political Science," November 28, 1949, Charles E. Merriam Papers, Special Collections, University of Chicago, quoted in Wallace, "Institutionalization," 121; Gertrude Stein, *Wars I Have Seen* (New York: Random House, 1945), 21. Giddings's main publications during this period were *The Principles of Sociology: An Analysis of the Phenomena of Association and of Social Organization* (New York: Macmillan, 1896); *The Theory of Socialization: A Syllabus of Sociological Principles for the Use of College and University Classes* (New York: Macmillan, 1897); *Democracy and Empire: With Studies on Their Psychological, Economic, and Moral Foundations* (New York: Macmillan, 1900); *Inductive Sociology: A Syllabus of Methods, Analyses and Classifications, and Provisionally Formulated Laws* (New York: Macmillan, 1901); *Readings in Descriptive and Historical Sociology* (New York: Macmillan, 1906). Harry Elmer Barnes, in an editorial comment to C. H. Northcott, "The Sociological Theories of Franklin Henry Giddings," in *An Introduction to the History of Sociology,* ed. Barnes (1948; Chicago: University of Chicago Press, 1965), 763–64, ranks Giddings with his contemporaries Durkheim and Weber. See also Bernhard J. Stern, ed., "Giddings, Ward, and Small: An Interchange of Letters," *Social Forces* 10 (March 1932): 305–18.

7. ECP, "American 'Society' I" and "American 'Society' II," *New Republic* 9 (1916): 184–86 and 214–16; Nietzsche, quoted by Frederic Jameson in Jean-François Lyotard, *The Postmodern Condition: A Report on Knowledge* (Manchester: Manchester University Press, 1984), xii. For her incipient feminism as a child, see ECP, "The Journal of a

Feminist, 1913–1914," unpublished manuscript, APS, 102. For the Clews family, see
Peter H. Hare, *A Woman's Quest for Science: Portrait of Anthropologist Elsie Clews
Parsons* (Buffalo: Prometheus Books, 1985), a delightful portrait of Parsons by the member of her family who assembled her private papers and deposited them in the APS
Library; and Rosemary Levy Zumwalt, *Wealth and Rebellion: Elsie Clews Parsons, Anthropologist and Folklorist* (Urbana: University of Illinois Press, 1992). The interpreta-
tion presented here derives from Desley Deacon, *Elsie Clews Parsons: Inventing Modern Life* (Chicago: University of Chicago Press, 1997). For the scandal, see Gore Vidal,
1876: A Novel (New York: Random House, 1976). For Lucy Clews, see ECP, Record of
Family Faculties, APS. Other accounts of ECP are Barbara A. Babcock and Nancy J.
Parezo, *Daughters of the Desert: Women Anthropologists and the Native American
Southwest 1880–1980: An Illustrated Catalogue* (Albuquerque: University of New Mex-
ico Press, 1988), 14–19; Louis A. Hieb, "Elsie Clews Parsons in the Southwest," in
Parezo, ed., *Hidden Scholars: Women Anthropologists and the Native American South-
west* (Albuquerque: University of New Mexico Press, 1993), 63–75; Paul Boyer, "Elsie
Clews Parsons," in *Notable American Women*, ed. Edward T. James, Janet Wilson
James, and Paul S. Boyer (Cambridge: Harvard University Press, 1971); Mary Jo
Deegan, "Elsie Clews Parsons," in *Women in Sociology: A Bio-Bibliographical Source-
book*, ed. Deegan (New York: Greenwood Press, 1991); Judith Friedlander, "Elsie
Clews Parsons," in *Women Anthropologists: Selected Biographies*, ed. Ute Gacs, Jerrie
McIntyre, and Ruth Weinberg (Urbana: University of Illinois Press, 1989); Alfred L.
Kroeber, "Elsie Clews Parsons," *American Anthropologist* 45 (1943): 252–55; Louise
Lamphere, "Feminist Anthropology: The Legacy of Elsie Clews Parsons," *American
Ethnologist* 16 (1989): 518–33; Gladys Reichard, "Elsie Clews Parsons," *Journal of
American Folklore* 56 (1943): 45–56; Rosalind Rosenberg, *Beyond Separate Spheres:
Intellectual Roots of Modern Feminism* (New Haven: Yale University Press, 1982); Leslie
Spier, "Elsie Clews Parsons," *American Anthropologist* 45 (1943): 244–51; and Leslie
White, "Elsie Worthington Clews Parsons," *Dictionary of American Biography* (New
York: Scribner, 1932–1964). For Beecher, see Kathryn Kish Sklar, *Catharine Beecher: A
Study in American Domesticity* (New York: W. W. Norton, 1976).

  8. ECP, "Sex and the Elders" and "War and the Elders," *New Review* 3 (1915): 8–10,
and 191–92. For psychosomatic illnesses of Jane Addams and Charlotte Perkins Gilman
as young women, see Allen F. Davis, *American Heroine* (New York: Oxford University
Press, 1973); Charlotte Perkins Gilman, *The Yellow Wallpaper*, with an afterword by
Elaine R. Hedges (1892, 1899; Old Westbury, N.Y.: Feminist Press, 1973); and Carroll
Smith-Rosenberg, *Disorderly Conduct: Visions of Gender in Victorian America* (New
York: Oxford University Press, 1985).

  9. Helen Lefkowitz Horowitz, *Alma Mater: Design and Experience in the Women's
Colleges from Their Nineteenth-Century Beginnings to the 1930's* (New York: Knopf,
1984), 142, 248.

  10. Ibid., 256–59.

  11. Henry James, *The Bostonians* (1886; New York: Bantam Books, 1984), 240–43.
For Stanton, see Elisabeth Griffith, *In Her Own Right: The Life of Elizabeth Cady Stanton* (New York: Oxford University Press, 1984).

  12. K. [Wadamoris?] to EC, December 3, 1899; Ralph [Paine?/Parry?] to EC, October 5, 1897, RHS. For summer, see Leslie Bright to EC, August 17, 1894, and November
12 [1894]; Kirk Brice to EC, September 5, 1894, RHS. For her youth, see Desley Deacon, "The Republic of the Spirit: Field Work in Elsie Clews Parsons's Turn to Anthropology," *Frontiers: A Journal of Women Studies* 12, no. 3 (1992): 13–38; EC to Sam
Dexter, November 19 [1893]; [December 22 and 27, 1893]; January 13, 1894; [February

6, 1894]; and March 12, 1894, APS. For Giddings's sociology, see Arthur J. Vidich and Stanford M. Lyman, *American Sociology: Worldly Rejections of Religion and Their Directions* (New Haven: Yale University Press, 1985), 105–25. See Deacon, *Elsie Clews Parsons*, and Elsie Worthington Clews, "Field Work in Teaching Sociology," *Educational Review*, September 1900, 159–69, for details of her work as Hartley House Fellow and director of fieldwork for Giddings's students from 1899 to 1902.

13. See Vidich and Lyman, *American Sociology* for Giddings; and ECP, "The Study of Variants," *Journal of American Folklore* 33 (April–June 1920): 87–90, esp. 90. See Zygmunt Bauman, *Legislators and Interpreters: On Modernity, Post-Modernity and Intellectuals* (Ithaca: Cornell University Press, 1987), for current discussion of concept of "legislator."

14. Alice Sterne to EC, October 13, 1896, RHS; Henry Holt to ECP, October 30, 1902, and December 23, 1902, APS; Tarde, *Les Lois de l'imitation* (Paris, 1890; 2d ed., 1895; 3d ed., rev. and enl., 1900); *The Laws of Imitation*, translated from the second French edition by Elsie Clews Parsons, with an introduction by Franklin H. Giddings (New York: Henry Holt and Company, 1903) remains one of only two translations of Tarde's work into English. *Les Lois sociales: esquisse d'une sociologie* (1898; New York, 1899) was translated by Howard C. Warren, assistant professor of experimental psychology, Princeton, with a preface by James Mark Baldwin, whose child development studies were strongly influenced by Tarde. For Tarde, see Giddings, introduction to *Laws of Imitation*, iii; Terry N. Clark, introduction to *Gabriel Tarde on Communication and Social Influence, Selected Papers*, ed. Clark (Chicago: University of Chicago Press, 1969), 8–9; Georges Guy-Grand, "Gabriel Tarde (1834–1904)," *Encyclopaedia of the Social Sciences*, ed. Edwin R. A. Seligman (New York: Macmillan, 1935), 513–14; Ruth Leys, "Mead's Voices: Imitation as Foundation, or, The Struggle against Mimesis," *Critical Inquiry* 19 (Winter 1993): 277–307.

15. Tarde, *Laws of Imitation*, preface to 2d ed. (Parsons trans., xviii); Clark, *Gabriel Tarde*, 21. Although Tarde used the word "law," he recognized that this was "a slight misuse of vocabulary" sanctioned only by "the convenience of monosyllables." See review of *La Logique sociale*, *Monist*, April 1895, 434–36.

16. Adrien C. Taymans, "Tarde and Schumpeter: A Similar Vision," *Quarterly Journal of Economics*, August 1950, 611–22; Tarde, "L'Accident et le rationnel en histoire d'après Cournot" (1905), quoted in Taymans, 613; idem, review of Durkheim, *Division of Labour* (1893), reprinted in Tarde, *Essais et mélanges sociologiques* (Paris, 1895), quoted in Steven Lukes, *Émile Durkheim: His Life and Work. A Historical and Critical Study* (Harmondsworth: Penguin, 1975), 304; Celestin Charles Alfred Bouglé, "Un Sociologue individualiste: Gabriel Tarde," *Revue de Paris*, May 15, 1905, 313, quoted in Lukes, 303; Tarde, "La Psychologie intermentale," *Revue internationale de sociologie* 9 (1901) ("Inter-Psychology," *International Quarterly* 7 [1903]: 59–84); idem, *La Logique sociale* (Paris, 1895), vi, quoted in Lukes, 305–6; Durkheim, "Crime and Social Health," *Revue philosophique* 39 (1895): 518–23, esp. 523, quoted in Lukes, 309–10; Tarde, "Criminalité et santé sociale," *Revue philosophique* 39 (1895): 148–62 (reprinted in *Études de psychologie sociale* [Paris, 1898], 136–58), esp. 158–61, quoted in Lukes, 310; and idem, "La Réalité sociale," *Revue philosophique* 52 (1901): 457–79, quoted in Lukes, 311.

17. Review of *L'Opposition universelle*, *Monist* 8 (1898): 142–44; Tarde, *Laws of Imitation*, preface to 2d ed. (Parsons trans., xviii–xix, xxiv).

18. Tarde, *L'Opinion et la foule* (Paris, 1901); idem, *Fragment d'histoire future* (Paris, 1905) (*Underground Man*, preface by H. G. Wells [London: Duckworth, 1905]); see Clark, *Gabriel Tarde*, 56–58.

19. See Carroll Smith-Rosenberg, "Mary Kingsbury Simkhovitch," *Notable American*

Women: The Modern Period, ed. Barbara Sicherman and Carol Hurd Green (Cambridge: Harvard University Press, Belknap Press, 1980); Kathleen Marquis, "Mary Melinda (Kingsbury) Simkhovitch, 1867–1951," finding aid, Schlesinger Library; *Current Biography* (1943); *Dictionary of American Biography*, supp. 5; *Encyclopedia of Social Work* (1971); obituary, *New York Times*, November 16, 1951; and Mary Kingsbury Simkhovitch, *Neighborhood: My Story of Greenwich House* (New York: Norton, 1938).

20. Smith-Rosenberg, "Simkhovitch," esp. 649 and 650 for Simkhovitch quotations.

21. When Mary Simkhovitch began plans for Greenwich House in 1902, Elsie helped her secure wealthy young bankers for her board, and she herself chaired the finance committee, whose immediate task was to raise money for the purchase and repair of premises on Jones Street. In addition to her major fund-raising role, she was responsible for channeling a number of talented young researchers to Greenwich House, advising them on their work, and arranging its publication. See Deacon, *Elsie Clews Parsons*.

For M. Carey Thomas see Rosenberg, *Beyond Separate Spheres*, 12; and Helen Lefkowitz Horowitz, *The Power and Passion of M. Carey Thomas* (New York: Knopf, 1994). For Jacobi (1842–1906), see Ruth Putnam, ed., *Life and Letters of Mary Putnam Jacobi* (New York: G. P. Putnam's Sons, 1925). For Croly (1829–1901), see Robert McHenry, ed., *Famous American Women: A Biographical Dictionary from Colonial Times to the Present* (New York: Dover, 1983). For Miller, see obituary, *New York Times*, August 23 and 24, 1942; Sue G. Walcutt, *Notable American Women*; Henry Wise Miller, *All Our Lives: Alice Duer Miller* (New York: Coward-McCann, 1945); Stanley J. Kunitz and Howard Haycraft, eds., *Twentieth Century Authors: A Biographical Dictionary of Modern Literature* (New York: H. W. Wilson, 1942), 958–59. For Emily James Putnam (1865–1944), see *Famous American Women*. For Annie Nathan Meyer, see Linda K. Kerber, *Notable American Women: The Modern Period*. Putnam reluctantly resigned due to "ill health"; see Dean Putnam to Brownell, April 13, 1900; note by Meyer re holding her to promise to resign if pregnant; both in Barnardiana File C Admin. (Corres. 1888–1911 Trustee Corres. Cttee Reports—also Dean Putnam's resignation), Barnard Library. For engagement, see EC to HP, April 20, 1899; Parsons family to EC, telegraph, May 4, 1900; Dolly Potter to EC, May 25 [1900]; Lowell to EC, June 3, 1900; A. R. Cross to EC, June 7 [1900]; Reynolds to EC, July 23 [1900]; Sarah Cohen to EC, July 19 [1900]; Susan Walker to EC, June 1 [1900], RHS; Walker [later Fitzgerald] was head of the West Side (Women's) University Settlement (later Richmond Hill House) from 1901 to 1904; see Mary Simkhovitch to ECP, October 17, 1905, RHS, for Fitzgerald's second baby.

22. ECP, "Diary of Elsie Parsons from the day of her birth, Tuesday, August 6, 1901"; Mary Simkhovitch to ECP, August 9, 1901, RHS. The diary breaks off with the sending of the telegrams and is never resumed. See also Alice Duer Miller to ECP, August 9, 1901, RHS, and August 21, 1901, APS; Elizabeth Crockett to ECP, August 20, 1901; John E. Parsons to HP, August 25, 1901, RHS; ECP to HP, October 11, 1901, APS; Mary Simkhovitch to ECP, June 27 [1902], RHS; and ECP, "Journal of a Feminist," 102.

23. Mary Simkhovitch to ECP [January? 1902], RHS, for Stephen's birth; Mary Simkhovitch to Edith [? 1902]; and E.K. to Mary Simkhovitch [? 1902], Schlesinger Library, for resignation; Mary Simkhovitch to ECP, May 28, 1902, for plans for new settlement; Mary Simkhovitch to ECP, May 29 [1902], and October 29 [1903], for help with children; Mary Simkhovitch to ECP, June 27 [1902], for pregnancy; Coman to ECP, November 5 [1903], RHS; Smith-Rosenberg, "Simkhovitch"; Marquis, "Simkhovitch."

24. ECP, "The Aim of Productive Efficiency in Education," *Educational Review* 30 (December 1905): 500–506; and idem, "The School Child, the School Nurse, and the

Local School Board," *Charities*, September 23, 1905, 1097–1104, esp. 1104. See also Dr. James Hamilton, "Is the Settlement a Permanent Institution?" *Charities*, October 14, 1905, 102–4.

25. See "The Imaginary Mistress" (1913), 1, unpublished manuscript, APS. For socialism and working conditions, see Paul Buhle, "Socialist Party"; Kathryn Kish Sklar, "Florence Kelley (1859–1932)"; Jon Bloom and Paul Buhle, "Intercollegiate Socialist Society and Successors," all in *Encyclopedia of the American Left*, ed. Mari Jo Buhle, Paul Buhle, and Dan Georgakas (New York: Garland Publishing, 1990), 716–23, 398–99, and 362–63. For WTUL, see Nancy Schrom Dye, *As Equals and as Sisters: Feminism, Unionism, and the Women's Trade Union League of New York* (Columbia: University of Missouri Press, 1980); and Elizabeth Payne, *Reform, Labor and Feminism: Margaret Dreier Robins and the National Women's Trade Union League* (Urbana: University of Illinois Press, 1988).

26. ECP, "Penalizing Marriage and Child-Bearing," *Independent*, January 18, 1906, 146–47. See also idem, "A Plan for Girls with Nothing to Do," *Charities*, March 4, 1905, 545–49; Celia Parker Woolley, Anna Garlin Spencer, Emily V. Hammond, Frances Greeley Curtis, Sadie American, and Cynthia Westover Alden, "Girls Who Have Nothing to Do," ibid., 520–23; and S.W.H., letter to editor, ibid., 601–2; Edith Eustis, "Why Should Girls Have Nothing to Do?" ibid., September 16, 1905, 1083–86; editor, "Mrs. Parsons, Mrs. Eustis and the 'Girl With Nothing to Do,'" ibid., 1080–81; ECP, "Girls With Nothing to Do: A Rejoinder from Mrs. Parsons," letter to editor, ibid., October 28, 1905, 124–25; and idem, "Division of Labor in the Tenement-House," *Charities and the Commons*, January 1906, 443–44.

27. ECP, "Sex Morality and the Taboo of Direct Reference," *Independent*, August 16, 1906, 391–92.

28. ECP, "The Religious Dedication of Women," *American Journal of Sociology* 11 (July 1906): 610–22; idem, *The Family*, 334–54.

29. Heywood Campbell Broun and Margaret Leech, *Anthony Comstock: Roundsman of the Lord* (London: Wishart & Company, 1928), 227–36; for Craddock, *Heavenly Bridegrooms*, Theodore Schroeder, "An Unintentional Contribution to the Erotogenetic Interpretation of Religion" (1915) cited in Ralph E. McCoy, *Theodore Schroeder, a Cold Enthusiast: A Bibliography* (Carbondale: Southern Illinois University Press, 1973), 26. For *Lucifer*, see Anne Braude, "Louise Waisbrooker" (paper presented at the American Studies Meetings, New Orleans, 1990); Martin Henry Blatt, *Free Love and Anarchism: The Biography of Ezra Heywood* (Urbana: University of Illinois Press, 1989); Linda Gordon, *Woman's Body, Woman's Right: Birth Control in America*, rev. ed. (New York: Penguin, 1990), esp. 501; Theodore Schroeder, "From the Free Speech League's Attorney," *Lucifer, the Light-Bearer*, January 3, 1907; Hal Sears, *The Sex Radicals: Free Love in High Victorian America* (Lawrence: Regents Press of Kansas, 1977); Fred Whitehead, *Lucifer, the Light-Bearer*, in *Encyclopedia of the American Left*, 440–41.

30. Macfadden was found guilty, but his sentence was suspended. See Broun and Leech, *Anthony Comstock*, 249–56. See Alice Wexler, "Emma Goldman (1869–1940)," in *Encyclopedia of the American Left*, 275–77; Richard Drinnon, *Rebel in Paradise: A Biography of Emma Goldman* (Chicago: University of Chicago Press, 1961), 87–94, 166–67, and 321. For anarchism, see Allen Ruff, in *Encyclopedia of the American Left*, 374–75; James M. Beck, "The Suppression of Anarchy," *American Law Review* 36 (March–April 1902): 190–203; Goldman, "The Tragedy at Buffalo," *Mother Earth*, October 1906, 11–16; Drinnon, *Rebel in Paradise*, 96–97. For Free Speech Leagues, see David M. Rabban, "The Free Speech League, the ACLU, and Changing Conceptions of Free

Speech in American History," *Stanford Law Review* 45 (November 1992): 47–114; Alice Wexler, *Emma Goldman: An Intimate Life* (New York: Pantheon Books, 1984), 116–18, 138; and Drinnon, *Rebel in Paradise*, 93–94, 118–19.

31. ECP, "Little Essays in Lifting Taboo" (1904–7), 1–4, unpublished manuscript, APS. See Theodore Schroeder to ECP, February 1906, APS. For Schroeder and the free speech battles of the period, see Rabban, "Free Speech League"; Mark Graber, *Transforming Free Speech: The Ambiguous Legacy of Civil Libertarianism* (Berkeley and Los Angeles: University of California Press, 1991), 54–62; Emma Goldman, *Red Emma Speaks: An Emma Goldman Reader*, ed. Alix Kate Shulman (New York: Schocken Books, 1982); and idem, *Living My Life* (London: Duckworth, 1932); Schroeder, *"Obscene" Literature and Constitutional Law: A Forensic Defense of Freedom of the Press* (New York: Da Capo Press, 1911); idem, *Free Speech for Radicals*, enl. ed. (New York: Free Speech League, 1916); and idem, *Conservatisms, Liberalisms and Radicalisms and the New Psychology* (Cos Cob, Conn.: Next Century Press, 1942). For cuts made to "Penalizing Marriage and Child-Bearing" by *Independent* editor Hamilton Holt, see Deacon, *Elsie Clews Parsons*, 414 n. 44.

32. Dr. Allan McLane, in his review of *The Family*, *Putnam's Magazine*, February 1907, 557, considered that the book surpassed G. Stanley Hall's *Adolescence* (1904). Other positive reviews came from Mary L. Bush, *Journal of Philosophy, Psychology and Scientific Methods*, August 15, 1907, 467–70; Franklin Giddings, *Educational Review*, September 1907, 202; and Theodore Schroeder, *Arena*, January 1907, 105–7. ECP was pregnant again in late February 1909. For pregnancies and jealousy, see Deacon, "Republic of the Spirit" and *Elsie Clews Parsons*. For her own fictionalized account, see ECP, "The Imaginary Mistress."

33. See Deacon, "Republic of the Spirit" and *Elsie Clews Parsons* for trips, fieldwork, and men and women friends.

34. ECP, "The Imaginary Mistress," esp. 18; Deacon, "Republic of the Spirit" and *Elsie Clews Parsons*.

35. ECP, "The Will to Power Among Sociologists" (1915), unpublished manuscript, APS; "Gregariousness and the Impulse to Classify," *Journal of Philosophy, Psychology, and Scientific Methods*, September 30, 1915, 551–53; "The Minority," letter to editor, *New York Tribune*, December 4, 1917. See Julius Weinberg, *Edward Alsworth Ross and the Sociology of Progressivism* (Madison: State Historical Society of Wisconsin, 1972), 149–76; and Edward A. Ross, *The Old World in the New* (New York: Century, 1914), for Ross's increasing nativism between 1907 and 1915; Vidich and Lyman, *American Sociology*, 105–50; and Franklin Giddings, *The Responsible State: A Reexamination of Fundamental Political Doctrines in the Light of World War and the Menace of Anarchism* (Boston: Houghton Mifflin, 1918) for Giddings's social engineering and apologetics for colonialism; and Graber, *Transforming Free Speech*, for minority opinion during war. For anthropologists, see Paul Radin, "Robert H. Lowie 1883–1957," *American Anthropologist* 60 (1958): 358–75; Robert H. Lowie, "Reflections on Goldenweiser's 'Recent Trends in American Anthropology,'" *American Anthropologist* 43 (1941): 151–63; Alfred L. Kroeber, "Pliny Earle Goddard," *American Anthropologist* 31 (1929): 1–6; William N. Fenton, "Sapir as Museologist," in *New Perspectives in Language, Culture, and Personality*, ed. William Cowan, Michael K. Foster, and Konrad Koerner (Philadelphia: J. Benjamins Publishing Co., 1986), 215–40 (for Goldenweiser).

36. Mach, *The Science of Mechanics: A Critical and Historical Exposition of Its Principles* (1883; Chicago: Open Court, 1893); idem, *Contributions to the Analysis of Sensations* (1886; Chicago: Open Court, 1897); idem, *Popular Scientific Lectures* (Chicago: Open Court, 1895); and idem, *Knowledge and Error: Sketches on the Psychology of*

Enquiry (1905; Dordecht: D. Reidel, 1976). For Mach, see Hugo Dingler, "Mach, Ernst (1838–1916)," *Encyclopaedia of the Social Sciences* (1935), 653; Irwin N. Hiebert, "Ernst Mach," in *Dictionary of Scientific Biography*, ed. Charles Coulston Gillespie (New York: Scribner, 1973); Robert S. Cohen and R. J. Seeger, eds., *Ernst Mach: Physicist and Philosopher*, Boston Studies in the Philosophy of Science 6 (Dordecht: D. Reidel, 1970); Robert H. Lowie, "Ernst Mach," *New Republic*, April 9, 1916, 335–37; Lyotard, *Postmodern Condition*, xxiv; Mach, quoted in P. Frank, "The Importance of Ernst Mach's Philosophy of Science for Our Times," in Cohen and Seeger, *Ernst Mach*, 219–34; Robert S. Cohen, "Ernst Mach: Physics, Perception and the Philosophy of Science," ibid., 126–64, esp. 128 and 129.

37. Robert H. Lowie, "Social Organization," *American Journal of Sociology* 20 (July 1914): 68–97, esp. 68. See also "Letters from Ernst Mach to Robert H. Lowie," *Isis* 37 (1947): 65–68; Cora Du Bois, *Lowie's Selected Papers in Anthropology* (Berkeley and Los Angeles: University of California Press, 1960); Lowie, "Relations with Boas," Robert H. Lowie papers, Department of Anthropology, University of California at Berkeley; idem, "An Ethnologist's Memories," *Freeman*, August 11 and October 6, 1920, 517–18 and 85–86; idem, "Reminiscences of Anthropological Currents in America Half a Century Ago," *American Anthropologist* 58 (1956): 955–1016; idem, *Robert H. Lowie, Ethnologist: A Personal Record* (Berkeley and Los Angeles: University of California Press, 1959); Harry Hoijer, "Paul Radin, 1883–1959," *American Anthropologist* 61 (1959): 839–43; Morris R. Cohen, *A Dreamer's Journey: The Autobiography of Morris Raphael Cohen* (Boston: Beacon Press, 1949).

38. See Desley Deacon, introduction to ECP, *Fear and Conventionality* (1914; Chicago: University of Chicago Press, 1997); ECP, "Sex and the Elders"; idem, "A Warning to the Middle Aged" and "War and the Elders," *New Review* 3 (1915): 62–63 and 191–92. See Melville J. Herskovits, *Franz Boas: The Science of Man in the Making* (New York: Charles Scribner's Sons, 1953); George W. Stocking, Jr., ed., *The Shaping of American Anthropology 1883–1911: A Franz Boas Reader* (New York: Basic Books, 1974); Theodora Kroeber, *Alfred Kroeber: A Personal Configuration* (Berkeley and Los Angeles: University of California Press, 1970).

39. ECP, *Social Freedom: A Study of the Conflicts between Social Classifications and Personality* (New York: G. P. Putnam's Sons, 1915), 1, 25; idem, *Social Rule: A Study of the Will to Power* (New York: G. P. Putnam's Sons, 1916), 2. See also *The Old-Fashioned Woman* (New York: G. P. Putnam's Sons, 1913).

40. *Social Rule*, 54–55; L. Lévy-Bruhl, *Les Fonctions mentales dans les sociétés inferiéures* (Paris: Félix Alcan, 1910); ECP, "Feminism and Conventionality," *Annals of the American Academy of Political and Social Sciences* 56 (November 1914): 47–53.

41. R. J. Seeger, "On Mach's Curiosity about Shockwaves," in Cohen and Seeger, *Ernst Mach*, 60–61; ECP, "Feminism and Conventionality," 48–49; idem, *Social Freedom*, 1; idem, "The Supernatural Policing of Women," *Independent*, February 8, 1912; idem, "Avoidance" and "Teknonymy," *American Journal of Sociology* 19 (1914): 480–84 and 649–50; idem, *Fear and Conventionality*, 205–18, esp. 210.

42. Ernst Mach, *Analysis of the Sensations*, cited in R. Von Mises, "Ernst Mach and the Empiricist Conception of Science," in Cohen and Seeger, *Ernst Mach*, 245–70, esp. 263; ECP, "Journal of a Feminist," 115.

43. ECP, "Privacy in Love Affairs," *Masses*, July 1915, 12.

44. ECP, "Friendship, a Social Category," *American Journal of Sociology* 21 (1915): 230–33; idem, *The Old-Fashioned Woman*; idem, "Must We Have Her?" *New Republic*, June 10, 1916, 145–46.

45. ECP, *Fear and Conventionality*, 209–10.

46. See Deacon, "Republic of the Spirit" and *Elsie Clews Parsons*; and Judith Ryan, *The Vanishing Subject: Early Psychology and Literary Modernism* (Chicago: University of Chicago Press, 1991), 226, for the "life without the self." ECP, *Pueblo Indian Religion*, 2 vols. (1939; Lincoln: University of Nebraska Press, 1996, with introductions by Pauline Turner Strong and Ramon Gutierrez); idem, *Mitla, Town of the Souls and Other Zapoteco-Speaking Pueblos of Oaxaca, Mexico* (Chicago: University of Chicago Press, 1936); idem, *Peguche, Canton of Otavalo, Province of Imbabura, Ecuador: A Study of Andean Indians* (Chicago: University of Chicago Press, 1945). For ECP's complete bibliography, including selected unpublished work, see Deacon, *Elsie Clews Parsons*, 485–99.

47. Randolph Bourne, "A Modern Mind," *Dial*, March 22, 1917, 239–40.

The "Self-Applauding Sincerity" of Overreaching Theory, Biography as Ethical Practice, and the Case of Mary van Kleeck

GUY ALCHON

> The past was always the underdog, and we sensed it was only right to be
> on its side against the bully future.
>
> —Patricia Hampl, *Virgin Time*

> Enthusiastic partisans of the idea of progress are in danger of failing to
> recognize—because they set so little store by them—the immense riches
> accumulated by the human race on either side of the narrow furrow on
> which they keep their eyes fixed; by underrating the achievements of the
> past, they devalue all those which still remain to be accomplished. . .
>
> —Claude Lévi-Strauss, *Tristes Tropiques*[1]

WILLA CATHER once remarked that "the world broke in two in 1922 or there-abouts." Overtaken by the "forward-goers," by those "in revolt against the homilies by which the world is run," the older virtues of endurance, sacrifice, and personal steadiness had been run to ground. In the United States, especially, the rush of progress was personified, in the words of Agnes Repplier, by "honest enthusiasts." This type, she continued, perhaps with some social scientists in mind, seemed "to think that if they stopped pushing, the world would stop moving." Skewering their quality of "self-applauding sincerity," Repplier found them unreflective and apparently not much troubled by doubt. "The more keen they are," she noted drily, "the more contemptuous they become."[2]

We are today more knowledgeable, if only marginally less keen, about pretensions to a "science of society." Having invested social science with tremendous responsibility for the ordering of a better future, even Americans now understand how cruelly the twentieth century has treated such hopes and have begun to doubt what Christopher Shannon terms the long "bourgeois attempt to construct a rational alternative to tradition."[3]

Scholars have turned both their keenness and their doubt to good effect by reconstructing the origins of the thing, by tracing out its professional, intellectual, and political struggles, and by setting these in a larger context of historical crisis and change. As a result, social science is now more firmly embedded within the history of American ideas and politics, and its history is now better understood as a heroic effort, if a fatally flawed and overreaching one, to negotiate a pact with modernity.[4]

More recently, many argue that our view of the subject is necessarily partial, having largely elided the problem of gender. But the usual corollary, that our chief task now is both to widen and sharpen our focus through the "lens" of gender analysis, seems less obvious. The more immediate task might be to take seriously the criticism of the modern disciplines that is at the heart of the best recent social science history. Dorothy Ross, among others, has made plain the consequences of the failure of self-consciousness and self-criticism endemic to the social scientific enterprise. And historians are among the indicted. "Like the social sciences," she writes at the end of *The Origins of American Social Science*, ". . . history has not accepted a fully historicized view of itself and hence not fully recognized its dialogic relation to the past."[5]

Nor, we could add, to the present. Despite a rhetoric that honors self-criticism and abjures the totalizing stance, the "honest enthusiasm" for gender analysis, even among historians, comes too close to the "self-applauding sincerity" typical of social science. Gender analysis, in other words, tends uncannily to recapitulate the transcendent claims and ahistorical hubris of social science, the very qualities it otherwise seeks to unmask and undermine.[6]

But why would this be surprising? Gender analysis is, after all, and whatever else its virtues, the latest enthusiasm of a disciplinary tradition capable of withering scrutiny of everything except itself and its own motives. "Disciplinarity," as Louis Menand admonishes, "makes us stupid." And if in thinking about gender and social science we are serious about avoiding such a fate, we ought to try to avoid the mistakes of the social sciences, their tendency, in their rush to escape from history, to embrace worldviews at once self-exculpatory, condescending, and ahistorical.[7]

This essay, then, advances a plea for caution in the effort to develop a history of gender in social science. It suggests that this story is as likely to be distorted as illuminated by gender analysis, an interpretive strategy at war with itself. For as currently employed, gender analysis, like the women's studies movement from which it emerged, is enmeshed in irreconcilable impulses. Simultaneously rejecting absolutist, universal, and totalizing approaches to the past, it remains linked, often quite consciously, to the absolutist, universal, and totalizing hopes that impelled its rise in the 1960s and 1970s. This admittedly creative incoherence is founded upon a long-standing enthusiasm for making feminist politics and scholarship, in the words of Joan Scott, "part of the same political project," one in which "the historian can interpret the world while trying to change it."[8]

Much of the work that has come from this political project, especially in women's history, has been creative and important; it "has intruded upon and destabilized virtually every element of the old narratives." But now that women's history has "progressed" from women to gender, from the history of women toward the transcendent claim to discern a "system of meaning" in socially constructed gender relations, the tension between its basic impulses has intensified. And we ought at least to wonder, then, how gender analysis can possibly escape the fate of all other such efforts to reconcile skeptical and totalizing impulses, to have it both ways at once, and the degree to which the feminist academic project depends upon evading and forgetting this question.[9]

The plea, then, is for a stance toward the past more honest because it is informed by a stance toward ourselves and our present less overweening and self-regarding. We need, that is, to ask more concertedly of ourselves why we are so eager to flatten history under a theoretical regime that argues for power, hierarchy, and subordination as the chief categories of human relations. Is the insight gained by such a method worth the resulting distortion, one in which other compelling qualities—character, grace, and grit, for example—are diminished in our calculus? Or does this distortion reflect the hubris of a project concerned more with present politics and jobs than with any respectful relation to the dead?[10]

These questions are far from arbitrary, for they go to the heart of the ethical problems posed by the course of academic feminism, by the history of social science, and by the life of one particular social scientist, the Christian radical Mary van Kleeck (1883–1972). Although hardly remembered today, from 1904 and her graduation from Smith College to 1948 and her retirement from the Russell Sage Foundation, van Kleeck was central to some of the vital streams and key events of the twentieth century. A pioneering student of women's labor, she led the foundation into a range of contentious labor-management arenas, including overtime in women's trades and employee governance in coal mining. During the First World War she ran the Labor Department's Woman in Industry Service and in 1919 became the first chief of the U.S. Women's Bureau. Van Kleeck's religious faith, social scientism, and identification with the labor movement led her leftward in the interwar years. Indeed, she devoted the peak years of her life and powers to advancing the cause of the Soviet Union and in advocacy of what she termed "world social-economic planning."[11]

Van Kleeck's life, like some of our lives, was fractured by an irreconcilable devotion to scholarly skepticism and the claims of a progressive hope always tending toward the utopian. Indeed, van Kleeck is interesting precisely because of how her struggles were so eerily similar to yet so demonstrably unlike our own. Perhaps more intensely than other women of her generation, she was continually in transit between worlds, between the sensibilities of tradition and the aspirations of scientism. Like Jane Addams, who was twenty years her senior, van Kleeck was raised in an explicitly religious framework, one that "privileged" self-sacrifice and bearing witness, a way of life alien to most of us. Yet, like us, and unlike Addams, van Kleeck embraced modernity's most ruthless norm, rule by technically enlightened elites. Like some of us, in other words, van Kleeck made an investment in progress that lived in tension with her commitment to skepticism and scholarship. As for us, this tension was for her a creative one. But it was also unsustainable. Eventually it undermined her capacity for introspection, encouraged a self-righteous and unprincipled stance, and worked ultimately to undermine both her scholarship and her politics.[12]

More likely to be helpful, then, to those who wish to understand what can be understood of gender's past is an approach chastened by the lessons we have learned from the history of the social sciences. It is an approach more serious about avoiding totalizing temptations, an approach exceedingly modest but ultimately surer in its "truth claims," an approach favoring the courtesy of particular context over the pressure of abstract argument. These qualities would be salutary in any historical approach. But the one in which they reign almost definitionally is biography, a reconsideration of which throws into sharp relief the virtues of a perspective circumscribed by life-stories, as against one unrestricted by anything but our own ambitions.

Biography is attractive because it elevates the particular and concrete over the general and abstract, more necessary than ever if we are to avoid the tendency of abstractions to run roughshod over real people and things. More pointedly, biography requires what Jacquelyn Dowd Hall terms "disciplined empathy." It can serve, in other words, as a discipline against projection, especially against the projection of our anxieties and hopes. It can operate to caution us, as in the case of Mary van Kleeck, against the perils of a life in which immersion in great social movements overwhelms the skeptical sense, in which scholarship succumbs to the press of "honest enthusiasm." And if gender analysis is any indication, biography is a practice whose virtues we should not automatically disdain, and to which we might profitably return.[13]

II

> I do not know for what reason this throng of educated women has been released
> into the larger life, just in the period when an old order of civilization is passing
> away, and the new order emerges in confusion.
>
> —Vida Dutton Scudder, *On Journey*[14]

It is no easy task to comprehend those often difficult predecessors who pioneered the passage from the late Victorian to the modern world. This is especially so with regard to the formative "utopian moment" within the history of American social science, and to Mary van Kleeck, one of its chief apostles.

Long discredited by events, and surviving now as a sort of "repressed memory," a utopian impulse once drove American social science. Animating the work of women and men, the professorial and those outside the academy, it arose from a crisis of faith common to many Americans in the years following the Civil War. Cresting in the 1880s and 1890s, a time when even the most visionary could be forgiven their ignorance of the terrible century to come, social science utopianism was most distinctively modern in its embrace of the idea of the planned future. Yet, even at their most overblown, such scholars as Richard Ely, Simon Patten, and John Commons, children of a mournful Protestant tradition and a world shaped by material scarcity, were ever aware of the pathos of human aspiration, and their utopian impulses lived in tension with a fearful humility largely unknown and inaccessible to us.[15]

Because of its theological roots, because it was essentially the distilled product of liberal Protestantism's crack-up, the utopian element in American social science is too easily relegated today to the status of antiquarian oddity. Accustomed as we are to worldviews that make little room for religious identity, and for which scientism usually functions as religion's antithesis, it is doubly difficult to comprehend.[16]

But much of this nonetheless can be discerned in the intertwined story of Social Christianity and social science. And no individual better personifies this story than Mary van Kleeck. Throughout a life that traversed the interesting terrain between the YWCA's industrial work program and Taylorism, between Vida Scudder's Companions of the Holy Cross and Communist fellow-traveling, van Kleeck embodied a striking amalgam of Social Gospel evangelism and the heady hubris of the emerging sciences of "social reconstruction." No one else, woman or man, managed to fuse as she did evangelical faith and social science mysticism into a career that did so much to shape the rise of a politically engaged institutionalist social science in the years from 1910 to 1940.

Van Kleeck's work combined the Social Gospel impulses of the first generations of college-educated women with the technocratic ethos of scientific management and the new social sciences. With the YWCA and, more emphatically, with the Russell Sage Foundation, she developed an institutional arena for the care and development of this most curious thing: a reformism that was at once a deeply religious scientism and a rigorously scientistic Social Christianity.

The YWCA had moved into "industrial work" in the 1890s. Van Kleeck was drawn to this and first approached the "social question" through the Y's work. The Russell Sage Foundation, building partly on the YWCA's precedent, pioneered in the organization of social work and industrial sociology, becoming in the years between 1910 and 1930 a nexus of reformist associational activities and a national institute for the advanced study of labor and the economy. As the director of its Department of Industrial Studies, van Kleeck was an intellectual and moral force behind these developments.[17]

Van Kleeck's role in advancing Christianity's passage into social science is the one feature of her life most at risk under the regime of gender analysis. There is much here to be missed, in other words, by an analysis driven by gender, much that is ironic, surprising, and otherwise inaccessible to the press of such an abstraction. This is nowhere so much the case as in the relationship between Mary van Kleeck and Taylorism, a relationship that crystallized her social scientism and intensified both her religious and her socialist commitments.

Van Kleeck's story begins to take evidential shape in 1900, the year of her high school graduation and matriculation at Smith College. It is a story that moves from a New York high school to Smith College, from Smith and the YWCA to New York City and the beginnings of her social science career. A story of how one young woman tightroped the difficult crossing from the late Victorian to the modern world, it is also, as is so often the case, a story that is both singular and representative.[18]

As the leading student among the ten girls and six boys in the Flushing High School Class of 1900, van Kleeck carried an academic average of 94 percent, took honors in classics and mathematics, and graduated with a Regents 96 Count Diploma, one of only four students ever to win such an honor in New York State. Skilled at argument, she led debate competitions within her English history class and between Flushing and other high schools. The town of Flushing had a history of political and religious dissent, and its high school by 1900 was a center of relatively advanced opinion. It was the sort of place where a classroom debate over Elizabeth I's treatment of Mary, Queen of Scots, could turn on the women judges' objections to one boy's reference to the impossibility of national peace were "two women" struggling for the crown; "two rulers" would be a better formulation, he was told. It was a school where girls usually ran the student paper and chose the class motto, where women were well represented on the faculty, and where students and faculty apparently were quite cognizant of debates over the status of women.[19]

"We are living in an age of disputes," the seventeen-year-old van Kleeck began her valedictory address in June of 1900, "and by no means the least among them is the question of woman and her rights." While numerous, she continued, those who comment upon this matter "make one great mistake—they bravely defend woman, but they forget that she needs no defense, they eloquently plead her release from the bonds of slavery, but they forget that she is not a slave." Instead, she argued, Shakespeare's plays offered a "grand testimony to the power of woman in the world."

For young Mary it was Portia in *The Merchant of Venice* who had most to say to the women of 1900:

> It has been in no frivolous mood that Portia has determined to disguise herself and plead Antonio's cause. . . . The display of intellectual powers of this woman of Shakespeare is remarkable and would make Portia an interesting type of womanhood even if no other side of her nature were shown us. But though her intellect is glorious, it is her womanliness which charms us. . . . Perhaps the twentieth century woman will come nearer this type of symmetrical womanhood, but if so, do not let us apply to her the repulsive name of "new woman," for she has existed in Shakespeare's plays for three centuries.[20]

How are we to account for the seventeen-year-old van Kleeck? And what are we to make of her strong identification with Portia, an identification at once prescient and premonitory? Courtship and marriage, to be sure, would not be Mary's. But in other regards Mary and Portia are similar. Mary shared with

Portia a father's too-early death. This could have spared her the burden of filial struggle, but more likely it left her, as it did Portia, compelled to obey, or mirror, a father whose meaning to his daughter was deepened by his absence. A distant man and unwell in Mary's childhood, Robert van Kleeck, Jr., had forsaken a lucrative legal career for the Episcopal ministry of his fathers and uncles. "This is a family of many ministers," according to Barbara Stevens Roberts, a distant cousin. And in a remark wickedly insightful of the woman Mary was to become, Roberts adds that "just because a daughter wasn't a minister, it didn't mean she didn't preach."[21]

Later, Mary would share a life passionately involved with the fate of "the Jew," in her case not an individual, Shylock, but a population of immigrants busy becoming trade unionists, New Yorkers, and Americans. And Mary, like Portia, was simply smarter than most people. Here, Mary's mother, Eliza Mayer van Kleeck, was probably decisive. "My mother always said," Barbara Roberts also recalls, "that it was the Mayer side of the family that had the brains."[22]

Eliza identified with a daughter who, like herself, was the youngest in her family. And she groomed her daughter for opportunity, writing to Mary almost daily while she was away at college. These letters reflect an intensity of maternal devotion and dependence, and make plain the extraordinary linkage between Mary and her mother. And having launched her daughter upon the cataracts of college and career, Eliza was eventually requited for her devotion, as Mary in 1919 would forsake her position as the highest-ranking woman in the federal government to care for her dying mother.[23]

Mary van Kleeck, then, was not without a sense of duty and historical self-consciousness. She had led in choosing her high school class motto, "Doe Ye Nexte Thynge," and she pledged herself and her classmates—"the last class of the nineteenth century"—to use their influence "for good in the century which is to come." She hoped the new century would be one in which women could achieve a "symmetrical womanhood." She could not have known how difficult such a thing would be. But, as early as age seventeen, and no doubt without full awareness, she had already identified for herself a possible alternative—the pursuit of the right and the good through an enabling disguise, one that would allow a woman to enter and influence the precincts of "life or death" questions. Such a disguise was still years away and would involve not the mask of Portia's judge but one better suited to the modern sensibilities of Social Christianity and scientism. And its construction would begin in the fall of 1900 at Smith College.[24]

Advocates of women's collegiate education in the latter half of the nineteenth century usually promised to develop women's minds without making them like men. The promise betrayed the perceived, if paradoxical, threat—that no matter how separate and wholly female they were, women's colleges were embarking upon a dangerous mixing of natures, if not sexes, by introducing women to higher education. Their founders minimized such dangers, but in their drive to bring to women some of the advantages enjoyed by men, Henry Durant, Matthew Vassar, and Sophia Smith, among others, did seek to enlarge women's authority. In doing so, they inaugurated institutions that for a brief historical moment made possible the raising not only of "new women" but of a new woman's secular priesthood, one that created new reformist vocations by grafting heretofore masculine training onto women's Social Christianity.[25]

This, Smith College certainly did for van Kleeck; it offered to attach her religiosity and seriousness of purpose to the unfolding crisis of American life, the collision between an older, Protestant America and the modernity about to overwhelm it. The few drafts of Mary's surviving college poems suggest that she was preoccupied in her junior and senior years by a mixture of fear and attraction to such a wider and disturbing world. And her tendency to cast life beyond college in the quasi-religious terms of a "call" and "calling" would be unremarkable were it not for the fact that she had devoted much of her college time to the most vital form of "extroversion" then encouraged—the exploration of the Social Gospel's ideal of service. Here one organization appears to have been especially vital.[26]

III

It is my prayer that every girl in college may long to say, as St. Paul said, that "To me to live is Christ."

—Mary van Kleeck, 1903

It would be possible to regard reform as the social gospel unconscious of its religious debts.

—Donald Meyer, *The Protestant Search for Political Realism*[27]

The Smith College Association for Christian Work (SCACW) was the chief student association at Smith. Just as the college brought young women together in their first national institution, the SCACW introduced them to a national network of Social Gospel and women's reform activities. Van Kleeck threw herself into the SCACW's work. A member of its Christian Union, College Settlements, Consumers' League, and Missionary Committees, she chaired its Extension Committee during her junior year. Her work here involved organizing boys' and girls' clubs, Sunday schools, and classes for factory girls in adjacent towns. But it was through the SCACW's connections to the YWCA's growing college and industrial work that the terms of van Kleeck's vocation began to take shape.[28]

The YWCA came under the influence of the Social Gospel late in the nineteenth century. The inadequacy of personal religion, along with the need for social salvation through greater involvement in the lives of the working classes, increasingly preoccupied the thousands of college women affiliated with the YWCA and the larger Student Christian Movement. For these women, Florence Simms, the YWCA's first national industrial secretary, was a compelling leader. At a time when the new National Women's Trade Union League and National Consumers' League had begun their secular campaigns to draw women into cross-class alliance, Simms drew heavily upon the Social Gospel to ignite the social passions of college women. "She found young women in the colleges," van Kleeck later recalled, "instinctively reaching out to prepare themselves for the new conditions of this generation."

> She believed firmly that true conversion to Christianity would come . . . through participation in the solution of social problems. She had seen with her own eyes that leading girls in the student movement had been won to Christianity by their contact with girls in industry. . . . In her view social righteousness was the essence of the Master's teachings,—the way, the truth and the life through which alone personal religion can be fully achieved.[29]

As SCACW president-elect in the summer of 1903 van Kleeck herself was one of the "leading girls" in the student movement as she led the Smith delegation to the YWCA's summer conference at Silver Bay, Lake George, New York. There, student delegates from northeastern colleges attended a program of lectures, classes, and small group discussions designed both to foster collegiality and to identify potential recruits for the industrial missionary work of the national organization. Van Kleeck found such conferences "essential to the carrying out of the Association['s] work." Their "practical suggestions" were helpful, she felt, "but it is in the spiritual force which characterizes them that their great value . . . lies and stronger, better service consists."[30]

There was more to this arid sentence than meets the eye. It was here at Silver Bay in the summer of 1903 that Mary, with the help of the mysterious Smith graduate Frances Bridges, experienced something akin to a conversion, a calling to "help others to find 'the Life that is in His Son.'" And in an age in which "the Social Question" preoccupied many, especially the supersensitive young vanguard of the women's colleges, it was probably inevitable that van Kleeck's conversion would soon conform to the ideal of "service."[31]

"Service" was the title of the only van Kleeck poem published in Smith's 1904 yearbook. It suggests that she had by then come to a tentative and unstable resolution of her vocational crisis. Like Jane Addams and others before her, van Kleeck was acutely aware of the simultaneous luxury and distress of her own condition. Safely tucked amidst the sheltering gentility of family, religion, and college, she had become an educated young woman. But through her immersion in women's social religion she had become not only a woman aware of a larger world but one driven by her faith to identify with that world's outcasts, and led by her education to value if not the outcast's at least the intellectual's allegedly disinterested point of view. In the tension between the intellectual and the religious, between disinterested inquiry and faith, the balance was always a delicate one, with the former tending to be handmaiden to the latter.[32]

Thus the vision of "service" with which van Kleeck left Smith College was very much pregnant with her coming achievements and, in the classical sense, her tragedy. Her adoption of the "service ideal," like that of so many other Progressives, betrayed not so much the enduring piety of Protestant culture as a frenzied quest to find a substitute for theologies, systems of belief, broken and demoralized by the end of the nineteenth century. If the quest was ultimately unsuccessful, it nonetheless carried cultural weight, creating new professions, institutions, and women who would help remake the modern United States.[33]

IV

The creation of the modern foundation and its legitimation as a national system
of social reform—a privately supported system operating in lieu of a
governmental system—carried the United States through a crucial period
of its development: the first third of the twentieth century.

—Barry Karl and Stanley Katz[34]

In 1944, reflecting upon the legacy of the Russell Sage Foundation's Department of Industrial Studies, van Kleeck wrote that "a watchtower is important for the scene it commands rather than for its own structure." Since the foundation's inception in 1907, her department had won a reputation for its work in the industrial sociology of women's work, employee-management relations, and economic planning. But as witness and student during a period that saw two world wars and four depressions, its significance, van Kleeck felt, was substantially achieved "by events affecting industry and its role in society, rather than by its own work alone."[35]

Belying this cool and unusually modest assessment, Van Kleeck's early career in the New York City of 1905–17 was characterized by a fierce advocacy of social research as the key to truth and social transformation. Social progress, she wrote in 1915, "will depend upon how clearly the community thinks. How clearly the community thinks will depend upon how much the community knows." Social science, she continued, "is not the making of many books without end, but a contribution toward the forming of the new social mind . . . which shall get things done through the force of opinion."[36]

Her entire career, she later told Mary Beard, had been dedicated to "seeking to accumulate facts regarding the life and labor of the workers of the United States; to analyze the significance of these facts; and to interpret them to those groups who are interested in some kind of action." Van Kleeck's was thus a technocratic faith, and one that first found expression amidst the sweated women and children, the candy, hat, and artificial flower makers, of early-century New York City.[37]

Following her graduation from Smith College, van Kleeck joined the New York College Settlement on Rivington Street in the fall of 1905. The settlement had been founded by Vida Scudder and other Smith graduates, and it was a joint fellowship from the Smith College Alumnae and College Settlements Association that launched van Kleeck upon her city career. There, she looked forward to following Frances Kellor, who had held the College Settlement Fellowship before her. "I read her book on employment exchanges," van Kleeck would later write, "and sought to follow in my subject her methods of getting first-hand information in such a study."[38]

Van Kleeck attended graduate classes at Columbia in the mornings, and her settlement work quickly introduced her to the mysteries of shoe-leather social research, lessons in what might be termed a rather intimate form of "standpoint epistemology." After one evening meeting of the Women's Trade Union League, for example, van Kleeck tried to strike up a conversation with the working "girl . . . sitting next to me." But "she was suspicious of questions—asked, in answer to [a] question of where she worked and whether conditions were good there, whether I was trying to find out something and what trade did I belong to[?]" Van Kleeck concluded that this incident was an "example of the impossibility of direct questions."[39]

Nonetheless, van Kleeck soon learned that many young working women had difficulty attending the girls' clubs because of excessive overtime in local factories. "It had become evident that this could not be controlled by prosecuting one employer," she noted, "but required a concerted effort to stimulate public opinion on the basis of facts secured from the workers themselves." And under the direction of Florence Kelley and Lilian Brandt, and with the sponsorship of the Consumers' League of New York and the New York Child Labor Committee, van Kleeck soon began a series of investigations of child labor and overtime in women's work. Reflecting upon their importance later in 1935, she remarked that for "a view of the industrial system which comprehends not only the factory but the homes of the people and the effects of industrialism upon civilization, the best subject of study is the status of women in industry."[40]

Van Kleeck's work soon came to the attention of the new Sage Foundation. Inaugurated in 1907, the foundation reflected the scientizing currents then running strongly through philanthropic circles, and the determination to move beyond charity and relief into the systematic study of poverty's causes. To this end, the foundation sponsored, among other things, the Pittsburgh Survey, the first social survey of an American city, dedicated itself to professionalizing social work, and would function for the next forty years as Mary van Kleeck's institutional base.[41]

Initially, the new foundation sponsored the continuation of van Kleeck's early researches, operating now under the auspices of an independent Committee on Women's Work chaired by Henry Seager, and in 1910 brought this committee formally into the foundation. Between 1910 and 1917, van Kleeck's department launched investigations of the poor conditions, night work, and unemployment suffered by New York City's women workers in the artificial flower, millinery, and bookbinding trades. "Intensive in method, dealing with a concrete, limited subject of inquiry," these studies, she explained, produced "not theories but evidence gathered slowly from those who know the facts through experience—the workers and the employers."[42]

Van Kleeck's investigations emphasized the disorganization and irregularity of business operations; called, among other things, for worker-management wage boards and employment exchanges to address these problems; and would lead directly in 1910 and again in 1915 to the establishment of state prohibitions against night work for women workers. By 1914, however, convinced by her work "that distress and poverty among women workers are but phases of" larger "industrial and social conditions," van Kleeck welcomed the foundation's decision to enlarge her department's scope to include study of men's as well as women's work. This broadened mandate was made formal in 1916 with the creation of a new Department of Industrial Studies under her leadership.[43]

These projects reflected a faith in the potential of social science to provide both the vision and the means necessary for social transformation. They were, she noted in 1915, "carried on in the faith that a well-informed community will develop, step by step, a new order, the outgrowth of a new philosophy pressing toward the control of the industrial causes of poverty and misery. . . ." Management and labor, in other words, would be brought to a more balanced and just accommodation through a public opinion informed by social research.[44]

In the meantime, the Department of Industrial Studies took shape as a collaborative venture, one that emphasized careful empiricism, collegial review, and cooperation with state and private agencies. As director, van Kleeck organized each project, in consultation with both the research associate handling it and the management and labor representatives whose business or trade was to be studied. Decisions regarding the preparation of data and the writing of research reports were made in staff conferences, with completed studies published under the names of such research associates as Ben Selekman, Mary LaDame, and Louise Odencrantz. The department's work, van Kleeck noted with pride, was "practical in purpose, . . . intensive in method . . . ," and ". . . gathered slowly from those who know the facts through actual experience—the workers and employers."[45]

Foundation executives occasionally had to protect the department's projects. John Glenn, the foundation's general director and a member of the Board of Trustees, had been a lawyer and charities executive in Baltimore, and at the Sage Foundation functioned for van Kleeck and others on the staff as editor and counselor. In 1911, amidst preparation for publication of her department's first studies, she thanked Glenn for his advice. "I have never before been able to carry on our work," she wrote, "in a way which seemed so thoroughly satisfactory as it has been under your guidance."[46]

Such guidance sometimes took the form of protection from the interference of disgruntled subjects of a van Kleeck–directed study. An investigation of the living conditions of women munitions makers at the Remington Arms plant in

Bridgeport, Connecticut, in the summer of 1916, so angered management that it appealed to Robert deForest, the foundation's vice president, to suppress the findings. The company had refused to let van Kleeck and her chief investigator, Amy Hewes, study conditions inside the plant, and deForest's response to its objections was to urge it to allow such an investigation. If he were in their position, deForest told company officials, he "would covet such an inquiry and could assure them of fairness." Similarly, when later in the 1920s representatives of Filene Bros. objected to the department's investigation of employee-management relations at their department store, Glenn once again defended van Kleeck and her staff.[47]

By the end of her department's first decade and the coming of war, van Kleeck's work had already brought her into a wider orbit of reformers, management engineers, and labor leaders similarly concerned with the social costs of business and economic mismanagement. Some of them, like Morris Cooke, were proponents of scientific management and members of the new Taylor Society for the Advancement of Management. Van Kleeck's wartime service with Cooke and others attempting to manage the conditions of women workers intensified both these concerns and these contacts, and suggested the possibility of national solutions through government action and more rational management of business operations. "The work is promising," she wrote Glenn in 1918, "and I see more possibilities in it every day."[48]

In a memorandum prepared for Glenn in 1919, van Kleeck made the case for expanding her department's technocratic function. "Research and investigation," she noted, "continue to be the chief tools of the Foundation in its relation to industry." And the foundation, she continued, enjoyed "in its reputation for accuracy" a "unique opportunity," beyond that available to any public agency. "The fact is," she argued, "that a public institution, dependent upon funds appropriated by legislative action, is less free to express the minds of its staff on controversial questions than a private agency." In the foundation's case, she concluded, the "procedure in carrying out investigations and publishing reports, and the policy of the trustees in leaving to the staff the responsibility for facts and conclusions insure a statement and analysis as true, unprejudiced and accurate . . ." as possible. And because her studies also indicated that management's shortsightedness lay behind unemployment, van Kleeck would soon be among those encouraging the fusion of scientific management and social work in the assault on economic instability.[49]

V

By 1915 and Frederick Taylor's death, scientific management had been moving for some time toward just such a wider application of its principles. Taylor's later writings and pronouncements, together with the popularization of his ideas by Louis Brandeis, Ida Tarbell, and others, strongly suggested the movement's applicability to the cause of national reform and renewal. Under Harlow

Person's presidency, the Taylor Society from 1914 through 1919 was increasingly receptive to the consideration of social ideals and to the participation of social scientists and reformers.[50]

Van Kleeck surely was aware of this ferment; while the origins of her association with the Taylor Society remain unclear, she first referred to Taylorism in a syllabus for a course on industrial problems at the New York School of Philanthropy, where she taught from 1914 to 1917. There, in 1915, she introduced students of social work to the proposition that scientific management's "big contribution" to their field lay in its "expert study of working conditions." Such study, she argued early in 1917, had already led some management engineers to recognize the inefficiencies of unemployment and haphazard personnel policies. Here she pointed approvingly to the ideas of Richard Feiss and Ordway Tead, and to the efforts of Robert Valentine to promote an "Industrial Audit" in which the management of human relations within firms would be subject to the scrutiny accorded the management of production. Taylorites, it seemed to van Kleeck, were beginning to share social work's preoccupation with the "human element"; in order to further these merging tendencies, she urged the adoption of the industrial audit as the first step in training social workers to assume personnel management positions in industry.[51]

As they developed from 1915 to 1925, van Kleeck's views on the relations between social work and scientific management were complex and contradictory. Convinced that both social workers and scientific managers had much to teach each other, she encouraged their merger and welcomed their contributions to the new field of personnel management. At the same time, she resisted the tendency of Taylorites and others to view the growing emphasis on human relations in industry as an improvement upon and departure from the ideas of Frederick Taylor. Occasionally, she seemed to suggest that scientific management needed no lessons in wider social vision from anyone. Because an unreconstructed Taylorism's scientific, and thus disinterested, approach to industrial management could help to rationalize the firm, she reasoned, it could not help but rationalize and make just the firm's relationship with its workers and community. Scientific management, for van Kleeck, was thus a social science of utopian potential. With its pretensions to transcendent authority, moreover, such a fundamentalist scientism likely held an additional appeal: it could enable insecure professions, social workers as well as management engineers, to cast themselves as social arbiters with important and independent roles to play in stabilizing the industrial system.

Van Kleeck was acutely conscious of social work's uncertain professional status. With its attention split between the results and the causes of human suffering, between casework and social reform, and lacking an esoteric technique and independent source of income, social work's identity was unclear, its disinterestedness in question. Since it functioned best as a "mediating" contact among various groups, van Kleeck argued, it should view its professional mission as one of encouraging other groups and professions to think in terms of the community, the social ideal. "Only as social workers are prepared consciously to formulate their experience as a guide for the practice of others . . . can they lay claim to the possession of technique." Recent "experience seems also to show," she noted, "that the more socialized the other professions become, the more they turn to social workers for light." The best evidence for this proposition, van Kleeck felt, lay in the warming relations between social workers and management engineers.[52]

The First World War's demand for labor management had intensified the linkages between these groups, encouraging both the development of the personnel management movement and fresh opportunities to illustrate scientific management's importance to women workers. Together with Morris Cooke, for example, van Kleeck had sought to advance the interests of wartime women workers by establishing labor standards through the Storage Committee and Industrial Service Section of the Ordnance Department. With the trade unionist Mary Anderson, she expanded upon this work in the Woman in Industry Service of the Labor Department, forerunner of the U.S. Women's Bureau. Despite employer resistance, exploitation, and discrimination, women workers, she found, often succeeded in men's work.[53]

"Hundreds of jobs," van Kleeck noted proudly, "became sexless." Such success, however, depended mostly upon intelligent and efficient business management. "The war record," she wrote in the *Atlantic Monthly*, ". . . is clear. Management in industry, and not feminism, opened the way to novel work for women." Nonetheless, van Kleeck suggested, feminism and scientific management shared ultimate goals. "Efficiency," she averred elsewhere, "is not the ultimate aim. . . . The goal is the establishment of just relationships."[54]

> . . . It is the method of industry to attach the individual to his limited, specified place in the whole scheme of production; while the aim of feminism is to make the whole recognize a hitherto unrealized obligation to the individual . . . .; it busies itself with the issues that the times create.
>
> The economic issues of the time, as they are reflected in women's industrial status, were never more baffling. She must win a more secure place in the shop as a skilled worker. She has as yet only a limited . . . recognition in the labor movement. . . . She is accused of aiming to undermine the home, just when she may be working hardest at uncongenial tasks to support it. So discouraging is the outlook . . . that one is almost inclined to agree with certain anti-feminists about the effects of industrialism on all our social institutions, including the family as a whole and women individually. Not feminism, however, but industrial organization, uncontrolled in the common service, has done the damage.[55]

Scientific management, van Kleeck was certain, could help undo the damage. And while in the immediate postwar years she would continue to work on behalf of women workers through her association with the U.S. Women's Bureau, by far the bulk of her energies would be devoted to furthering the merger of social work and Taylorite perspectives. Here, her own ties to scientific management would intensify, as she would be elected to the Nominating Committee and the Board of Directors of the Taylor Society.[56]

"The management engineer and the social worker," van Kleeck concluded in 1922, "have found cooperation necessary." "The management engineer has discovered . . . that the efficiency and cooperative attitude of a labor force is directly affected by the organization of life in the community." The social worker, "approaching from a different direction[,] has also arrived at the place where recognition of the relations of these two groups . . . becomes highly desirable for the success of each. . . ." Van Kleeck was probably right, although in more ways than she admitted. During the years just before and after the world war, elements within each group were interested in securing greater influence and autonomy, both within and without the corporation: engineers by claiming possession of a scientifically informed social vision, social workers by establishing a new professional authority resting on the research and skills they could deploy in analyzing the economic sources of social distress. "Industry," she proclaimed, "is being invaded by social workers, who are bringing their experience to bear upon problems of personnel and research as they affect human relations." For a social worker like van Kleeck, eager to see her profession take up an important role in social reconstruction, the assault was providential.[57]

Closer ties to scientific management, van Kleeck seemed to think, would help to "scientize," and thus make more effective, social work's claim to a place in the larger postwar debate over capitalist instability and unemployment. Personnel management already had emerged, in part, from this linkage, and van Kleeck looked forward to further developments along these lines, toward an entirely new profession for industrial sociologists like herself. For a time in 1921 and 1922, she worked with Lucy Carner, Frances Perkins, Molly Dewson, Louise Odencrantz, and George Soule, attempting to organize a field of "industrial social work," but nothing came of this effort. Still, as she reminded her friend, Morris Cooke, "the analogy is close between social work and engineering." "We wish," she continued, "that we could find a more inclusive title than social work which has been so strongly associated with case workers." Briefly, she considered the term "social engineering" but regarded it as inaccurate and confusing. Still, "a term of that kind which denotes our interest in constructive social problems and in research would give us the broader basis necessary for . . . professional organization."[58]

While van Kleeck welcomed the development of mutually informing links between social work and scientific management, ties that would alter each movement, she resisted any suggestion that Taylor's thought had ignored the "human element." "My own experience," she would tell the Taylor Society in 1924, "began with what is called the human element in industry, and I saw it first outside the shop in the community." There, her search for solutions to the long hours and repetitive unemployment characteristic of women's work "led back into the causes of these conditions in the shop itself, and nowhere did I find so many questions in process of being answered as in the Taylor Society."[59]

Those answers did not relate merely to what is called the human element in industry, conceived as a separate problem in a different compartment of the manager's desk. My interest in the contribution of scientific management . . . was not solely in its emphasis upon personnel relations, but in the technical organization of industry as it affects wage-earners. The constructive imagination which can spend seventeen years studying the art of cutting metals is the imagination which can make industry and all its results in human lives harmonize with our ideals for the community. That kind of constructive imagination, though it may deal with one technical problem, will not fail to envisage the whole significance of industrial management. Nor will it be content merely to increase profits. The philosophy and the procedure which it represents will ultimately build a shop whose influence in the community will be social in the best sense, because the shop and all its human relations are built on sound principles.

Therefore, my interest in the Taylor Society is not directed toward challenging the technical engineer to give attention to problems of human relations. I am not worried about that, because if he is a good engineer he cannot fail to contribute to human relations. I am concerned rather with the other end of the story. I am eager to have those people who see the present disastrous results of industrial organization in the community realize how the art of management in the shop can fundamentally change those social conditions in the community.[60]

VI

During the interwar years, van Kleeck would emerge as a leader of the scientific management, national planning, and interfaith social justice movements. She devoted her mature career to the merger of the Christian socialist concern for a "just materialism" with Taylorism's promise of abundance through planning. This pursuit of what she later termed "social-economic planning" animated her defense of protective legislation for women against the Equal Rights Amendment, her alliance with Herbert Hoover's macroeconomic planning efforts, and even her role in cleaning up the Hollywood labor rackets through the creation of the Central Casting Corporation in 1926.

By the late 1920s, van Kleeck's life and work would take on a decidedly "internationalist" cast. She began, first, a lifelong union with the charismatic Dutch welfare worker Mary "Mikie" Fledderus. Together they devoted the interwar years to building the International Industrial Relations Institute (IRI), a Euro-American association of women personnel managers, progressive employers, Catholic socialists, modernist architects, Theosophists, Communists, and Taylorites committed to international economic planning. By the late 1920s she had also become the object of a considerable, if hardly unusual, courtship by Soviet and American Communist officials, apparently eager to draw a woman of such independent and authoritative reputation within their orbit. The implicit messianism of Stalin's first Five-Year Plan could not have been better designed to do just that, appealing as it did to fundamental aspects of van Kleeck's Christian and Taylorite faiths. And with the advent of the Great Depression, van Kleeck felt simultaneously confirmed in her disillusionment with Christian and social science gradualism, and freed to embrace the most militantly salvationist of the mutually reinforcing elements within the Social Christian, Taylorite, and Stalinist religions.[61]

Throughout the 1930s, then, van Kleeck played an unusual role in public debate. She was the only prominent American who could claim, for better or worse, simultaneous reputations in the worlds of social science, Christian social action, and Communist fellow-traveling. And she lent her energy then, and through her retirement in 1948, to an array of enterprises. She was, for example, a member of the original editorial board of the *Encyclopaedia of the Social Sciences*; an ally of the American Communist Party in its struggles to shape unemployment and social insurance; and a leading figure in that remarkably influential sisterhood of Episcopal women, the Society of the Companions of the Holy Cross.[62]

Prominence in these areas brought van Kleeck into alliance and combat with a range of people, including John Dewey, Sidney Hook, Elizabeth Gurley Flynn, Earl Browder, Wesley Mitchell, Alice Hamilton, Corliss Lamont, Vida Scudder, and Anna Louise Strong. Throughout, she was an unabashed fellow traveler, refusing to countenance criticism of the Soviet Union, and contemptuous of those who did.[63]

There was nothing appealing, in other words, about the quality of van Kleeck's fellow-traveling after the early 1930s. A "vital difference" separated the benign socialist from the malevolent fascist form of dictatorship, she argued. The purges were a "major victory against international fascist aggression." And the Soviet invasion of Finland, although possibly an error, was justifiable. Many people thought and felt this way, of course, but most had come to a hard-earned change of mind by the 1950s. Not, however, van Kleeck. By then, isolated, jobless, and old, she had retired with Mikie Fledderus to Woodstock, New York, where she endured the repeated attentions of the FBI, the State Department, and Senator Joseph McCarthy.[64]

When balanced, the intellectual and religious impulses underlying this life were powerful and creative. In tandem they helped to design the YWCA's industrial work, a new urban and industrial sociology, and the larger range of women's reform that remade American urban and political life early in the century. When unbalanced, when the secret "desire of the Social Gospel" for personal and social salvation overwhelmed reason and intellect, when "honest enthusiasm" degenerated into the traps of "self-applauding sincerity," it went badly wrong.[65]

"Nothing could have been more revealing," Christopher Lasch noted over thirty years ago, "than the pervasiveness of the ideal of 'service' among the very people one might have expected to have been its most outspoken critics." Almost from the instant of their late-nineteenth-century appearance, Lasch argued, American intellectuals "could find comfort and meaning . . . only in large, encompassing movements of masses of people, of which they could imagine themselves a part." This seems to have been especially the case if such a movement appeared to promise a fusion of the Social Gospel and scientific progress. To van Kleeck and many others, the rise of the Soviet Union seemed to promise exactly that, and she was prepared to defend all its works as necessary to the survival of the world's single most important experiment in social salvation.[66]

VII

Mary van Kleeck, then, explodes some of what we thought we already knew about gender and social science. Her career indicates, among other things, that the idea of a division between female practitioners of a "soft" reformist social science and male academics intent upon "hardening" and "disciplining" their fields is inadequate. Such a view ignores the attractions of the scientific management movement for a woman who would "plan" the world. As an early and ardent Taylorite, van Kleeck embraced a fundamentalist Taylorism far "harder" than that propounded by Henry S. Dennison, Harlow Person, Henry S. Seager, or any of her other male colleagues in the Taylor Society and in the academy. Efforts to "engender" social science history will thus remain sentimental until they make room for Taylorism, and unless they recognize that women Taylorites, not only van Kleeck but Ida Tarbell and Lillian Gilbreth, too, were nobody's victims. Rather, they were crucial accomplices in the construction of a cold, technocratic authority.

Also inadequate is a history of American social science that views religion as little more than a hobbling atavism, a tradition to be shucked, rather than as the organizing principle whose crisis impelled some of the most devout to give themselves over to social scientism. And to neglect the profound part such nonstatist institutions as the YWCA and the Sage Foundation played in building the modern public sphere is to misconstrue not only social science's history but that of liberalism itself.

Despite or because of these things, van Kleeck is scarcely remembered and difficult to apprehend. Like her life, the ideas and institutions she advanced often stood poised in the shadows between the historical and political definitions we commonly use to explain the twentieth century. Organizational history, for example, preoccupied with the abstractions of managerial ideology and institution building, has tended to "depopulate" history. It especially misses the large role of women in the elaboration of the social sciences and the philanthropic foundation, phenomena it otherwise rightly emphasizes as critical to the exceptional development of the modern American public sphere.[67]

The YWCA, and later the Sage Foundation and the Taylor Society, were not only central to van Kleeck's story, they were potent elements in a larger historical stream of nonstatist social analysis and ordering; linked, however tenuously, in a shifting relation with the state, these institutions helped to reshape and complicate the meanings of such categories as the "social," the "private," and the "public" during the first half of the twentieth century. Much of their work, to be sure, was eventually overtaken by the state authorities they had helped—indeed, had intended—to construct. Yet, while their authority attenuated, these institutions did not entirely disappear; they persist to this day, the intensifying arguments over their place and influence part of the larger eruption of interest in "civil society."

Their history and significance is stubbornly obscured, however, mostly by our parochial tendency to equate politics and government, and by our readiness to subsume varieties of political activity under the notion of "state build-ing." Too often we seem to view these institutions as significant only in terms of their function as "midwives" to the birth of the more important, modern, constituted state. Some continue to assume, in other words, that the public activity of most consequence is state activity, and that government policy is the highest expression of the political impulse. My point is not simply that this view primarily reveals our progressive assumptions and location in a statist world (although, of course, it does), nor is it to deny the statist intentions of Mary van Kleeck and other social scientists of her time, nor the centrality of the state in modern life. Rather, it is to suggest that despite these things, we risk historical distortion by insisting on seeing such institutions simply as vehicles for the delivery of the future, instead of recognizing them for the enduring, and pecu-liarly American, cultural formulations they are.[68]

Women's political history, the one field most sensitive to the varieties of political activity, has also, and paradoxically, been one of the fields most steeped in progressive assumptions. Some of its practitioners, in other words, have tended, if only implicitly, to regard voluntarist, associational, and philan-thropic institutions as "spear-carriers" in the teleological drama of the rise of the modern state.[69]

Such an emphasis may be appropriate to much of recent history, particularly the two world wars, the 1930s, and the 1960s, periods of significant statist ex-pansion. It is one, however, that works to diminish those women, activities, and institutions that cannot be fit obviously within the activities of the progressive state. And, as inquiry into the years from 1900 through the 1920s is making plain, this was a period of intensive ideological and institutional innovation, one in which women were central, especially as social scientists, philanthropic en-trepreneurs, and ideologists, to the rise of a new public sphere in which the state was but one of the constituents.[70]

Set thus against the achievements and blind spots of women's history, gen-der analysis may be less a theoretical advance than a solipsistic and ahistorical turn. If, in other words, "concern with gender as an analytic category has emerged only in the late twentieth century," then, perhaps, this says more about us than about anything else, and perhaps it is to this that we should first attend. But "concern with gender," so it often seems, encourages study of al-most everything except our own situation—as scholars and protagonists—within history.[71]

As scholars, we have become used to living in times of epistemic stress and upheaval, and we prefer, naturally, to put a happy face on things, interpreting our times as a portent of fresh enlightenment to come. We can readily admit that our disciplines, our universities, even our self-conceptions, have been rudely handled by events, but this, too, can be interpreted as healthy flux and a prelude to better times. We can, it seems, admit almost anything except the possibility that we have got it all wrong, that our optimism is the only standing artifact from a scientific and progressive age impossible now to recapture.[72]

As protagonists, as interested parties in the gender wars, perhaps the most appropriate thing to do before we subject the past to gender analysis would be to direct our zest for theory and analysis at ourselves. How is our work helped and hindered by our necessarily intimate knowledge of the issue? None of us, after all, is untouched by the times we live in; all of us, to some degree, have lived lives buffeted by and complicit in the increasingly brittle relations between the sexes. So whether we regard the late twentieth century's preoccupation with gender as a predicament or a liberating opportunity, as an occasion for lament and bad conscience or as a belated opening toward a more equitable future, or some amalgam of these things, we ought at least to admit that the lens of gender analysis, like other tools of our trade, is inevitably clouded by the messes and spills we have all made of and with our lives.

Missing from the idea of gender analysis, in other words, is a more realistic sense of our own situation in history. Missing is an appreciation of the possibility that the gender strife and disorganization of the late twentieth century is unusual in its intensity, and how our own complicity in it necessarily, if unclearly, must influence our approach to our work. Such an appreciation suggests the need to adopt a more skeptical stance toward ourselves, toward our "broad field of dissatisfaction," which somehow is never broad enough to include our own biases and impulses. It is our self-consciousness about gender, then, more than gender itself, that needs historicizing.[73]

VIII

> Begin with an individual, and before you know it you find that you have created a type; begin with a type, and you find that you have created—nothing.
>
> —F. Scott Fitzgerald, "The Rich Boy"[74]

Biography, then, "one of the great observed adventures," has never been more timely. Long suspected of lacking metahistorical ambition, it has retained an allure out of proportion to its otherwise pedestrian reputation. This has much to do with the autobiography necessarily lurking within. And if today's bull market in the gauzy art of the memoir suggests anything, it is that the entire middle-aged carnival of the chattering classes, not only academics, is hungry to tell a tale, the story of a generation. It is this pull toward autobiography, as much as anything, that lies behind biography's recent rehabilitation. It is thus especially appropriate that feminist biographers have been busy plumbing this connection, particularly its ethical dimension.[75]

That some of this writing is fundamentally dishonest, more concerned with the scholar than the subject, more interested in biography's psychotherapeutic possibilities than is ever admitted, is no doubt true. "Remedial biography," as Carol Brightman calls it, commits its own sins of projection. Referring to recent biographies by Sharon O'Brien (Willa Cather) and Lynda Wagner-Martin (Sylvia Plath), Brightman says that "it is not their subjects' stories that enthrall them, but their own."[76]

Even without these problems, biography inevitably carries heavy baggage—overidentification with the subject and the tendency to ask the subject to bear an era's interpretive burden. But these are also, and inescapably, the source of biography's strength. And it is the strengths of the form that we need to consider, now perhaps as never before. For biography, "art under oath," in Dee Garrison's memorable phrase, is nothing if not an ethical practice, almost lawful in its mandate for honesty, and for an honest regard for the boundary between scholar and subject.[77]

Biography, in other words, is hostile to unchecked projections of hope and ambition. It is chastening, as opposed to arrogating. And because it is ultimately more committed to the imaginative enterprise than we might assume, it has little patience for a scholarly self unable to discriminate between imagination and the pressure of theoretical overreach.

Only in biography, and not in fiction, to paraphrase Janet Malcolm, "does the question of what happened and how people thought and felt remain open." And it is because of this, because of the ultimate seriousness of the enterprise, that biography, as Reed Whittemore puts it, is "a genre in which, finally, humility must be the best policy."[78]

"History," Israel Metter concludes, "finds it easy to explain the fate of an entire class, but to explain the life of an individual is beyond it." But we do not have to go quite that far, nor must we all become biographers, to profit still from biography's virtues. Resistant to grand theory, but especially receptive to ethical inquiry, biography earns for itself a discipline, if not a guarantee, against "forward-going" delusions of the sort that entrapped Mary van Kleeck. Little else in our scholarly armamentarium, least of all the vaulting abstractions of gender analysis, can yet claim such a distinction.[79]

NOTES

1. Patricia Hampl, *Virgin Time* (New York: Random House, 1992), 60; and Claude Lévi-Strauss, *Tristes Tropiques* (New York: Atheneum, 1974), 393.

2. Willa Cather, *Not Under Forty* (New York: Knopf, 1936), prefatory note; and "Paul's Case," in *Youth and the Bright Medusa* (New York: Knopf, 1920), 233. Agnes Repplier, "The Chill of Enthusiasm," in *Americans and Others* (Boston: Houghton Mifflin, 1912), 171; and Marcus Klein, introduction to Cather, *My Mortal Enemy* (New York: Knopf, 1961).

3. Christopher Shannon, *Conspicuous Criticism: Tradition, the Individual, and Culture in American Social Thought, from Veblen to Mills* (Baltimore: Johns Hopkins University Press, 1996), 188.

4. Among more recent studies, see, for example, Judith Sealander, *Private Wealth and Public Life: Foundation Philanthropy and the Re-Shaping of American Social Policy,*

1903–1932 (Baltimore: Johns Hopkins University Press, 1997); Mary O. Furner, "Social Scientists and the State: Constructing the Knowledge Base for Public Policy, 1880–1920," in Leon Fink et al., *Intellectuals and Public Life: Between Radicalism and Reform* (Ithaca: Cornell University Press, 1996); John M. Jordan, *Machine-Age Ideology: Social Engineering and American Liberalism, 1911–1939* (Chapel Hill: University of North Carolina Press, 1994); David C. Hammack and Stanton Wheeler, *Social Science in the Making: Essays on the Russell Sage Foundation, 1907–1972* (New York: The Russell Sage Foundation, 1994); Steven Brint, *In an Age of Experts: The Changing Role of Professionals in Politics and Public Life* (Princeton: Princeton University Press, 1994); Mark C. Smith, *Social Science in the Crucible: The American Debate over Objectivity and Purpose, 1918–1941* (Durham, N.C.: Duke University Press, 1994); Clarence Wunderlin, Jr., *Visions of a New Industrial Order: Social Science and Labor Theory in America's Progressive Era* (New York: Columbia University Press, 1992); John L. Recchiuti, "The Origins of American Progressivism: New York's Social Science Community, 1880–1917" (Ph.D. diss., Columbia University, 1992); Dorothy Ross, *The Origins of American Social Science* (Cambridge: Cambridge University Press, 1991); James Allen Smith, *The Idea Brokers: Think Tanks and the Rise of a New Policy Elite* (New York: The Free Press, 1991); Martin Bulmer et al., *The Social Survey in Historical Perspective, 1880–1940* (Cambridge: Cambridge University Press, 1991); Ellen Condliffe Lagemann, *The Politics of Knowledge: The Carnegie Corporation, Philanthropy, and Public Policy* (Middletown, Conn.: Wesleyan University Press, 1989); Robert C. Bannister, *Sociology and Scientism: The American Quest for Objectivity, 1880–1940* (Chapel Hill: University of North Carolina Press, 1987); Barry D. Karl, "History and Social Science: The Paradox of American Utopianism," in Nobutoshi Hagihara, Akira Iriye, et al., *Experiencing the Twentieth Century* (Tokyo: University of Tokyo Press, 1985); and David M. Ricci, *The Tragedy of Political Science: Politics, Scholarship, and Democracy* (New Haven: Yale University Press, 1984).

5. Ross, *Origins*, 474.

6. Joan Scott's writings on gender analysis and academic politics best epitomize this tendency, renouncing totalizing explanatory schemes while celebrating the transformative possibilities of today's "critical scholarship." Joan W. Scott, *Gender and the Politics of History* (New York: Columbia University Press, 1988), introduction; idem, "Gender: A Useful Category of Historical Analysis," *American Historical Review* 91, no. 5 (December 1986): 1053–75; and idem, "The New University: Beyond Political Correctness," *Perspectives* 30, no. 7 (October 1992).

7. Louis Menand, "The Advocacy Trap," *Lingua Franca* 5, no. 5 (August 1995): 60; Ross, *Origins*, epilogue.

8. Daphne Patai once remarked, with an approval she would no longer confer, that "feminism . . . is the most utopian project around. That is, it demands the most radical and truly revolutionary transformation of society. . . ." Daphne Patai, "Beyond Defensiveness: Feminist Research Strategies," *Women's Studies International Forum* 6, no. 2 (1983): 177–89; and Patai and Noretta Koertge, *Professing Feminism: Cautionary Tales from the Strange World of Women's Studies* (New York: Basic Books, 1994).

Scott, *Gender and the Politics of History*, 6. Scott is quite clear, on p. 50, about the utopianism that underlies this linkage between scholarship and politics. More recently, however, she has worried about the dangers of moralizing as a substitute for argument, of a dogmatism which "insists that its truths are immune to criticism or change," in "Academic Freedom as an Ethical Practice," *Academe* 81, no. 4 (July–August 1995).

9. The quoted phrases are from Linda K. Kerber, Alice Kessler-Harris, and Kathryn Kish Sklar, eds., *U.S. History as Women's History: New Feminist Essays* (Chapel Hill: University of North Carolina Press, 1995), 6.

The implicit progressivism of the turn toward gender, its allegedly theoretical superiority, is made explicit by Linda Gordon in "Gender, State, and Society: A Debate with Theda Skocpol," *Contention* 2, no. 3 (Spring 1993): 144–46, 188.

Masculinity and manhood are also ripe for imitative attention. See, for example, Mark C. Carnes and Clyde Griffin, eds., *Meanings for Manhood: Constructions of Masculinity in Victorian America* (Chicago: University of Chicago Press, 1990); and E. Anthony Rotundo, *American Manhood: Transformations in Masculinity from the Revolution to the Modern Era* (New York: Basic Books, 1993). These, however, should be supplemented by Christopher Lasch's "The Mismeasure of Man," *New Republic* 208, no. 16 (April 19, 1993): 30–35.

None of this is to suggest that feminists and women's historians have not long been alive to the contradictions and tensions within an academic project that seeks at once to serve truth and to serve political desire. See, for example, Linda Gordon, "What Should Women's Historians Do: Politics, Social Theory, and Women's History," *Marxist Perspectives* 1 (1978): 128–36, and the symposium titled "Politics and Culture in Women's History," *Feminist Studies* 6, no. 1 (Spring 1980): 26–64.

10. A "potentially explosive approach . . . ," gender implies "not only difference but power . . . ," editorial, *Gender and History* 6, no. 1 (April 1994): 3–4. The relation of gender analysis to matters of power is also a theme in Linda Kerber, "Separate Spheres, Female Worlds, Woman's Place: The Rhetoric of Women's History," *Journal of Women's History* 75, no. 1 (June 1988): 39; and idem, "Diversity and the Transformation of American Studies," *American Quarterly* 41, no. 3 (September 1989): 429.

11. Biographical essays on van Kleeck include Eleanor M. Lewis, "Van Kleeck, Mary Abby," in *Notable American Women: The Modern Period*, ed. Barbara Sicherman and Carol Hurd Green (Cambridge: Harvard University Press, Belknap Press, 1980), 707–9; and Jan L. Hagen, "Van Kleeck, Mary Abby," in *Biographical Dictionary of Social Welfare in America*, ed. Walter Tratner (Westport, Conn.: Greenwood Press, 1986), 725–28. The course of her social-economic planning is traced in my "Mary van Kleeck and Social-Economic Planning," *Journal of Policy History* 3, no. 1 (1991): 1–23.

12. Jean Bethke Elshtain has interesting things to say about Addams in "A Return to Hull House: Reflections on Jane Addams," in *Power Trips and Other Journeys: Essays in Feminism as Civic Discourse* (Madison: University of Wisconsin Press, 1990).

13. Jacquelyn Dowd Hall, "Second Thoughts: On Writing a Feminist Biography," *Feminist Studies* 13, no. 1 (Spring 1987): 26.

14. Vida Dutton Scudder, *On Journey* (London: J. M. Dent & Sons, 1937), 64.

15. Having led in the founding of the American Economic Association in 1885, for example, Richard Ely noted that a "new world was coming into existence," one in which "the forces of life were getting beyond the control of individuals," and in which a new and technocratic economics, possessing "the potency of life," would be decisive. Richard T. Ely, *Ground under Our Feet: An Autobiography* (New York: The Macmillan Co., 1938), 152–54. See, also, Simon N. Patten, *The New Basis of Civilization* (New York: The Macmillan Co., 1907); Daniel M. Fox, *The Discovery of Abundance: Simon N. Patten and the Transformation of Social Theory* (Ithaca: Cornell University Press, 1967); John R. Commons, *Myself* (New York: The Macmillan Co., 1934); and Wunderlin, *Visions of a New Industrial Order*.

On the persistence of utopianism in our times, see, especially, Krishan Kumar, *Utopia and Anti-Utopia in Modern Times* (Oxford: Basil Blackwell, 1987), and John Ralston Saul, *Voltaire's Bastards: The Dictatorship of Reason in the West* (New York: Free Press, 1992).

16. On the religious dimensions of this story, see Charles Howard Hopkins, *The Rise of the Social Gospel in American Protestantism, 1865–1915* (New Haven: Yale University Press, 1940); Donald Meyer, *The Protestant Search for Political Realism, 1919–1941* (Middletown, Conn.: Wesleyan University Press, 1960, 1988), chaps. 1–2; Henry F. May, *Protestant Churches and Industrial America* (New York: Harper, 1949), pt. 4; Ann Douglas, *The Feminization of American Culture* (New York: Knopf, 1977); and David Danbom, *"The World of Hope": Progressives and the Struggle for an Ethical Public Life* (Philadelphia: Temple University Press, 1987).

17. On the YWCA, see, for example, Elizabeth Wilson, *Fifty Years of Association Work among Young Women, 1866–1916* (New York: National Board of the YWCA, 1916); and Annabel M. Stewart, *The Industrial Work of the YWCA* (New York: The Woman's Press, 1937). On the Russell Sage Foundation, see Hammack and Wheeler, *Social Science in the Making*; and the two-volume history by John M. Glenn, Lilian Brandt, and F. Emerson Andrews, *Russell Sage Foundation, 1907–1946* (New York: The Russell Sage Foundation, 1947).

18. Van Kleeck was long thought to have destroyed almost all of her personal and familial material. But in the spring of 1992 a trove of such things came to light. It consisted of a fifty-nine-pound box of letters, photos, daily appointment books, poems, short stories, expense accounts, and more (hereafter, the "59-lb. box").

19. On van Kleeck's high school accomplishments, see the undated news clipping in Box 1, Folder 16, Mary van Kleeck Papers, Sophia Smith Collection, Smith College, Northampton, Mass. (hereafter, MvK Papers), and the record of her Regent's Exam scores, Flushing High School Archives. Her debate experience is captured in *High School Folio*, January 1898), 10–12, and June 1899. Flushing's reputation is remembered in Margaret Treadwell, "Reminiscences of Old Flushing," *High School Folio*, January 1898, 6–8; George L. Smith, *Religion and Trade in New Netherland: Dutch Origins and American Development* (Ithaca: Cornell University Press, 1973), 224–27; John Webb Pratt, *Religion, Politics, and Diversity: The Church-State Theme in New York History* (Ithaca: Cornell University Press, 1967), 20–21. On the selection of the class of 1900's motto, see "Class History," *High School Folio*, June 1900, 18.

20. Van Kleeck, "The Woman of Shakespeare," valedictory address, Flushing High School Commencement, 1900, in *High School Folio*, June 1900. 22–24.

21. Frank van Kleeck, "The van Kleeck Family" (1900), 16–17, Box 2, Folder 23, MvK Papers; Obituary of Robert Boyd van Kleeck, Jr., *New York Times*, May 18, 1892. Interview with Barbara Stevens Roberts, Stockbridge, Mass., July 10, 1990.

22. Barbara Stevens Roberts interview.

23. These letters make up more than half of the "59-lb. box." Van Kleeck was appointed the first chief of the new Women's Bureau of the Department of Labor on July 14, 1919. She resigned the post within a few weeks.

24. "Class History," 18. Portia's boldness, androgyny, and sense of justice are treated in Diane Elizabeth Dreher, *Domination and Defiance: Fathers and Daughters in Shakespeare* (Lexington: University Press of Kentucky, 1986), chap. 6. Juliet Dusinberre contends that "disguise makes a woman not a man but a more developed woman" in *Shakespeare and the Nature of Women* (London: The Macmillan Press, 1975), 233.

25. David F. Noble, "Women in a World without Women," in *A World without Women: The Christian Clerical Culture of Western Science* (New York: Knopf, 1992), chap. 10; Lynn D. Gordon, *Gender and Higher Education in the Progressive Era* (New Haven: Yale University Press, 1990), 26; Thomas Woody, *A History of Women's Education in the United States*, vol. 2 (New York: The Science Press, 1929), chap. 4; Mabel Newcomer, *A Century of Higher Education for American Women* (New York: Harper & Bros., 1959); Barbara Miller Solomon, *In the Company of Educated Women: A History of Women and Higher Education in America* (New Haven: Yale University Press, 1985).

26. In one of her poems, "In the Valley," van Kleeck writes, "Grant me to know the touch of Thy hand . . . Till the call comes to go from the Valley—alone through the land." In another, "Voices," she refers to voices calling to her. "But I knew I dared not follow, for my heart was full of fear." Still, as the poem's refrain echoes, "Far away from toiling cities . . . they called me. . . . Will you go?" These appear in van Kleeck's college scrapbook, a rich source of pamphlets, notes, and scraps, in the author's possession. Jane Addams examined the vocational crises of college women during this period in "The Subjective Necessity of Social Settlements," reprinted in her *Twenty Years at Hull House* (New York: Macmillan, 1910). See, too, Joyce Antler, "'After College, What?': New Graduates and the Family Claim," *American Quarterly* 32 (1980): 409–34; and Christopher Lasch, "Jane Addams: the College Woman and the Family Claim," in *The New Radicalism in America, 1889–1963: The Intellectual as a Social Type* (New York: Vintage, 1965).

27. Van Kleeck to Frances Bridges, September 13, 1903, the "59-lb. box." Meyer, *The Protestant Search for Political Realism*, 3.

28. On van Kleeck and the SCACW's activities, see "Annual Report of the Extension Committee, 1902–1903," 53–56, and "Report of the General Secretary of the SCACW, 1902–1903," 82–83, both in *SCACW Annual Reports, 1902–1903*, SCACW materials, College Archives, Smith College.

29. On Florence Simms and the early college and industrial work of the YWCA, see Marian O. Robinson, *Eight Women of the YWCA* (New York: National Board of the YWCA, 1966); and Richard Roberts, *Florence Simms* (New York: The Woman's Press, 1926). Van Kleeck's remembrance of Simms is found in "Florence Simms," *Woman's Press*, April 1923, 194. See, too, Wilson, *Fifty Years of Association Work among Young Women, 1866–1916*, chaps. 10, 11, 21; Stewart, *The Industrial Work of the YWCA*, chap. 2; Genevieve M. Fox, *The Industrial Awakening and the Young Women's Christian Association* (New York: National Board of the YWCA, 1920); Mary S. Sims, *The Natural History of a Social Institution—the Young Women's Christian Association* (New York: The Woman's Press, 1936); Mary Frederickson, "Citizens for Democracy: The Industrial Programs of the YWCA," in *Sisterhood and Solidarity: Workers' Education for Women, 1914–1984*, ed. Mary Frederickson and Joyce L. Kornbluh (Philadelphia: Temple University Press, 1984), 75–106; Ronald C. White, *Liberty and Justice for All: Racial Reform and the Social Gospel, 1877–1925* (New York: Harper & Row, 1990), introduction, chap. 12; Regina Bannan, "Management by Women: The First Twenty-Five Years of the National Board, 1906–1931" (Ph.D. diss., University of Pennsylvania, 1994); and Nancy Marie Robertson, "'Deeper Even Than Race?': White Women and the Politics of Sisterhood in the YWCA, 1906–1949" (Ph.D. diss., New York University, forthcoming).

30. The quoted phrases are from SCACW Minutes, April 1902–April 1905, 9–13; *SCACW Annual Reports, 1902–1903, 1903–1904*, 104; *Eleventh Eastern Student Conference for Young Women, 1903*, a pamphlet, all in SCACW materials. I am grateful to

Elizabeth Norris, librarian and YWCA historian, for her insights into the significance of the YWCA's summer conferences: Norris to author, July 25, 1989. See, too, Esther Kelley's account of another Silver Bay Conference in *Smith College Monthly* 9 (June 1902): 607–8.

31. The quoted phrases are from SCACW Minutes, April 1902–April 1905, 9–13; *SCACW Annual Reports, 1902–1903, 1903–1904*, 104; *Eleventh Eastern Student Conference for Young Women, 1903*, a pamphlet, all in SCACW materials. A brief correspondence between van Kleeck and Bridges in the fall of 1903 indicates the power of their summer meeting at Silver Bay. These letters were among the many survivors in the "59-lb. box."

32. Van Kleeck, "Service," *Smith College Class Book, 1904*, 134.

33. Christopher Lasch once argued that "it was the waning of theology rather than the persistence of piety that created the cultural climate out of which the social settlement in particular and progressivism in general emerged." See Lasch, "Jane Addams: The College Woman and the Family Claim."

34. Barry D. Karl and Stanley N. Katz, "The American Private Philanthropic Foundation and the Public Sphere, 1890–1930," *Minerva* 19, no. 2 (Summer 1981): 243.

35. Van Kleeck, "Industrial Studies of the Russell Sage Foundation: A Record of Thirty-five Years of Fact Finding on the Social Aspects of Industry," 1944, introduction, Box 99, Folder 1549, MvK Papers.

36. Van Kleeck, "Industrial Investigations of the Russell Sage Foundation," September 17, 1915, 4, Box 13, Folder 28, Mary van Kleeck–Russell Sage Foundation Industrial Research Collection, Reuther Library, Wayne State University (hereafter, MvK/R Papers).

37. Van Kleeck to Mary Beard, November 18, 1935, Box 1, Folder 3, MvK Papers.

38. On Scudder, see, for example, her "Socialism and Spiritual Progress—A Speculation," *Publications of the Church Social Union*, ser. A, no. 10 (January 1, 1896); and idem, "Some Signs of Hope," *Intercollegiate Socialist* (Union Theological Seminary), April–May, 1915. Also, idem, "The College Settlement, 1888–1914," Russell Sage Foundation Library Collection, City College of New York Archives; van Kleeck to Mary Dreier, March 3, 1952, Box 9, Folder 152, Mary E. Dreier Papers, Schlesinger Library, Radcliffe College; van Kleeck, "Memorandum No. 1," November 2, 1956, and "Memorandum No. 2," November 14, 1956, both addressed to the Smith College Library, in Box 1, Folder 18, MvK Papers; van Kleeck to Beard, November 18, 1935.

39. Van Kleeck studied with Henry R. Seager, Franklin Giddings, and Samuel McCune Lindsay, working on a dissertation even as late as 1926, but never took the Ph.D. See the Mary van Kleeck folder, Samuel McCune Lindsay Papers, Butler Library, Columbia University. Her early encounter across the class divide is recorded in a journal, "Daily Record, The College Settlement . . . ," October 12, 1905, Box 77, Folder 1202, MvK Papers.

40. Van Kleeck, "The Sixty-hour Law for Factory Women in New York," "Seventeenth Annual Report of the College Settlement, October 1, 1905–October 1, 1906," Box 77, Folder 1203, MvK Papers; van Kleeck to Beard, November 18, 1935; van Kleeck, "Working Hours of Women in Factories," *Charities and the Commons*, October 6, 1906, 13–21, and "Child Labor in New York City Tenements," *Charities and the Commons*, January 18, 1908, 1405–20, both in Box 26, Folder 504, MvK Papers. See, too, Ellen Fitzpatrick, *Endless Crusade: Women Social Scientists and Progressive Reform* (New York: Oxford University Press, 1990); Frances Kellor, *Out of Work* (New York: G. P. Putnam's Sons, 1904); Josephine Goldmark, *Impatient Crusader* (Urbana:

University of Illinois Press, 1953); Nancy Schrom Dye, *As Equals and as Sisters* (Columbia: University of Missouri Press, 1980); and Peter Seixas, "Unemployment as a 'Problem of Industry' in Early-Twentieth-Century New York," *Social Research* 54, no. 2 (Summer 1987): 403–30.

41. "Russell Sage Foundation: Confidential Bulletin No. 1," 1907, Box 18, Folder 19, MvK/R Papers; Glenn, Brandt, and Andrews, *Russell Sage Foundation*; David Hammack, "Russell Sage Foundation," in *Foundations*, ed. Harold Keele and Joseph Kriger (Westport, Conn.: Greenwood Press, 1984), 373–80; Hammack and Wheeler, *Social Science in the Making*; and *Pittsburgh Surveyed: Social Science and Social Reform in the Early Twentieth Century*, ed. Maurine W. Greenwald and Margo Anderson (Pittsburgh: University of Pittsburgh Press, 1996).

42. See, for example, van Kleeck, "The Artificial Flower Trade in New York City," November 30, 1909, Box 13, Folder 3; van Kleeck to John M. Glenn, Russell Sage Foundation, March 31, 1910, Box 13, Folder 4; and van Kleeck, "A Program for a Committee on Women's Work," April 25, 1910, Box 13, Folder 6, all in MvK/R. See, too, idem, "Memorandum Regarding Investigations for the Winter of 1910–1911"; and the several letters from van Kleeck to John Glenn, all in Box 15, Folder 132, Russell Sage Foundation Papers, Rockefeller Archive Center (hereafter, RSF Papers). Several of these studies were published under van Kleeck's name as *Artificial Flower Makers* (New York: The Russell Sage Foundation, 1913), *Women in the Bookbinding Trade* (New York: The Russell Sage Foundation, 1913), and *A Seasonal Industry* (New York: The Russell Sage Foundation, 1917). See, also, the studies of lawless boys and neglected girls written by Pauline Goldmark, Ruth True, Katharine Anthony, Josephine Roche, and others, compiled in *West Side Studies* (New York: The Russell Sage Foundation, 1914); and Louise Odencrantz, *Italian Women in Industry* (New York: The Russell Sage Foundation, 1919). The quotation is from van Kleeck, "Industrial Investigations of the Russell Sage Foundation," 4.

43. On the role of van Kleeck's *Women in the Bookbinding Trade* in the prohibition of women's night work, see Hammack and Wheeler, *Social Science in the Making*, chap. 1; Glenn, Brandt, and Andrews, *Russell Sage Foundation*, 154–56; and the brief prepared by Louis D. Brandeis and Josephine Goldmark on behalf of the *People of the State of New York v. Charles Schweinler Press*, Cases and Briefs, NY Court of Appeal, 214 N.Y. 395, 108 N.E. 643 (1915). The quotations are from van Kleeck to Mary Beard, November 18, 1935, Box 1, Folder 3; and van Kleeck, "Memorandum Regarding Investigation of Industrial Conditions By Russell Sage Foundation," October 26, 1915, Box 100, Folder 1564, both in MvK Papers. On the creation of the Department of Industrial Studies, see Glenn, Brandt, and Andrews, *Russell Sage Foundation*, 161.

44. Van Kleeck, "Industrial Investigations of the Russell Sage Foundation," 4; idem, *Women in the Bookbinding Trade*, 235–36.

45. Van Kleeck, "Industrial Investigations of the Russell Sage Foundation," 4. On the department's collaborative operations and relations with other agencies, see, for example, idem, "Memorandum No. 6," November 29, 1956, Box 1, Folder 18, MvK Papers; idem, "A Program for a Committee on Women's Work," April 23, 1910, Box 13, Folder 6; "Memorandum of Conference with Mr. Glenn and Professor Seager," October 5, 1911," Box 13, Folder 10; "The Artificial Flower Trade in New York City," undated, Box 13, Folder 3, all in MvK/R Papers. See, also, Odencrantz, *Italian Women in Industry*; Ben M. Selekman, *Sharing Management with the Workers* (New York: The Russell Sage Foundation, 1924); and Mary LaDame, *The Filene Store* (New York: The Russell Sage Foundation, 1930).

46. Van Kleeck to Glenn, July 3, 1911, Box 15, Folder 132, RSF Papers. An example of Glenn's encouragement is evident in Glenn to van Kleeck, August 9, 1916, Box 14, Folder 123, RSF Papers. A fascinating and important figure, Glenn remains largely unstudied. The best account of his life is still the unpublished biography by his longtime colleague Shelby Harrison. See Harrison's typescript, "John Mark Glenn, And First Steps Toward Better Living Conditions," John M. Glenn Papers, Butler Library, Columbia University. See, too, the essay on Glenn by Jane Andrews in *American National Biography* (Cary, N.C.: Oxford University Press, forthcoming).

47. Amy Hewes and Henriette Walter, *Women as Munition Makers* (New York: The Russell Sage Foundation, 1917); deForest's views are recounted in Paul U. Kellogg to van Kleeck, December 7, 1916, in a casefile, Box 15, Folder 133, RSF Papers. The Filene Study controversy, and Glenn's views, are documented in van Kleeck, "Memorandum," September 24, 1929, and surrounding casefile, Box 14, Folder 123, RSF Papers.

48. Van Kleeck to Glenn, February 5, 1918, Box 15, Folder 132, RSF Papers.

49. Van Kleeck, "Memorandum," October 25, 1919, Box 23, Folder 456, MvK Papers.

50. This section on Taylorism has appeared previously in my "Mary van Kleeck and Scientific Management," in *A Mental Revolution: Scientific Management after Taylor*, ed. Daniel Nelson (Columbus: Ohio State University Press, 1992). Harlow Person, "The Manager, the Workman, and the Social Scientist," *Bulletin of the Taylor Society* 3, no. 1 (February 1917): 1–7; Nelson, *Frederick W. Taylor and the Rise of Scientific Management* (Madison: University of Wisconsin Press, 1980), chap. 7; Hindy Lauer Schachter, *Frederick Taylor and the Public Administration Community: A Reevaluation* (Albany: SUNY Press, 1989); and Martha Banta, *Taylored Lives: Narrative Productions in the Age of Taylor, Veblen, and Ford* (Chicago: University of Chicago Press, 1993).

51. "New York School of Philanthropy, Course 3a," October 1914–January 1915; van Kleeck, "Memorandum Regarding Preparation of Students for Industrial Service," January 26, 1917, both in Box 90, Folder 1412, MvK Papers. On scientific management and the "human element," see Lillian Gilbreth's remarks in *Scientific Management: Addresses and Discussions at the Conference on Scientific Management*, ed. Harlow S. Person (Hanover, N.H.: Dartmouth College, 1912), 356; Richard A. Feiss, "Personal Relationship as a Basis of Scientific Management," *Bulletin of the Taylor Society* 1, no. 6 (November 1915): 5; Robert G. Valentine, "The Progressive Relation between Efficiency and Consent," *Bulletin of the Taylor Society* 2, no. 1 (January 1916): 7–11; and Louise Odencrantz, "Personnel Work In Factories," May 18, 1923, Box 25, Folder 4, YWCA Records, College Archives, Smith College.

52. "New York School of Philanthropy—Memorandum Regarding Report on Curriculum . . . ," November 27, 1916, Box 90, Folder 1412, MvK Papers; van Kleeck and Graham Romeyn Taylor, "The Professional Organization of Social Work," *Annals* 101 (May 1922): 163–64; van Kleeck to Mr. Glenn, February 5, 1921, Box 19, Folder 7, MvK/R Papers.

53. See, for example, van Kleeck to Morris Cooke and reply, July 23, 24, 1917, Box 11, Folder 182; van Kleeck, "Storage Bulletin No. 9," October 24, November 24, 1917, Box 72, Folder 1125, both in MvK Papers; idem, "Memorandum Regarding the Work Done During the War," Box 1, Entry 1, Folder: Labor Department (Secretary of Labor), RG 86, Papers of the U.S. Women's Bureau, National Archives; idem,, "Women in the Munitions Industry," *Life and Labor* 8 (June 1918): 113–22; A. L. Alford, "An Industrial Achievement of the War," *Industrial Management* 55 (February 1918): 97–100; Mary

Winslow, *Woman at Work: The Autobiography of Mary Anderson as Told to Mary Winslow* (Minneapolis: University of Minnesota Press, 1951), chaps. 9–12; and Glenn, Brandt, and Andrews, *Russell Sage Foundation*, 256–58.

54. The quotations are from van Kleeck, "Women and Machines," *Atlantic Monthly* 127 (February 1921): 250–52; and idem, "Industrial Studies of the Russell Sage Foundation," September 16, 1943, 53, Box 99, Folder 1549, MvK Papers.

55. Van Kleeck, "Women and Machines," 255–56.

56. On van Kleeck and the Women's Bureau, see Winslow, *Woman at Work*; and the reports and correspondence in Box 71, MvK Papers, and Box 1 of the Mary Anderson Papers, Schlesinger Library, Radcliffe College. For van Kleeck's positions in the Taylor Society, see *Bulletin of the Taylor Society* 5, no. 1 (February 1920): 9; and H. S. Person to J. H. Williams, Mary van Kleeck, et al., September 8, 1927.

57. Van Kleeck and Taylor, "The Professional Organization of Social Work," 164.

58. Van Kleeck to Cooke, June 9 and 11, 1921, Box 16, Morris L. Cooke Papers, Franklin D. Roosevelt Library; van Kleeck, "Notes for Speech on Industrial Basis of Social Work," March 14, 1922, Box 24, Folder 487; "Minutes, Committee of Industrial Social Work," December 22, 1921, January 13, 1922, Box 99, Folder 1450, both in MvK Papers.

59. Van Kleeck to Person, July 4, 1922, Box 117, Folder 344; "Remarks of Mary Van Kleeck at Annual Business Meeting of the Taylor Society, December 4, 1924," Box 24, Folder 488, both in MvK Papers.

60. "Remarks of Mary Van Kleeck . . . ," December 4, 1924.

61. It is difficult to mark with any precision the beginnings of van Kleeck's alliance with the Soviet Union and the Communist Party of the United States. Her IRI activities had taken her to Europe several times in the 1920s, and preparations for the IRI's "World Social-Economic Congress" in August 1931, in Amsterdam, produced a flurry of correspondence with Soviet economic officials and with Amtorg's New York representative, Peter Bogdanov. Following the congress, van Kleeck spent six weeks in the Soviet Union, and throughout the 1930s her positions on public matters closely mirrored those of the Party. See, for example, the casefile of correspondence with Bogdanov, Box 10, Folder 156, MvK Papers.

At first, while the Ukrainian famine was under way and before the purge trials, there was an almost winsome quality to van Kleeck's fellow-traveling. Shortly after returning from the Soviet Union in the fall of 1931, she apparently authored a letter extolling the Soviet Union from the point of view of a foreign engineer. See "Dear Mr. and Mrs. Blank," March 30, 1932, Box 68, Folder 1084; and in an article apparently intended for *Soviet Russia Today*, she wrote of a train ride where the "comrade conductor" explained that "the intelligentsia must be in the vanguard" of the revolution. See van Kleeck, "Comrade Conductor to the Intellectuals of America," Box 26, Folder 513, both in MvK Papers.

62. Van Kleeck wrote the essay on "Women in Industry" for the 1935 edition of the *Encyclopaedia of the Social Sciences*, ed. Edwin R. A. Seligman and Alvin Johnson (New York: The Macmillan Co., 1935).

Before Congress and in the pages of the *New York Times* and the *Daily Worker*, van Kleeck usually joined Earl Browder, Herbert Benjamin, Ernest Lundeen, and other friends and members of the Communist Party in the push for a "National Economic Council," better labor standards, unionization of professionals, and a more thorough going scheme of social insurance. See, for example, "Establishment of National Economic Council," a transcript of Senate hearings, Box 28, Folder 533; "Investigation of

Economic Problems," an extract from Senate hearings, Box 28, Folder 533; van Kleeck, "A Planned Economy as a National Objective for Social Work," *Compass*, May 1933, 20–24, Box 26, Folder 513; "An Open Letter from Mary van Kleeck," *Social Work Today*, March 1934, Box 26, Folder 514, all in MvK Papers; and "Mary van Kleeck Urges House to Act on Social Insurance Bill," *Daily Worker*, February 22, 1934; and Kenneth M. Casebeer, "Unemployment Insurance: American Social Wage, Labor Organization and Legal Ideology," *Boston College Law Review* 32, no. 259 (March 1994): 292–304, especially.

Joining van Kleeck on the left wing of women's Social Christianity, from 1900 through the 1940s, were, among others, Vida Scudder, Ellen Gates Starr, Mary Kingsbury Simkhovitch, Mary Wilcox Glenn, and Grace Hutchins. All were members of the Society of the Companions of the Holy Cross. Scudder has left an especially profound record of the spiritual and political exertions of this group. See, for example, *Socialism and Character* (Boston: Houghton Mifflin, 1912); "The Christian Attitude toward Private Property," in *New Tracts for New Times* (Milwaukee: Morehouse, 1934); and *On Journey*. See, too, Peter J. Frederick, *Knights of the Golden Rule: The Intellectual as Christian Social Reformer in the 1890s* (Lexington: University of Kentucky Press, 1976); Mary S. Donovan, *A Different Call: Women's Ministries in the Episcopal Church* (Wilton, Conn.: Morehouse-Barlow, 1986); and Bernard K. Markwell, *The Anglican Left: Radical Social Reformers in the Church of England and the Protestant Episcopal Church, 1846–1954* (Brooklyn, N.Y.: Carlson, 1991).

63. Not even a sympathetic Eleanor Flexner was spared van Kleeck's anger on this score. When Flexner, sometime in 1957 or 1958, ventured a mild criticism of "Red China," van Kleeck "went up like a rocket." Interviews with Eleanor Flexner, April 19 and June 1, 1989.

64. Van Kleeck, "Dictatorships and Democracy," *Soviet Russia Today*, November 1933, Box 26, Folder 513, MvK Papers; "The Moscow Trials—A Major Victory against International Fascist Aggression," radio broadcast by van Kleeck, March 22, 1938, Mary van Kleeck folder, Tamiment Library, New York University; "Postscript on Finland, December 27, 1939," apparently a page proof of a piece by van Kleeck in *Social Work Today*, Box 1, Folder 3, MvK Papers. See, too, van Kleeck, "Soviet Democracy and Peace," November 5, 1937, Box 4, Folder 11, and "Comment and Correspondence— The Moscow Trials, Box 4, Folder 12, both in MvK/R Papers.

The best published account of van Kleeck's activities in the 1930s is Jacob Fisher's *The Response of Social Work to the Great Depression* (Cambridge, Mass.: Schenkman, 1980). Fisher was a younger social worker, a Party member, and friend of van Kleeck's, helping her to organize the so-called rank-and-file movement of social workers and the Interprofessional Association for Social Insurance.

65. Meyer, *The Protestant Search for Political Realism*, 193.

66. Lasch, "Woman as Alien," in *The New Radicalism in America*, 64.

67. On organizational history and the public sphere, see Samuel P. Hays, "The New Organizational Society," in *Building the Organizational Society: Essays on Associational Activities in Modern America*, ed. Jerry Israel (New York: The Free Press, 1972), introduction; Louis Galambos, "Technology, Political Economy, and Professionalization: Central Themes of the Organizational Synthesis," *Business History Review* 57 (Winter 1983): 471–93; Brian Balogh, "Reorganizing the Organizational Synthesis: Federal-Professional Relations in Modern America," *Studies in American Political Devlopment* 5 (Spring 1991): 119–72; Karl and Katz, "The American Private Philanthropic Foundation and the Public Sphere," 236–70; Judith Sealander, *Grand Plans: Business Progressivism*

and Social Change in Ohio's Miami Valley, 1890–1929 (Lexington: University of Kentucky Press, 1988); and Jerold E. Brown and Patrick D. Reagan, eds., *Voluntarism, Planning, and the State: The American Planning Experience, 1914–1946* (New York: Greenwood, 1988); and Ellis W. Hawley, "Economic Inquiry and the State in New Era America: Antistatist Corporatism and Positive Statism in Uneasy Coexistence," in *The State and Economic Knowledge: The American and British Experiences*, ed. Mary O. Furner and Barry Supple (Cambridge: Cambridge University Press, 1990), 287–324.

68. Sealander, *Private Wealth and Public Life*; Peter Dobkin Hall, *Inventing the Nonprofit Sector, and Other Essays on Philanthropy, Voluntarism, and Nonprofit Organizations* (Baltimore: Johns Hopkins University Press, 1992), chap. 1; and Karl and Katz, "The American Private Philanthropic Foundation and the Public Sphere."

69. This sensitivity to the varieties of political history is evident in Kathryn Kish Sklar, *Florence Kelley and the Nation's Work: The Rise of Women's Political Culture* (New Haven: Yale University Press, 1995); Theda Skocpol, *Protecting Soldiers and Mothers: The Political Origins of Social Policy in the United States* (Cambridge: Harvard University Press, 1992); and in *Women, Politics, and Change*, ed. Louise A. Tilly and Patricia Gurin (New York: The Russell Sage Foundation, 1990). Paula Baker and Linda Gordon have also called for a more expansive definition of the political. See Baker, "The Domestication of Politics: Women and American Political Society, 1780–1920," *American Historical Review* 89, no. 3 (June 1984): 620–47, and Gordon, ed., *Women, the State, and Welfare* (Madison: University of Wisconsin Press, 1990), 24. Still, a "teleology of the state" is implicit in women's historiography of modern political life. For example, see Susan Ware, *Beyond Suffrage: Women in the New Deal* (Cambridge: Harvard University Press, 1981); Robyn Muncy, *Creating a Female Dominion in American Reform, 1890–1935* (New York: Oxford University Press, 1991); Theda Skocpol, *Social Policy in the United States: Future Possibilities in Historical Perspective* (Princeton: Princeton University Press, 1994), introduction; and *Rethinking the Political: Gender, Resistance, and the State*, ed. Barbara Laslett, Johanna Brenner, and Yesim Arat (Chicago: University of Chicago Press, 1995).

70. Fitzpatrick, *Endless Crusade*; Sealander, *Private Wealth and Public Life*; and Jordan, *Machine-Age Ideology*.

71. The quoted phrase is from Scott, *Gender and the Politics of History*, 41.

72. These themes are developed in my "Policy History and the Sublime Immodesty of the Middle-Aged Professor," *Journal of Policy History* 9, no. 3 (1997): 1–17.

73. Agnes Repplier, *Eight Decades: Essays and Episodes* (Boston: Houghton-Mifflin, 1937), 156.

74. F. Scott Fitzgerald, "The Rich Boy" (1926), reprinted in *The Stories of F. Scott Fitzgerald*, ed. Malcolm Cowley (New York: Charles Scribner's Sons, 1951), 177.

75. The quoted phrase is from Henry James, in Leon Edel, "The Figure under the Carpet," in *Biography as High Adventure: Life-Writers Speak on Their Art*, ed. Stephen B. Oates (Amherst: University of Massachusetts Press, 1986), 21. On feminist biography, see, for example, the essays in Sara Alpern et al., *The Challenge of Feminist Biography: Writing the Lives of Modern American Women* (Urbana: University of Illinois Press, 1992).

76. Brightman is referring, in addition, to such theorists of biography and biographers as Carolyn Heilbrun, Jill Kerr Conway, and James E. B. Breslin. See Carol Brightman, "Character in Biography," *Nation* 260, no. 6 (February 13, 1995): 210.

77. Dee Garrison, "Two Roads Taken: Writing the Biography of Mary Heaton Vorse," in Alpern et al., *The Challenge of Feminist Biography*, 67.

78. Janet Malcolm, *The Silent Woman: Sylvia Plath and Ted Hughes* (New York: Knopf, 1994), 108–9; and Reed Whittemore, *Whole Lives: Shapers of Modern Biography* (Baltimore: Johns Hopkins University Press, 1989), 10.

79. Israel Metter, *The Fifth Corner of the Room* (New York: Farrar, Straus, Giroux, 1989, 1991), 9.

INDEX